The Bank Culture Debate

The Bank Culture Debate

Ethics, Values, and Financialization in Anglo-America

HUW MACARTNEY

OXFORD
UNIVERSITY PRESS

OXFORD
UNIVERSITY PRESS

Great Clarendon Street, Oxford, OX2 6DP,
United Kingdom

Oxford University Press is a department of the University of Oxford. It furthers the University's objective of excellence in research, scholarship, and education by publishing worldwide. Oxford is a registered trade mark of Oxford University Press in the UK and in certain other countries

First Edition published in 2019

Impression: 1

Published in the United States of America by Oxford University Press
198 Madison Avenue, New York, NY 10016, United States of America

British Library Cataloguing in Publication Data
Data available

Library of Congress Control Number: 2019934018

ISBN 978–0–19–884376–4

DOI: 10.1093/oso/9780198843764.001.0001

Printed and bound by
CPI Group (UK) Ltd, Croydon, CR0 4YY

'Sa aking apat na pinakamamahal: Ang Diyos Ama, Raquel, Asia at Levi.
Kayo ay isang maliit na piraso ng kawalang-hanggan sa mundong eto'

Acknowledgements

The writing of this book has taken several years, but my interest in bank culture began in the late 1990s. I remember the Saturday in 1997 for example, when I visited all four of the big UK retail banks and signed up for credit cards that came with £50–£100 rewards for opening the account. Looking back now it seems rather bizarre that someone in the bank moved a step closer to meeting their sales target by opening an account for a student NINJA (no-income-no-job-or-assets). But as an undergraduate at Manchester University the prospect of a little extra beer money was most welcome. The culture of banking did not seem so bad to me that day.

Later, as a graduate in the early 2000s, I worked for a financial company. I distinctly recall the day one client called to withdraw money from his investment fund to pay for his daughter's wedding. I remember his shock and anger to be told of the penalty charges he would face for early withdrawal, and the fact that the fund had actually declined in value. As we spoke on the phone it became clear that he had been misinformed by our sales executive who had visited his home. Our executive was apparently more concerned with earning his commission than explaining the fine print of our investment product. The culture of financial services became a little more disturbing to me that day.

Those thoughts, however ill-formed, were an important reason behind the PhD I later wrote in the mid-2000s. I had never wanted a career in banking, mainly because I had hated maths at secondary school; but also because I soon became aware that sales roles—where a large portion of my pay was tied to my ability to manipulate the truth—brought out an unpleasant part of my character. Nonetheless I became increasingly fascinated by banks. It puzzled me for example that companies which in many ways were just utilities—like the post office or the rail service—had such allure; held such sway in the British economy; and paid such high bonuses at senior levels. I was therefore always intrigued and yet somehow troubled by what I saw of the banks from the outside.

I then managed to write a PhD and my first book from this outsider's perspective, by focusing on banks' lobbying efforts in shaping EU financial market integration. I spent years sifting through the annual reports of these large banks, searching for keys to understanding the mystery and power that surrounded these institutions. At one level I was fascinated by what I found. But the experience was also deeply dissatisfying. Annual reports tell you what the banks wish to present to shareholders; they are the public face of the banks. If all I knew of my best friends was their public Facebook profile then our relationship would be very shallow.

Then in 2014–15 I stumbled across the bank culture problematique. I remember watching the public ‘interrogation’ of the bankers by the Treasury Select Committee in 2008–10, and the questioning of Sir John Vickers after the LIBOR scandal in 2012. He was asked whether the Treasury had required the Independent Commission to address banking culture in the drafting of the UK ring-fence. His response puzzled me somewhat, because he explained that the Treasury had only asked them to focus on stability and competition concerns, rather than culture directly. Subsequent discussions with other policymakers made clear that bank culture only became a priority in its own right after the LIBOR scandal. This seemed rather odd to me, given that culture was arguably the most fundamental driver of the banking activities that negatively affected stability and competition. In 2015 I then had the privilege to sit with Sir John in his office in Oxford as he elaborated on the culture debate. At that point I began to realize that whilst I could write something about the political efforts to change bank culture—from an outsider’s perspective—I really needed to fill in the blank in my knowledge by better understanding how banks work on the inside. To extend the Facebook analogy, I felt the need to visit my Facebook friends, sit with them in their living rooms, and listen to them describe their world.

Thanks to British Academy funding (SG151841) I was given the financial means to achieve this goal. Getting access to bank employees however, was an entirely different matter; that whole process was at the same time frustrating and illuminating. I lost count of the thousands of emails sent to US and UK financial institutions, and for legal reasons I will say no more on this matter. But to those who met with me to discuss what was changing in their organizations, I am eternally grateful. Most importantly though, it allowed me to glimpse inside the banks and see something of their private profile.

Versions of the argument for this book were then presented at the ECPR Joint Sessions in Salamanca (2014), the same Joint Sessions in Nicosia (2018), and at various other universities and practitioner workshops across the UK and North America between 2015–18. I am extremely grateful for all the feedback provided by participants at these various outings. I am particularly grateful though to members of the FCA, the Banking Standards Board, and other practitioners and academics who attended the British Academy workshop on Banking Culture which I convened in April 2018. They gave generously of their time and the discussions were especially helpful in refining the key arguments of this book. On that note, I also need to thank Fitch Connect, Thomson Reuters, the Bank of England, the CMA, the Federal Reserve, the US Census, Gallup, Edelman, and Ipsos Mori for permission to use their data, and Verso books for permission to reproduce a figure. All errors in the reproduction and interpretation of that data are my own.

I would also like to thank the University of Birmingham undergraduate students who worked as interns, gathering data and analysis during the summers of

2017 and 2018: Stefano Kalyvas, Joseph Woodman, Emily Roberts, Paola Calcagno, Lewis Patterson, Ellena Hannon, and Nadia Hamid were tireless researchers. I am also extremely indebted to the hundreds of Politics and International Relations students at the University of Birmingham in recent years. You have been guinea pigs for the arguments I present in this book, and the thought-provoking discussions we have had in lectures and seminars have proven to be invaluable. I should also thank John Andrews, James Ingram, David Drinkwater, and Chris Wood, my friends in the City of London and New York, for their help at various stages of the project.

There are a number of people who played an especially important role in shaping the argument of this book. I would like to Randall Germain, Rachel Epstein, and David Howarth for flying to the UK to comment on the draft manuscript in November 2017. Although it was rather soul-destroying having the manuscript dissected, I am very confident that the final product is significantly improved as a result. I would also like to thank Tim Haughton, my then Head of Department, for his consistently supportive approach to the book project and for having agreed to fund the one-day workshop on the draft book manuscript.

But perhaps the two people who deserve a special note of thanks are my friend Mat Watson and my late PhD supervisor Mick Moran. I am not sure whether Mat realizes it or not, but during the course of the writing process he made two decisive interventions. Both times he explained to me—with typical clarity—what exactly I was attempting to argue. Nobody I have ever met writes an email like Mat; nobody writes comments on draft manuscripts like Mat; and few people are able to clarify your own argument—rather than imposing theirs on your work—with the simplicity that Mat does. Thank you my friend. I fear though that you may now be inundated with emails from a fresh batch of academics looking for 5* feedback...

As for Mick Moran, he sadly passed away recently and it is with a heavy heart that I recognize that I will never get to thank him for the role that he played in framing this book. During the mid-2000s when I wrote my PhD, Mick was more than a PhD supervisor; he was a friend and mentor. I remember sitting in his dimly lit office in Dover Street, Manchester, bugging him with questions about academia and life. More than anyone else I have encountered in my academic career he taught me about the joys of what he called 'getting your hands dirty' in rich, empirical research. But as I got to know Mick, I also gained a huge amount of respect for how he prioritized his family life as well. In every sense then, he was a fabulous role model and I am so very grateful for the influence he had on my life and work.

Finally, I want to thank the people who mean the most to me. If I learned anything from Mick, it is that academia has its place, and it is secondary to family and faith. I know that writing a book places extra pressure on those around us. I am very grateful to my parents for their financial and emotional support over the years, and to my wife, for giving me the freedom to travel in researching this book. I am particularly grateful to my children, Asia and Levi, for demanding that I stop work and go cycling with them. Our afternoons in the park remind me of everything that is good in life. But they are also the *ultimate* guinea pigs for some of the arguments in this book. For example, my daughter—who is currently nine—was asked what daddy works on, and quickly replied 'banking and crisis'. I have obviously succeeded as a father.

But lastly, the past few years have been filled with some truly gut-wrenching experiences that have made me especially grateful for the God that I have put my faith in. My opinion—for what it is worth—is that some people dismiss the idea of a Creator because of inconclusive evidence to affirm his existence; whilst others assume his existence without examining the evidence or considering the opposing view. Neither of those two positions are intellectually satisfying to me. But having reasoned and wrestled with the evidence for more than two decades I can firmly say that God has been my rock (Psalm 18: 2) in recent years. Put simply, I find answers to both the kinds of (mis)conduct brought to light by the bank culture debate and the personal challenges I have experienced during the writing of this book, in the scriptures. And so I feel that it would wrong not to thank Him last and the most.

HM, January 2019

Contents

List of Figures

List of Tables

List of Abbreviations

BCBS	Basel Committee of Banking Supervisors
BIS	Bank for International Settlements
BoA	Bank of America
BoE	Bank of England
BCBS	Basel Committee of Banking Supervisors
BIS	Bank for International Settlements
BSB	Banking Standards Board
CFPB	Consumer Financial Protection Bureau
FCA	Financial Conduct Authority
FDIC	Federal Deposit Insurance Corporation
FFETF	Financial Fraud Enforcement Task Force
FSA	Financial Services Authority
IMF	International Monetary Fund
LIBOR	London Interbank Offered Rate
MBB	Market-Based Banking
PCBS	Parliamentary Committee on Banking Standards
RBS	Royal Bank of Scotland
SEC	Securities and Exchange Commission
TBTF	Too Big To Fail
TSC	Treasury Select Committee (UK)

1
Introduction
The Bank Culture Puzzle

Everybody knows that the global financial crisis exposed some serious cultural problems in Western banking systems. Judging by the headlines about fraud, mis-selling, extravagant bonuses, and corrupt bankers, the media and general public certainly know it. In researching this book though I have spoken to over 150 individuals working in financial services, as well as dozens of regulators, politicians, academics, and lawyers and almost all of them admitted that there were some deep-seated problems with banking, and particularly in the financial systems of the UK and the US (henceforth Anglo-America). Regulators, policymakers, lawyers, and the banks themselves subsequently made extensive efforts to address these so-called 'cultural shortcomings'. Reform after reform was introduced; billions of dollars in fines were handed out; comprehensive training programmes were initiated. Yet the cultural problems plaguing Anglo-American banking simply will not go away. The aim of this book is to explain why.

The Culture Debate

On 21 March 2017, the UK Banking Standards Board hosted a discussion panel at the Bank of England where the Governor of the Bank, Mark Carney, the President of the Federal Reserve Bank of New York, William Dudley, and the Lord Chief Justice of England and Wales were the keynote speakers. The title of the event was 'Worthy of Trust? Law, Ethics, and Culture in Banking'. Governor Carney was the first to speak and he began with the following statement:

> we are here because over the course of the last decade banking has suffered two crises: the crisis of solvency and the crisis of legitimacy...The first, has really been addressed, by comprehensive reforms and as a consequence we have a banking system that is stronger, more liquid, and much more focused. But that immense progress risks being overshadowed by a crisis of legitimacy. A series of scandals ranging from mis-selling to manipulation have undermined trust in banking, the financial system, and, to some degree, markets themselves.
>
> (Carney 2017)

A 2015 paper by the Bank of International Settlements (BIS) confirmed this conclusion, stating that 'behaviour and culture at banks have never been so high

The Bank Culture Debate: Ethics, Values, and Financialization in Anglo-America. Huw Macartney, Oxford University Press (2019). © Huw Macartney.
DOI: 10.1093/oso/9780198843764.001.0001

a priority of the agenda of regulatory agencies worldwide' (BIS 2015: 3). In other words, an argument could be made that the *culture* of banking was the most pressing issue facing Western financial systems in the mid-2010s.

Carney and the BIS were not the first to express this view though. In fact, regulators and policymakers (henceforth state managers) had recognized the centrality of cultural problems since the early stages of the financial crisis. To understand this we must first offer a preliminary definition of what state managers and banks mean by bank culture, though we will explore this concept more fully in Chapters 2 and 3. For now, the following will suffice: the culture of banking has been defined as the norms (beliefs and ideas) and behaviours (activities) within banks. As one US banker noted, 'a bank's culture exists in the hearts, minds and actions of every banker in its employ' (American Banker 2015). Or as the chairman of the US Federal Reserve stated, 'Culture relates to the implicit norms that guide behaviour in the absence of regulations or compliance rules—and sometimes despite those explicit restraints' (Dudley 2014). 'Bank culture, especially at large institutions, can [therefore] range from how a [cashier] interacts with customers to how highly paid traders make decisions and weigh obligations to their clients against the bank's' (*WSJ* 2015a).

For those familiar with banking, this definition raises one immediate problem. To speak of *the* culture of banking is of course a gross oversimplification. There are multiple cultures in any one bank just as there are in any other corporation with divisions covering different business activities. That aside, regulators, politicians, and even many in the banking sector itself accepted the assertion that problems stemmed from a culture that prioritized a bank's own interests above those of their clients and customers (G30 2015: 11, see also Obama 2012). As the New York Federal Reserve explained, this constituted 'a narrow cultural focus on short-term gain and disregard of broader social consequences' (New York Fed 2015a). Or as the US Securities and Exchange Commission noted, 'the financial crisis... [was] yet another reminder of the fundamental need for stronger ethics, risk management and regulatory compliance' (SEC 2011).

Two Views of Culture

From Misconduct to Financialization

The perceptive reader will already notice another important point that requires clarification though; and it is one that strikes at the heart of the argument in this book. State managers described the culture of banking problem, on the one hand, as banks prioritizing their own interests over wider societal concerns; whilst on the other hand arguing that the solution was ethical, managerial, and compliance-related reform. For them, this was a simple case of bankers behaving badly. Bad culture was about misbehaviour. And misbehaviour was defined as conduct that did not abide by acceptable (read liberal) market ethics. It was conduct that undermined the market. State managers would regularly refer to it as 'misconduct', because it was perceived to be out of keeping with *appropriate* market conduct.

The implicit assumption was that misbehaving individuals needed reminding of the correct behaviours; the culture of banking would then re-align with the culture of the market; and this would allow the market to function properly again. To put it rather bluntly—and at the risk of oversimplifying—the problem was with the agents and their behaviour, whilst the structure of the market was beyond contestation. In this book I will argue that this was a flawed assumption, because to a large degree the *structure* determines the culture of Anglo-American banking.

The view adopted by state managers led to a very public debate about improving *behaviour* in banks, and countless reforms of the ethics and norms—the ideas and principles—in Anglo-American banking. The crux of the argument of this book however, is that the problematic culture of US and UK banking has far deeper roots than misconduct; bad bank culture stems, in large part, from the financialization of Anglo-America. This process of financialization—which arose from the slowdown in profitability in both economies and has led to wage stagnation and high levels of private debt—distorts the very structure of US and UK economies within which the banks operate. As a result, the benign assumptions that underpin the narrower bank debate are flawed. Financialization fuels: economic inequality; financial instability; the bloodthirsty search for yield to satisfy shareholder demands (Froud et al. 2002); as well as engendering rent-seeking behaviour (Stiglitz 2015); and it empowers the financiers, which also distorts democratic politics (E. Warren 2018). Thus *financialization*, I will argue, is the more fundamental driver of the culture of banking problem.

This distinction—between the narrow debate about bank culture and the broader, structural version—is hugely important. This is because, by narrowing the debate to misbehaviour and misconduct the political efforts were limited in two ways: firstly, they were limited *temporally*; and secondly, they were limited in *scope*. The reforms state managers implemented were limited temporally, because they will have a very limited lifespan; the reforms will almost certainly be undone by the overriding pressures of financialization. But even more importantly, the reforms were also limited in scope, because important features of the culture of banking—like disproportionately high pay in the finance sector for example—were excluded from the political debate.

From Financialization to Legitimacy

Why was the political debate unnecessarily narrow? One argument that this book will develop is that in spite of differences between more conservative and more radically minded US and UK state managers, a broad consensus emerged about the nature of the bank culture problem. This consensus accepted the misconduct diagnosis. For conservative and more radically-minded state managers the cultural problem was all about a few 'bad apples'; re-embedding the right rules and re-educating bankers was therefore the main priority. There were heated debates amongst the political classes, and differences of opinion over individual pieces of legislation. But these were differences of degree, rather than more fundamental disagreements about the causes of the bank culture problem. Almost all of the political debate therefore accepted that culture could be fixed by fostering better value systems amongst bankers; structuring incentives to promote more socially responsible investment strategies; and improving accountability mechanisms.

Why did this consensus emerge? I will argue that it emerged for two reasons: one was a matter of timing and urgency. Anglo-American state managers were faced with a crisis of legitimation characterized by historically low levels of trust in the institutions of government. The financial crisis—followed by public spending cuts—risked degenerating into a political crisis of the state. State managers urgently needed to restore trust. Conservatives and radicals recognized this. They therefore used the culture of banking problem as a 'political weapon' (Interview 20160518). Eye-watering financial penalties, public interrogations of bankers, and big speeches about punishing the banks accompanied the conduct reform agenda. But this was an attempt by both US and UK state managers to re-assert the appearance of their autonomy from the banks that they had previously bailed out. It was a populist attempt to present themselves as champions of the general will of the people against the profligate banks (Mudde and Kaltwasser 2017).

The other reason for the consensus though is unnervingly obvious: financialization is hard to fix. When we understand that financialization in Anglo-America has resulted from political and corporate responses to a longer-term crisis of accumulation—a slowdown in profitability—since the 1960s and 1970s, that affects the entire model of economic growth and a full range of financial and non-financial companies' strategies, then it is easy to see why change is challenging (Kay 2016: 301). It would not be too much of a stretch to argue that financialization in Anglo-America is now considered part of the natural order of things; too deeply embedded to be fundamentally reconfigured. In light of this we can understand why the culture of banking debate narrowed to the simpler and more easily identifiable problem of promoting responsible conduct. But the underlying message of this book is that Anglo-American state managers abdicated responsibility for dealing with the more fundamental, structural problems at the heart of their financial systems.

Defining Bad Culture as Misconduct

We are getting ahead of ourselves though. To start with we should present a brief survey of the cultural problems as state managers defined them. The Basel

Committee on Banking Supervision (BCBS) and the EU Commission presented three categories of misconduct or, put differently, three interrelated symptoms of a cultural problem in banking: the mis-selling of financial products to retail and business clients; the violation of national and international rules (tax rules, anti-money laundering rules, anti-terrorism rules, economic sanctions); and the manipulation of financial markets (LIBOR [London Interbank Offered Rate] rates and foreign exchange rates) (BCBS 2015). Again, though this book focuses on Anglo-America, these types of cultural shortcomings were not limited to Anglo-American institutions. Connor (2014) for example, gathered data from around the world on antitrust investigations relating to price-fixing by multinational banking cartels. Over 400 cases of large banks being involved in market manipulation were identified, and most of the largest banking groups in Japan, Switzerland, the UK, Australia, and the US have been involved in such price-fixing cartels since 1990.

Having identified and framed the debate around bank culture as being defined by poor ethics and misconduct, state managers set about remediation. In response to the cultural shortcomings, from an early stage (around 2009) and with a renewed sense of urgency after the 2012 LIBOR (rate-fixing) scandals, first UK and then US state managers set about reforming bank culture. The first phase of responses to the global financial crisis focused primarily on stabilizing banking systems—through bailouts—expanding supervisory powers and establishing resolution plans to avoid a repeat collapse (Interview 20160419). In the US the Troubled Asset Recovery Plan (TARP) was effectively a bailout package to (primarily) support struggling banks, and was initially set at $700bn. In the UK, a series of measures ranging from the Special Liquidity Scheme (£200bn) to the Bank Recapitalization Fund (£25bn) sought to achieve the same goal, albeit by slightly different means (Woll 2014). Then came the Dodd Frank Wall Street Reform and Consumer Protection Act (the Dodd Frank Act) in the US, and several Banking Reform Acts in the UK. Together these aimed at giving supervisory authorities greater legal powers to manage and intervene in struggling financial institutions. Even at this early stage however, there was a recognition of cultural problems exposed by the crisis and the role that these problems had played.

Initially the diagnosis focused primarily on risk management and the perverse incentives to take on too much risk that had in turn left the taxpayer exposed through the government bailouts. Opinion is divided over how exactly this so-called *moral hazard* works or whether financial rewards actually incentivize greater risk-taking. It certainly makes for good headlines if you believe that under 'casino capitalism' (Strange 1998) traders in large banks sit gambling away taxpayer money hoping to make a quick buck for their firm and walk away with a million-dollar bonus at the end of the financial year, safe in the knowledge that if the bet fails (on a large scale), governments will intervene to rescue the bank because they are deemed Too Big To Fail (TBTF). This is to assume a degree of

(1) *bad intent*—that these traders lack any social responsibility; (2) *consciousness*—that they are completely aware of the potential cumulative implications of their individual transactions; and (3) desire for *financial reward*—when in fact status and the pecking order might be even more important, that is both hard to believe and is not supported by available research. In other words, the gambling analogy in casino capitalism only goes so far.

But, at the very least, Anglo-American state managers recognized that corporate governance and managerial (as well as supervisory) oversight had become complacent with regards to the risks their firms were assuming. Though bonuses and pay were features of these early discussions in the US and the UK however, the general conclusion was that cultural issues could probably be resolved by banning or separating out certain higher-risk activities (the Volcker rule in the US and the Vickers Reforms in the UK) and restructuring the banking system so that banks bore greater responsibility for their own activities (inter alia via shareholder bail-out plans). It was assumed that the threat of failure would prove to be a powerful disincentive; and, ultimately, that tightening market discipline would weed out cases of misbehaviour. Put differently, the underlying business strategies of banks under financialization—including, but not limited to, the search for yield and the reliance on non-interest income—were already conspicuously absent from the debate; instead the debate moved further towards an idealized vision of the market, where existence-threatening levels of risk-taking were curbed. Conduct which threatened the market would be outlawed.

We might also note that although—post-LIBOR—the UK took a lead in narrowing the culture debate to focus on ethics and values, even at an early stage of the financial crisis the starting point for discussions over problematic elements of banking was therefore noticeably constrained. Even the emphasis of ring-fencing reforms—for example—was simply to reduce the worst negative externalities of trading-related activities. The fact that these trading activities are essentially a mechanism for the redistribution of wealth amongst the financial sector was—at best—a secondary concern (Hardie and Macartney 2016).

By 2012 however, the second phase, or what Mark Carney referred to as the legitimacy crisis, became an even more pressing priority. Several years of austerity and public protest following the bank bailouts created a newfound sense of urgency for state managers. Public opinion would not tolerate a second banking crisis without a strong(er) political response. The immediate catalyst for the legitimacy crisis was the LIBOR rate-fixing scandal and, for reasons I will explain later in the book, was particularly important in the UK. It was during this second phase of the crisis that the political response to the culture of the banking problem crystallized.

Since the LIBOR scandal was so pivotal to the subsequent political response, an explanation of how the scandal unfolded is warranted. In a certain sense, LIBOR was just another important example of the three kinds of misconduct outlined above. In another sense though, the change in tone and approach of the UK and US responses can be directly attributed to this particular scandal. As the Federal Reserve would later explain, the Fed's 'interest in reforming culture [was] a product of events since the Financial Crisis [in particular] the manipulation of LIBOR and foreign exchange rates' (New York Fed 2015b). This was because, 'though the many post-crisis reforms to banks' balance sheets' from the Dodd–Frank Act to Basel capital adequacy 'had provided necessary bulwarks against systemic risk…those new laws, regulations, and standards [had] done little to curb banker misconduct' (ibid.). The assumption that tightened market discipline would be sufficient to promote good conduct had been undermined. The already narrow debate on culture therefore narrowed even further.

The LIBOR Scandal

The London Interbank Offered Rate (LIBOR) is a benchmark interest rate overseen by the British Bankers Association in London. LIBOR was calculated each business day by averaging the interest rates at which the Contributor Panel (designated banks) estimated they could borrow unsecured funds from other banks across ten currencies. The panel would electronically submit perceived borrowing rates for fifteen different borrowing periods (maturities)—ranging from overnight to one year—to Thompson Reuters by approximately 11.10am each working day. Thompson Reuters would then rank the submissions by currency and maturity from highest to lowest, exclude the four highest and four lowest submissions, and average the remaining submissions. By approximately 12pm the LIBORs—multiple averaged rates—were sent, amongst others, to servers and traders of LIBOR-based financial products around the world. These LIBOR rates were used as the basis for the pricing of fixed-income futures, swaps, options, and other derivative instruments. Traders made predictions based on where LIBORs would be set in future, and on this basis often entered into multiple derivatives contracts; the profit and loss that resulted from those contracts was therefore directly affected by the relevant LIBORs on specific dates. If the relevant LIBORs moved in the direction that favoured the traders' position, then the respective trader and their institution stood to benefit and vice versa. The point though was that since traders often took large derivative positions, even relatively minor shifts in LIBOR could result in significant gains or losses.

But the LIBOR rates were not simply influential because of their impact on trading-related gains and losses. Financial institutions around the world frequently used LIBOR to set their own reference interest rates which were related to both financial instruments and consumer lending products such as mortgages, credit cards, student loans, and so on. In fact, money market rates are used as a benchmark to set payments on up to $800 trillion worth of financial instruments globally (EU Commission 2015: 174). In other words, LIBOR affected the global flow of money on a day-to-day basis. Although the LIBOR averages were intended to be an objective set of estimations based on designated banks' submissions, if a bank was therefore able to coordinate its submission with another Contributor Panel bank submission its potential to manipulate the average increased (USDC 2015: 4).

On 16 April 2008 the *Wall Street Journal* published an article claiming that larger banks may have been understating their borrowing costs during the 2008 credit crunch (*WSJ* 2008a). The evidence for this at the time was that LIBOR rates had remained largely unchanged until the day before the financial turmoil began, whereas other interest rates and CDS (Credit Default Swap) spreads had increased (*WSJ* 2008b). In other words, other market measures for the borrowing costs of the largest banks—and, in particular, Citigroup, West Landesbanken, HBOS, JPMorgan Chase, and UBS—suggested that these banks were keeping their reported rates artificially low. This would present a picture of the banking system 'doing better than it was at critical junctures in the financial crisis' (*WSJ* 2008b). Initially, authorities were sceptical of the claims, responding that there was no hard evidence of manipulation (BIS 2008:70). Indeed, in the International Monetary Fund's (IMF) Global Financial Stability Review of October 2008, it stated that '[a]lthough the integrity of the US dollar LIBOR fixing process has been questioned by some market participants and the financial press, it appears that US dollar LIBOR remains an accurate measure of a typical creditworthy bank's marginal cost of unsecured US dollar term funding' (IMF 2008: 76). Yet subsequent investigations revealed that reporting banks had indeed manipulated quotes, sometimes at the request of senior management, and other times simply based on the discretion of traders themselves, who stood to gain from (typically) higher estimates of a banks' borrowing costs.

In the immediate aftermath of the LIBOR revelations, UK state managers went into overdrive. US authorities subsequently followed suit. This sequencing was important, because one reason for the already narrow debate focusing increasingly on culture-as-ethical-conduct was due to the framing of the British authorities. The result of the British response was twofold: on the one hand the focus on improving ethics and conduct led to modest but noticeable changes in accountability and compliance. This set of changes is painfully apparent to those working in the largest US and UK banks now. But the second effect was that the speed and shape of the UK response meant that the focus of the debate shifted even further from a broad-based discussion about financialization itself. Even more critical voices—such as Andrew Tyrie MP who led the UK Parliamentary response and US Senator Elizabeth Warren—were rapidly co-opted into the ethical conduct narrative.

Following LIBOR, financial penalties were meted out by both UK and US regulators against the largest banks in a form of populist statecraft. But the LIBOR scandal was nonetheless a defining moment in the shift towards reforming norms and ethics. The UK Parliamentary Commission on Banking Standards was established in August 2012 producing a four-hundred page report entitled 'Changing Banking for Good'. As a result of that report three big culture-related initiatives were undertaken in the UK: the Banking Standards Review Council (which would later become the Banking Standards Board) was established as an industry-led, standard-setting body; the earlier Vickers ring-fencing of certain core banking activities from higher risk trading activities was revisited, resulting in a stronger system of disincentives for the banks to test the ring-fence (euphemistically called 'electrifying' the ring-fence); and the Senior Managers and Certified Persons Regime was established, to increase the personal accountability of those responsible for various types of risk-taking (PCBS 2013a). Initially the responses of US state managers were less wide-ranging, with the Department of Justice, the NY Department of Financial Services and other federal and state regulators sticking to their strategy of deferred and non-prosecution agreements and large financial penalties. Over the course of 2012–13 US authorities handed out fines of \$360 million to Barclays, \$1.2bn to UBS, and \$475 million to RBS for their part in the LIBOR scandal. Admittedly these were only a small proportion of the \$162 billion in fines dispensed by US regulatory authorities between 2007–18. But by 2015 US authorities led by the NY Federal Reserve had also begun a process of cultural standard-setting that specifically imitated the UK example (New York Fed 2015b).

Revisiting the Broader Culture Debate

The Two Big Arguments

In summary, the question which this book addresses is why, given the vast array of efforts employed by the US and UK authorities and their banks, have many of the issues associated with the culture of the banking problem persisted? This book offers two arguments: firstly, from the political perspective, the cultural problems persist because state managers in both the UK and the US have been primarily concerned with addressing the legitimacy crisis their institutions of government have been facing (Streeck 2014). As a result the kinds of substantive (and more radical) banking reforms required have largely been overlooked. The urgency of the legitimacy crisis is why both critical and conservative state managers have been drawn into a narrower debate about culture as ethical conduct. The legitimacy crisis is also the reason for the populist statecraft invoked by state managers, which I will discuss below.

Secondly, from the perspective of the banking system itself, the deep financialization of these two Western economies goes a long way to explaining the stubborn persistence of bad culture. Structural, demand-side factors are arguably the more important determinant of bank culture in Anglo-America. This book argues that financialization engenders a process of wealth abstraction without a similar growth in productive and innovative activity (Kay 2012: 1); or leveraging control over something that already exists, and manipulating your expertise or ownership of this asset or service (Bregman 2017). Economist Roger Tootle described this as a distinction between creative and distributive activity, arguing that 'part of the answer to why there is so much financial activity in relation to the gains this produces for society is that much financial activity produces huge distributive gains; that is, gains that are of no net overall benefit' (Bootle 2012: 18). This view of financialization helps to explain why bank culture is as it is. It helps to explain what was missing from the political debate. And it certainly helps to explain why profits and wages are so high in the banking sector whilst wage and productivity growth are so anaemic in other parts of the economy.

We therefore return full circle to our argument about legitimacy. For Anglo-American state managers have needed to address bank culture because it has become socially unacceptable not to. The public has contested, inter alia, bank bailouts whilst social spending on areas such as education and healthcare has been cut (Burnham 2011). This is part of the legitimacy crisis UK and US state managers have faced. Their responses to the culture of banking problem therefore reek of populism, as they have engaged in a political point-scoring exercise—being seen to address the banks—without wanting to address the underlying financialization of Anglo-America. As a result they have bought themselves time, but simply offset the inevitable legitimacy challenges associated with banking culture and financialization. These two pieces—*legitimacy* and *financialization*—therefore form the basis of the conceptual argument presented in this book.

Three Parts of the Book

This book is divided into three parts: the first part provides some of the historical and conceptual context; the second part then tells the story of how state managers, having defined the bank culture problem as one of misconduct and poor ethics, set about addressing it. Aside from significant legislative and industry-led reforms, which have indeed had a marginal impact on US and UK banking (see Chapter 9), state managers also used the banks as scapegoats in a populist attempt to address their own (political) legitimacy crisis. This is the case that I make in Part II of the book.

Part III then shows what has changed in the banks. Here a puzzle emerges because in Chapter 9 I will show that the world of banking has undergone some modifications, whilst in Chapter 10 I will argue that very little of substance has actually changed. In conducting the research behind this book between 2014–18 I wrestled long and hard with this puzzle. Those I spoke to working in financial services now feel that banking is entirely different: tougher controls; more accountability; a heavy emphasis on values; and less fun to be had and money to be made. This is what I was told again and again.

But as I stood back and surveyed Anglo-American banking in its broader context, what I realized is that the paradox that everything and nothing has changed is—to some degree—a matter of perspective. More importantly though, it is a question of what we consider to be *acceptable* and *unchangeable* features of the political economies of Anglo-America. If we simply accept (for example) that disproportionately high pay in the financial sector; high levels of household debt which feeds pernicious lending practices; the disconnect between profits in financial services and the social benefits to non-financial firms and the wider economy; and the financial instability that stems from the incessant search for yield, are beyond the realm of debate, then we are left to focus on tinkering with incentives and values and ethics. We accept that the financialized markets of Anglo-America are fit-for-purpose, and so we are left to encourage appropriate market conduct—conduct befitting these purportedly healthy, functioning markets. And this is precisely the political move state managers have attempted. For more conservative voices this was a deliberate attempt to depoliticize—or remove from scrutiny—the financialization of Anglo-America; and for more radical voices, they were co-opted into a banal debate about culture as good conduct.

The Academic Contribution

There are four major contributions developed by this book: one is that it provides a more comprehensive account of both the problems facing Anglo-American banks and the political reforms of bank conduct than other non-academic texts; secondly, it provides a more elaborate conceptual understanding of the failures of political reforms than other similar legal accounts; thirdly, it contributes to the growing political economy literature on post-crisis financial reform; and fourthly, it provides one of the first systematic, critical political economy studies to focus on bank culture.

On the first contribution, the argument of this particular book distinguishes it from a series of other recent accounts. In relation to the banking element of our study, these accounts have ranged from informal biographical texts—such as *Swimming With Sharks* (2016)—and popular novels—such as *CityBoy* (2009) and *The Big Short* (2011)—to more academic accounts such as *Other Peoples Money* (2016), *The End of Alchemy* (2017), and *Between Debt and the Devil* (2017). In particular the academic accounts have tended to opt for a nostalgic version of the traditional financialization argument, proposing a range of solutions and policy prescriptions that basically amount to a return to the past; to a simpler and narrower form of banking with stricter limits, controls, and firewalls on more radical types of trading activity. In essence, this has been their answer to the culture problem. The solution has tended to be proposed by writers who grieve the financial revolution of the 1980s and 1990s; and it is essentially a stricter version of that which has already been proposed by US, UK, and EU authorities. One of the most significant policies implemented by state managers for instance has been the banning of higher risk trading activity; and these academic accounts have simply called for tougher versions of the same thing, or what is called a return to 'narrow banking' (Kay 2009).

To understand why we have failed to achieve these more radical reforms the above accounts have tended to rely—often implicitly—on an accepted version of bank lobbying power. A range of arguments, from *The Bankers New Clothes* (2013), to *Fragile by Design* (2015), *This is Our Fight* (2017), or *The End of the Experiment?* (2014) have implicitly or explicitly emphasized the overweening influence of the largest banks, and policymakers' fear of challenging them. This leads us to the second contribution, because this version of events resonates with accounts from legal studies. Here we find a range of studies that also accept the elision of good culture with good conduct, but then highlight the inefficacy of political efforts to promote reform. Legal scholars have for example, noted the inadequacy of deferred and non-prosecution agreements (discussed in Chapter 8) on the part of US state managers (Karpoff 2012, Garrett 2016). These agreements are intended to reduce financial penalties or prosecutions in exchange for promises of improved behaviour by firms.

The explanation for why these political efforts have failed however, is undertheorized. It rests primarily upon the fear of authorities to tackle large corporations (Eisinger 2017); or on the type of prosecution pursued, where civil lawsuits generally result in modest fines and little retribution, whilst criminal prosecutions are watered down by plea bargaining (Shapiro 1984). As Rena Steinzor has argued, the main reason for the lack of corporate reform is 'the deeply ingrained tendency amongst investigators and prosecutors to take the route of least resistance' (2014: 6). For legal scholars though, this strategy is determined by the fact that proving corporate misconduct 'beyond reasonable doubt' is highly problematic; but also the fact that prosecutors are deterred by: the risk of losing; limited resources; and 'apprehension about the intensity of the potential defence' (ibid.).

I argue that the legal studies contribution is nonetheless a relatively basic explanation for three reasons: first, it understates the social and ideological relations between political authorities and capitalist enterprises that the critical political economy account in this book foregrounds (Burnham 1994). Secondly, and relatedly, the fact that states appear deferential to the banks is highly contingent in the legal accounts. That is, the structural conditions (financialization) that empower the financiers are underspecified (see Bieler and Morton 2008 for a critique). Thirdly, legal accounts struggle to conceptualize the power of ideas and rhetoric. They therefore limit our understanding of the ways in which populist discourses impact upon the *intangible* but very *real* crisis of legitimation (Macartney and Calcagno 2019).

This of course leads us towards our third academic contribution, which relates to the political economy literature. There is by now a wide political economy corpus focusing on post-crisis reform in the banking sector (Epstein 2017). One simple way of categorizing this literature is to divide it between those accounts focused on regulatory reform; and those accounts focused on bank practices and models. The vast majority of the regulatory literature has targeted big structural reforms, from changes in capital adequacy ratios, to resolution and ring-fencing measures (Moschella and Tsingou 2013). Accounts of changes in banking practices have suggested that despite a general shrinkage of investment banking operations in the largest banks, there has been a remarkable continuity in the business models of the largest banks (Bell and Hindmoor 2018). In particular, the heavy emphasis on shareholder metrics and non-interest income are seen as indicators of the continued financialization of Anglo-American banking systems, and market-based banking (Mayfield et al. 2017, Erturk 2016).

In relation to corporate misconduct in the financial sector, political economists have drawn contradictory conclusions. In partial contrast to this book some scholars have argued that the strategic position of the US gives its enforcement agencies a structural power over international banks (see Emmenegger 2015 for an overview). These authors claim that international banks depend on access to US markets, allowing authorities to apply pressure during negotiations with firms. Instead, the evidence in this book shows the limits to authorities' power. In our case, at the risk of oversimplifying, the structural conditions lead to the opposite outcome; domestic authorities—in both the US and the UK—are limited to a significant degree by the embeddedness of financialization as the organizing principle for their respective economies. In that sense our argument confirms the findings of Malcolm Campbell-Verduyn (2017), who is sceptical about the capacity for states to promote deep cultural change amongst the largest banks (2017: 352).

Moreover, our account of how financialization shapes both banking and political responses coincides with the conclusions of Krippner (2011), who explains that the restructuring of capitalism in recent decades was oftentimes simply the product of contingent decision-making given a very limited range of policy options. Krippner ends however, on a more optimistic note, by suggesting that financialization is in terminal decline; on this point I disagree, because the evidence seems to suggest that financialization has been in an *almost permanent* state of decline. It is discredited but has become even more deeply embedded because of political and central bank responses to the financial crisis. I will return to this point in the Conclusion, where I will argue that although state managers have bought themselves a little time (Streeck 2014) in their response to the bank culture debate, the legitimacy and instability-threatening aspects of financialization have not been resolved.

This brings us to the fourth and final contribution, because populism features very prominently in our discussion of the short-term, reactionary strategy of US and UK state managers. I will explain the connections between populism and the legitimacy crisis more fully in Chapter 3. Suffice it to note that at the time of writing populism has arguably become the buzzword of the 2010s for comparative politics and political economy (Mudde and Kaltwasser 2017). Whilst populism is often conflated with its right-wing, nativist version though, there is also a left-wing version of populism (Deegan-Krause and Haughton 2009). The former strand of populism is most commonly associated with xenophobia and nationalism; whilst the latter strand, which is far more relevant to this book, is focused on economic grievances, inequality, and the economic elite—in our case, the bankers. At its core, populism is a thin ideology based on capturing anti-establishment sentiment; and this is why it became such a powerful tool in tackling the legitimacy crisis, by re-asserting the independence of the political classes from their embattled banks, and by claiming to be representing the general will of the public. This reading in turn helps to explain why superficial differences between radical and more conservative responses to the bank culture problem collapsed into a narrow, reactionary, populist statecraft.

Methodological Matters

To be very clear, the point of the book is not that all banking is bad. Elsewhere there is certainly evidence, for example, of socially-oriented strategy in large banks (see Epstein 2017). But—to reiterate—this book focuses on Anglo-America for a number of reasons: firstly, though the financial sector, as a proportion of the domestic economy is far larger in the UK than in the US, the 'marked shift towards financial activity as a form of profit generation since the 1980s' (French et al. 2011: 807) meant that these two countries were the first to undergo the shareholder revolution from the 1970s (Stockhammer 2005). Secondly, the inequality trends in the US and UK are remarkably similar. Between 1979 and 2007 in the UK, the top 10 per cent increased their share of total income by 14 percentage points, from 28.4 per cent to 42.6 per cent; whilst the top 1 per cent saw their share rise from 5.9 per cent to 15.4 per cent. In the US, the magnitude of the gains are almost identical, with the top percentile of US workers seeing their share of total income rise from 8.0 per cent to 18.3 per cent (Bell and van Reenen 2013: 1). In particular, wages in the finance sector—and bonuses in the finance sector—were the major driver of this inequality (Lindley and McIntosh 2014). This has been labelled the 'finance sector premium'—or the disproportionate wage gains for workers in the finance sector—and the UK and US are leading economies based on this indicator (ibid.: 36). Finally, not only did the global financial crisis have a distinctly Anglo-American emphasis, but so did the subsequent scandals and cases of misconduct, with large Anglo-American banks being at the forefront. Ethical and conduct-related reform efforts have therefore been most pronounced in the US and UK, whilst there is also strong evidence that deeper cultural problems continue to abound. This makes these two economies ideal test cases.

As I will explain, only by employing a wide-ranging methodology can the limitations to state managers' and banks' efforts be understood. The research behind this book therefore draws heavily upon official publications from the US and UK regulatory authorities in question. It also draws extensively upon speeches and publications from government officials, their central banks and Treasury departments. Further, the book mobilizes a wide range of statistical data, including a comprehensive list of all the fines levelled by UK and US state managers that I have compiled in recent years. Together these sources allow us to compare and explore the stated intentions and motivations of state managers with actual measures, legislative and otherwise, that have been employed in relation to the bank culture issue. By using these sources it is possible to trace the narrowing of the bank culture debate to focus on conduct and ethics, and to situate the populist narratives that accompanied this narrowing in the context of the legitimacy crisis.

The second part of the book focuses almost entirely on the banks themselves. For reasons of practicability and because they have been at the forefront of the most important structural changes in recent decades and at the centre of the misconduct sanctions, I focus primarily on the *largest* UK and US banks. Much of this material is therefore drawn from the annual reports and financial statements of the largest banks in our survey. In addition to these official data, the findings of the book draw extensively on a wide range of semi-structured interview data compiled between 2014–18. These interviews include over 150 conducted with employees in financial services firms on both sides of the Atlantic, as well as over forty conducted with regulators, politicians, lawyers, and journalists. For legal reasons not all of this interview material can be attributed in this book, though the material nonetheless heavily informs the argument.

Plan of the Book

The argument unfolds as follows. Chapter 2 examines the sources of bank culture. It begins by outlining the view that good culture is about good behaviour that abides by liberal market norms. This is the view that state managers and the banks have subscribed to. Then the chapter develops an account of financialization. The aim here is to show the underlying conditions, rooted in crises of accumulation, changing models of banking, and the indebtedness of Anglo-America, that are strong determinants of bank culture but which have been relatively absent from the political debate.

Chapter 3 then has two purposes, both of which focus on understanding what US and UK state managers have been attempting in tackling the culture problem. Through a re-reading of Smith and the German ordo-liberals the chapter first explains that—during early responses to the global financial crisis—Anglo-American state managers followed what I call a liberal blueprint (based on their conception of culture-as-acceptable-market-conduct). Their aim, as Smith and the ordo-liberals had indicated, was to shape behaviour by tightening market discipline; supply-side reform. If bankers bore the costs of their decisions there would be more incentive to act responsibly. The second half of the chapter develops the notion of the legitimacy crisis. Witnessing the limitations of market discipline to shape good behaviour, state managers shifted towards normative, ethical reforms—alongside another wave of financial penalties and new regulations; again, supply-side in character. The aim however, was to address the legitimacy crisis. Here I turn to the work of Jürgen Habermas on legitimacy. Habermas argued that the benefits of the capitalist economy are disproportionately weighted in favour of the rich and powerful. This tension becomes particularly acute and apparent in the management of crises. The requisite level of public support thus declines. Rather than fundamentally reconfigure the economic system however, state managers revert to point-scoring or populist strategies (Macartney 2014). These insights help to explain the agency of UK and US authorities in Chapters 4–7.

Part I of the book argues that there were two overarching imperatives shaping state managers responses to the culture crisis since 2007: the belief that improving bank culture could predominantly be solved by tightening the market mechanism and making banks more responsible for their actions; yet with time, as the legitimacy crisis developed, the goal changed somewhat to restoring trust in the financial system and, perhaps more importantly, in the executive leadership of state managers themselves.

Part II begins with Chapter 4 and focuses on the emergence of the culture crisis in the US, by beginning in the early 2000s. It shows how, following a period of regulatory intensity after the Dot.com and Enron scandals, regulatory complacency set in. Using a range of opinion survey data, this chapter also tracks a rather unnerving correlation between popular confidence in the banking system and regulatory activity, for example, in areas like prosecutions for misconduct. The chapter then shows that, as the financial crisis hit in 2007–8, though the main priority was stabilization, there was already an attempt to address (so-called) cultural shortcomings. The final section of the chapter shows how the legitimacy crisis unfolded in the US in 2010–11. In the context of severe budget cuts (or austerity) by the Obama administration, and the emerging Occupy movement, the perception that the government was going easy on misconduct in the banking system became politically unsustainable.

Chapter 5 then continues this argument by looking at the approaches US state managers employed to address this legitimacy crisis. These are broadly divided into *harder* and *softer* measures. In keeping with US tradition, the harder measures tended to revolve around prosecutions and fines. The chapter examines new institutions that were set up at the time such as the Consumer Financial Protection Bureau and the Financial Fraud Enforcement Task Force. Yet, even here, the chapter presents evidence of the importance of legitimacy and a quasi-populist response—hitting the big banks with unprecedented fines as a way of point-scoring—particularly in the emergence of the NY Department of Financial Services (DFS). The chapter then turns to the softer approaches to the legitimacy crisis that began to emerge, particularly from 2014–15 onwards. Here we focus closely on the New York Federal Reserve, which spearheaded the standard-setting, normative agenda to reform banking culture through workshops and closer scrutiny of the boards of the largest banks.

Chapter 6 then continues the argument about the legitimacy crisis as a central theme shaping state managers' responses, by looking at the UK. The UK was less affected by the post-Enron regulatory flurry but equally guilty of the regulatory complacency in the mid-2000s. As with the US, as the financial crisis unfolded the first wave of responses focused primarily on tightening market discipline via resolution planning and the ring-fence, though once again culture and legitimacy were evident in the thinking of state managers. One obvious example discussed early in this chapter is the public hearings held by the Treasury Select Committee in an attempt to defuse public anger. This chapter then focuses on the second wave of the crisis following the LIBOR and Forex scandals. Tracking a range of opinion polls and combined with an examination of rising austerity measures from 2010 onwards, as well as London anti-banking protest movements, the chapter closes by showing how the legitimacy crisis unfolded in the UK.

In turn, Chapter 7 examines the hard and soft approaches of UK state managers to the legitimacy crisis. In terms of harder responses, the chapter focuses on new legislation and institutions that were introduced immediately following the LIBOR scandal, focusing in particular on the Senior Managers Regime (SMR) and the electrification of the ring-fence. The Senior Managers Regime for example is widely considered to be one of the most significant and toughest culture-related reforms anywhere in the world. As I explain later in the chapter though, the SMR itself was significantly diluted by the efforts of more conservative UK Treasury officials who were cautious—on the one hand—to appear to be taking a hard line with the banks whilst—on the other—to avoid imposing too onerous a requirement on senior bankers (Interview 20170611). The chapter then examines the extensive standard-setting, normative approaches by UK state managers, focusing in particular on the Parliamentary Commission on Banking Standards. The chapter closes however—by way of confirming the argument about legitimacy as a driving mechanism for addressing bank culture—by showing that by 2015, as public resentment towards bank bailouts and the scandals of 2012 began to abate, so did the political will for substantive reform.

Part III of the book is focused on examining the extent of the changes taking place in banking culture. For reasons of space and because they have been at the forefront of both the misconduct issues and regulatory reform agenda, Part III of the book focuses primarily on the largest UK and US banks: Barclays, Lloyds, RBS, and HSBC, as well as Citibank, Bank of America, JPMorgan, Morgan Stanley, Goldman Sachs, and Wells Fargo.

Part III begins with Chapter 8 by examining the effectiveness of financial penalties as a mechanism for promoting cultural reform in the banks. In the first part of the chapter I explain the emphasis placed by state managers on financial penalties as a disincentive for misconduct; but I also explain that, from the perspective of regulatory authorities, the mechanism for change is not directly linked to the financial penalty itself, but to the rise in compliance and risk management systems adopted following the imposition of a fine. These are supposed to create a more cautious approach to—inter alia—risk-taking and ethical decisions. The main argument of the chapter however, is that the effectiveness of these fines is not convincing. The chapter examines for example, the impact that the penalties had on the share prices and profitability of the banks. I show that, contrary to what one might have assumed, the banks that received the largest fines oftentimes also performed the best financially, suggesting that the fines did not bear a direct relationship to economic performance. The chapter then explains this claim by dissecting the fines themselves. It shows that, relative to the size of the misconduct the penalties were rather negligible; that large portions of the penalties were tax-deductible; that the structure of the penalties—for example as charitable donations or orders to increase lending to poor communities—also dampened their effectiveness; and that the compliance reforms often incorporated within the penalties were weak and poorly enforced.

Chapter 9 then examines what exactly *has* changed in the culture of these largest Anglo-American banks. Using the supply-side, good conduct concept the chapter explains why—from the perspective of bank employees—so much has changed in bank culture. The first section focuses primarily on the annual reports of the banks between 2007–16 to show—despite certain important differences between the UK and the US banks—the growing emphasis placed on customers, risk, and ethics. It also shows a surprising continuity between these value statements pre- and post-financial crisis. The banks believed that their employees *knew* and *accepted* proper market norms, but had probably *forgotten* them. The second and third sections of this chapter then explore how these value statements emphasizing risk and compliance became embedded in the day-to-day operations of these banks. The fourth section then examines changes to one of the most politically controversial culture-related issues, that of remuneration (fixed pay and bonuses). It examines the ways in which pay became more closely connected to longer term performance rather than short-term risk-taking, as well as considering the rising emphasis of values and ethics in performance reviews for bank employees. The main argument of this chapter is that, certainly from the perspective of bank employees, significant changes were made to banking culture.

Chapter 10 however, then explains what has not changed. Here I return to the argument that financialization is the most important determinant of bank culture in Anglo-America. The chapter is divided into three parts. I begin by showing that, on various measures, financialization has increased in the aftermath of the financial crisis. Quantitative easing and low interest rates have only compounded the emphasis of the US and the UK economies on profits from financial activities. The second part of the chapter then examines how austerity and wage stagnation, plus the emphasis on consumption-led recoveries, led to heightened consumer indebtedness. Here I show how Anglo-American banks continue to employ business models that exploit the heavily indebted. In the third and final section I return to the issue of pay and bonuses. Though—as Chapter 9 showed—there has been a heavy regulatory focus on the bonus culture, the existence of the finance sector premium—disproportionately high pay in the financial sector—remains. Not only is this evidence of rent-seeking behaviour but I close the chapter by showing the ongoing legitimacy challenges associated with high pay in the banking sector juxtaposed against wage stagnation in the rest of the economy.

In the Conclusion I point to the fact that in the political realm in the US and the UK the bank culture debate lost traction by the late 2010s. Recovery and a new president in the US, and Brexit and economic stagnation in the UK, have distracted attention away from the problem at hand. Political discussions about bank culture have been marginalized. Political discussions about the malign impacts of financialization are also conspicuously absent. State managers are living on borrowed time however, because the wave of anti-establishment sentiment that led to the 2016 Brexit vote and the Trump election are of the same order as the legitimacy crisis evoked by the bank culture problematique earlier in the 2010s.

PART I
RETHINKING BANK CULTURE

2
Bank Culture
Behaviour and Ethics, or Financialization?

The aim of this chapter is to examine the sources of bank culture. It begins by outlining the view that good culture can be established by ethical reform and curbing socially harmful behaviour through improving incentives and accountability. This is the view that state managers and the banks have subscribed to. I will argue however, that the emphasis on values, ethics, and socially responsible conduct is a very superficial way to approach some of the worst cultural problems in Anglo-American banking. Ethical reform and penalties *may* therefore succeed in limiting behaviours that cheat or distort the market mechanism—as in the case of LIBOR; but a fuller understanding of the structural pressures and incentives faced by the Anglo-American banking sectors helps to understand why, despite the 'successes' in improving conduct, many of the more disturbing (political and economic) idiosyncrasies inherent to US and UK banking remain unchecked. The difference between these two explanations of what drives bank culture is hugely important, because if financialization drives culture it not only means that many ethical improvements will at some stage be undone by the pressures of financialization, but it also means that certain things—like disproportionately high pay in the finance sector—that are marginalized from the political debate, can also be brought into view.

In developing this argument about an alternative explanation for bank culture we also move one step closer to answering the question about why state managers have narrowed the bank culture debate. The broader structural, historical conditions that states responded to and banks capitalized on help to explain the stickiness of financialization. The answer this chapter arrives at—and which is pursued further in Chapter 3—is that state managers therefore opted for the simpler response because financialization is difficult to fix.

Culture as Behaviour

To begin with we will briefly examine a range of academic accounts of organizational culture. We can keep this discussion brief because many of these themes—on how to use financial incentives to promote responsible behaviour and how to disseminate good ethics throughout a bank, for example—are explained more

The Bank Culture Debate: Ethics, Values, and Financialization in Anglo-America. Huw Macartney, Oxford University Press (2019). © Huw Macartney.
DOI: 10.1093/oso/9780198843764.001.0001

fully in Chapters 4–7 and 9. Though the academic accounts are informative in and of themselves, they are also important for our argument because they show the intellectual basis for state managers and the banks defining good culture as ethical, socially responsible conduct. This conception of culture has underpinned both the harder political responses aiming to change behaviour via tightening the market mechanism, as well as the softer, normative changes that banks and states have pursued.

The introductory chapter provided some indication of the contemporary usage of the term culture when referring to an organization or firm. The academic debates however go much further. There has, of course, been a broader political economy focus on the relationship between culture, identity, and globalization (Best and Paterson 2009). Instead this opening section addresses the sources and definitions of *corporate* cultures. In the 1950s anthropologists recorded 164 definitions of culture used in their field. They concluded with a working definition: 'Culture consists of patterns, explicit and implicit, of and for behavior acquired and transmitted by symbols' (Kroeber and Kluckhohn 1952: 35). A recent survey of 933 executives showed how the findings of anthropologists manifest in an organization such as the firm. The survey recorded answers ranging from 'a beliefs system', to 'a coordination mechanism', 'an invisible hand', 'a standard of behaviour', 'part work ethic, part ambiance of the work environment', and 'the tone for what type of company this is' (Graham et al. 2015: 5). Similarly, culture has elsewhere been defined as 'the collective assumptions, expectations, and values that reflect the explicit and implicit rules determining how people think and behave within the organization' (Thakor 2016: 7). It is easy to see why the political debate swiftly narrowed to issues of executive leadership, value statements, and remuneration practices as determinants of the norms within a firm.

Two features of the academic debate on culture are worth noting, for they framed much of the political response and the narrowing of the debate: the first is the alignment between values and strategy; and the second is on incentives. Though issues of executive leadership also featured prominently in the political debate, the main focus was on removing the distortive impact that 'misconduct' had on the otherwise efficient market mechanism. Values and incentives were therefore pivotal to the debate about promoting the right kind of market conduct. I therefore focus this first section on these two issues.

Values and Strategy

As Schein noted, the organizational studies view of culture is that it comprises 'a pattern of shared basic assumptions that was learned by a group...that has worked well enough to be considered valid and, therefore, [is] taught to new members as the correct way to perceive, think, and feel in relation to [the group's] problems' (2004:17). Moreover, once a culture is established, firms will often tend to hire employees with similar personality traits, and those whose characters most closely fit with the corporate culture will tend to perform better over time. This creates a feedback loop reinforcing a particular culture. This implies that organizational cultures are hard to reform.

As will become apparent in Chapters 4–7 and 9 though, the fact that corporate cultures are hard to change does not guarantee that they produce optimal outcomes. In particular, arguably the most important academic work on culture as ethical conduct highlighted that organizations often struggle to align values and strategy. In other words, firms may recognize and accept good, liberal market norms; but they may then struggle to align these values with their business strategy. Instead, they settle for a simpler task which is to produce value statements and ethical codes—that are oftentimes posted on webpages and posters around the office—and assume that this will suffice. The assumption is that if employees internalize the message from these value statements, they will behave in the right way. These big value statements however, have been shown to have limited impact on the day-to-day activity of employees. Or, as Thakor (2016: 8) has it, 'in organizations [that settle for this hands-off approach] culture has little impact on the execution of strategy'.

Another reason for the misalignment of culture and strategy—according to the literature—is that as organizations become larger and more complex, they are likely to develop subcultures in different divisions (Cremer 1993). This creates challenges for senior management in developing a uniform culture that guides the activities of its employees. Similarly, other research showed that for organizations which expand at speed, training new employees with the existing culture becomes problematic, and hence inbuilt values and ethics often disintegrate (Van den Steen 2010).

In other words, the academic reference point for state managers regarding the bank culture problem led to two conclusions: firstly, academic findings implied that if culture had led to adverse outcomes then there must have been a breakdown between what banks *believed* and how they *behaved*. The literature focused attention on the disconnect between good values and good business strategy. In that case various measures—such as market discipline and re-education—were required to re-align values and strategy.

Secondly, the literature implied that firms might have actually adopted the *wrong* set of values in the first place. Values might have become deeply entrenched in a firm, but the values themselves might not have been appropriate. Admittedly the academic literature had less to say on this point. But the implicit assumption was that there were indeed *proper* and *widely accepted* (read liberal) market norms in an abstract sense. Somewhere there existed an unquestioned code of market conduct; and abiding by this code would produce positive market outcomes. I will return to this point in Chapter 3. For now, suffice it to note that if firms had the *wrong* values in the first place then they needed reminding of the liberal market code.

The one thing that the literature simply did not address was the possibility that the structure of the market itself might actually produce malign (read inequitable and unstable) outcomes. Put differently, the academic literature reinforced the view that there were two potential entry points for political intervention: to re-align values and strategy; or to re-educate agents with the proper market norms. At no point was there consideration of the efficacy of the (financialized) *structure* of the market; and role that this *structure* would play in determining corporate culture.

Incentives

The second major academic discussion that shaped the political debate was the focus on incentives. Regarding the impact that culture has on the performance of the firm (see Akerlof and Kranton 2010), accounts have been broadly divided between: a more straightforward neoclassical view that behaviours (ergo culture) are determined by financial incentives in a direct or linear relationship; and a range of other behavioural perspectives which problematize this simplistic view. A crude version of the orthodox economics perspective on *non-financial* determinants of culture suggests that they are almost irrelevant. Individuals respond (primarily) to *financial* incentives—perks and penalties—we are told (see Lo 2016: 19 for a critique). Matters such as performance, risk-taking and ethical decisions are therefore thought to be reducible to financial logic. Restructuring the cash versus equity elements of financial incentives (which I discuss further in Chapters 9 and 10) is therefore seen as sufficient to induce more socially responsible risk strategies, for example. In other words, employee behaviour is rational; employees are motivated by money; thus, get the financial calculations right and you can create the right culture.

As De Bondt and Thaler (1995: 385) contend however, this neoclassical view risks replacing the 'realistic characterizations of human conduct with representative agent models in which everyone in the economy is assumed to be as smart as Sandy Grossman and everyone looks toward the future in a way that would make econometricians proud'. Their point is that humans in these models are reduced to rationally thinking robots, where normative, nebulous determinants of culture are irrelevant.

More recently though, a range of other accounts have argued that *non-financial* determinants of culture do indeed make a noticeable difference to performance: 'firms with superior financial performance are typically characterized by a strong set of core managerial *values* that define the ways they conduct business' (emphasis added Barney 1986: 656, Denison and Mishra 1995). In more specific terms, these core values relate to how employees, customers, suppliers and so forth are treated. In more abstract terms it points to the fact that linear relationships between pay and performance are questionable. Indeed, a series of social psychology experiments in the 1960s and 1970s effectively demonstrated that 'monetary incentives are a completely insufficient explanation for behavior' (ibid., see also Milgram 1963).

This conclusion is confirmed by the behavioural economics literature. Individuals do not necessarily respond as rational actors; other cultural features can induce cooperation when traditional models emphasizing bargaining costs and asymmetric information would suggest that such behaviour is overly costly or unfeasible. By implication, the reverse may also be true: non-monetary cultural factors can induce undesirable behaviours which contrast with traditional models of rationality. For example, Kreps (1990) found that non-monetary determinants of culture can even promote outcomes that models of rational behaviour would not have predicted. In particular, these behavioural accounts have been useful because of their normative character; they have been used by business leaders seeking to promote a more successful business model by developing their non-monetary cultural environment (Bouwman 2013).

Where does this brief overview of how the organizational studies literature views culture leave us? Put simply, these accounts tell us that culture matters. But 'culture is more than just a set of guidelines that define ethical behavior in the organization' (Thakor 2015: 8); in fact, on this reading culture may actually be the key factor determining the day-to-day operating decisions of a firm. To be very clear, I agree with this conclusion. What I disagree with is the narrower definition of how to manipulate and improve this culture. If the political debate is the litmus test, these academic studies have been taken to mean (1) that if a corporation can promote the right values throughout the organization; (2) align its profit-making strategies with these values; (3) if the monetary and non-monetary incentive structures are right; and if, as a last resort, (4) there is sufficient accountability in place to deal with deviant behaviour; then (5) an ethical, socially responsible culture can be created.

Put differently, these accounts accept—without question—the liberal vision of the market. Proper, appropriate market conduct is axiomatic. The market functions, producing socially desirable outcomes. The solution to the culture problem lies in fixing the behaviour—the conduct—of market participants. It is therefore easy to understand why this view of culture as ethical, socially responsible conduct appealed to state managers; it made changing bank culture a seemingly much more manageable task. Yet the core argument of this book is that this narrow framing of the role and constituents of culture is a very superficial approach to the *cultural* problems facing Anglo-American banking.

From Financialization to Bank Culture

The remainder of this chapter explains how the process of financialization in Anglo-America is arguably the most important determinant of bank culture. It will also help to explain why this bank culture is therefore so hard to change, and—perhaps more importantly—why this bank culture is so problematic in legitimacy and stability-threatening terms. The argument I will make is that this bank culture is problematic for two big reasons: one is that, on various *economic* measures, it preys on and exacerbates weakness rather than strength in the economy. Deeply financialized economies tend to be more prone to financial instability and crises; profits in financialized economies become progressively detached from (healthy) output and growth in the non-financial economy; wages in the financial sector then also become disproportionate to either the value-added of the sector or wage gains in other sectors, suggesting evidence of rent-seeking behaviour (a term we will return to in due course). This all gives rise to the second, *socio-political* problem with bank culture under financialization, that of declining credibility and legitimation problems (the big theme of Chapter 3). Inequality breeds contempt amongst subaltern social groups (Brosnan and de Waal 2003); and disproportionately large gains in the financial sector make bankers an obvious target for social discontent.

Financialization is a broad and oftentimes poorly defined concept. French et al. (2011) divide this broad literature into two camps: one *narrower* set of accounts focus on describing 'the *processes* and *effects* of the growing power of financial values and technologies on corporations, individuals and households' (emphasis added ibid.: 799); that is, these accounts take financialization as a given and focus primarily on how it manifests and the impact it is having via shareholder value and the diffusion of financial metrics. The second set of accounts adopt a *broader* lens, to consider both the *causes* of financialization in relation to changing patterns of accumulation and what this might mean for the health of an economic system (Foster 2007). In other words, whereas one might intuitively assume that a thriving financial sector is dependent on a thriving economy, instead there is a complex relation where 'financial expansion feeds not on a healthy real economy but on a stagnant one' (Sweezy 1994). The latter set of accounts include, but are not limited to, Marxian and Keynesian versions. It is this latter perspective which will be employed in this book.

Following Krippner, financialization is—by definition—problematic to examine and measure because it does not necessarily show up in national economic statistics on the tasks performed by an economy, or what is produced by an economy. But a useful proxy for examining financialization is considering 'where profits are generated in an economy', indicative of the 'growing weight of finance' (Krippner 2005: 175, 174). Similarly, John Bellamy Foster also describes financialization as 'the shift in gravity of economic activity from production...to finance' (2007: 1). The major added advantage of this approach to financialization is that it gets beyond some of the limitations of the political science, 'bank power' approach, which focuses specifically on the lobbying efforts and influence of the financial services sector in the US and the UK. Yet by also addressing the (structural) causes and implications of the expanded role for finance in economic activity (Kotz 2008: 2), it does not negate the fact that the influence of financial firms—and policymakers' deferential approach to them—has also increased.

That said, the relationship between financial firms and the state is complex. Indeed, even in Anglo-America though the turn towards financialization was oftentimes facilitated and actively encouraged by the state it was largely an attempt to 'avoid a series of economic, social, and political dilemmas that confronted policymakers' (Krippner 2011: 2). Thus financialization was not, by and large, a 'deliberate outcome sought by policymakers but rather an inadvertent result of the state's attempts to solve other problems' (ibid.). Likewise, secondly, though banks were major beneficiaries of the process of financialization and they may even have contributed to the crisis of profitability in the non-financial economy, the crisis did not orginate with them nor was this part of a coherent project or long-term plan by the financial services sector. To quote Polanyi, banks only capitalize on 'that which is falling and hold on to that which, under its own steam, is moving their way. It may then seem as if they had originated the process of social change, while actually they were merely beneficiaries, and may be even perverting the trend to make it serve their own aims' (Polanyi 1957: 28 cited in van der Pijl 1998: 62). This is simply a way of emphasizing that to understand the pressures and incentives facing banks and states in this book, and the struggles between political and economic actors to either solve or resist addressing cultural problems in banking, a deeper analysis of the underlying structural conditions that brought Anglo-American banking to this point is required—an approach that embeds agents within their appropriate structural conditions.

The Crisis of Profitability

Before we can examine the changes in bank structure in the contemporary era and the implications these have had for bank culture, we must begin by briefly outlining the crisis of accumulation in Anglo-America. In recent years, there has much been talk about the productivity slowdown and the productivity puzzle in many advanced economies (IMF 2018). This usually refers to something quite specific, in the form of a decline in Total Factor Productivity (TFP), which is a measure of productive output after discounting for inputs. The crisis of accumulation in Anglo-America covers the productivity slowdown, but is far broader. It refers to a shift in the political, economic, and social patterns of accumulation that had characterized the post-war consensus, towards one increasingly dominated by financial activities. In its simplest form though, this accumulation crisis reflected declining opportunities for profitable investments in traditional, productive activity (Magdoff and Sweezy 1983). Given the potential for double-digit asset growth in capital markets, compared to the single-digit growth achievable in most real product markets, the shift towards financial activities is entirely understandable (Froud et al. 2002, French et al. 2011: 803). This was no benign process however. Firms in financialized economies are increasingly myopic, as they jeopardize long-term integrity, stability, and the interests of wider societal stakeholders, in favour of a short-term focus on fluctuating share prices (Zysman 1983, Albert 1991). A significant part of this reading of financialization is that 'it carries [more than] a whiff of disapproval by suggesting a problematic relationship between finance and the rest of the economy' (Lapavitsas 2013: 794).

The reasons for the decline in profitability in the non-financial sector differed somewhat in the US and the UK. In the UK the decline was primarily caused by a failure to innovate in British industry in the post-war period; the rapid redevelopment of war-torn Europe and other advanced economies that surpassed British competitive advantages; coupled with the longstanding structural bias towards the financial and merchant elite in the British economy (Gamble 1994, Longstreth 1979, Middlemas 1979). The result was that the Eurodollar markets and the 1980s Big Bang marked the ascendancy of finance and the nail in the coffin of British industry as a globally competitive force (Moran 1991, 2009). Whereas in the US, the financialization of the economy was, until the mid-1990s, characterized by spurts of reasonably strong performances in the non-financial sector. The point however, was that across the last three decades of the twentieth century the slowdown in profitability in the real economy—in both the US and the UK—led a majority of larger non-financial corporations to expand their financial activities as a means of supplementing profits.

The decline in productive investment in the UK has a far longer history than in the US, and can arguably be traced back to the historical origins of the UK as a merchant and financial centre, prior to the industrial revolution; a fact which also contributed to the emergence of industry in the UK relatively autonomous from the largest banks domiciled in the City of London (Moran 2009, Ingham 1984). All this was simply a precursor to the subsequent overweening power of the City of London in British economic planning. In parallel to the sluggishness of British industry in the post-war period then, successive UK governments made strategic decisions, culminating in the 1986 Big Bang, to prioritize the interests of the City of London over domestic industry. What ensued was an exponential growth in financial activity that went hand-in-hand with a decline in productive investment: for example, investment in financial services grew 320 per cent between 1979–89, compared to only a 12.8 per cent rise in investment in manufacturing (Coates 1995: 6).

In the US however, the economy expanded during the late 1930s and early 1940s, benefiting significantly from powerful war-time demand and capitalizing on the fact that Japanese and Western European economies were decimated by war (Block 1977). Nonetheless the very conditions set in place during this early period of growth subsequently became constraints: the high fixed costs attached to initially advanced technology; its internationally hegemonic position driven by big corporations, the banks and the state; and the resistance of its residually powerful working class (Brenner 2003: 11). In this sense, both the US and the UK benefited initially from technology and markets in the immediate post-war period whilst suffering in coming decades from the decline of their competitive advantage compared to a boom in Europe and Japan (Kindleberger 1967). Paradoxically though, US progress through this initial period also depended crucially upon their rivals' national economic development and the growth of their domestic markets, to accommodate US exports. For a time then although this was a period of uneven development it also created a certain synergy in economic interests between the US and later developing economies. This synergy was short-lived. The time came, by the mid 1960s, when the US' economic rivals were themselves producing more cost-competitive products than their US imports, leading to falling rates of returns for US firms. By the early 1970s however, the manufacturing sectors of the G-7 economies as a whole were experiencing a decline in profitability of about 25 per cent (between 1965–73) (Armstrong et al. 352).

The point is that the boom in the US contributed to—or at least depended upon—the boom elsewhere, whilst laying the basis for the decline, first of the US and then of its Western rivals. The process of financialization therefore occurred against the backdrop of economic stagnation in the early 1970s that was effectively global in scale. By the 1990s for example, the advanced capitalist economies displayed less dynamism and grew more slowly than they had during the 1980s, when they had expanded less rapidly than during the 1970s (Brenner 2003: 7). From the early 1970s then, this was the end of the end of the post-war boom. Against this crisis of accumulation, the fact that financialization was most pronounced and fastest to develop in Anglo-America was largely a product of particular state strategies that sought to capitalize on the comparative and competitive strength of New York and the City of London as financial centres. From the 1950s, for example, the emergence of the Eurodollar markets had reinvigorated both the City and New York (Macartney 2010). Decisions to liberalize and promote competitive re-regulation of these respective financial markets was both a response to and an exacerbating factor behind the crisis of Anglo-American capitalism (Harvey 2005).

What this meant for many non-financial firms in both the US and the UK was pronounced structural change, characterized by heightened indebtedness. Three interrelated issues therefore developed in the context of the declining profitability of the Anglo-American non-financial sector: the emergence of shareholder value;

the politics of tight money; and rising household indebtedness. These three elements of financialization are important determinants of the bank culture problems in the US and UK, and highlight the limitations of the political debate on culture focused on ethical, socially responsible conduct.

Shareholder Value

Firstly, shareholder value is a means of assessing the financial performance of a firm based on Return on Equity (ROE)—the investment, or capital, of the shareholders (Hillman and Keim 2001: 126). This metric became increasingly significant through the 1970s and 1980s because the ownership structures and emphasis on financial activities within non-financial corporations grew. From the 1980s private sector debt was now no longer primarily used to fund increased expenditures on plant and equipment; henceforth it was increasingly used to finance share buybacks and mergers and acquisitions (Brenner 2003: 58). The relationship between the slowdown and this type of financial activity is complex and is not one-directional. That is, it would be misleading to claim that firms *only* turned to financial activity to supplement declining rates of profit, though it is clear that financial activities became a lucrative and sizeable profit-making opportunity. Debate over the precise order of events is less significant for the purposes of this book however, than the indisputable restructuring of non-financial and financial corporations which took place predicated on both declining returns on productive investments and increased access to cheap capital (Engelen et al. 2011: 110). The result was a shift from productive investment to financial activities. Between 1984–9 US non-financial corporations, for example, spent an annual average of $184bn on mergers and acquisitions, compared to an average of $84bn on fixed investment (Pollin 1996: 4).

The spiraling indebtedness made non-financial firms fragile, by making investment and stockholding more sensitive to interest rate changes (Clarke 1988: 309). Moreover, financial strategies such as buybacks were deliberately designed with one goal in mind: to manipulate equity prices. Thus began the heightened emphasis on shareholder value as the guiding principle shaping corporate activity. Under the more traditional model of accumulation, non-financial firms would tend to issues shares as the most cost-effective way of gaining investment and expanding capacity. Yet instead, from the 1980s, non-financial firms actually reverted to borrowing in order to purchase their own equities, with the aim of maximizing shareholder value by directly fattening up share prices (Smithers and Wright 2000: 152–3). The result was that 'with more wealth put into these [financial] assets, there was less invested in real productive capital' (Stiglitz 2012: 9).

Equally importantly, research into the *social* and cultural implications of an obsession with shareholder value suggests that as financial performance—measured by ROE—is targeted, the interests of other stakeholders—employees, customers, and communities—become, at best, peripheral concerns (Hillman and Keim 2001: 126). This claim should be qualified: firms which act in socially responsible ways to their closest stakeholders—their own employees and customers—may, for example, improve their financial performance by promoting loyalty amongst their workers and customers (Freeman 1984). Beyond that however, research indicates that there is no financial incentive—at least to shareholders—to consider wider societal interests (Mitchell, Agle, and Wood 1997). Again, this is another reason why simply improving incentives and values will have very limited impact. Thus, for the purposes of this book the shift towards financialization pushed shareholder value and the importance of equity markets to the forefront of corporate strategies; empowered the financial agents (banks in our case) with access and informational privileges; and exacerbated a *culture* of placing financial performance above other interests.

The Politics of Tight Money

The second related issue at the heart of the financialization of Anglo-America is the role that state managers played in enabling and actively encouraging the process via the politics of tight money. The result was that the financialization empowered the financial sector and laid the basis for the exploitative or higher risk activities symptomatic of the culture of banking problem. Of course, in a narrow sense policymakers were responsible for the liberalization and re-regulation of financial markets during the 1980s and 1990s (Moran 1991). But our aim is to also explain the broader state strategies that precipitated and followed the liberalization of the financial sector. The state managers' strategy came in two symbiotic, yet ultimately toxic, forms: firstly, prioritizing price stability and the interests of the *marktvolk* (international investors) as tax revenues fell and states turned to financial markets for funding (Streeck 2014). This shift from tax state to debt state helps to explain the rationale behind austerity and spending cuts, as expansionary spending becomes an acutely sensitive issue in the eyes of international investors (Blyth 2013). Simultaneously and secondly though, Anglo-American state managers also actively encouraged the expansion of the credit economy to corporates and households. The shift towards cutting state spending and the public deficit (the politics of tight money) therefore necessarily also involved the ratcheting up of private and household indebtedness to plug the gap and maintain demand. Those at the lower end of the income distribution are particularly vulnerable because of their previous dependence on government social spending. The twofold strategy led Colin Crouch (2011) to adopt the term 'Privatized Keynesianism' to describe this form of statecraft.

On the issue of the *marktvolk* and tight money, the more embedded the financial activities of Non-Financial Corporations (NFCs) became, the more attuned the US and UK governments became to the interests of lenders and speculators. This is important for our understanding of why tackling financialization is difficult: it is not simply that state managers are captured by the banks; the broadest spectrum of financial and non-financial institutions in Anglo-America are configured around financialization and stock market performance. As I will explain below, price stability therefore became the order of the day; this offered insurance to investors and lenders that inflation would not diminish their profits—either by guaranteeing the value of their loans or enabling them to profit from rising asset prices (Brenner 2003: 128). Since our argument concerning the culture of banking problem is as much about the condition of the non-financial sector in Anglo-America, and the agency of state managers, as it is about the banks themselves, it is worth pausing to examine the crisis of public finances that is integral to financialization.

The orthodox economics interpretation presents this as a crisis of democracy whereby democratic discretion led to overspending; the orthodox solution is that public finances must be shielded from democratically generated demands and the overall size of the public budget must be trimmed (Brittan 1977). This explanation for the crisis of public finances is fundamental to both the Obama and Conservative government's post-crisis response and to the unravelling legitimacy crisis (see Chapters 3, 4, and 6). Put differently, another reason for steering the bank culture debate away from financialization was the almost unquestioned consensus amongst more radical and more conservative state managers on the politics of tight money. Instead however, the long-term fiscal crisis of the state in the US and the UK is more accurately the product of declining economic performance and the consequences of a lower tax base (Streeck 2014: 49). That is, it is not a result of high or rising social or welfare spending, but of low or declining tax receipts (O'Connor 1973). Fig. 2.1 shows the general trend of falling tax

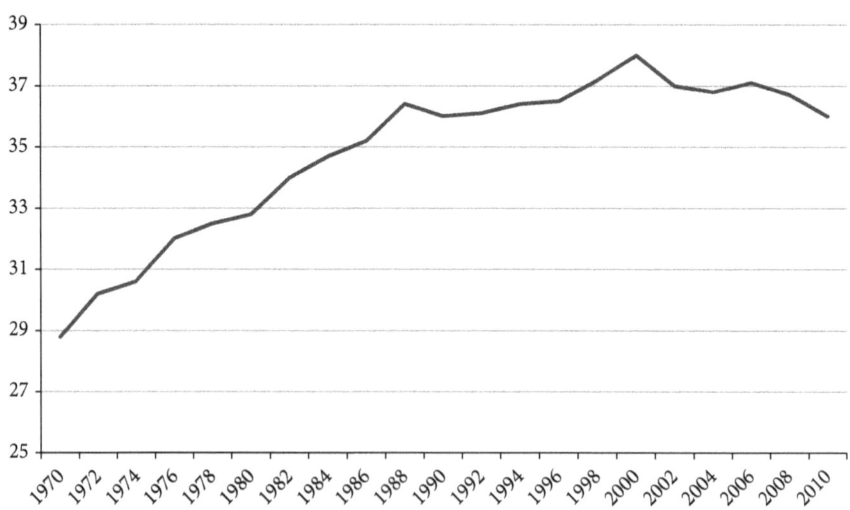

Fig. 2.1 Total tax revenue as a percentage of GDP, selected OECD countries, 1970–2010
Source: Streeck 2014: 12.

revenue for a range of OECD countries from the 1980s onwards. In this way it is interwoven within the crisis of Anglo-American accumulation outlined earlier.

A major component of this pressure on the public purse was a product of the slowdown in profitability from the 1970s; whilst the fast-growing internationalization of the economy in the 1990s then gave even greater freedom to larger firms to shift their profits to lighter tax regimes and offset their profits against tax deductible expenses in higher tax regimes. The result of this tectonic shift in the financing and functioning of the state meant that it needed to cover a growing portion of its expenditure 'through borrowing rather than taxation...thereby accumulating a debt mountain that it has to finance with an ever greater share of its revenue' (Streeck 2014: 72). Thus the 'proliferation of the finance industry...was connected in many ways with the fiscal crisis of the rich democracies' (ibid.: 49). Greater freedom for financial services in the 1980s in the US was intended to correct the balance of payments deficit by encouraging inflows of capital, but also to help the government finance its own public deficit. Then, in the 1990s the Clinton administration encouraged a further period of financialization, in part to sustain demand via cheap credit in the face of dramatic cuts to social spending to address the deficit once again. Thus the influence that shareholders may hold over firm strategy under financialization is similar to the influence that bondholders hold over governments in what Streeck calls 'debt states'; the 'trust of creditors require[s] that governments persuade or compel their citizens to moderate their claims on the public purse' (ibid.: 80).

The impact that this profitability crisis had on state policy was that it increased pressure for fiscal stringency, further limiting social policy spending; whilst involving the state and central banks in the struggle to moderate wage demands. Either this was a deliberate strategy to respond to the demands of productive capital—particularly in the US—by constraining wages within the limits of profitability (Clarke 1988: 305, 307); or, on repeated occasions in the post-1980s inflation-targeting era, US and UK central banks were simply responding to rising inflation by raising interest rates, with the indirect consequence that wage gains were effectively diluted (Stiglitz 2016). Either way, the emphasis on tight money brought about by the crisis of accumulation acted as a transmission mechanism from the economy to the state to the household. Meanwhile the banking sector, as we shall, was greasing the wheels of this process of financialization as it unfolded.

Household Debt

The other major component of state managers' responses to the economic slowdown was to encourage the expansion of the credit economy. Higher rates of profit in the early post-war decades allowed both economies to generate large surpluses, making it possible to maintain high rates of investment and relatively rapid growth in productivity (at least, certainly compared to the period from the late 1970s onwards). This also allowed for relatively consistent real wage growth

(Brenner 2003: 9). One product of the slowdown in productivity in the US and the UK was therefore a limited tolerance for wage increases. The shift under Thatcher and Reagan was therefore primarily an attempt to raise profitability by increasing unemployment so as to dampen the growth of wages. By abandoning a commitment to full employment, the financialization process since the 1980s has occurred against the backdrop of stagnant (or slow-growing) real wages. Under normal circumstances one might therefore have expected low productivity and stagnant wages to have resulted in the rise of classical labour movements (Postone 2016). But as I will explain more fully in Chapter 3 on legitimacy, this did not occur for two reasons: greater coercion contributed to the decline in power of organized labour; and state managers also encouraged the expansion of the credit economy and home ownership as a way of diluting social class antagonisms (Langley 2006). Both of these elements are obviously pivotal to our analysis of bank culture. Here the credit economy is deeply political: it acts as a 'neutralising agent' (Bonefeld 1996: 216) allowing low and middle income households to engage in the 'project of prosperity' (Marx 1990 [1867]: 765, Macartney 2009: 114). The result was a massive proliferation of both (secured) mortgage debt and (unsecured) credit card debt and personal loans over this period.

The explosive growth of household and corporate indebtedness crystallized the shift from the recovery of the (export-oriented) US manufacturing sector and towards the growth of domestic consumption. At key moments the rise of corporate and household debt was propelled forward by the Federal Reserve and Bank of England, using loose monetary policy to re-inflate the stock market and prop up debt-financed consumer demand. In the UK, one particularly important decision for the shift towards consumption-driven growth came after the ejection of the UK from the European Exchange Rate Mechanism (ERM) in 1992. The devaluation of sterling which ensued led, in turn, to repeated cuts in interest rates (Hay 2013: 23). In the US in the early to mid-1990s, an artificially low Federal Reserve rate and interest rate on long-term bonds also induced a similarly dramatic fall in the cost of borrowing (Bernanke and Lown 1991).

This meant that by the early 2000s the financialization of the UK and US economies was well embedded: investment and consumer demand had become dependent on the wealth effect of rising equity prices (Brenner 2003: 289). The cuts in interest rates in response to the Dot.com collapse only exacerbated the problem of indebtedness, despite the fact that the rate cuts achieved their desired effect, reviving the buoyancy of the stock market. In fact, the stock market had by then become the key barometer of the health of the economy rather than productivity and output; as Brenner noted, 'hitherto the growth of equity prices was basically driven by the growth of the economy and profits…[now it had taken on] a life of its own' (2003: 142). This meant that consumption-driven growth and indebtedness were not perceived to be problematic so long as equity markets were buoyant. Culturally speaking though, this involved the desensitization of the British and American public to living with personal debt in a way that was unthinkable in the earlier post-war period, and remains morally objectionable in other Western economies to this day (De Goede 2004, Langley 2010). This is another example of the spatial specificity of some of the problems examined in this book. It is not that the culture of banking problems—the bloodthirsty search for yield, the instability of excessive risk-taking, disproportionately high wages, and so forth—cannot and have not arisen elsewhere. But it is hardly surprising that they were most extreme in Anglo-America.

Most importantly for our purposes, the rise in household indebtedness was capitalized on by Anglo-American banks. In light of declining opportunities of productive investments, banks turned to various non-interest sources of income. Credit card fees and overdraft charges, alongside arrangement fees for loans and mortgages, became absolutely integral revenue streams. As Johnna Montgomerie pointed out, 'targeting existing revolving debtors became central to new marketing strategies. Extensive market research found that the more often people used their credit cards, the more likely they were to overspend and not pay their full balance. The desire for a larger proportion of revolving debtors meant new marketing strategies focused on luring individuals with existing debts' (2009: 8).

The Culture of Banking

Thus far, the chapter has highlighted the slowdown in profitability in Anglo-America, the agency of the state—either in suppressing wages to induce a recovery, or liberalizing finance and loosening credit access, which contributed to increased indebtedness—and the impact that these macroeconomic and political changes had on household finances. The aim of the remainder of this chapter is to position the Anglo-American banks within this wider process of financialization, and to outline the cultural changes at work.

As such, there are three big developments that shaped the culture of banking and are deeply interwoven in the changing patterns of accumulation outlined above: the rise of Too-Big-To-Fail (TBTF) and its impact on risk-appetite; market-based banking and the development of non-interest income; and remuneration. To reiterate, we began this chapter by affirming the view that culture matters in an organization; but the central argument of this book is that reducing bank culture to ethical, socially responsible conduct is misleading. Instead, the pressures and incentives generated by financialization are far more important in determining a type of bank culture with massive political and economic weaknesses.

We should begin by noting though that there is a risk here in homogenizing Anglo-American bank culture. We must caution against this oversimplification. Not all banks are the same, and hence the cultural problems will manifest in different ways. Taking the financial crisis as an obvious example of the importance that different bank cultures and structures played, the crisis affected smaller, newer lenders such as Bradford and Bingley and Northern Rock—through their over-reliance on short-term wholesale sources of funding—as well as Bear Stearns and Lehman Brothers—larger US investment banks that were over-leveraged (Engelen et al. 2011: 115). The wide range of interviews conducted during the course of writing this book confirmed the vast cultural differences between different divisions within the *same* bank, and those between different banks *themselves*. Nonetheless, the argument of this book is that a wide range of cultural problems evidenced in Anglo-American banking are connected by the fact that they are products of the financialization of these two economies. As Simon Clarke (1988: 3) noted then, 'to stress the distinctiveness of the variations is to ignore the underlying theme'.

To outline the alternative determinants of bank culture proposed by this book, the remainder of this chapter now moves from the big, structural changes in relation to concentration and consolidation of the banking sector, or the rise of Too-Big-To-Fail banks; to internal strategic developments *within* the banks, entitled Market-Based-Banking; and then to changes in remuneration policy. At one level, all three of these features shaped *behaviour*, the determinant of culture outlined at the start of this chapter. Yet I have repeatedly cautioned that these behavioural features need to be embedded in the deeper, structural processes of financialization of the Anglo-American economies to be fully understood and in order to understand why focusing the political debate solely on constraining unethical and socially irresponsible behaviour is futile.

TBTF

We begin, firstly, with the rise of Too-Big-To-Fail (TBTF) banks. A combination of the slowdown and shift towards finance, the liberalization of financial markets by the state, and more aggressive expansion by larger firms also gave rise to TBTF, which had an important cultural impact. Not all of the banks in Anglo-America that have been embroiled in mis-selling or other unethical behaviours would be classified as Systemically Important Financial Institutions (SIFIs) or TBTF. But as Chapter 8 will explain, most of the worst cases have involved TBTF firms. Equally importantly, the ways in which larger (TBTF) firms responded to and shaped financialization also led to cultural changes in smaller and medium sized banks. Understanding TBTF is therefore an important starting point for examining the ways in which the banking sector as a whole responded to and exacerbated financialization.

It is probably not unreasonable to argue that the cultural implications of Too-Big-To-Fail banks originated in the response to the banking collapses of the 1930s and the Great Depression. Then, more than ever, the implications of allowing banks to fail became acutely apparent (Volcker 2005: vii). The root of TBTF therefore sprang from heightened creditor expectations of government protection (Stern and Feldman 2004: 11). That government protection comes in three forms: liquidity insurance (protecting wholesale deposits), deposit insurance (protecting retail deposits), and capital insurance (protecting shareholder equity) (Alessandri and Haldane 2009: 3). Liquidity insurance dates back to the early nineteenth century, but deposit insurance and capital insurance have a shorter history, emerging after the Great Depression. Ironically though, deposit insurance became the most influential factor in TBTF banking. Of course, this was not immediately apparent in the half-century following the 1930s. The 'scars of the depression and bank failures led to a more conservative, risk-averse approach by bankers themselves' (Volcker 2005: viii) which meant that deposit insurance and the stability of state aid during economic turmoil was not seen as a premise for higher risk investment strategy.

A decisive moment came in 1982 however, when one of the largest American commercial lenders, Continental Illinois National Bank and Trust Company (CINB), collapsed. Here the Federal Reserve and the FDIC stepped in to recapitalize the bank, going well beyond the narrow remit of the small depositors insurance required by the post-1930s legislation. CINB had traditionally been a highly conservative bank. But in the mid-1970s—around the early stages of financialization in the US—its management embarked on an aggressive strategy, expanding its commercial and industrial (C&I) lending from approximately $5bn to $14bn. As the nation's seventh-largest bank at the time then, CINB's collapse proved to be a watershed moment for bank regulators. Not only did it call into question the regulators' ability to supervise the largest financial institutions, but the methods adopted in the resolution of CINB were also highly controversial. Debate centred on whether large banks had to be treated differently to smaller institutions (FDIC 1987: 112). What was different in the CINB case was the scale of the rescue and guarantee, and the change in perception that it caused. The lengths that authorities would go to prevent resolution or actually having to deliver on the depositor payout promise was suddenly apparent. Again, state agency played a pivotal role in buttressing financialization; this time by circumventing the market mechanism and preventing a bank collapse. This too was another instance where the pristine (neoliberal) model of self-regulating markets in banking gave way to the reality of needing government bailouts to prevent financial Armageddon.

Earlier, we highlighted that financialization broadly reflected 'the shift in gravity of economic activity from production...to finance' (Foster 2007: 1). The difficulty is that the scale and concentration of the growth in the banking system escalated expectations of state support. In turn, these expectations generated lower funding costs which further encouraged expansion and concentration. This has been described as a self-perpetuating 'doom loop' (Alessandri and Haldane 2010). The point is that the expectation of state support has been shown to make share and bond prices, as well as the cost of debt for these largest banks, less sensitive to risk (Lindh and Schich 2012, Hau, Langfield, and Marques-Ibanez 2013, O'Hara and Shaw 1990, Morgan and Stiroh 2005, Balasubramnian and Cyree 2011, Acharya, Anginer, and Warburton 2014). That is simply a way of saying that markets were less concerned about the risks associated with the largest banks, because the expectation of public support from the state had grown (Siegert and Willison 2015: 4); bank creditors who 'do not face the full cost of the failure of their bank lose some of the incentive to monitor and assess its riskiness' (Stern and Feldman 2004: 17). TBTF status reduces a bank's debt costs because a bailout would 'keep a bank from defaulting on its obligations' (Siegert and Willison 2015: 7). Risk assessments will tend to affect the prices creditors require before they invest their funds, so that higher risk banks should face higher prices from creditors. Risk assessments can also affect the *quantity* of funds provided by creditors. Lack of funding therefore affects the ability of a bank to carry out its business (Stern and Feldman 2004: 17). The implicit (or explicit) government guarantee simply distorts these market mechanisms. As such, it is not (necessarily) that bankers sit in a dark room actively seeking to defraud the government or make reckless investment decisions. Instead, in terms of the risk–reward calculations they perform, given the prices and quantity of funding they receive, bankers are making optimal decisions: the problem is that the prices and quantities confronting them 'do not fully reflect the risk of their institutions or of their activities' (ibid.: 18).

This brings us closer to the culture issue then and poses a fundamental challenge to the ethical, socially responsible behaviour agenda; if bank strategies—ergo their culture—are determined to a greater or lesser degree by misleading price signals it is already unclear how far better value statements (for example) will influence culture. And this is just one part of the problem with the narrow bank culture debate. Returning to the TBTF question though, a range of other studies set out to investigate whether TBTF banks behave differently by looking at balance-sheet data (Gropp, Hakenes, and Schnabel 2011), syndicated loans (Brei and Gadanecz 2012), and bank z-scores (Brandao Marques, Correa, and Sapriza 2013). Arguably the most important study however, was conducted by a team from the Federal Reserve Bank of New York (Afonso, Santos, and Traina 2014). Using a new Fitch rating designed to provide a more accurate and comprehensive assessment of whether a bank would receive government support, their study found that a greater likelihood of support does indeed lead to a rise in bank risk-taking (ibid.: 42). The main proxy for the higher risk activities of these TBTF banks was measures of impaired loans on the books of these banks. Impaired loans are those that are in default or close to default. Across a range of 224 banks in forty-five countries, with panel data over 1739 quarters, the authors found that banks with higher levels of (implied and actual) state support had higher ratios of impaired loans to total assets (ibid.: 50). Other measures for riskier lending were also used, including net charge-offs (unrecoverable debts minus previously collected written-off debts), tier 1 capital ratios, return on assets (ROA), and trading asset ratios relative to total assets. On all these measures, the results showed a statistically significant relationship between state support and the riskiness of activities in TBTF banks. For this reason, the emergence of TBTF as both cause and effect of financialization fuels a particular culture: within the bank itself the full effect of risk is diluted; and, within society, one implication is that the bank might be willing to overextend itself via cheap credit. For our purposes here the data supports the conclusion that more heavily financialized economies can have extremely negative impacts on their respective state—society complexes.

Market-Based Banking

Secondly, having outlined the big structural changes in the banking industry accompanying and driving financialization, the literature on Market-Based Banking (MBB) is arguably the best account of strategic shifts *within* the banks that were not simply limited to TBTF firms (Hardie et al. 2013). As such MBB also helps to explain why cultural problems were not limited to the narrower subset of TBTF banks. MBB explains how bank structures and practices have adapted to and reinforced processes of financialization (Maxfield et al. 2017:1005). Indeed, the emergence of market-based banking appears to be a 'necessary, if not sufficient, condition for extensive financialization' (ibid.: 1007).

Under market-based banking, the central activity of loan-making is done with the intention of selling the loans to the market and where the purchase of those loans is partially financed through 'wholesale' borrowing (Hardie and Maxfield 2013: 59). Two of the key features outlined above are therefore explained: securitization enables almost limitless lending for consumption, which is a key contributor of household indebtedness under conditions of wage stagnation; whilst MBB also enables the debt-financed boom of share buybacks and financial activities on the part of non-financial firms that we witnessed earlier in this chapter (Maxfield et al. 2017: 1007). Moreover, it also helps to explain the tendency towards higher-risk, short-term speculative activities that detract from more efficient intermediation of savings to investment (Grabel 1997: 252).

Simply, MBB allowed banks to prosper despite the slowdown in the productive economy. The early 2000s is a case in point. Anglo-American banks benefited significantly from the relatively *low* interest rates of the early 2000s (Blackburn 2008: 68, Hay 2011). At face value, this should appear to be rather odd, for the traditional business of banking depended largely on income generated through interest; higher interest rates were assumed to be integral to bank profits. Instead, under market-based banking, lower interest rates enabled banks to borrow extensively in order to sponsor hedge funds, private equity buyouts, and their own structured investment vehicles. Market-based banking therefore points towards a further two structural changes with cultural dimensions: leveraging and non-interest income.

Leveraging

Leveraging here reflects the practice of banks themselves borrowing to produce a (hopefully) positive multiplier effect. As Haldane (2009, cited in Engelen et al. 2011: 108) noted, banks' impressive performance in the lead-up to the financial crisis was not the result of economies of scale and scope or high value-added innovation. Instead 'the driver was financial engineering in the form of higher leverage, new sources of funding, and an increasing velocity of transactions'. There were a number of concerning features with this trend. One was that banks' targeting Return on Equity was 'benchmarked by peers' performance', creating what Haldane defined as an 'important cultural influence' of 'keeping up with the Jones's' (2009: 3). The second was that where returns on *assets* were insufficient to meet these increasingly competitive return on *equity* targets, banks 'resorted to leveraging their balance sheets' at increasingly unsustainable levels (ibid.). The difference between return on assets and return on equity is that the latter is magnified by leverage (debt). Engelen et al. (2011: 109–11) found that for US and UK banks the contrast between slim returns on assets and substantial returns on equity was very stark. All large US and UK banks had returns on assets of less than 1.5 per cent, but converged on 15+ per cent return on equity. Indeed, this leveraging was so systemic by the time of the financial crisis that the funding gap—the difference between the loans extended and the deposits held—for UK banks had risen from near zero in 2000 to £530bn in 2006 (Bank of England 2003: 135; 2007: 29; IFS 2007: 153, Macartney 2014). Put differently, UK banks themselves were heavily indebted (or exposed) to wholesale borrowing, in the hope of producing the aforementioned multiplier effect and boosting returns (see Admati and Hellwig 2014 for a critique).

The details are complex, but the idea is not: bank culture changed—in many respects for the worse—in line with the crisis of Anglo-American capitalism and the slowdown in profitability in the non-financial sector. Banks therefore developed innovative ways of extracting profits which no longer required strong output and growth in the economy. In fact, as we shall see in the remainder of this chapter, consumption and indebtedness became important avenues for non-interest income (the next subsection); and together this allowed for wages to grow disproportionately to the value-added of the financial sector and out of sync with wages in other sectors (the final subsection).

Non-interest Income

It has often been remarked that the culture which came to predominate could be described as a sales culture. More accurately, this sales culture stemmed from a search for non-interest sources of income. The implication from the Market-Based Banking account is that structural changes within banking had important cultural dimensions that are almost entirely absent from the narrow culture-as-ethical-or-socially responsible-conduct debate. In the orthodox economics literature, banks are traditionally thought of as simply financial intermediaries channelling funds from creditors to borrowers, and resolving informational asymmetries—by gathering information on the creditworthiness of the borrower for example. This is however, a rather simplistic and anachronistic view of banks. In particular, commercial (or what we have called retail) bank structures have changed fundamentally since the 1980s (Kaufman and Mote 1994). A major component of the sales culture was the growing importance of fee income on bank balance sheets.

In 1999, the Federal Reserve Bank of Minneapolis noted that increased competition from deregulation and technological innovation was driving banks to seek new sources of revenue to remain profitable (Feldman and Schmidt 1999). The result was that, in the face of these new competitive threats and opportunities, many banks—and in particular the larger firms—drastically altered their operating strategies. In both the UK and the US, banking industry deregulation from the 1980s onwards removed a whole range of restrictions on the efficiency of financial products markets. A major component of this was the development of high volume, automated lending technologies based on credit scoring and securitization—a business model which allowed for large amounts of non-interest income to be generated (Kroszner and Strahan 1999, DeYoung and Rice 2004: 7). These high-level changes in bank structures however had important implications for the cultural divide between larger and smaller banks: larger banks tended to take advantage of their size in the production, marketing, securitization, and servicing of consumer loans (DeYoung, Hunter, and Udell 2004). They became more like efficiency-driven banking machines. Smaller community banks and building societies tended to remain embedded in their local markets with stronger relationships with their depositors and borrowers.

What was clear however, was that for the larger banks in particular the sales culture (and 'cross-selling') associated with these changes in bank structure became important sources of revenue, and important means of diversifying that revenue (DeYoung and Rice 2004). As a result, these larger banks began hiring sales staff from other industries to promote cross-selling (Interview 20170511). Originally, in the 1980s, fee revenue compared to income earned from interest was low; but by 2001 the non-interest income in the US commercial banking system for example, had increased from 0.77 per cent to 2.39 per cent of aggregate banking industry assets, and increased from 20.31 per cent to 42.20 per cent of aggregate banking industry operating income (DeYoung and Rice 2004: 3). As we shall see in later chapters, these fees are generally comprised of service charges on deposit accounts as well as overdraft, ATM, and account maintenance fees. By 2009 then,

US banks alone generated over $46 billion a year from deposit account fee revenue (Pew 2016).

In particular this meant that many of the traditional (cultural) distinctions between retail and investment banking were diluted. In films such as *It's a Wonderful Life* (1946), just as in some academic accounts outlined in the introductory chapter, retail banking was seen to be safer and more mundane; here banks were simply functional intermediaries channelling savings into productive investments. The structural changes outlined by MBB however, enabled retail banks to provide packages of loans—via securitization—to be sold on by their investment banking arm, with the accompanying fee and commission structures a lucrative revenue stream (Interview 20160415, Engelen et al. 2011). The 'sales culture' that had previously characterized investment banking now spilled over into retail banking (Saltz Review 2013). This is also why—despite differences between banks—it is possible to speak of important cultural pressures—stemming from financialization—that the majority of Anglo-American banks are exposed to.

Put simply, Market-Based Banking helps to explain the structural changes that were taking place inside Anglo-American banks that allowed them to profit in spite of the declining dynamism of the UK and US economies. Lower interest rates enabled banks themselves to borrow, oftentimes through wholesale or interbank markets, whilst securitization—or the selling of loan portfolios to the market—contributed to a sales culture permeating a wide range of banking divisions, driven by the search for non-interest forms of income. At one level then, the claim is that despite their differences, many of the cultural problems in Anglo-American banking—from exploitative lending practices, higher risk short-termist strategies in the search for yield, and declining investments in the non-financial economy—were connected by important structural shifts within the banking sector as part of the process of financialization.

Remuneration

The third and final cultural issue to consider is how financialization affected pay in the financial sector. Financialization is not solely an Anglo-American phenomenon; nor are the cultural problems in banking isolated in the US and UK. But the disproportionate wages in the banking sector are most extreme in Anglo-America, making it crucial to our analysis for two reasons: one is that it feeds into our claim about so-called rent-seeking behaviour; and the other is that the disproportionate rise in pay in the financial sector relative to any wage gains in the rest of the economy is a major cause of the inequality at the heart of the legitimacy crisis.

As we shall see in Chapter 3, this inequality exacerbates the legitimacy crisis, which in turn has led to a superficial, populist response and the narrowing of the bank culture debate. Between 1979 and 2007 for example, in both the US and the UK, the top decile increased their share of total income by 14 percentage points, from 28.4 per cent to 42.6 per cent in the UK; whilst the top 1 per cent accounted for fully two-thirds of these gains, seeing their share rise from 5.9 per cent to 15.4 per cent in the UK and from 8 per cent to 18.3 per cent in the US (Bell and van Reenen 2013: 1). Yet these wage gains were not evenly spread across all sectors: in both economies the finance sector saw the lions' share of these increases, with the majority of the gains coming from elevated bonuses (Kaplan and Rauh 2010). And whilst not all positions in the finance sector receive huge salaries, there is evidence of a premium for employees working in the finance sector compared to employees doing similar jobs in other sectors (Lindley and McIntosh 2014). In other words, financialization in Anglo-America not only drove a shift towards financial activities, but disproportionately high wage gains in the financial sector; and in particular in variable remuneration (bonuses).

The idea of rent-seeking behaviour usually refers to sectors which lobby governments to secure special privileges—by distorting competition (Deaton 2017). In the political economy literature on financial services this is often referred to as the bank power thesis or regulatory and political capture (see Hacker and Pearson 2002). In a broader sense though, the idea of rent-seeking can apply to our conception of financialization as the shift away from productive activities towards financial activities; and the accompanying slowdown in the non-financial economy, with profits increasingly made from finance-led activities. Here the focus is on wealth abstraction without a similar growth in productive and innovative activity (Kay 2012: 1); or leveraging control over something that already exists, and manipulating your expertise or ownership of the asset or service (Bregman 2017). Roger Tootle described this as a distinction between creative and distributive activity, arguing that 'part of the answer to why there is so much financial activity in relation to the gains this produces for society is that much financial activity produces huge distributive gains; that is, gains that are of no net overall benefit' (Bootle 2012: 13). This has been referred to as profit-without-producing (Lapavitsas 2013); socially useless activities (Turner 2009); or 'an increase in the value of wealth that is unaccompanied by any increase in the flow of goods and services' (Stiglitz 2012: 9).

The financial sector in Anglo-America has always refuted criticisms of its social function and profit-producing mechanism in a number of ways: by highlighting the contribution of financial services to tax revenue and employment; by emphasizing the link between remuneration and performance within each individual firm; and by arguing that even seemingly opaque and complex trading activity contributes vital liquidity to the financial system (Hardie and Macartney 2016). Indeed, orthodox economic thought contends that in any given sector pay is correlated to the value-added to the economy (Mankiw and Taylor 2008). As one CEO contended, 'if you examine our practices on compensation, you will see a complete correlation throughout our history of having remuneration match performance over the long term' (cited in the *Times* 2009).

Yet the pay-for-performance claim is dubious at best. First, the contribution of the financial sector to the Anglo-American economies is highly questionable (Erturk et al. 2011). Indeed, although the financial sector in both economies is undoubtedly profitable, it has been shown that the share of the financial sector is not dependent on its share of total output unlike, for example, the manufacturing industry. The correlation coefficient between the share of profits and the share of output for the financial sector is in fact statistically insignificant (Moosa 2016: 289). This is just one indicator that a profitable finance sector does not necessarily reflect or contribute to a healthy economy.

Secondly, a wide range of evidence also challenges the claim that pay in the finance sector is based primarily on merit. A number of studies sought to explain the so-called 'finance sector premium' by testing for the effects of higher cognitive skills; higher education levels; differences in job characteristics; or technological change across a range of seventeen OECD countries. The conclusion of these studies was that whilst these factors have some influence, 'none of the possible explanations for the finance sector pay premium, involving the characteristics of the workers in the finance sector, or aspects of the jobs that they do, can fully explain why finance sector workers are paid more than non-finance sector workers, or why the same worker moving between the two sectors sees his/her pay rise or fall accordingly (depending on direction of movement) even when doing the same job in both sectors' (Lindley and McIntosh 2014: 20). The result is 'a level of pay in financial services…out of all proportion to their contribution to society' (Bootle 2012: 14). For now, suffice it to note that the claim that pay reflects performance is highly questionable.

Instead it is far more plausible that high pay in the banking sector is at least partially evidence of rent-seeking behaviour, made possible by the privileged and protected status afforded the financial services industry in Anglo-America (Martens and Martens 2015). Indeed many of the cultural problems highlighted by this book were driven by profit-making activity with no obvious social value: profits were generated by fixing the London Interbank Offered Rate (LIBOR) and the foreign exchange market; misleading clients into purchasing certain financial products whilst shorting the market in the expectation of a massive decline in the prices of the same products; and developing business models to exploit heavily indebted, poorer customers with punitive charges, to name but a few (Moosa 2016: 290). In this book I therefore describe this dynamic of profit-making as *exploitative*, because in contrast to marginal productivity theory which suggests that 'those at the top only get what they add', exploitation here describes how those at the top benefit *at the expense of* those at the bottom (Stiglitz 2012: 6).

Most importantly though, we do not need to definitively prove that rent-seeking is the cause of disproportionately high pay in the banking sector to be able to show that high pay has legitimacy-threatening effects—the other negative outcome of bank culture highlighted by this book. As I will explain in coming chapters, when disproportionately high pay in the banks is juxtaposed against stagnant or declining real incomes it simply exacerbates existing levels of inequality (Piketty and Saez 2003). This inequality was not *caused* by the banking sector per se, but by processes of neoliberalization—specifically the weakening of redistributive, progressive policies (Shields 2014)—actively promoted by US and UK state managers. Yet financialization and the shifting emphasis towards financial activities empowered the banking sector; and technological innovation and deregulation enabled disproportionate gains. This helps to explain why the rising share of wealth accrued by the top percentiles had a distinctly finance-sector character to it.

Closing Remarks

This chapter began by briefly outlining the academic literature that contributed to the narrow banking debate. This literature accepted the liberal vision of the market and appropriate market norms. It therefore suggested entry-points for political intervention to re-align values and strategies with these liberal market norms. This supports the political debate about bank culture focused on behavioural and conduct-related reform. The rest of the chapter however, explained how the structure of the financialized markets of Anglo-America not only (1) fundamentally condition banking culture but also (2) mean that that banking culture has serious instability and legitimacy threatening outcomes. The next chapter now examines the liberal market norms and the accompanying legitimacy crisis in more detail.

3
Culture and Legitimacy

We began this book by questioning how it is possible that those working in Anglo-American banking perceive dramatic transformation in their organizations, whilst so many of the problematic cultural elements remain unchanged. Our central argument is that the political debate about bank culture narrowed, defining good bank culture as ethical, socially responsible conduct. This led to certain changes in the banks. As Chapter 2 explained however, the far more significant pressures and incentives shaping bank culture in the US and UK stem from financialization. Chapter 2 therefore concluded that one reason for the narrowing of the political debate was because of the embeddedness of financialization itself. This present chapter now explains the second reason for the narrowing of the debate, arguing that state managers resorted to a populist statecraft to fight the legitimacy crisis confronting them.

Before we address populism and the legitimacy crisis however, this chapter lays the conceptual basis for understanding the early (2007–12) responses to bank culture. Here too state managers conceived of good culture as socially responsible conduct; already the broader discussion on the adverse costs of financialization was conspicuously absent. Instead, the political debate was characterized by implicit assumptions about the merits of the liberal market. The aim of political intervention was therefore to fine-tune and tweak the balance between risks and rewards to improve market discipline. The LIBOR scandal (2012) prompted a greater emphasis on values and ethical reform. But the assumptions that underpinned both the early focus on dealing with culture via market discipline and the later emphasis on normative reform, were largely the same.

The political debate was essentially characterized by liberal assumptions about the merits of the market; and the emphasis for intervention was therefore on sifting out individual or clustered instances of misconduct. Misconduct, on this reading, was conduct that deviated from liberal market norms and hence jeopardized the pristine market. Put differently, the market—and, by extension, the structural conditions of financialization—were taken as a given; the aim was to tinker with behaviours which hindered the efficient functioning of the market. The purpose of this chapter is therefore to explain why Anglo-American state managers responded to the culture of banking problem as they did: firstly by explaining the liberal blueprint for improving market discipline; and then by explaining what is meant by a legitimacy crisis.

The Bank Culture Debate: Ethics, Values, and Financialization in Anglo-America. Huw Macartney, Oxford University Press (2019). © Huw Macartney.
DOI: 10.1093/oso/9780198843764.001.0001

To understand the liberal blueprint, the first half of the chapter presents a critical re-reading of Adam Smith and the German ordo-liberals. Orthodox (read neoclassical) economic thought has relatively little to say about the state's role concerning culture. The assumption is that if the rewards and risks are properly structured then unethical conduct should be disincentivized, whilst risk-taking would be moderated by the threat of failure. This was evident in Chapter 2 where we discussed the orthodox approach to financial incentives. The state is mysteriously written out of the picture, it would seem. This orthodox economics reading apparently draws its inspiration from the thinking of Adam Smith, and is an extension of the 'invisible hand' of the market, the semi-automated mechanism of market self-regulation (see Watson 2006 for a critique).

Yet a large body of economic thought, also rooted in a reading of Adam Smith, argued that the market—left to its own devices—would tend towards moral degradation. A strong, interventionist statecraft would be required to maintain commercial society (Bonefeld 2014). But the role of the state, according to this more robust version of liberal thought, would be to remove impediments to the proper functioning of the market; bad culture—in this view—is misconduct which distorts market competition. The point is that—as we shall see in Chapters 4–7—early responses by state managers were in this vein; the aim was to bring into being the pristine model of the market.

One key message of this book however, is that these efforts to strengthen the market mechanism were not enough during the first phase of the crisis response. Cultural problems kept emerging. Scandals kept coming to light. And the wider economic context, of fiscal consolidation (austerity) and inequality, gave rise to a secondary, quasi-populist form of statecraft. Because this secondary response is also agent-centered and supply-side, it too fails to address the underlying structural problem.

To understand this claim the second part of this chapter turns to the work of Jürgen Habermas and his writings on legitimacy. As with Chapter 2 which argued that crises constitute a rupture in existing patterns of accumulation, Habermas developed this notion in relation to what he called the 'steering problems' experienced by state managers during crisis periods. Habermas was particularly concerned with the notion of what is socially accepted and reified—such as the asymmetrical distribution of chances, wealth, and power—and how an economic crisis can in turn give rise to a social and political crisis as disadvantaged groups begin to turn their criticism towards the state.

These kinds of growing antagonisms require a response from the state, not only to protect the given socio-economic order, but also to protect the institutions of government itself. Why this is important and distinctive however, is that Habermas contended that the state is not a neutral, agnostic organization negotiating compromises between interest groups as certain pluralistic accounts would have us believe. Instead it is instrumental in maintaining a system predicated on inequality. This is hugely important, for you could be forgiven for reading the later chapters about state managers and legitimacy as a story of performative, institutional politics and governmental elites simply trying to hold on to power and gain votes. But this is only half the story. The account presented in this book contends that struggles between agents must be embedded in their proper structural context; and that the perceived neutrality of the state must be challenged. With this in mind we can see why the culture of banking problem risked degenerating into a political crisis for the state.

Smith and Culture

This first section begins to move towards understanding why culture matters in the *political* realm, a central aim of this chapter. In so doing however, we will also show how the necessity for political intervention also presupposes the particular *form* of that intervention. The liberal state is the strong but limited state, removing impediments to the proper functioning of the market. Put crudely, the previous chapters established why culture would matter to business executives, both as it relates to enhancing profits and as it concerns minimizing adverse behaviours. In what follows I will argue that important strands of the economic liberal tradition explain not only why state managers would target bank culture but the methods they would use—via market discipline and the rule of law—to do so. The issue that these liberal writers addressed—as far as it concerns us—is how participants in the market economy can be induced to do the right thing, or act in an ethical and socially responsible way. It is somewhat perplexing though, given the repeated attempts to appropriate the work of Adam Smith in modern economic theory, that his writings on human nature and ethical behaviour—as well as the need for strong political intervention—are given scant attention. As Mat Watson pointed out, 'the popular conception of *The Wealth of Nations* is that it represents a populist defense of the market economy' (2006: 47). The error here is twofold, since Smith portrays anything but a utopian vision in *WoN* and, more broadly, Smith always considered the 'moral dimension of economic life' in his writings (ibid.). But the real issue which this chapter explores is not simply the fact *that* state managers would intervene in dealing with culture, but the *methods* they would employ and the *purpose* that intervention would pursue. This is what I mean by the—albeit at times incoherent—*liberal* intellectual blueprint used by Anglo-American state managers.

The Glaring Absence of Culture and Politics

This is a book about the debate on bank culture. The emergence of the term 'culture' only came to the fore after 2012 however. But although the word culture was rarely used in early responses to the financial crisis, the diagnosis by state managers of what was wrong with banking was remarkably similar both pre- and post-2012. Though it was not necessarily labelled a 'cultural' problem, state managers targeted excessive risk-taking, irresponsibility, and hubris from immediately after the 2007–8 bank bailouts. Bankers were dragged before Senate and Treasury Committees to explain their conduct; ring-fencing and proprietary trading measures were introduced to limit the contagion effects of bad investment decisions; resolution plans were introduced to avoid the need for further publicly funded bailouts; and remuneration reforms began, to encourage greater prudence. State managers rarely spoke of bank culture; but the parallels between these political initiatives and the more explicit post-2012 culture reform debates are stark.

Early initiatives focused on limiting excesses and promoting social responsible behaviour via greater market discipline; later efforts focused on similar goals via ethical reform. The diagnosis suggested that (minor) adjustments to incentives and accountability would promote the right culture. The debate was therefore limited because the assumption was that by disciplining bad conduct, the proper functioning of the market could be achieved. The assumption is that the market is unquestionably the best form of social organization and resource allocation. But this is a distinctly liberal assumption that needs to be explored further, if we are broaden the debate about bank culture; because, as we will see in later chapters, the evidence suggests that the market under financialization consistently fosters disruptive, malign consequences that simply do not square with the pristine, liberal vision of the market. The difference is that the vision state managers invoke implies that negative outcomes can be reduced to near zero; that negative outcomes do not need to be the accepted norm. Instead, one implication of our focus on financialization as a driver of (bad) bank culture is that malign outcomes are the exact opposite; that is, they are indeed the norm.

To make this point this chapter must move through three stages: firstly, we must quickly dismiss the orthodox economics account which provides only a limited view of culture and political intervention; secondly, by examining the work of Smith and then the ordo-liberals (in more detail) we will see where both the liberal vision of the pristine market derives from and also the emphasis on market discipline and ethical reform to achieve this vision. This account is hugely important to understanding (conceptually) what US and UK state managers have sought to achieve. The third section moves away from the liberal vision of the market, to show the inherent biases and asymmetries that are integral to capitalism and the market. This leads towards our discussion of legitimacy and populism, as ways of explaining how state managers attempted to square the circle; seeking public approval by depoliticizing the inequalities and struggles that financialization engenders.

Culture in Orthodox Economics

Put simply, neither culture nor politics are major themes in orthodox economic thinking. This is because the single most important endeavour for orthodox economics has been to create models for market interactions where amorphous and discretionary variables—like culture and politics—are considered superfluous. A number of important texts in recent years have challenged this scientization or mathematicization of economics (Fine and Milonankis 2009, Watson 2017). Yet these critiques can also be applied to our understanding of culture, and why the concept was progressively written out of the economics canon and therefore the type of applied economics used to address market structures and market behaviour in the pre-crisis period. As we shall see in Smith's own writings, in both his philosophical and economic work he was referring to real life examples of the emerging commercial society around him (Smith 1776: I.ii.2, Watson 2017). As a result, he addressed *economic* matters such as the failure of markets to clear—a condition that can be said to be satisfied when 'every buyer has access to sufficient stocks of the products to satisfy their optimal consumption plan and every seller exhausts their previously unsolved inventorying of stocks' (Watson 2017: 25)—just as readily as he did *cultural* factors—such as the distortive effects of power and greed on the functioning of that market. Since his starting point was the world he witnessed around him, economic and socio-cultural relations were rather obviously interwoven. By contrast, the neoclassical economics which followed became increasingly abstracted from these real-life conditions. For example, instead of exploring the self-interested exercise of power (hypothetical) rational actors in the neoclassical models are 'well behaved and act solely on the basis of the cues that they take from price signals' (ibid.). Politics and culture have no place in this sanitized world of abstractions.

The marginalist revolution of the late nineteenth century began this process, whilst general equilibrium theorists pushed the dependence on mathematic equations and therefore abstractions even further. As Milonakis and Fine (2009: 92) have argued, 'following the *Methodenstreit* and the rise of marginalism, interest in method [and the wider social context of market interactions] declined, focusing more on the extent to which it did or did not conform to…*theoretical and technical terms*, discarding anything that did not so conform, and often blundering forward without regard to methodological implications' (emphasis added). This constituted a major rupture with earlier economic thought. The result was that, by the twentieth century, leading economists in the field no longer considered it necessary to keep re-reading the economics of previous generations; all the big debates had been resolved, and any outstanding debates would find only 'out of date' answers in the classical economists (Stigler 1969: 218, see also Samuelson 1992). In other words, if the aim is to understand why liberally minded state managers would adopt market discipline and ethical reform in order to influence bank culture, the orthodox economics canon is relatively inconclusive. The preponderance with abstract models of markets had no need of political intervention; and rationality made culture and ethics of negligible importance.

A Return to Smith

Where did this deification of the market begin? Supposedly, the traditional point of reference in Smith's work is the *Wealth of Nations* (*TWON*) and the invisible hand that guides the market economy (Watson 2017). But it is his *Theory of Moral Sentiments*, written thirty years before *TWON* which provides his most substantive account of ethical struggle. In *Moral Sentiments*, Smith comes much closer to the depiction of culture as unethical behaviour that has characterized recent political rhetoric. Smith shifts between the flawed nature of man and society around him, and the idealized, aspirational view of man he wishes to promote. In fact, Smith operates with three different conceptions of man: the (external) man who acts; the (internal) man who thinks and feels and exists within the man who acts; and the (hypothetical) idealized man, who is the embodiment of good conduct. Smith contended that there is, in every individual, an innate desire to consider the interests of others: 'that to feel much for others and little for ourselves, that to restrain our selfishness, and to indulge our benevolent affections, constitutes the perfection of human nature' (Book I.I.44). He continued though that the ability to exercise 'self-government' may not always be 'able to stifle, altogether, the voice of human weakness, or reduce the violence of passions' (Book I.I.47).

In other words, though knowing the proper conduct, man will not always be able to exercise self-control. Indeed, this inability to contain and control passions posed a particular dilemma for Smith, for he recognized that commercial society is itself reproduced by the triumph of man's selfish and vain ambitions over his moral compass. Smith writes, 'The rich man glories in his riches, because he feels that they naturally draw upon him the attention of the world' and this itself is a driver of innovation and a fantastic motivation towards enterprise (Book I.III.16). Yet this 'disposition to admire, and almost to worship, the rich and the powerful...is...the great and most universal cause of the corruption of our moral sentiments' (I.III.28); 'Market society, with its spectacle of riches and its constant appeal to desires that might be satisfied, has a potentially corrupting influence on the individual' (Watson 2006: 50). Indeed, this corruption of the ethical order extends to the fact that respect and attention are more strongly directed towards wealth and power than they are towards wisdom and virtue (I.III.29). So, at one and the same time, Smith recognized that this is an inversion of the proper moral order, yet fundamental to the vitality of the market economy. And if we dismiss orthodox liberal economics, we see firstly, that these cultural questions were integral to the earlier liberal economics tradition; secondly, that they took as axiomatic the merits of the market; and thirdly, that they therefore focused on the narrower question of tackling unethical and uncompetitive behaviours that interfered with market competition.

In Smith's writings it was not simply the recognition of a struggle within market society though, but the importance of the state as organizer and enforcer of market competition—a theme which re-appeared later in the work of liberal scholars like Milton Friedman (1962: 15). For Smith there is a clear struggle between moral and immoral man; between the ethical man we know we ought to be, and the base instincts. This gives rise to a paradox that Smith was unable to overcome: the continued existence of commercial society requires the presence of his idealized moral man; but commercial society came into being and thrives on the base instincts that lead to moral corruption (Verburg 2000: 36–7, Watson 2006: 51). It is in the context of this paradox that his writings on the political and the state should be understood. Though much of what Smith writes focuses upon the moral struggle nascent within individuals rather than the external imposition of a moral order, there is also an implicit claim that justice requires an agent. In this sense Smith is a realist: he wishes to exhort moral man towards self-control and moderation; but he recognizes that without an external authority 'the whole fabric of society…must crumble into atoms' (II.II.18). 'Beneficience…is less essential to the existence of society than justice' (II.II.17). Indeed 'men, though naturally sympathetic, feel so little for one another…[that] justice is the main pillar that upholds the whole edifice' of commercial society (II.II.18, Bonefeld 2010). He concluded then, that the market 'cannot subsist unless the laws of justice are tolerably observed' (II.II.20). Away with the abstract theoretical models of orthodox economics; and away with the notion of non-intervention; his vision of the market economy required a market police state to overcome the avarice and moral corruption that would undermine the extant social order.

Moreover Smith was not alone among the early liberal political economists in recognizing the challenge that moral degradation would have on the maintenance of commercial society. 'Men being naturally selfish', wrote Smith's contemporary David Hume, 'they are not easily induc'd [*sic*] to perform any action for the interest of strangers, except with a view to some reciprocal advantage'. This meant that commerce was, for the most part, dominated by self-interest, although the more 'generous and noble intercourse of friendship' could still exist between family and friends (Hume T.3.2.5.8 and 3.2.5.10). Much rested then on the capacity for men to exercise moderation and fulfil moral obligations. He concluded for example, that 'we must govern ourselves by rules, which are more general in their application, and more free from doubt and uncertainty' and which must 'frequently prove contradictory both to men's wants and desires'. For to 'allow every man to seize by violence what he judges to be fit for him, would destroy society' (Hume T.3.2.4.1). Yet Hume too recognized that men would nonetheless oftentimes prefer 'any trivial advantage' to the maintenance of order in society and the observance of justice (T.3.2.7.3). Put differently, 'men are always much inclined to prefer present interest to distant and remote' (T.3.2.8.1). The result was that, as with Smith, Hume recognized the need for government—inter alia—to help enforce economic obligations: promises and commitments, he concluded, were the foundation of economic life in all large and civilized societies, making government a 'necessity' (T.3.2.8.7). Indeed, his three fundamental rules of justice—the stability of possession, its transference by consent, and the performance of promises—would be meaningless without the 'separate sanction of government' (T.3.2.11.1).

The purpose of this first section can be simply stated then: critics have often highlighted the disjuncture between the theory and the practice of neoliberalism. In theory neoliberalism—by which we mean the neoclassical skein of orthodox economics and the philosophical contributions of, inter alia, Hayek and Rand—refers to 'free markets liberated from state interference', whilst in practice it has entailed 'a dramatic intensification of coercive, disciplinary forms of state intervention to impose market rule upon all aspects of social life' (Brenner and Theodore 2012:.5). Arguments about light-touch, arms-length intervention clearly shaped the pre-crisis approach to the banking sector (Turner 2009). Yet in the writings of Smith and Hume we find three themes which are common to the liberal tradition, and which informed the liberal policy responses by state managers to the bank culture debate: that the market was benign and the pristine textbook vision of the market realizable; that the cause of dysfunctional outcomes was therefore a problem of unethical behaviour and failure to abide by the norms of market competition; and that this framing of the problem necessitated political intervention and pre-determined the *form* of that intervention as well. As others have argued, mainstream political parties in Anglo-America almost universally accept the liberal virtues of the market (Ryner 2010). Against this backdrop the narrowing of the bank culture debate to a liberal focus on perfecting the market is entirely understandable.

Ordo-liberals and Culture

If our aim is to understand (conceptually) the worldview of state managers as they reduced the bank culture debate to a focus on socially responsible behaviour and tightened market discipline, the German ordo-liberals provide an even more systematic explanation of the liberal perspective. Their relevance here is twofold: firstly, the work of the German ordo-liberals in the twentieth century is much more contemporary than that of Smith et al., and there is evidence that ordo-liberal thinking has actually framed a wide range of policy responses to the global financial crisis (Young 2017); and secondly, their work helps us to overcome the aforementioned paradoxical gap between what policymakers practice and orthodox economists preach, by highlighting the ordo-liberal emphasis on the strong state to bring the pristine model of market interactions into being. We therefore see that a parallel strand of economic liberal thought—ordo-liberalism—provides a much more robust account of how state managers addressed the bank culture debate.

Ordo-liberalism originated towards the end of the Weimar Republic (1918–33) in Germany and constituted a major contribution to liberal economic and political thought. Many of the conditions that the founding ordo-liberal thinkers—Walter Eucken, Franz Bohm, Alexander Rustow, Willhelm Ropke, and Alfred Muller-Armack—sought to address however, have strong historical parallels with both Western political and economic conditions following the financial crisis in general, and the ways that state managers conceived of bank culture more specifically. As with Smith in the previous section, much of the ordo-liberal thought should be read as a critique of so-called laissez-faire liberalism for its neglect of the state. The economy, so they argued, does not comprise an independent reality: the belief in economic liberty as a self-contained system in which 'self-dependent processes [are] whirring away automatically' was incorrect (Ropke 2017: 51, Bonefeld 2017). Rather the economy is a social construct, an 'artificial order' (Mueller-Armack 1947: 86) which has to be actively sustained through a strong and independent state.

Similar to Smith's conception of the importance of self-interest and innovation, for the ordo-liberals market competition was the goal, as the means of ensuring individual freedom and autonomy (Bonefeld 2017: ch. 2). As Alfred Muller-Armack noted, 'competition is indispensable as an instrument of social organization' (1978: 326). Competition takes two forms: it is a mechanism for promoting the continual inducement of maximum performance on the part of both workers and capitalists; and it is a device for regulating and ordering the economic process, that is, governing supply and demand (Ropke 1957: 95). Put differently, the ordo-liberals were firm believers in the capacity of the free price mechanism to regulate between multifarious individual preferences (Muller-Armack 1978: 327, Bonefeld 2013). Again, negative outcomes—such as some symptoms of a problem with bank culture—were therefore not conceivably a fault with the market itself, but with the disruptive influence of individual and clusters of bad behaviour.

Were there forces within the market that provoked this bad behaviour? Yes and no was the answer given by the ordo-liberals. As Smith had also suggested, unbridled competition is at odds with social integration. Competition destroys the 'substance of binding forces' that hold society together (Muller-Armack 1979: 152); competition was a 'category of disunity and strife, self-interest and greed, abuse and coercion' (Bonefeld 2017: ch. 2). The question was how to sustain a society of 'greedy self-seekers' (Rustow 1932: 255). Managing these tendencies that form the driving impulsion of the market economy is therefore a matter for the state. Imposing order and rules is the function of government. 'Changes in the law could make firms liable for some of the "disbenefits" they cause. Discrepancies between private costs and the spillover costs imposed on others can be corrected' by the state (Brittan 1977: 50). The market fed on self-interest; but the state was required to prevent destructive excesses.

There are two particular features of the ordo-liberal writings on state intervention then which are relevant to this book, both of which provide a more convincing account than the orthodox (neoliberal) economic alternatives: the first concerns what the ordo-liberals tell us about the state and private interests. The second concerns what the ordo-liberals tell us about culture. In both respects there are strong parallels with the writings of the classical economists discussed above. The logical conclusion of the ordo-liberal challenge to laissez-faire liberalism is that there is no such thing as a non-interventionist state. Instead it is the *purpose* and *method*, the *objective* and *aim* of intervention which differs; even the laissez-faire state is a form of intervention. The ostensibly light-touch state is in fact a state that is deferential to particular private interests. It intervenes, but to protect privileged groups. It is therefore a *weak* state that has succumbed to private interests. Instead, the ordo-liberal state intervenes not for specific social ends or on behalf of powerful private interests. It intervenes to ensure that all participants are exposed to competitive pressures. It intervenes to ensure that no participants are insulated from competition or from the effects of the decisions they make. As Bonefeld contends, the ordo-liberals 'also make clear that freedom entails responsibility, that is, the economic agents are liable for the consequences of their decisions, removing the state as a public insurer for private risk taking' (2017: ch. 2).

Thus the 'market form of complete competition surrenders each one to the control of the market' (Eucken 2004: 237). This is because commercial society is constantly threatened since competition 'appeals... solely to selfishness' and that same self-interest drives interest groups to subvert competition itself (Rustow 1942: 272). This happens in two ways: on the one hand free competition is threatened by capitalists, via economic domination and concentration in the form of monopolies; whilst on the other hand it is threatened by democratic movements. Labour unions were seen as one form of mass democratic demand, whereby workers sought to insulate themselves from the pressures and incentives of competition (Ropke 1957: 30). Likewise, monopolies formed by particular business groups distorted the free price mechanism. The rent-seeking discussed in Chapter 2 is an example of profiteering from uncompetitive behaviour. In other words, state managers approaching the culture of banking problem from a liberal perspective would see clusters of financiers disrupting the functioning of an otherwise healthy market mechanism; and the behaviour of these financiers therefore needed to be exposed to greater market competition and market discipline, to correct their 'misconduct'.

This leads to a liberal vision of the state's role in subjecting individual agents to the rule of money and of law; the vision that is merely obfuscated by laissez-faire economic thought. The state must remain autonomous from particular private interests to enforce the law of competition. Indeed even Hayek concluded that laissez-faire is 'a highly ambiguous and misleading description of the principles on which a liberal policy is based' (Hayek 1976: 84). But Smith, the ordo-liberals, and—in a different vein—Marxian-inspired accounts recognized that 'the state secures the general interest of capital... *not by overriding* the rule of the market, but by *enforcing* the rule of money and of law, which are the alienated forms through which the rule of the market is imposed not only on the working class, but also on all particular capitals' (emphasis added Clarke 1988: 124).

This first element of ordo-liberalism pushes the Smithian argument to its logical conclusion: as market police the state must act in the collective interest of competition which necessarily involves a willingness to impose competition itself on—inter alia—firms in the market. The state is not simply the instrument of the capitalists, as some theories would imply; this is far too simplistic, and would undermine the functioning of the market economy which relies on competition. Some explanations of light-touch policy prior to the financial crisis indicate that Anglo-American state managers had succumbed to lobbying efforts of the large banks (Morgan 2012). When we argue in coming chapters that state managers sought to strengthen market discipline then, this reflects an attempt to prioritize systemic interests—competition—over particular private interests (the banks). Though the term 'culture' was rarely used in the political debate early in the financial crisis, the implicit notion was that the right kind of culture was one of improved competition, because the excessive risk-taking and subsequent bailouts were evidence that market competition (and the associated price signals) had somehow been diluted. Competition would produce the right kind of culture. The state strategies outlined in Chapters 4 and 6 explain these struggles as attempts to impose the so-called 'rules of the game' on the banks, whilst also reducing welfare provision and promoting workfare for the poor (Jessop 1993). This is the ideal at the heart of the liberal blueprint: a limited but strong state, less deferential to big corporations and less responsible for welfare recipients (Bonefeld 2015). The first phase of crisis responses—guided by this (renewed) liberal vision—places culture within the wider strategy of improving competition and market discipline; and it shows why, even at an early stage, broader questions about the structure of the market under financialization were absent from the political debate.

Before we move to consider the other big conceptual theme of this chapter—the legitimacy crisis—however, we find one other key insight in the writings of the ordo-liberals. Specifically, the ordo-liberals focused explicitly on the importance of the state to ethical reform. Though orthodox economics made every effort to render the functioning of the market economy a technical exercise and thereby remove the need for discretionary state intervention (see Best 2005 for a critique), few (political) liberals would contest the need for the state as market police

(Brittan 1989: 202). What is less well recognized however, is the importance of the state to matters of corporate ethics. Certainly the academic literature on culture-as-behaviour discussed in Chapter 2 placed a premium on values and leadership *within* the firm; the role of the *state* in promoting these good ethics was less apparent.

In contrast, the ordo-liberals acknowledged—as Smith had—that the struggle to sustain commercial society also involved a *moral-ethical* dimension that would require political authority. Enforcing the rules of competition disciplines behaviour. But competition also degenerates—argued the ordo-liberals—when participants in the market economy fail to abide by 'bourgeois' ethical and moral principles (Ropke 1957: 98). Simply appealing to people's enlightened self-interest by trying to convince them that 'they serve their own best advantage by submitting to the discipline of the market and of competition' will not suffice (ibid.: 123). Though the ordo-liberals were firm believers in the market economy—that is 'a system where supply and demand move prices and thereby govern production'—they also highlighted that 'society as a whole cannot be ruled by the laws of supply and demand' (Ropke 1957: 91). That is, 'the market economy is not enough... Economic life naturally does not go on in a moral vacuum. It is constantly in danger of straying from the ethical middle unless it is buttressed by strong *moral* supports' (ibid.: 124).

This is a step beyond the earlier emphasis on state managers' enforcing the technical, legal framework for market competition. Here the ordo-liberals were also thinking of the *moral* prerequisites for the market and competition being 'furnished from outside' (ibid.: 126). This made the ordo-liberals attentive to 'social structure and... the definite spiritual and moral setting' of the market economy (Ropke 1957: 93). This function of the state points to an understanding of the importance of *educating* market participants in the correct norms and behaviours. As we will see in Chapters 5 and 7, this softer, normative role ascribed to the state by liberal thinkers resonates with more contemporary, benchmarking efforts by the New York Fed and the Banking Standards Board.

In closing, the first two sections of this chapter have presented a re-reading of Smith and the ordo-liberals to argue that unethical and irresponsible behaviours by market participants, as well as attempts to distort the market, were major themes in liberal thought. Orthodox economics largely ignores questions of ethics and culture (Di Tella and MacCulloch 2014) and almost certainly underemphasizes the importance of the state in sustaining market discipline and educating participants in the right values. Yet there has always been a tension between what orthodox economists preach and what policymakers practice (Rodrik 1995: 1458). That tension is resolved if we return to Smith and the ordo-liberals. Anglo-American state managers have, in this way, followed the economic liberal playbook: assuming that the problems derived from sources other than the structure of the market itself; and focusing instead on deviant behaviour, which led them first to tighten market discipline and then to promote ethical reform. If our aim is to understand why the great bank culture debate narrowed, then this liberal worldview is an important piece of the jigsaw puzzle.

Habermas and Legitimacy

Having laid the intellectual foundation for understanding the liberal attempt to tackle culture as just another component of improved market competition, the remainder of this chapter now examines the concept of the legitimacy crisis. For reasons that will become clear, improving the market mechanism was not enough. Not only did scandals—LIBOR, Wells Fargo and so forth—continue to emerge, but the practices of the limited state—curbing social spending and austerity—as well as the prolonged experience of inequality in Anglo-America only grew worse. Public perceptions of selective intervention—privatizing the gains and socializing the losses—only worsened as the 2010s progressed (Burnham 2011). The resulting legitimacy crisis required a (populist) political response; and one that would not require a full reconstitution of the financialization of Anglo-America, for all the structural reasons outlined in Chapter 2. In other words, another reason why the bank culture debate narrowed was the need for an immediate (simple) response. Thus the populist response to the legitimacy crisis also helps to explain why the world of banking feels so different to employees (Chapter 9); whilst to the informed observer it is clear that the *real* cultural problems—disproportionately high wages, bank models exploiting the indebted, financial instability, and the divide between the financial sector and the economy—remain unchanged.

Jürgen Habermas was the first to systematically explore the concept of a legitimacy crisis. His aim was to develop the Weberian—Marxian notion of socio-economic crises (1973: 2). Unlike the idea of a strictly economic crisis—whatever that might mean—Habermas suggested that crises emerge from 'unresolved steering problems' (ibid.: 4). Like Marx and Hegel, Habermas contended that conflicts at the political level are only the surface appearance of underlying contradictions though. Simply, a political crisis—or a crisis of crisis management (Clarke 1991: 7)—emerges when the state is no longer able to reconcile the conflicting demands made upon it. Under late capitalist societies, the principle form of organization is the relationship of wage–labour and capital (Habermas 1973: 20). This was foreseen by Smith who contended that private property was a consequence of the development in the division of labour. In turn, it gives rise to the social differentiation of society into distinct social classes, which increases value creation, which in turn leads to the expansion of private property. This expansion 'lays the foundation for the separation between civil society and the state in capitalism' (Bonefeld 2010: 18). In its most abstract form then, the state derives its purpose from the needs of private property. Class society though means that the interests of capital and labour are not aligned: the 'workmen desire to get as much, the masters to give as little as possible' (Smith 1976: 83).

Here the liberal capitalist state has a structural and ideological bias, for it operates under the belief that the resolution of class conflict can only lie in sustained progressive accumulation (Offe 1974: 36). Put differently, it suspends the democratic demands of the working classes for rising wages or welfare provision in favour of prioritizing capitalist accumulation. The state achieves this by 'fixing in a system of observed norms the asymmetrical distribution of legitimate chances to satisfy needs' (Habermas 1973: 96). This function of the market mechanism was viewed as relatively benign by the economic liberals, who assumed that since workers would—they argued—benefit somewhat from progressive accumulation they too had a vested interest in sustaining the asymmetry at the heart of the market. Though workers resist tougher working conditions and reductions in aggregate pay, Smith contended for example, 'workers do well not to struggle, because with the increase of revenue' the demand for workers also increases (1976: 86–7). In fact they gain little from the 'violence of those tumultuous' efforts to rebel against market discipline (1976: 84). Thus (so the liberal blueprint implies) it is in the interest of the state to maintain progressive accumulation—in the belief that it leads to the increase in national wealth—and override the short-term pleas of workers.

Both the historical materialist critique and the historical record confirm however, that the proceeds of progressive accumulation are not equally distributed. As Marx noted, it is not simply the distribution of chances (in an abstract sense) that is weighted in favour of the bourgeoisie, but the market mechanism itself produces genuine, wealth inequality: 'How lame an anti-climax!', Marx contended, 'If the working-class has remained "poor," only "less poor" in proportion as it produces for the wealthy class "an intoxicating augmentation of wealth and power," then it has remained relatively just as poor. If the extremes of poverty have not lessened, they have increased, because the extremes of wealth have' (2004: 715–16). We do not need to develop this critique further here since our focus is on the politics of state intervention and banking culture that function at a more concrete level of abstraction. But, at the very least, we can point to the fact not all political economists agreed with the liberal assumption that the market mechanism was benign.

This function of the state in maintaining the legitimacy of the capitalist order does not mean however, that we should conflate the priority of the state with particularistic bourgeois interests (Habermas 1973: 61). The state is not simply or necessarily captured or co-opted by the rich and powerful. But it does indicate, as Smith had also earlier contended, that 'bourgeois culture as a whole was never able to reproduce itself from itself' (ibid.: 77). In this sense the challenge that Habermas confronts is markedly similar to that outlined by Smith and the ordo-liberals. The accumulation of capital requires free competition; but the 'supporting conditions of this competition—the social foundations of the production of surplus value—cannot themselves be reproduced by capitalist means. They require a state that confronts individual capitalists as a non-capitalist' (p. 50). How then do we get from this claim to the notion of a legitimacy crisis and the political response to the bank culture debate?

Legitimacy challenges emerge from this class structure within capitalist society (Habermas 1973: 73). This is due to the aforementioned 'asymmetrical distribution of chances for the legitimate satisfaction of needs' (p. 27). People are not entirely ignorant; they recognize that social and economic inequalities abound under advanced capitalism. Put simply, the rich—for a variety of reasons ranging from private wealth, to education and social opportunity, as well as the fact that the capitalist economy and the state are rigged in their favour—are more likely to achieve 'the satisfaction of their needs' than the poor are. The rich (or the bourgeoisie) are, in general, reasonably willing to live with the existing economic order during prosperous times. Acceptance of this bourgeois ideology and the 'socially integrative effects of the value form may be restricted, by and large, to the bourgeois class' though; whilst the 'loyalty and subordination' of the lower (poorer) classes requires either a 'fatalistic willingness to follow' or 'naked repression' (p. 22). The rich—on balance—are net beneficiaries and so actively consent to and benefit from the status quo. The poorer classes are more likely to experience tougher living and working conditions, though their participation is as equally necessary as that of the richer bourgeoisie. Manufacturing the consent of the working classes is therefore an active struggle (Bruff 2008), albeit one that is significantly easier during times of prosperity and economic growth.

The opposition of interests comes to a head during economic crises, or the interruption of the process of accumulation (Habermas 1973: 23). Marx made a similar point about the realization of the illusory character of some profits from financial activity during a crisis of accumulation of course; here Habermas was applying a similar conception to the social and political implications of a breakdown in the rhythms of accumulation. Thus an *economic* crisis can develop into a *social* crisis—where the class divide becomes starker—and, in turn, develop into a *political* crisis for the state as it struggles to revitalize the accumulation process whilst containing class antagonisms in the interim. This is a case of trying to get the genie back into the bottle however.

To jump two steps ahead of ourselves, it is no coincidence then that the culture of banking debate has emerged against the backdrop of three underlying challenges for the Anglo-American state managers: the upwards redistribution of wealth (or rising inequality) which has been taking place since at least the 1970s; the equally long-term withdrawal of state spending on social policy (or austerity);

and the more immediate challenges in restarting economic growth in the UK and the US in the 2010s. These three trends have made the class divide between rich and poor ever more apparent and exposed state managers to ever-greater criticism. Wolfgang Streeck, drawing on Habermas, refers to this is as the crisis of (Western) democratic capitalism (Streeck 2014: 6–9).

This is how we draw together the arguments of Chapters 2 and 3. Financialization is the shift towards financial activity that occurs against the backdrop of the crisis of accumulation in Anglo-America; this same financialization also empowers the *marktvolk*, leading to the politics of tight money; this tight money, and the attempt to restore profitability, places further cost of living pressures on lower and middle income individuals; and these pressures thereby act as the transmission mechanism for the crisis of accumulation, exacerbating both greater indebtedness and rising discontent and politicization. The point is simply that *this* is the political crisis confronting state managers, and it reflects unresolved steering problems—or the political challenge of sustaining the capitalist order when its inequalities are starkly apparent and the neutrality of the state is in doubt (Burnham 2011).

Returning to Habermas (1973), the political crisis can take two forms: a rationality crisis, and a legitimacy crisis. A rationality crisis occurs when the administrative system does not succeed in reconciling and fulfilling the imperatives received from the economic system (p. 46). A legitimation crisis emerges though when the requisite level of mass loyalty dissipates. The rationality deficit means that the state is losing the ability to steer the economic system; a legitimacy deficit means that the state is unable to maintain effective normative structures (p. 47). Habermas' commentary on the legitimacy crisis will prove to be important in Chapters 4–7.

As he saw it, a legitimation crisis begins to emerge when the expectations of the populace cannot be fulfilled either by the available quantity of value or the rewards that the political and economic system generates (p. 74). Intervention by the state—for example via bank bailouts—produces 'unintended unsettling and publicizing effects', 'weakening the justification potential of traditions that have been flushed out of their nature-like course of development' (p. 72, see also Burnham 2011: 494). This 'stirring up of cultural affairs that are taken for granted' further politicizes areas of life that the state had sought to insulate from scrutiny and questioning. Indeed, as 'belief in the legitimacy of the existing order vanishes the latent force embedded in the system of institutions is released' (Habermas 1973: 96). This is simply another way of saying that the depth of the class antagonisms that had previously been vacuum-sealed in the container of the existing institutional structures, breaks loose; in such cases we would expect to see angry and often violent protests of the type experienced in Occupy movements in London and New York.

Populism as a Response to the Legitimacy Deficit

It is here that we turn to the debate around populism. Much like the terms globalization and neoliberalism have been buzzwords for academia in previous decades, populism is arguably the most commonly referred to theme for academics and the media in the 2010s. In this final subsection I will argue that the ideologically thin, simplistic anti-establishment character of populism made it an ideal response to the legitimacy crisis for Anglo-American state managers. This is because populism is, by very definition, designed to score cheap political points by presenting a black and white picture of 'them versus us' that is superficially appealing to the electorate. Populism is therefore an important reason for the narrowing of the bank culture debate and the fact that the more challenging task of reforming financialization was largely ignored. The fact that populism overrides traditional distinctions between the political left and the political right however, also helps to explain why more conservative and more radically-minded state managers congregated around the narrower debate.

Populism is often mistakenly conflated with its right-wing, nativist variant (Mudde and Kaltwasser 2017). Post-financial crisis however, a left-wing populism has been equally prevalent (Mounck 2014). Both left and right-wing versions share the fact that they are ideological thin—insofar as they often attach to other existing ideologies and generally lack a specific policy programme of their own (Mudde and Kaltwasser 2017). What they have in common however, is their depiction of a corrupt 'elite' and a deprived 'people' (Bale et al. 2009). In this sense it has been argued that we should talk about populist narratives attaching to more traditional ideological positions, rather than simply analysing populist 'parties' in a narrower sense (Deegan-Krause and Haughton 2009). Populist discourses have thus permeated mainstream—Conservative and Labour, Democrat and Republican—narratives, with state managers presenting policies such as bank fines as a defence of the general will of the people (see Kriesi et al. 2012 for an overview).

The capitulation of social democratic parties in Western Europe (including the UK) to neoliberalism, and the immanence of neoliberal ideology amongst the American political classes already constrained the range of ideological alternatives (Bruff 2014, Ryner 2010). The fact that the financialized model of capitalism was not central to the bank culture debate is in some ways unsurprising. Yet the growing divide between the (worsening) lived experiences of lower and middle income households and the promises of prosperity attached to the neoliberal project fuelled the legitimacy crisis, whilst the political classes had an ever tighter ideological space within which to manoeuvre (see Streeck 2014: 6–9). To be clear, the legitimacy crisis Anglo-American state managers have been fighting is not solely the product of financialization. A legitimacy crisis refers to a decline in mass consent for the political strategies of the ruling classes (Streeck 2014). This has as much to do with ill-advised military campaigns, the long-term decline in welfare provision, and the failed promises of neoliberalism, as it does with financialization and the global financial crisis. But, as we shall see in Chapters 4 and 6, there is a clear correlation between both the bank bailouts and the subsequent austerity agenda, and the fall in public confidence in both the banks and the political classes. Populist strategies such as public denigration of the bankers and large financial penalties were an obvious response aimed at re-establishing the perception of an independent state apparatus, rather than a state beholden to the whims of the embattled banks. Of course the point is however, that this populist statecraft was almost entirely performative (Macartney 2014). It was part of a wider attempt to deflect criticism, and whether inadvertently or deliberately the result was that the broader, more challenging debate about bank culture and financialization dissipated.

Closing Remarks

This book has set out to explain why the bank culture debate narrowed to a focus on ethical and socially responsible conduct. The answer provided by Chapters 2 and 3 is that financialization is deeply embedded and therefore harder to reform; this chapter has also explained why the immanence of certain (positive) liberal assumptions about the market also meant that when state managers were looking for causes of the bank culture problem the answer had to lie somewhere other than the structure of the market itself; and finally this chapter has also argued that the early responses to the financial crisis—the bailouts and subsequent austerity measures in Anglo-America—exacerbated an already slowburning legitimacy crisis that necessitated an urgent response by state managers. The result was a form of superficial populism that once again deflected attention away from the effects of financialization on bank culture. The following Chapters 4–7 now apply these conceptual insights to examine the political responses to the first and second phases of the bank culture problematique.

In the Conclusion to this book however, we will return to these broader questions. If financialization is the underlying cause of problematic culture in the banking sector in Anglo-America—from disproportionately high pay, to the divide between the finance sector and the rest of the economy, and stability-threatening risk-taking as well as predatory lending practices focused on the heavily indebted—then state managers have only bought themselves time by refusing to deal with the structural causes. At the time of writing academic accounts tend to dissect and interrogate the financial crisis, anti-establishment voting (Brexit and Trump), inequality, the delayed economic recovery, and fiscal consolidation as relatively separate phenomena. Yet the conclusion of this book argues that the bank culture problem and the political responses it engendered are merely the tip of the iceberg. And that a political crisis of the state might be unfolding, as the legitimacy crisis reaches a tipping point. For now, we put these considerations on hold in order to examine (Part II) the responses of US and UK state managers and (Part III) changes within the banking system.

PART II
STATE RESPONSES

4

US Responses and the First Phase

The aim of this book has been to explain why, despite the claims of those working in the banking sectors of Anglo-America that their working environment has changed quite dramatically, many of the more problematic features of Anglo-American banking culture have changed very little. In particular this book has highlighted the disproportionately high pay in the banking and financial sector, the relationship between the banking sector and the rest of the economy, and bank business models that continue to prey on the heavily indebted as some of the most problematic concerns. I have argued that so little change has taken place because good culture was defined in the political debate as ethical and socially responsible conduct—achievable via the right kinds of checks and incentives and via normative reform. Instead, I argue that we need a much broader-based discussion about the effect that the financialization of Anglo-America has on bank culture.

Before we examine what has and has not changed in the US and UK bank culture in Part III of the book, Part II traces the political response of state managers. First this response to culture-related problems involved tightening market discipline and changing incentives; then it focused more explicitly on reforming values. This narrow focus however, stemmed—in large part—from the fact that the legitimacy crisis state managers were facing demanded an immediate (but ultimately rather superficial) policy response. In Chapter 3 I described this policy response as a form of populist statecraft because it was an ideologically thin attempt to score political points. But although the culture reform agenda was partly a response to popular discontent, it should not be interpreted as a reassertion of democratic politics over the liberal market economy. Instead, state responses were an attempt to impose the rule of the market—of competition—upon the bankers themselves.

The main aim of this chapter then is to examine the unfolding financial and bank culture crises that added fuel to a slow-burning legitimacy crisis, which in turn prompted a response from US state managers. But—as noted above—the chapter cautions against reading the politico-regulatory response as a defence of lower and middle income Americans. Instead, bank culture became a particularly important target for US state managers because, as one NY Federal Reserve official explained 'culture is the precursor to the rule of law' (Interview 20160419). Thus, although much of the political response was couched in terms of 'consumer

The Bank Culture Debate: Ethics, Values, and Financialization in Anglo-America. Huw Macartney, Oxford University Press (2019). © Huw Macartney.
DOI: 10.1093/oso/9780198843764.001.0001

protection' and a defence of the '99 per cent', in reality it was a liberal attempt to protect and fortify the market mechanism by targeting the distortive misconduct of the bankers. In other words, though populism is ultimately ideologically thin, Anglo-American state managers also exhibited a deeply rooted set of (economic liberal) beliefs in the merits of the market.

In Chapter 5, we will see how the efforts to improve the market mechanism did not resolve either the culture problem or the accompanying legitimacy crisis. The present chapter however, unfolds in two broad sections. The first section discusses the lead up to the financial crisis and the early phase of the crisis itself. It argues that in contrast to what was happening in the UK prior to the crisis where the main regulator, the Financial Services Authority, essentially became a promotional agent for the banking sector, US regulators at the start of the 2000s did indeed have a tough approach to the US banking sector. This pressure eased off though in the mid 2000s only to emerge again with a vengeance as the crisis hit. Suffice it to say that misconduct—one of the identifiers of cultural problems according to state managers—was a big issue earlier on in the US than it was in the UK case.

The second section of this chapter examines the crisis of legitimacy. It argues that falling confidence was very pronounced at the early stage of the financial crisis in the US, and continued to fall through to 2012. Opinion poll data is used to support this claim. This section also argues that New York became the epicentre for the populist, anti-bank movement, which is particularly important in understanding the responses of state managers. Indeed, the context of austerity and fiscal consolidation further exacerbated the legitimacy crisis, highlighting the inequality in the US and being exemplified in the high-paid individuals on Wall Street. This struggle over inequality and Wall Street, against the backdrop of austerity, formed the basis for state managers' responses to the culture of banking problem.

Early Phase

Early 2000s

In Chapter 2, I explored many of the more fundamental changes that had occurred in the business practices and structures of the world's largest banks, and how these changes had unfolded in the US banking system during the late 1980s and through the 1990s. From a regulatory perspective though, the changing approach of US policymakers and regulators as the financial crisis emerged in 2007–8 should be juxtaposed against two earlier periods in the decade leading up to the crisis. The first section of this chapter therefore begins with (i) a brief overview of the Enron and Dot.com crises and the regulatory approach which followed, before then examining (ii) the regulatory lull during the mid 2000s.

Enron

Given that this is a book about the culture of banking debate it might appear odd to begin this chapter with the energy company Enron. Yet much of the financial manipulation that took place within Enron mirrors the corporate scandals which have hit Wall Street in recent years; and the collapse of Enron was also a major factor, alongside the bursting of the Dot.com bubble, shaping US regulatory practice in the early 2000s. Enron was born from the merger of Houston Natural Gas and Internorth, a Nebraska pipeline company, in 1985. In the process of this merger however, Enron incurred massive losses and was forced to hire a consultant, Jeffrey Skilling, from McKinsey and Co. to reformulate their business strategy. Skilling however had a background in banking and asset management, and so he proposed to create a 'gas bank', in which 'Enron would buy gas from a network of suppliers and sell it to a network of consumers, contractually guaranteeing both the supply and the price, charging fees for the transactions and assuming the associated risks' (Thomas 2002). This was the beginning of the energy derivative.

Through the course of the 1990s then, Skilling set about transforming Enron into a trading business. Not only did Enron begin to compete with the largest investment banks in recruiting the top talent, but it placed a major emphasis on the bonuses it awarded its top traders. Together this gave rise to a corporate culture that became infamous for valuing profits above all else. It soon became common knowledge for example, that employees who were unable to keep up the pace were routinely fired within six months. Towards the end of the 1990s Skilling and Lay then began applying the same business model to the electricity sector, turning Enron Capital and Trade Resources into the nation's largest wholesale buyer and seller of natural gas and electricity. The result was that in August 2000 Enron stock hit an all-time high of $90.56 and was seen as one of the most innovative companies in the world.

A comprehensive summary of Enron's downfall is unnecessary. Suffice it to note that the widespread use of mark-to-market accounting by Enron allowed the company to post record, and ultimately fallacious, profits; an important theme in our discussion of financialization. Under mark-to-market rules, companies with outstanding energy related or other derivative contracts on their balance sheets at the end of a quarter must adjust them to fair market value; long-term futures contracts in commodities such as gas though create significant problems, because there are often no quoted prices on which to base valuations. Enron, which was under such extreme pressures to surpass earnings estimates, considerably overstated those earnings. Towards the end of the 1990s other energy companies began to follow Enron's lead, which placed downward pressures on Enron's profits. At the same time, energy prices themselves began to fall in the first quarter of 2001. Meanwhile, a variety of analysts began to question the opacity of Enron's financial disclosures and trust in the company began to erode.

What concerns us most in this chapter though, is the regulatory response to the kind of financial scandal witnessed at Enron. In October 2001, Enron reported a $618 million third-quarter loss and announced a $1.2 billion reduction in shareholder equity. This was the catalyst for the US Securities and Exchange Commission (SEC) to begin a formal investigation into the reported losses, followed in January 2002 by a criminal investigation into the collapse of Enron by the US Justice Department (*NY Times* 2001 Click here to enter text.). What followed was a lengthy investigation into failures in financial reporting by Enron itself and the accounting firm Arthur Anderson, followed by criminal prosecutions of a number of Enron's senior personnel. Then in 2002, a Senate committee began an investigation into the SEC's regulation of Enron, unearthing a 'systemic and catastrophic' failure by the SEC to adequately supervise Enron (*WSJ* 2002). The Senate's report concluded that although their 'investigation found no wilful malfeasance by the Commission with respect to Enron, [they] concluded that the Commission's largely hands-off approach to the company... allowed inaccurate and incomplete information to flood the market, leading to significant financial losses for thousands of Enron employees and an even greater number of investors' (Committee on Government Affairs 2002: 46). The nature of the scandals and subsequent collapse at Enron, coupled with the strength of the regulatory response—outlined below—bear unfortunate parallels with the global financial crisis later in the 2000s.

Dot.com

The second pivotal event which would shape the regulatory response in the early 2000s was the collapse of the 'Dot.com' boom. In the late 1990s, a range of new, trendy Internet companies sparked massive overinvestment in the belief that these companies had reinvented traditional business models. Rather than basing investment decisions on existing business plans and the idea that the stock price of a company reflected its actual, existing profits, stock market valuations of these companies became increasingly detached from any real fundamentals (*NY Times* 2000); this is a recurring theme of the analysis in this book and points to the distributive gains under financialization outlined in Chapter 2. The result was that stocks traded at record multiples of earnings.

Part of the issue was that in this new Internet technology era, many argued that earnings no longer mattered, and so a variety of other metrics and financial information were relied upon to generate estimates of future profitability. In March 2000 the Dot.com bubble began to burst, with stocks falling in price and companies collapsing. Once again, as with the Enron debacle, the Dot.com boom highlighted a tendency within the financial system whereby logic and moderation give way to profit; and where passive regulators watching the exuberance from the sidelines were suddenly called into action when market volatility became apparent. As with Enron, the US Securities and Exchange Commission was the regulatory institution which gate-crashed the party. In December 2001 they issued an advisory statement cautioning public companies against misleading investors (SEC 2001).

In terms of the regulatory response then, the collapse in Enron and Dot.com in particular sparked 'one of the busiest and most successful periods' ever witnessed in US prosecutions (*FT* 2011). The energy company's bankruptcy was quickly followed by a series of other revelations of fraud at firms like Tyco, Adelphia Communications, Worldcom, and HealthSouth. The result was that Enron's chief executive and chief financial officer as well as nearly two dozen top executives from the other firms were imprisoned; and banks and the other companies were forced to pay more than $15 billion in fines and payouts to investors. In turn, the US Congress passed the controversial Sarbanes–Oxley corporate accountability law which toughened the rules for auditors and corporate boards in issues relating to accounting fraud. Indeed, a former lawyer at the Securities and Exchange Commission contended that the Enron fraud 'raised the bar for law enforcement' (cited in *FT* 2011).

The above two cases are significant because: as highlighted, they point to a disturbing trend of post ad hoc regulation; and because despite the tough regulatory responses that emerged following Enron and the Dot.com bubble, by the mid 2000s the US again experienced a regulatory lull. Ironically, this was partially sparked by the lowering of interest rates after the Dot.com bubble burst, which led to the surge in market activity through the 2000s and brought to a head many of the cultural problems that are endemic to financialization and which are the major theme of this book. The reason these tendencies reared their ugly head again in 2008, so soon after Enron and Dot.com, was arguably because then as in the post-2008 period, state managers narrowed the debate to promoting good conduct rather than tackling the structural conditions of financialization.

Mid-2000s

The aim of the first sections of this chapter is not to show through some kind of regression analysis a precise causal mechanism which gives rise to increased regulatory activity and prosecutions. The aim is much more modest than that. Instead it is to provide some context to the treatment of bank culture post-2008. Most importantly, the chapter as a whole aims to highlight the two goals—responding to the legitimacy crisis and tightening market discipline—which shaped post-2008 responses. To show what changed though as the global financial crisis unfolded it is necessary to have in mind what regulatory action looked like in the preceding period. Simply put, though the Enron and Dot.com crises prompted tough regulation and litigation, this was followed by a regulatory lull. More pithily though—in the subsequent sections—I argue that there appears to be an unsettling relationship between public opinion and regulatory activity. It is widely recognized that regulation can tend to follow a business cycle. Here I argue that regulatory and supervisory activity—for all its technical language—is also deeply influenced by politics, responding to public criticisms and the 'mood of the times' (Stanley 2014). In other words, in the early 2000s the desire for a high-profile and immediate political response shaped and narrowed the debate; and this pattern repeated itself with the great bank culture debate in the 2010s.

This subsection maps the regulatory lull of the early 2000s. Fig. 4.1 below highlights this general trend across the range of US regulatory and prosecution authorities. It includes data from the Federal Reserve Board of Governors, and the Securities and Exchange Commission. It highlights that, particularly in the case of the SEC, after a significant round of litigation cases early in the 2000s, the volume of cases being launched by these two regulatory institutions fell significantly in the lead up to 2007. The data also then shows a significant spike, as one would expect, around 2008. We will explore this spike more fully in subsequent sections of this chapter.

Another way of contextualizing the changing approach of the US authorities as the financial crisis hit is not simply to examine the volume of litigation cases, but the kinds of enforcement action taken. One particularly important proxy for understanding the mindset of regulators during this period became known as the 'deferred prosecution' agreement. Developed during the 1930s as a means of

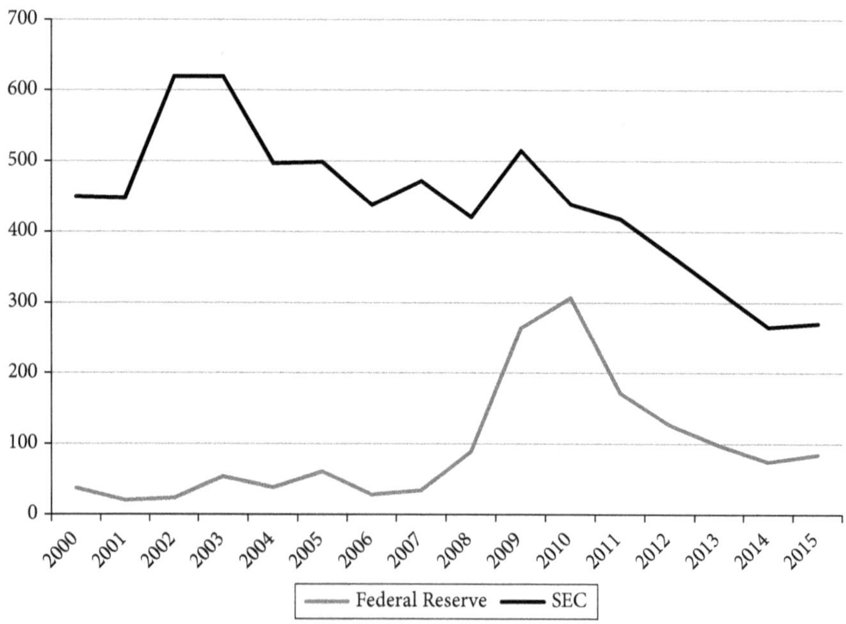

Fig. 4.1 Enforcement actions by US regulatory institutions (2000–15)
Source: Various Federal Reserve and SEC records.

reforming juvenile offenders, federal prosecutors began using deferred prosecution agreements with major corporations and large financial institutions with increasing frequency from the early 1990s onwards. These agreements are particularly relevant to our discussion of corporate culture.

In the typical arrangement, the authority would agree to defer prosecution on the understanding that in addition to paying a financial penalty the company itself would introduce 'prophylactic' measures designed to prevent similar crimes occurring in the future and also to 'rehabilitate' the company's culture (Rakoff 2015). Many of the changes in prosecution strategy in the 1990s can be traced back first to the work of academics in the 1980s, who suggested that one of the most effective ways to promote good culture within corporations was to provide in-house ethical training and to enlarge internal compliance programmes. In other words, this was one of the ways—highlighted in Chapter 2—in which academic definitions of bank culture also contributed to a narrowing of the political debate. These academic ideas gained traction with the US Sentencing Commission who in 1991 introduced the Corporate Sentencing Guidelines, whereby the existence and quality of a firms' internal compliance programmes became the most important factor in determining the size of the fine imposed upon that firm. In other words, these regulatory and legislative changes were underpinned by the philosophy that the internal culture of the firm was the responsibility of the firm itself, and that prosecutors would look favourably on the existence of good compliance programmes in the belief that, if misconduct did occur, it was a case of individual deviance from the corporate cultural norm, rather than a problem with the corporation itself. In very simplistic terms, we might think of this as a light-touch or arms-length regulatory approach. If we were to push the argument a little further, we might imply that this type of framing reinforced the liberal conception of a pristine market model and supported the view that any 'cultural' problems could not lie within the structure of the financialized market itself, but rather the behaviours of individual deviants.

In turn, the US Department of Justice published the Thompson, McCallum, and McNulty Memoranda indicating that another important factor in deciding on the nature and size of the prosecution against a firm was evidence of the attempts to establish or improve compliance programmes. This also gave rise to the deferred prosecution agreements, as firms increasingly argued that 'the best response to alleged misconduct was not to punish them...but to rehabilitate them' (Rakoff 2015). As Garrett argued, this represented an 'ambitious new approach to governance in which federal prosecutors [sought to] reshape the policies and culture of entire institutions', but in a very discrete manner (Garrett 2014:41). Yet as the 2000s progressed, there was a growing sense—made acutely apparent in the global financial crisis—that deferred prosecution agreements and self-regulation by the firm were quite ineffective in promoting change in corporate culture (Garrett 2014). Indeed, 'many, perhaps most such agreements...fail[ed] to achieve meaningful structural or ethical reform within the company itself' (Rakoff 2015). Yet despite their limitations, state managers continued to promote deferred and non-prosecution agreements (DPAs and NPAs)—alongside tightened market discipline—as measures to improve ethical and socially responsible conduct. In fact, Chapter 8 will also argue that the populist character of the political response made DPAs and NPAs the ideal instrument, because they gave an appearance of an active state response to bank culture, without imposing too many additional costs on the banks themselves.

The final point to make in the mid-2000 period concerns the unnerving correlation between (i) the relative slowdown in regulatory activity (as measured by prosecutions and litigation); (ii) a marked boom within the banking sector itself and wider economic growth; and (iii) public confidence in the banking sector. Again, to reiterate, the purpose of this chapter is not to argue that this relative regulatory lull derived entirely from public satisfaction, nor that the subsequent legitimacy crisis that unfolded with the 2008 banking collapses and scandals was the only motivation behind regulatory action from 2008 onwards. But the evidence does indeed suggest that regulatory action is closely correlated with what might be termed 'the mood of the times' (Widmaier 2004, Stanley 2014). For this reason I argue in this and subsequent chapters that much of the political and regulatory push was driven by a populist statecraft rather than a serious attempt to change the culture of banking.

The Crisis Hits: 2007–9

As noted above, in a cruel twist of fate it was the low interest rates introduced after the Enron and Dot.com crises of the early 2000s—accompanied by the savings glut and steady inflow of capital from Asia and petroleum exporters—which led to the lending boom and, eventually, the financial collapses of 2007–8. There is little sense in retelling this story again, except to provide some context to the two important issues at the heart of this chapter: (1) the fall in public confidence and subsequent legitimacy crisis; and (2) the two major shifts which took place in the regulatory and policy-making response to the 2008 crisis. As suggested above, in the 2000s it was not simply the economic boom or the pronounced growth in the US banking system in an abstract sense that gave rise to either the regulatory lull or growing public confidence in the banks. Instead, perhaps the best proxy of a booming banking sector and ease of access to household credit in the US case is levels of homeownership (Langley 2010). Fig. 4.2 compares the rising homeownership figures with levels of public confidence in the banking system. The correlations would seem to be readily apparent.

In the summer of 2007 falling US house prices and higher default levels signalled the beginning of the downturn. The complex bundling of obligations

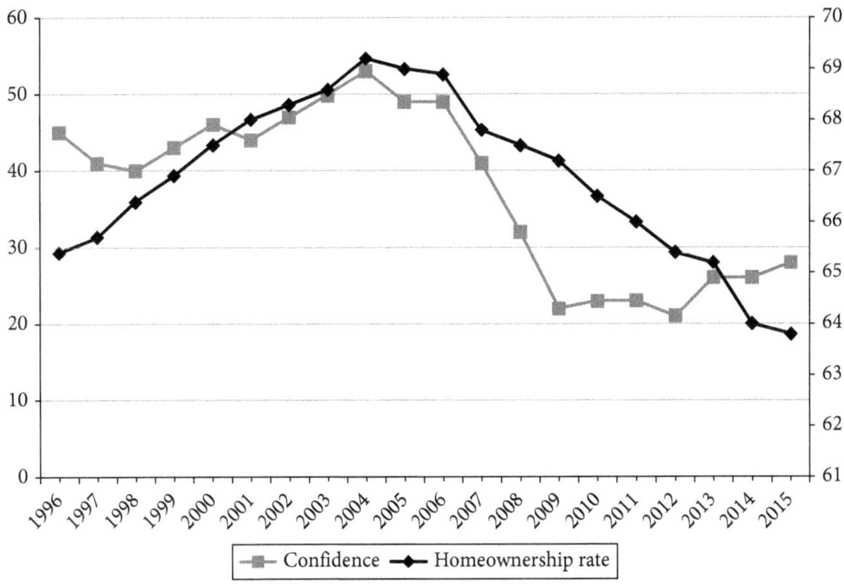

Fig. 4.2 Homeownership (%) vs. confidence in the US banking system (% respondents answering 'Great deal' and 'Quite a lot'
Source: US Census 2016; Gallup Polls (1996–2006).

however, simply amplified the risks and effects of the collapse in housing markets (Reinhart and Rogoff 2008). Many accounts have been written trying to trace the mechanisms of the so-called economic and financial aspects to this crisis; from mortgage defaults, to toxic assets, to the slowdown in interbank lending, to the credit crunch, to the slowdown in economic output, and—alongside the massive public bailouts themselves—how this slowdown contributed to escalating public debt, in turn leading to the fiscal consolidation campaign. Far fewer accounts though have dealt in any meaningful way with the impact of the crisis on public perceptions of banking and the financial system and, in turn, how this shaped the (populist) political response.

In part, this lack of systematic treatment of falling public confidence is due to the fact that the first and most noticeable range of political responses were focused on restoring financial stability (Interview 20160419). In this regard, financial stability presents itself as a technical, structural issue detached from public perceptions and the legitimacy crisis this chapter seeks to address. We will therefore return to the legitimacy crisis argument after briefly examining the first phase of the US crisis response, focused on recovery of the failing financial system and setting in place stability and resolution mechanisms. Even at the early stage though, the structure of these first responses was targeted at improving the market mechanism; whilst they were not *explicitly* framed as culture-improving measures the underlying assumption was the same as that which underpinned later responses. The first responses therefore already began the process of narrowing the political debate—saving financialized capitalism from itself and moving one step closer to the idealized pristine market of liberal economics.

First Phase Responses: Stability and Resolution

The Dodd–Frank Wall Street Reform and Consumer Protection Act is arguably the most influential early crisis response, and typifies the stability and resolution agenda—with culture more of an afterthought. In the view of US authorities, the 'broken financial regulatory system was a principal cause' of the crisis. It was deemed to be 'fragmented and antiquated', providing little supervision to important parts of the financial system (Obama 2010). To be sure, addressing the concerns of US taxpayers was central to the reform bill. Yet the most fundamental aspects to Dodd–Frank viewed consumer protection through the lenses of financial stability; the aim behind these early measures was to establish frameworks to either guarantee the robustness of the banks (capital adequacy), or to impose future losses on the banks' shareholders themselves (resolution) and thereby avoid taxpayer bailouts. This is why I describe them as market tightening measures.

If the events surrounding LIBOR were a game-changer (see Chapter 1) in terms of the cultural reform agenda, then the week of 15 September 2008 was a game-changer in terms of financial stability. The mid 2000s regulatory lull came to an abrupt halt. It was that week that Lehman Brothers filed for bankruptcy protection under chapter 11 and US authorities bailed out the insurer AIG. As Randall Germain has pointed out, at that point 'there were no legal means by which the government could seize control of its institutions in the name of the public good, which in this case revolved around the stability of the nations financial system' (Germain 2016). Dodd–Frank specifically responded to this regulatory deficiency in at least three ways. Under Title II of the reform bill it centralized authority to deal with failing systemically significant institutions within the hands of the FDIC, the Fed, and the Treasury (the troika); it increased the judicial powers of these institutions to exercise their Orderly Liquidation Authority (another way of saying that the troika had almost ubiquitous power to close down a failing financial institution); and it gave the troika total control over disposition of assets. Alongside the Volcker Rule, which sought to diminish the ability of larger banks to operate proprietary trading activities (trading on their own account and solely for their own profit) which were not related to serving customers, Title II was undeniably the cornerstone of the Dodd–Frank post-crisis response. Consumer protection, in the guise of financial stability and taxpayer interests, was central to this. As the ordo-liberals argued, this was a strengthening of the state so that financial firms would bear the costs of poor investment decisions; and as the liberal economists believed, the interests of lower income social groups were best served by restoring (financialized) accumulation. But despite these liberal assumptions it would be an understatement to suggest that bank culture was much more than an afterthought in the drafting of Dodd–Frank.

There was however, even at this early stage in the crisis, a clear recognition that much of the excessive risk-taking which Dodd–Frank sought to address was a 'cultural' problem—even if it was rarely named as such. Even if Dodd–Frank did not deliberately set about redressing it, both the Final Report of the National Commission on the Causes of the Financial Crisis (FCIC) and the Dodd–Frank text acknowledged this culture of prioritizing bank profits and short termism over those of the consumer. According to one managing director, banks' culture had changed from one 'resembling a university academic department to one which values revenue at all costs' (Eric Kolchinsky, cited in FCIC 2011: 207). In Dodd–Frank this recognition of cultural problems manifested in at least two ways: one was the attempt to redress the misplaced priorities of the banking sector by reducing aggressive lending practices. Specifically, section 913 of Title IX was an explicit attempt to assess whether the activities of broker-dealers and investment advisers provided sufficient, and sufficiently comprehensible guidance to retail consumers (SEC 2011). Dodd–Frank also established the Consumer Financial Protection Bureau (CFPB) to enforce existing laws banning 'unfair, abusive and deceptive practices'. Previously, authority for consumer financial activity had been distributed between the FTC, Federal Reserve, and the Department of Housing and Urban Development. Aside from its enforcement responsibilities, the CPFB's other main objective was to protect and educate consumers as well as regulating bank and non-bank entities in order to prevent large-scale financial disasters, like the most recent mortgage crisis. As I will show in Chapter 10, this shifts the focus away from inequality and exceptionally high levels of consumer debt in Anglo-America, and towards simply ensuring that banks do not defraud consumers. Already then our caricature of two competing debates about the causes of bad bank culture were evident, though the political discussion was already focused on a far narrower account.

The second culture-related issue raised in Dodd–Frank, Subtitle E, 'Accountability and Executive Compensation' dealt with the contentious issue of bank bonuses. Though many of the crucial details took a further six years to negotiate—ultimately failing to reach a conclusion—Dodd–Frank introduced the requirement for shareholders to hold a 'separate resolution' vote to approve executive compensation and on 'golden parachutes'. Though the decisions of this special shareholder vote would not be binding on the final decisions of board members with regards to bonuses, the aim was to introduce another check on executive pay (Scully 2011: 38). I will examine the executive compensation issue more closely later. For our purposes though, suffice it to note that bank bonuses were significant because they were perhaps the most obvious early target of public discontent—and symptomatic of everything the public perceived to be wrong with the culture of banking.

But the focus of the debate about bonuses was reduced to—inter alia—measures to promote socially sustainable portions of cash and equity instruments, rather than the structural conditions that gave rise to disproportionately high pay in the banking sector.

To summarize, though it is widely recognized that improving stability was the first goal of political responses, the less widely acknowledged assumption was that the (idealized) free market had been distorted by particularistic interests (Bonefeld 2013: 238). Thus the bank bailouts were the product of a corruption of the market code, rather than the product of the market code itself. Improving market discipline for example, via resolution planning (to allow failing banks to collapse), would expose these same market participants to the right kind of market competition. Thus although culture appeared as a named theme later, the groundwork for the great culture debate was being laid in the early crisis responses.

Second Wave Responses: LIBOR, Sanctioned Countries, and Money-laundering

As I have argued, explaining the political response to the cultural problem can be attributed to a series of factors: at a more concrete level, responding to the bank culture issue was a populist point-scorer and a major money-spinner (see Fig. 4.3); more abstractly, authorities were responding to the legitimacy crisis and attempting to impose the rule of law. In both concrete and abstract terms though, the revelations of corporate misconduct from 2012 onwards prompted a marked shift in regulatory and juridicial activity. Fig. 4.3 uses the amount of US dollars paid in fines by the biggest banks as a simple heuristic device to convey this point. I therefore characterize these corporate scandals as a second wave of the financial crisis.

Here an important methodological point related to causation and timing must be noted though. On causation, simply put, there is a degree of spillover that complicates the narrative. Scandals prompted regulatory action which in turn brought further cases of misconduct to light, in turn leading to tougher regulatory action. Likewise, as the fines began to roll in, institutions such as the New York Department of Financial Services recognized that prosecuting the banks was a lucrative business. We will consider these issues more systematically in Chapter 8. The point is that our simple heuristic tool does not, alone, substantiate the claim that there was a second wave to the crisis, or that there was a relationship between these scandals and the legitimacy crisis. The three 'variables'—the scandals, regulatory action, and public opinion—do not easily lend themselves to a linear analysis (x caused y which caused z); social reality is always more complex than this (Hay 2002). Nonetheless, a brief survey of the timing issue provides sufficient context for one of the main claims of this chapter: that state managers were

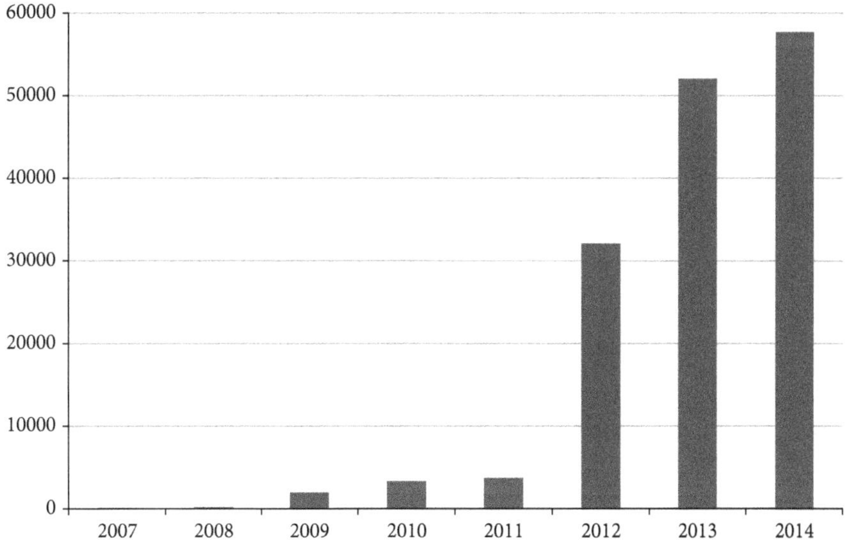

Fig. 4.3 Total amount of bank fines for all banks (US$millions)
Source: data calculated from *FT* 2016.

responding to more than just the financial stability issue, and that the legitimacy crisis became increasingly prominent in their thinking. I will examine the specifics of this regulatory action in subsequent sections. For now we should simply note that although many of the prosecutions and fines came from 2014 onwards, the activities banks such as—inter alia—Standard Chartered, HSBC, and Credit Suisse were being penalized for had occurred in the pre-2014 period. The revelation of these activities therefore constituted a second phase in the financial crisis.

In particular, the relationship between the world of banking and the US security agenda meant that there were three overlapping skeins to growing public and political discontent with the banking industry: LIBOR and Forex were one skein; the second was certain banks' engagement in financing sanctioned countries and the anti-money laundering agenda; whilst the third was the longer series of mis-selling scandals (Interview 20170627). On the first issue, the LIBOR and Forex scandals were discussed at length in earlier chapters. As with the British case, these revelations were hugely important to understanding the regulatory response in particular. As one interviewee noted, 'when Bill Dudley [chairman of the New York Federal Reserve] heard about Forex he was disgusted' (Interview 20160419). As the Federal Reserve would later explain, their 'interest in reforming culture [was] a product of events since the Financial Crisis [in particular] the manipulation of LIBOR and foreign exchange rates' (New York Fed 2015b). This was because, 'though the many post-crisis reforms to banks balance sheets' from the Dodd–Frank Act to Basel capital adequacy 'had provided necessary bulwarks against systemic risk…those new laws, regulations, and standards [had] done little to curb banker misconduct' (ibid.). Again, we should note the language used: bad culture was about 'misconduct', that is, not abiding by the right market code. Simply put though, LIBOR and Forex were pivotal to the US regulatory response, but they were accompanied by two other types of scandal.

Whereas LIBOR and Forex were *only* considered to be cases of large-scale corporate fraud, US authorities took a particularly hard line on a second type of misconduct: the dealings of banks with sanctioned countries and the Anti-Money Laundering agenda. In particular, foreign banks were found to be guilty of breaching US rules in areas such as economic sanctions imposed on third-countries like Sudan, Iran, and Cuba. Explaining why foreign (non-US) banks had been targeted by US prosecutors, the Executive Vice-President of the New York Federal Reserve argued that 'some foreign institutions, unlike their American counterparts, did not see the values that motivate and support US economic sanctions' (Baxter 2014). The Federal Reserve official contended that foreign institutions had 'looked at economic sanctions as technical "American" rules that were not seen as consistent with the organization's and the home country's larger value system' (ibid.). In this instance, US authorities believed that their own domestic institutions understood the 'value system underlying the technical American legal rule', that of preserving national security, whereas they believed that foreign institutions had failed to 'correlate the rule with the value' (ibid.). The result was that on 1 July 2014 France's largest bank BNP Paribas was fined nearly $9bn for evading US sanctions between 2004 and 2012 (FBI 2014), and Credit Suisse was similarly fined $536 million in 2009 for violations of the International Emergency Economic Powers Act (US Dept. of Justice 2009).[1]

The sanctioned country issue was related to the broader anti-money laundering agenda. Here, 2013–14 also saw increased regulatory activity for breaches of the US Patriot Act, the Bank Secrecy Act, and Anti-Money Laundering laws, reflecting the intersection of the political stance towards the banking system and the US national security agenda. Following 9/11 for example, the US Patriot Act 2001 had tightened anti-money laundering laws in an effort to cut off terrorist financing. Once again, though domestic and foreign banks alike came under increased scrutiny it was the foreign banks that were at the heart of the scandals, and hence facing the largest fines. In 2010, HSBC was issued a cease and desist order by the US Office of the Comptroller of the Currency (OCC), culminating in a $1.9bn fine in 2012 (Fitch Ratings 2013). Then in 2013 Standard Chartered Bank was fined $667 million after the New York Department of Financial Services had earlier (in 2012) set in place increased internal surveillance processes within the bank (NY DFS 2014).

The third issue was that of mis-selling scandals brought to light in sub-prime mortgage markets and—albeit over a longer period—the sale of Payment Protection

[1] On a related note, Credit Suisse was later fined $2.6bn in May 2014 for helping US citizens to avoid their tax obligations to the Federal Government (*FT* 2014b).

Insurance (PPI) in the UK during the 1990s and early 2000s (see Chapter 6). The purpose of this brief overview of the three different types of banking scandal is straightforward. At one level it is simply to provide some context to the regulatory activity and falling public confidence discussed in the next section. At another level it is also to provide context to the claim that increased regulatory scrutiny of the banks and the lucrativeness of prosecutions were not the only reason for yet tougher regulation and fines—a kind of regulatory momentum described by the business-cycle critics of regulatory activity. Instead, it also sets the scene for the claim that the activity of state managers (including regulators) was also a response to falling public confidence in the banks and the government: part of a wider legitimacy crisis.

Legitimacy Crisis

The aim of this section is threefold: firstly, I provide evidence to support the claim that although LIBOR and Forex were arguably less pivotal to the declining confidence in the US banking system than in the UK, there is a correlation between the banking crisis and what I will term the *credibility* crisis facing the North American banking system. Before examining the political and regulatory action in the final section of this chapter though, in the second subsection I will further contextualize the credibility crisis facing the banking sector. This is where I depart even further from a business-cycle theory of pro-cyclical regulatory activity. The reason, I argue, that the credibility crisis fuelled a populist political response was because it was in the context of governmental efforts to implement fiscal discipline. This is a crucial point. Falling confidence in the banking (a credibility crisis) does not, a priori, fuel a political problem for the state (a legitimacy crisis). In contrast though, falling confidence in the banks that had been bailed out and thereby protected by the state, whilst average Americans were then confronted by social spending cuts, turns a credibility for the banks into a legitimacy crisis for the state. Finally, I will then show how the declining confidence manifested itself in rising protests. In this way I show how the already narrow political debate on saving financialized capitalism from the financiers narrowed even further into a populist response aiming to re-assert the (impression of) independence of the political classes from the embattled banks.

Opinion Polls

I begin by charting the credibility crisis facing the US banking sector. Public opinion is a notoriously slippery topic. In essence, it is hard to measure the *impact* and *effect* of the ideas and opinions held by individuals or groups of individuals (Hay 2002: 123). As I noted previously, social reality (opinions, ideas, norms) does not easily lend itself to straightforward, linear analysis. That said, the academic literature tells us that there are two relatively distinct tendencies when examining public sentiment. On the one hand, there are modest yet discernible shifts in public opinion that are relatively cyclical. These cyclical models tend to point to the importance of election and business cycles—that might, for example, manifest in changes in inflation, interest rates, consumer spending patterns and so forth—as producing slight shifts in opinion (Kenworthy and Owens 2011). On the other hand though, there is also a substantive literature to show that major social events, such as crises and scandals, result in demonstrable changes in public opinion (Lipset and Schneider 1983).

Fig. 4.4 shows the pronounced drop in confidence associated with the banking crisis of 2007–9. By the time of the poll late in 2007 those registering 'very little' confidence and those registering 'some' had increased by an average of 3.5 per cent, whereas those registering a 'great deal' and 'quite a lot' had fallen by an average of 4 per cent. A second conclusion can be drawn from this data, that based on all four responses the period 2011–12 was the low point in this credibility crisis. During that two-year period those with 'very little' confidence rose to the highest

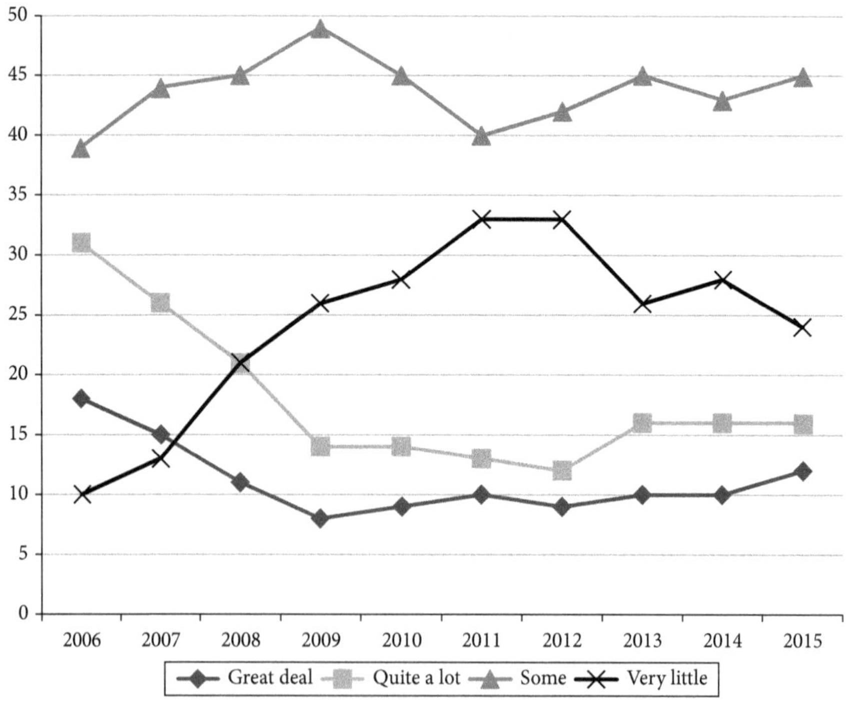

Fig. 4.4 Confidence in the US banking system, 2006–15 (%)
Source: Gallup polls.

level since the polls began in 1983 (33 per cent), and those registering a 'great deal' also fell (between 2009–12) to the lowest level on record (8–9 per cent). A third conclusion is also worth noting. Those recording high levels of confidence in the banking system (great deal or quite a lot) remained at historically low levels through the latter end (2012–15). This is significant because it suggests that whilst there was a moderate recovery in those recording explicitly negative levels of confidence ('very little' recovered from 33 per cent to 24 per cent by 2015) there was little change in those recording 'great deal' (fluctuating between 8–12 per cent between 2009–2015).

Finally, it is also worth noting that though the subsequent scandals—LIBOR, Forex, money laundering and so forth—may not have resulted in a significant drop in confidence in the US, they may have compounded the low levels of confidence.

Other data arguably provides an even more nuanced account of the prolonged low-levels of trust in financial services. Simply put, by 2016 richer people trusted the banks more than poorer people; and confidence amongst richer people had recovered to a greater extent than amongst poorer individuals. On the first point, the data suggests—as we will also see in the UK in Chapter 6—that higher income, better educated individuals recorded greater increases in levels of restored trust than did lower income, less well educated individuals. This arguably coincides with the asymmetric dynamics—the fact that poorer individuals tend to be disproportionately disadvantaged by the banking system—discussed in Chapter 2 and which we will return to in Chapter 10.

In 2016 the Edelmann Trust Barometer asked participants to indicate 'how much trust you have in each of the following industries to do what is right'. Defining the 'informed public' as those between the ages of 25–64; college educated; in the top 25 per cent of income in their respective country; and reporting significant media consumption and engagement in business news, and the 'mass population' as those not included in the informed public category, the US recorded the highest disparity between levels of trust of all the twenty-eight countries surveyed. Fig. 4.5 shows this. The countries are ordered by the size of the disparity in levels of trust between higher and lower income individuals. The US has the largest gap (31 percentage points), followed by France (at 29 percentage points) and so forth.

On the other related point, the recovery in confidence showed evidence of income-related disparity as well. Levels of trust had risen faster amongst higher-income individuals than amongst lower-income individuals. Fig. 4.6 shows this. With an 8 per cent increase in the gap between levels of trust amongst top earners and lower income earners between 2012–16, the US experienced the third largest change of the countries measured. Piecing together the data from Figs 4.4, 4.5, and 4.6, this indicates that although levels of trust in the US banking system appeared to be recovering, the recovery was primarily amongst higher income

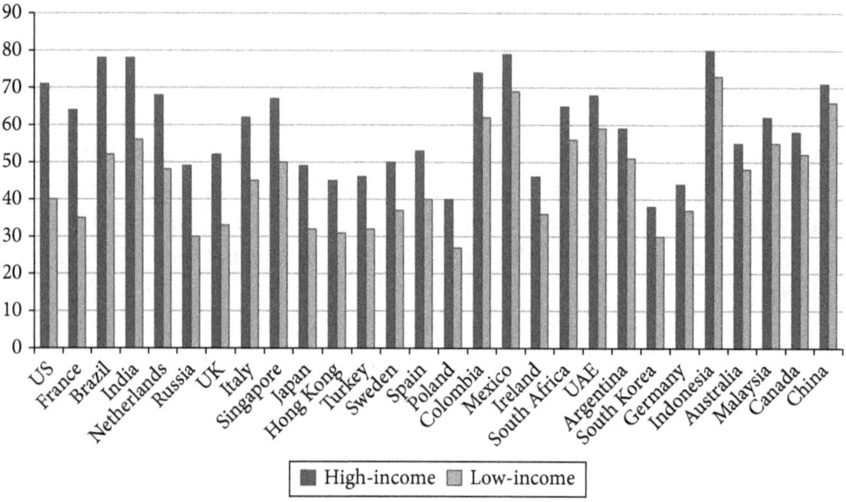

Fig. 4.5 Trust in banking sector by top 25% and bottom 25% of earners (2016)
Source: Edelman 2016.

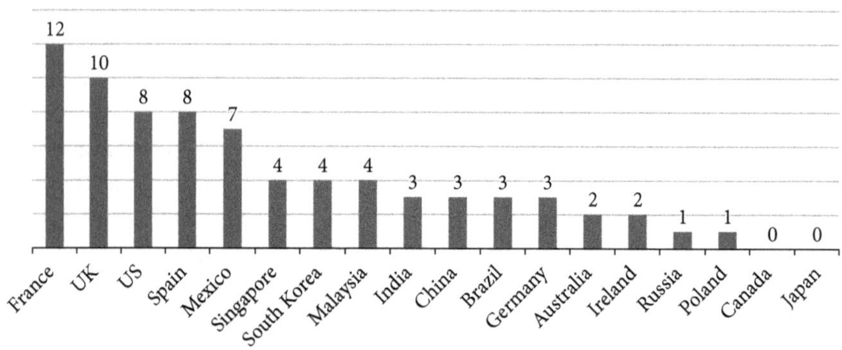

Fig. 4.6 Percentage point change in the 'trust gap' between top 25% of earners and lower income individuals (2012–16)
Source: Edelman 2016.

individuals. This is a robust and important conclusion. Although it is not the aim of this chapter to conclusively demonstrate why lower income individuals continued to trust the banks less, the next subsection of this chapter begins to develop the argument that this was primarily due to an association between the banks and inequality (see also Chapter 10). And it was the public response to inequality—with the highly paid bankers in the immediate firing-line of this counter-movement—which state managers felt compelled to diffuse via their turn to populist statecraft.

Austerity and Recovery

A comprehensive overview of inequality in the US is beyond the remit of this chapter. Instead, this subsection provides some context to the falling confidence levels (in the 'Opinion Polls' section) and the rise of protest movements (see section 'Protests' below). Put simply, neither the bank failures of the first phase of the crisis nor the subsequent scandals occurred in a political vacuum. Instead, they became characteristic of the divisions within American society. This divide between the rich and poor was thus a recurrent theme early in the crisis response. Perhaps the most obvious and well-known example was the Committee on Oversight and Government Reform hearing on 6 October 2008 where Richard Fuld, CEO of Lehman Brothers Holdings, was taken to task over his $700 million compensation package as his bank failed. In his questioning, Representative Henry Waxman explained to Mr Fuld, 'what's fundamentally unfair about the collapse of Lehman is its impact on the economy and on taxpayers'. He went on to state, 'the bottom line is that since 2000 you have taken home more than $480 million dollars... and that's difficult to comprehend for a lot of people. Your company is now bankrupt, our economy is in a state of crisis, but you get to keep $480 million. I have a very basic question for you: is this fair?'

This theme of divided fates only worsened as fiscal consolidation took hold in the US. This claim may appear surprising to some readers, who associate the Obama administration with pro-poor measures like Obama-care. Nonetheless, cuts to the federal budget post-2008 were so dramatic that James Crotty labelled this a one-sided class war (Crotty 2011: 3). He argued that 'the richest and most economically powerful segments of society, in concert with conservative political forces, have demanded that the deficits be eliminated by public-sector austerity' (ibid). As has been the case in the UK and Western Europe, government spending cuts have specifically focused on the forms of social spending that support the poor and middle classes as well as reducing public investment in education, healthcare, infrastructure, and technology. At the same time, larger corporations and conservative politicians have demanded tax cuts for wealthy households and corporations. This is completely in keeping with the long-term trajectory of centre-right and centre-left governments' fiscal policy in the West and reflects the immanence of the neoliberal consensus discussed in Chapter 3 (Streeck 2014). Tax revenues as a percentage of GDP have fallen consistently since the late 1970s and the structure of the tax system itself has become increasingly less progressive. This is simply another way of saying that as wealth became increasingly concentrated in the hands of top earners, the distribution of wealth amongst lower and middle classes decreased. Meanwhile, aggressive periods of fiscal consolidation from the 1990s onwards had disproportionately targeted public services—and thereby the most vulnerable members of society—in a bid to cut deficits.

As the financial crisis erupted the US budget deficit hit 10.1 per cent of GDP in 2009. By 2012 it was down to 7 per cent and by 2013 it had dropped to 4 per cent (Congressional Budget Office 2015: 3). At the peak the Congressional Budget Office issued a warning that the aging US population and rising health care costs were two of the main strains on the deficit, and that if the federal debt continued to expand faster than the economy 'the risk of a fiscal crisis will increase' (Congressional Budget Office 2011: 1). In particular it highlighted spending on Social Security and mandatory health care programmes (Medicare, Medicaid, the Children's Health Insurance Program, and health insurance subsidies) (ibid.: 3). It also explained that to solve these problems lawmakers would have to (i) restrain the growth of spending or (ii) raise (tax) revenues significantly above their historical share of GDP (ibid.: 5). Though the recovery of the US economy helped reduce the deficit, so did spending cuts. Indeed, by 2011, President Obama explained that 'now that the worst of the recession is over, we have to confront the fact that our government spends more than it takes in. This is not sustainable... [as a result, we will] freeze annual domestic spending for the next five years.' He continued 'this freeze will require painful cuts... [for example] I've proposed cuts to things I care about deeply, like community action programs' (Obama 2011). The result was that on 8 April 2011 the US Congress passed a revised spending bill, cutting $38 billion from the budget in what was hailed as the 'biggest annual spending cut in history' (Barack Obama, cited in Burnham 2011: 493).

Thus, in seeking to rationalize the need for so-called fiscal prudence and social spending freezes US state managers also invoked the banking crises in a type of populist rhetoric. In his 2012 State of the Union address for example, President Barack Obama spoke of the need for 'those banks that were rescued by taxpayers [to be given] a chance to repay a deficit of trust' (Obama 2012). But it was also apparent, from the framing of the issue, that state managers were concerned that the American public viewed the US government as complicit in the credibility crisis facing the banking system. Obama continued, 'Let's never forget: Millions of Americans who work hard and play by the rules every day deserve a government and a financial system that do the same. It's time to apply the same rules from top to bottom. No bailouts, no handouts, and no copouts. An America built to last insists on responsibility from everybody' (ibid.). Likewise, the Director of the Federal Deposit Insurance Company also noted, 'Who will agree to make sacrifices for the good of the country if they judge that reforms will be poorly or unfairly applied? How can we possibly convince Americans that the fiscal steps will be equitable when we bailed out the largest banks and yet they remain—larger, more powerful, and insulated from the market's discipline?' (Hoenig 2012). In other words, overcoming these challenges was problematic 'if the public fails to trust its financial and *governmental* institutions' (emphasis added, Hoenig 2012). The rhetoric was therefore pregnant with liberal assumptions about the capacity of the market to generate equitable outcomes.

Protests

Understanding the themes of inequality and 'class war' becomes particularly important when examining the protests against the banking sector as the legitimacy crisis unfolded. Arguably the most high profile and influential was the Occupy Wall Street movement. In their July 2011 edition, the Vancouver-based anti-consumerism magazine *Adbusters* proposed the idea of a 17 September 'occupation' of Wall Street. In response, a loose-knit group of organizers and hundreds of protesters gathered in Zuccoti Park, Lower Manhattan. The founders, Kalle Lasn and Micah White drew inspiration from the use of social media in the revolts in Tunisia and Egypt (Lasn 2011). Equally significantly for the purposes of our argument, the Occupy protests also stemmed from a disillusionment with the political left in the United States. As Kalle Lasn explained, 'the political left needs [Occupy] because people are losing their jobs, people losing their homes, and young people cannot find a job. [Meanwhile]...the people who gave us this mess—the financial fraudsters on Wall Street—haven't even been brought to justice yet' (Lasn 2011). Though the protests began and remained relatively decentralized and refused to make immediate demands of policymakers, it was symptomatic of the sense of injustice and a perceived failure of mainstream parties to respond to this concern. And again, the framing by Occupy leaders—of corrupt bankers against the victimized public—provided an ideal narrative for state managers to exploit.

In October 2011 a survey conducted by *CBS News* and the *New York Times* found that 43 per cent of those surveyed agreed with the aims of the Occupy movement, contending that wealth should be more evenly distributed across America (*CBS* 2011). Similarly, a *Time Magazine* poll found that 54 per cent of participants agreed with the Occupy protests against 'policies that favour the rich, the government's bank bailout and the influence of money in the political system' (*Time* 2011). This indicates that the general public were already hugely receptive to a populist framing of the problems in US banking. Over the coming year a range of critics pointed to the ineffectiveness of the movement, after the initial media flurry that accompanied it (*WSJ* 2012). By November 2011 for example, the New York protesters had been evicted from the site without having established a clearly articulated set of demands. Meanwhile the New York protest quickly sparked parallel occupations around the US and the world. Yet the true significance of the Occupy movement was that it was symptomatic of a growing intolerance of injustice and inequality. As one banner in Zuccotti Park read 'Dear 1%, we fell asleep for a while. Just woke up. Sincerely, the 99%.'

Most importantly, this ground swell of public opinion—exemplified in the Occupy protests—quickly began filtering through into the political discourse. A simple comparison of President Obama's State of the Union addresses in January 2011 and January 2012 supports this conclusion. The message of the 2011 address was that 'two years after the worst recession most of us have ever known, the stock market has come roaring back. Corporate profits are up. The economy is growing again.' The President went on to discuss the challenges for American workers competing in a globalized and technologically advanced economy, before focusing extensively on the need for reform in the education system and for better infrastructure. He briefly discussed tax reform, but the message was of the need to 'lower the corporate tax rate for the first time in 25 years'. The remainder of his speech focused largely on specific measures to cut the deficit. As a simple illustration of the point, terms like fair, fairness, inequality, and injustice were not mentioned. There was however a sense that policymakers were aware of the growing legitimacy crisis facing the institutions of government. As Obama noted towards the end, 'in the coming year, we will also work to rebuild people's faith in the institution of government... because the American people deserve to know that special interests aren't larding up legislation with pet projects' (Obama 2011).

By the 2012 address the tone of the message had changed; this was populism, clear and simple. The two issues of faith in government and inequality dominated much of the President's discourse. He explained that the defining issue of our time', was giving '*every* American... a chance to share [in the] story of success' (emphasis added, Obama 2012). He went on to explain that 'We can either settle for a country where a shrinking number of people do really well while a growing number of Americans barely get by, or we can restore an economy where everyone gets a fair shot.' On the first theme, inequality, the idea of representing the 99 per cent permeated the address: he spoke of folks at the top who saw their incomes rising, whilst hard-working Americans struggled with stagnant wages and personal debt; he retold the story of the 2008 crisis where banks had made huge bets and bonuses with other peoples' money and regulators had turned a blind eye or been powerless to prevent it; he spoke of tackling tax avoidance amongst multinational corporations; he noted that for families struggling with rising costs and stagnant wages, taxes should not go up, whilst those earning more than $1 million a year should face tax increases; and he explained his desire to oppose any effort to return to the same policies that led to the economic crisis.

But the second theme, that of a public disillusionment with the institutions of government, also featured prominently. Indeed, he stated that 'millions of Americans who work hard and play by the rules everyday deserve a government and a financial system that do the same. It's time to apply the same rules from top to bottom.' Specifically, he emphasized that he would not 'go back to the days when Wall Street was allowed to play by its own set of rules' (Obama 2012). The deficit of trust was not simply a problem facing Wall Street and regulators however, but Washington itself. As he candidly explained, most Americans have little faith in their political institutions because they believe that 'Washington is broken'. This was not simply a disconnect between Wall Street (high finance) and Main Street (everyday Americans) then, but a growing belief that 'nothing will get done in Washington this year, or next year, or maybe even the year after that' (ibid.).

Closing Remarks

In short, the main (populist) themes which had characterized the Occupy movement late in 2011—inequality typified by the banking culture of Wall Street, and the loss of confidence in political institutions to be able to resolve America's socio-economic crisis—were becoming increasingly prominent in the political agenda from 2012 onwards. This supports the main claim of this section of the chapter: a collapse in public confidence in the banking sector does not, a priori, indicate a political problem for state managers to respond to. The wider context to the banking crises and scandals however, that of inequality, disillusionment with mainstream politics, and the government agenda for fiscal consolidation, turned a banking crisis into a crisis of legitimation for state managers. Chapter 5 will show how state managers responded to the culture of banking problem—also reflecting a populist statecraft—as a means of addressing this legitimacy crisis.

5
US Responses and the Second Phase

The aim of this chapter is not to provide a comprehensive summary of all the measures taken by state managers in response to the culture of banking crisis. Instead, the aim is to explain the political motivations behind these responses. The big claim of this chapter is that both the reason for focusing on bank culture and the form of the political response itself were fundamentally shaped by the unfolding legitimacy crisis. As with the first phase of the crisis response, the liberal assumptions about the pristine market remained unquestioned. But efforts to improve market discipline (see Chapter 4) had not been enough. Bank culture therefore presented an opportunity to tackle the legitimacy crisis, and populist statecraft was the strategy employed. This political crisis reflected a prolonged decline in mass support. It became unsustainable though in the context of social spending cuts and bank bailouts; an urgent response was needed, but one which did not involve a more fundamental restructuring of financialized America. In so doing then, the debate on what was wrong with Anglo-American banking narrowed even further.

In addressing bank culture, there were, broadly speaking, two relatively distinct approaches pursued by the different US authorities: a tougher approach including prosecutions and fines; and a softer approach revolving around standard-setting and benchmarking. As I explained in earlier chapters, these measures are built upon the assumption that good culture is about ethical, socially responsible conduct. This chapter will examine these two different approaches in turn.

The Hard Approach

As I argued in Chapter 4, the unfolding culture of banking crisis prompted a significant toughening in the approach of US state managers. Fig. 4.1 has already highlighted the significant rise in fines and prosecutions from 2009 onwards, and the fines will be explored in greater depth in Chapter 8. Suffice it to note here that from an early stage in the financial crisis US regulators used large financial penalties—ostensibly to penalize misconduct (and therefore promote responsible behaviour), but also as part of the populist strategy by presenting the state as championing the general will of the public against the profligate financiers. This was significant, because the nature of the fines revealed that they were not simply

The Bank Culture Debate: Ethics, Values, and Financialization in Anglo-America. Huw Macartney, Oxford University Press (2019). © Huw Macartney.
DOI: 10.1093/oso/9780198843764.001.0001

meted out for *illegal* activity, but for activity that contradicted the *values* US authorities believed to underpin these legal requirements. As the ordo-liberals had argued, the goal was to educate market participants in the correct market ethics. What is particularly important though is that these underlying attempts to impose the rule of law—the same rules from top to bottom as Obama had put it—crystallized in new institutions, expanded powers, and a re-reading of previously benign pieces of legislation.

Institutions

The first point to highlight in relation to the US institutions was the sheer number of actors with a stake in promoting so-called cultural reform. This fact became increasingly important in the volume of fines and prosecutions brought against financial services firms. These institutions ranged from the Federal Deposit Insurance Corporation, the Federal Emergency Management Agency, the Federal Reserve itself, the Federal Trade Commission, the Office of the Comptroller of the Currency, and the US Department of the Treasury, to the Securities and Exchange Commission, the US Justice Department, and the New York Department of Financial Services. Three new institutions established during the two phases of the banking crisis warrant specific attention however, epitomizing the more coercive approach applied by the state.

Consumer Financial Protection Bureau

The first was the Consumer Financial Protection Bureau (CFPB). The CFPB was one of the most significant institutions brought into life under the Dodd–Frank Act. Its main objective was to protect and educate consumers as well as regulating bank and non-bank entities in order to prevent large-scale financial disasters. Previously, this authority for consumer financial activity had been distributed between the Financial Trade Commission, the Federal Reserve, and the Department of Housing and Urban Development. The new CFPB however, was an attempt to concentrate powers to write and enforce rules for mortgages, credit cards, student loans, and debt collection (*NY Times* 2010a). As the White House would later explain, before the CFPB was established 'no single agency had effective tools to set the rules and oversee the whole market' (White House 2012).

The CFPB is a prime example however of the kind of political struggle which this chapter seeks to highlight. From the outset the CFPB reflected a deeply populist agenda, addressing the dissipation of mass loyalty (Habermas 1973: 43) by invoking notions of elites (Wall Street) versus the people (Main Street). As one of the cornerstones of President Obama's post-crisis financial reform agenda, the consumer watchdog was part of a wider attempt to 'put in place the strongest consumer protections in history' (Whitehouse 2011). As Michael Barr, a law professor at the University of Michigan who was heavily involved in setting up the CFPB stated, 'we saw in the financial crisis [that] we didn't have anybody looking out for American families' (cited in NPR 2011). In other words, from the perspective of lawmakers, the culture of banking problem sprang from the fact that the interests of bankers were prioritized over those of the end consumer, and the CFPB was an attempt to address this.

This three-way struggle though, between (1) state managers attempting to respond to the demands of (2) American households, and yet facing opposition from (3) conservative segments of the political elite and banking sector, threatened to de-rail the CFPB from the outset. During its passage through Congress for example, banking and business representatives complained that tough and restrictive policies by a new consumer bureau would actually hurt the availability of credit (*WSJ* 2010). Nonetheless, after a range of deals struck between leading Republicans and Democrats the CFPB was established as part of the Dodd–Frank reforms. In turn, President Obama first chose Senator Elizabeth Warren as acting head (in 2010) before later appointing Richard Cordray as the first Director. Warren had been credited as the intellectual founder of the agency which she advocated in 2007, and was known for being an extremely vocal critic of the banking industry's mistakes and her 'aggressive advocacy of the middle-class' (*Huffington Post* 2010). But Warren's polarizing stance set her in opposition to other officials in key economic policy positions within the White House and the Treasury. Most notably, alums of the Hamilton Project—the initiative partly founded by Citigroup Chairman Robert Rubin—including Larry Summers and Timothy Geithner challenged her nomination by President Obama. Unlike the Roosevelt Institute, a progressive organization dedicated to New Deal-like reforms, with which Senator Warren was associated, the Hamilton Project were not known for their progressive economic policy positions or their advocacy of middle- and lower-income families. Thus, once again, we begin to see how the political attempt to reform bank culture was deeply embedded in even more fundamental issues related to inequality and class. But as we have argued from the outset, even these distinctions between radical and more conservative voices collapsed into an unhelpfully narrow debate about the right checks and balances needed to promote good behaviour amongst bankers.

Meanwhile, Cordray had already established himself as Ohio's attorney general, recovering billions of dollars in—inter alia—pension funds, and by tackling unscrupulous lending practices. But his nomination to the CFPB—marking an attempt to strengthen consumer protection—also met with opposition from vested interests in the financial services sector and in Congress. In December 2011 then, Senate Republicans blocked Cordray's appointment, claiming that having a single director rather than a five-member commission was unacceptable; and arguing for tighter oversight of the agency's decisions by other regulatory bodies (*Washington Post* 2011a). Behind these objections though, lay a more specific concern about the (moderately) tougher approach to the bank culture debate that Cordray represented, and the potential autonomy of the CFPB as an institution. As we will see throughout the remainder of this chapter, representatives from the banking industry and conservative minded elites sought to dilute the imperatives of the rule of the market and the rule of law via political, institutional struggles. This is another way of saying that the debate shifted away from addressing the underlying issue—that of financialization—because of the influence of coalitions of financiers (empowered by financialization) and conservative elites (with a vested interest in protecting the status quo).

One particular concern was the two types of authority granted to the Consumer Financial Protection Bureau at its inception in July 2010. The first was a set of powers previously distributed amongst the other seven governmental agencies, which were now moved to the new body; most notably the power to supervise banks. But the CFPB was also granted a set of new powers which included the ability to initiate investigations tied to anything 'abusive', without actually specifying what that term would entail. Proponents of the new bureau contended that this broad new power was necessary given the wide-ranging and controversial lending practices within the financial services industry and how many consumers had been adversely affected (*Economist* 2012). Critics on the other hand challenged the undefined prosecutorial powers this afforded the bureau, also pointing to the fact that special provisions of the law meant that overturning an action by the bureau would be nearly impossible. Nonetheless, despite these protestations, on 4 January 2012 President Obama circumvented the Senate's objections and appointed Cordray whilst lawmakers were in recess (*NY Times* 2012d). Most importantly for our argument however, these minor gains that granted moderately tougher powers to bodies like the CFPB were sufficient to give the impression that radical critics had won a victory. In reality though these minor skirmishes distracted from the war over financialization itself, which was already almost a lost cause.

Quickly the bureau set about issuing a series of rules to govern mortgage lending and enforcement actions against some of the larger banks for abusive lending practices, whilst the political struggle between Republicans and Democrats continued into 2013 (*Washington Post* 2013). Finally, in July 2013 the Senate voted sixty-six to thirty-four in favour of confirming Richard Cordray, in large part simply because undoing the President's decision would have involved a complex and uncertain Federal Appeals Court process, but also because the government agreed to certain concessions whereby the bureau would also increase its oversight of other non-bank institutions. This partially responded to banking industry concerns that it alone would experience heavy-handed treatment from the CFPB.

In short, it is tempting to read the establishment of the CFPB and the appointment of Cordray as simply a victory for consumers over the market and the banks. But this is only partially accurate. Instead, the CPFB is an institutional embodiment of the liberal vision. Republican senators and business lobbyists contended that the CPFB was precisely the opposite: limiting the market mechanism and evidence of a so-called 'nanny state' (Forbes 2013). Yet the CPFB was a politico-regulatory agency tasked with monitoring and challenging attempts by the banking industry to distort the 'rules of the game'. This made the CPFB an enforcer of the market mechanism. This is why the *strong* state is the precondition for the *free* economy, rather than its antithesis (Bonefeld 2010). In an ironic twist then, the CFPB and the appointment of Cordray appeared as victories for the radicals, but in reality these successes only reinforced the fact that the debate over improving bank culture was being fought between two remarkably similar intellectual positions. Both sides of this debate shared very similar assumptions about the (financialized) market and nature of the bank culture problem.

Financial Fraud Enforcement Task Force

A second important new institution to emerge in the debate over bank culture was the Financial Fraud Enforcement Task Force (FFETF). In 2009, President Obama established the FFETF comprising more than twenty federal agencies including the Department of Justice, the Consumer Financial Protection Bureau (CFPB), the Securities and Exchange Commission (SEC), the Internal Revenue Service, and the banking regulatory agencies. This made it the 'broadest coalition of law enforcement, investigatory and regulatory agencies ever assembled to combat fraud' (FFETF 2016, Bloomberg 2013a). Again though, the emphasis and focus of the FFETF is telling. This was not an attempt to distort the market mechanism in favour of weaker and disadvantaged social groups, though as a response to the legitimacy crisis it was presented under the populist rubric of consumer protection and defending the 99 per cent. Instead, the Task Force was another attempt to protect and improve the market mechanism, reflecting shared assumptions between more radical and conservative voices.

Later, in his 2012 State of the Union address, President Barack Obama announced a further financial crimes unit entitled the RMBS Working Group, as part of the FFETF. Its remit was to 'crack down on large-scale fraud and protect people's investments' and comprised a special unit of federal prosecutors—drawn from the Justice Department, the Securities and Exchange Commission, the FBI, and the Department of Housing and Urban Development, amongst others—to 'expand…investigations into the abusive lending and packaging of risky mortgages that led to the housing crisis' (Obama 2012). Part of the rationale for the establishment of this latter task force was a degree of frustration that regulators and the Justice Department had experienced in pressing criminal charges up to 2012 (Bloomberg 2012). In 2009 a federal jury had for example acquitted two former Bear Stearns hedge fund managers of continuing to sell investments it knew to be of dubious quality, on the grounds that the Justice Department prosecutors failed to prove the case 'beyond reasonable doubt' (ibid.). This failed prosecution of the Bear Stearns fund managers was a landmark case for the US authorities. The fund managers were charged with a $1.6bn securities fraud in connection with the funds that they managed. Many had assumed that this would be the first of many criminal prosecutions by the Department of Justice, but in November 2009 the jury acquitted the fund managers on all counts, due to the lack of sufficiently compelling evidence given the higher requirements for criminal prosecutions. The FFETF and subsequent RMBS Working Group were attempts to centralize and strengthen this regulatory capacity in order to make any enforcement action more effective. Again though, removing or shaming one or two bad apples was seen as sufficient to reinforce the correct market norms.

Equally importantly, the establishment of the FFETF was also accompanied by a re-reading of the existing legislative powers, also in a bid to enhance enforcement. The most important example of this was the Financial Institutions Reform, Recovery and Enforcement Act (FIRREA). The FIRREA was passed on 9 August 1989 in response to the US Savings and Loans crisis. Several of the features of the FIRREA were quite specific to the context of the S&L (Savings and Loan) crisis of the 1980s: it provided $50bn to close failed banks and stop further losses; and it set up a new government agency called the Resolution Trust Corporation (RTC) to resell S&L assets and to pay back depositors. These were essential features in the wake of a crisis that had effectively caused half of the nation's Savings and Loans banks to fail. But the FIRREA also came to be particularly important in the aftermath of the 2008 financial crisis because it gave the Justice Department powers to probe poor quality loans. In effect, though FIRREA had originally been established to protect banks from fraud by third parties, following the global financial crisis it came to be used by the Financial Fraud Task Force and the Department of Justice to prosecute banks for themselves being participants in the predicate fraud (Mondaq 2013). This was a moderately effective way of toughening market discipline on the banks themselves.

Once established then, the Financial Fraud Enforcement Task Force reverted to the FIRREA due to the fact that section 951 of the FIRREA allowed for *civil* cases to be made—with a lower burden of proof than is required for a criminal prosecution (FDIC 1989). Early in 2012, the Task Force used FIRREA when it issued more than a dozen civil subpoenas to top financial institutions, including Citigroup. The subpoenas related to mortgage-backed securities offerings between 2006 and 2008. In relation to the big themes of this book, the establishment of the FFETF, the RMBS Working Group, and the expanded use of FIRREA are hugely significant. As the then Attorney General, Eric Holder, explained at Columbia University in 2012, 'We found that much of the conduct that led to the financial crisis was unethical and irresponsible. But we have also discovered that some of this behavior—while morally reprehensible—may not necessarily have been criminal' (cited in *NY Times* 2012c). The task forces and FIRREA were important examples of state managers' efforts to expand the reach of the rule of law to target poor culture and conduct in the banking sector. They therefore fit with our argument that conditions for banks have indeed become somewhat more restrictive; whilst the real, structural causes of bank culture have barely been addressed.

NY Department of Financial Services

A third major institution to emerge in the fight against bank culture was the New York Department of Financial Services (DFS). It too reflected the populist, political agenda of appearing responsive to 'Main Street', whilst also becoming a leading enforcer of the rules of the game. The Department of Financial Services was a new state agency established in October 2011 by the Democrat Governor of New York Andrew Cuomo. Cuomo—rather like Elizabeth Warren—was a leading protagonist of the (so-called) radical campaign against bank culture, but his liberal mindworld and populist strategy revealed his true colours. The DFS merged together the New York State Insurance and Banking departments into a single financial services regulator. As a result the DFS was given responsibility to supervise over 3800 financial institutions, with assets of more than $7 trillion. It was also given the ability to revoke bank licences, and impose big fines on the financial services industry (*NY Post* 2015). It was brought into being under the Financial Services Law, signed in April 2011, and gave the superintendent expansive rule-making authority and enforcement powers over previously unregulated financial products and services and the entities providing them (Lexology 2011). In short, from its inception the DFS became arguably one of the foremost regulatory agencies tasked with penalizing poor conduct in the banking industry.

The way in which the DFS crystallized these struggles between the legitimacy crisis and attempts to impose the rule of law was manifest in three areas. The first was the way in which it remained an overtly political institution. The second was the size and scale of the financial penalties it imposed. And the third was the change in regulatory approach it embodied. In terms of its political rationale and populist undertones, the relationship between the Governor of New York and the Superintendents of the DFS are noteworthy. As with the other institutions outlined above, the establishment of the DFS was part functional centralization of powers previously distributed amongst a range of regulatory agencies, and part motivated by a political move by Governor Andrew Cuomo (Interview 20160418). Prior to the establishment of the DFS, Benjamin Lawsky was a former US attorney, spending four years as the top financial crimes prosecutor for the then New York Attorney General Cuomo. In this role, Lawsky had assisted Cuomo in his battle to force banks that had received taxpayer bailouts to disclose sensitive information about bonus payments (Bloomberg 2011a). When Cuomo won the election as New York's governor in 2010, he immediately appointed Lawsky as his chief of staff. It was significant that in his inauguration speech, governor Cuomo made his political agenda very clear: in a populist vein, he emphasized that 'the state faces a competence deficit, an integrity deficit, and a trust deficit', because 'too often government responds to the whispers of lobbyists before the cries of the people' (cited in *WSJ* 2011). Alongside his financial and economic policies then, Governor Cuomo also introduced the Public Integrity Reform Act of 2011, with the aim of increasing transparency and accountability and restoring public trust (NY Assembly 2011).

In the lead up to the Financial Services Law (2011) though, there was significant evidence that Cuomo wished to maintain and exercise his political voice in the running of the new DFS—which would otherwise have been an independent agency. In the draft proposals for example, it was suggested that the governor would be able to maintain many of the powers he had previously exercised as the attorney general (Coffee 2011). These proposals were later abandoned, but a little recognized fact about the DFS was that at the inception, Governor Cuomo did succeed in amending legislation to afford him powers of dismissal of the Superintendent, a right not afforded to other Governors over their Superintendents (Interview 20160418). This was an important legal change which characterized the degree of political discretion the governor sought to exercise over the DFS. Whilst the partnership between Lawsky and Cuomo (2011–15) was highly effective then, the enforcement and legislative actions pursued by the Department were largely determined by Cuomo himself; and it was the Governor who sought to take the credit for these successes.

The financial and *political* importance of the high profile fines and prosecutions achieved by the DFS (see below) should not therefore be understated. In other words, in keeping with his earlier populist rhetoric, the governor framed his agenda in terms of an aggressive approach towards Wall Street and a defence of New York homeowners. This was an explicit attempt to 'walk the tightrope', strengthening the state against the preferential, deferential treatment it had afforded particularistic private interests (the banks) whilst seeking to restore trust and credibility in the eyes of subaltern social groups (Burnham 2011). Yet the political confrontation with the bankers was also a significant point-scoring exercise given New York's austerity drive. As noted above, the bankers' credibility crisis morphs into a legitimacy crisis for the state when fiscal consolidation and inequality are on the table. On taking office in 2010 the governor set about a radical project of fiscal consolidation, turning a \$10 billion deficit into a \$2 billion surplus by 2014 (Cuomo 2014). Despite his Democrat affiliation this was a typical liberal agenda of cutting state spending on social projects. Spending on Medicaid programmes and the local school budget were both cut by \$2.85 billion each, whilst simultaneously refusing to extend a temporary state income tax increase on wealthy residents of New York (*NY Times* 2011). The overall tenor of his Governorship was an attempt to strengthen the state against special interests of various kinds—lower- and middle-income households on the one hand and banks on the other—whilst engaging in a lucrative point-scoring political exercise by prosecuting the financial services community (Bonefeld 2012).

The other two issues exemplifying the crystallization of the legitimacy and market discipline struggles—prosecutions and a changed regulatory approach—are best dealt with together. This is because although the official remit of the DFS was to promote 'strong, smart targeted regulation' (DFS 2013: 2), it quickly adopted an aggressive and expansive approach, meaning that it adapted its regulatory stance to pursue the goal of high profile prosecutions. This too is entirely in keeping with our conception of populism as an ideologically thin form of pragmatic statecraft. Beginning late in 2011 the Department set about forcing insurers to lose control of $100 million in unpaid death benefits to surviving family members, as well as dispatching countless subpoenas to banks, and pressing lenders to reduce their over-aggressive foreclosure practices (*NY Times* 2012b).

One particular illustrative example was the $340 million fine levelled against Standard Chartered bank in September 2012, for attempting to conceal approximately 60,000 transactions with Iran, cleared through its New York branch between 2001–7. It was the first instance in which the newly formed DFS threatened to exercise its right to revoke a firm's banking licence. Standard Chartered had argued that until 2008, federal law permitted foreign banks to transfer money for Iranian clients through their American subsidiaries to another foreign institution (*NY Times* 2012a). Yet even throughout the 2012 legal proceedings, Standard Chartered refused to admit that the transactions in question actually violated federal law, and Justice Department officials seemed to confirm this claim. It was at this point that the DFS shifted strategy, in line with similar adaptations witnessed with the FFETF and FIRREA. As it appeared that Standard Chartered might escape prosecution on the basis of a lack of clarity over the offence, the DFS changed tack and decided to base its case on the claim that the bank had masked the identities of its Iranian clients, lied to regulators, and thwarted US efforts to detect money laundering (*NY Times* 2012a), a more flexible allegation. In other words, the approach of the DFS revealed a genuinely more aggressive stance towards the bank and a more elastic strategy. Indeed, this willingness to pursue the *spirit* and not just the *letter* of the law had been written into the constitution of the DFS, enabling it to regulate a far wider range of activities not covered by existing legislation (see SEC 2011 for more on this distinction).

Another obvious example of this interventionist and expansionist stance was the DFS's investigations into the use of computer algorithms by Barclays and Deutsche Bank, in the manipulation of foreign exchange rates. In November 2014, the UK's Financial Conduct Authority and the US's Commodity Futures Trading Commission fined UBS, Citigroup, JPMorgan Chase, HSBC, Royal Bank of Scotland, and Bank of America more than $4bn for their role in the Forex rate-rigging scandal (*FT* 2014a, see Chapter 8). But the US Department of Justice and the Department of Financial Services continued with their investigations, placing monitors at the largest banks to study possible cases of manipulation from inside the banks and continued their investigations throughout 2015 (Reuters 2015b). Once again, the difference from the lighter-touch, pre-2008 approach was undeniable.

By 2014 then, the Department of Financial Services had established itself as the leading New York banking regulator. It had also developed a reputation of going further than the other regulatory authorities, spurred on by Governor Cuomo's populist zeal. Traditionally, following settlements over illegal activity, for example, US regulators would not continue to closely monitor the progress the respective banks made in addressing the underlying causes which had led to the offence. This was, as previously noted, a key weakness of the deferred prosecution agreements (Garrett 2014). But this was not the case with the DFS, meaning that in the case of Standard Chartered a further $300 million fine was introduced in 2014 for failure to resolve the anti-money laundering compliance problems (Forbes 2015). In addition, Promontory Financial Group—one of the industry's leading consultants—became embroiled in the Standard Chartered affair. The DFS claimed that Promontory had watered down its compliance reports on Standard Chartered, stating that Standard only had a mere $14 million worth of transactions that were outside of compliance requirements, compared to the $250 billion that Standard later admitted to (*WSJ* 2015c). In response, the DFS effectively prohibited Promontory from advising banks in New York. Amidst the populism the DFS therefore did indeed have an effect on conduct and culture; but, in the grand scheme of things, the DFS was something of a sideshow compared to the real bank culture problematique.

The investigation into Promontory is significant for the purposes of the main argument of this book for another reason. Implicit in the claim that the culture of banking debate has led to a strengthening of the market liberal state is the idea that segments of the banking community had previously escaped effective forms of market discipline. This claim is particularly evident in relation to Promontory. Promontory Financial Group is a leading strategy, risk management, and regulatory compliance consulting firm with offices in North America, Europe, Asia, Australia, and the Middle East (Promontory 2016). Importantly though, Promontory had gathered a whole range of former regulatory officials within its management structure, from the chairman, former US Comptroller of the Currency Chief Gene Ludwig, to former Fed vice chairman Alan Blinder, former SEC chairman Mary Shapiro, and former OCC general counsel Julie Williams. Founded in 2001, approximately one hundred of the 400 Promontory employees were former Washington regulators, and the consultancy firm became known as the 'ultimate revolving door between Washington and the private sector' (Bloomberg 2013b). These regulatory officials had given Promontory an air of legitimacy and inside knowledge which it sought to exploit in the Standard

Chartered case. The DFS investigations into Promontory should therefore be read as an attempt to re-impose the rule of the law and money on a financial advisory organization that had previously epitomized the blurred lines between (public) regulator and (private) regulated entities.

Deferred Payments

Moving beyond institutional changes, as we explained earlier in this chapter, perhaps one of the most important issues in relation to credibility and bank culture was that of remuneration. We will consider what actually changed in bankers' pay in Chapters 9 and 10. For now, we will simply focus on some key measures adopted by US authorities. The US Financial Crisis Inquiry Report (2011) repeatedly found that poor incentive structures were fundamental to the mis-selling that lead to the crisis (FCIC 2011: 6, 18, 61–3), whilst banker's pay and bonuses also became a focal point for anti-austerity and inequality campaigns from civil society. But pay was also intrinsically linked to issues of corporate culture and conduct. Earlier 1993 legislation had already attempted to mitigate the short-termist tendencies of bank compensation policy by making compensation in excess of $1 million taxable for the corporation unless performance-based. The financial industry had therefore begun using stock options, 'allowing employees to buy the company's stock in the future at some predetermined price, and thus to reap rewards when the stock price was higher than that predetermined price' (ibid.: 68). The unintended consequence of these pay structures however, was that it created incentives to increase both risk and leverage to promote larger rises in a company's stock price (ibid.).

As the second wave of the crisis unfolded, US authorities proceeded to emphasize that one of the most important means for the industry to influence behaviour was via 'two species of recognition': compensation and promotion (Baxter 2015). In the view of state managers, both of these measures of recognition should be tied to ethical considerations. As one figure noted, 'if the only consideration with respect to compensation and promotion is how much money the individual made for the firm, then that communicates a message that is inhospitable to a strong ethical culture' (ibid.). As a result, 'changing the time horizon for compensation' was deemed to be a 'significant feature of meaningful cultural reform' (ibid.). In other words, higher levels of pay, structured in such a way that reflected immediate, year-on-year profits in particular business lines, had incentivized a culture of short-termism; and implicit in this culture was the prioritization of bank interests and profits over those of the consumer. As a result, remuneration and incentives formed a central part of the Dodd–Frank act and years of subsequent struggle between the financial lobby and the Democrat political elite. As I will explain in Chapter 10 however, the structural causes of disproportionately high pay in the finance sector and wage stagnation in other parts of the economy were firmly outside of the purview of this type of bank culture debate.

But the issue of deferred payment and remuneration are also a particularly important case study in the kinds of dynamics we are outlining here. Banker's bonuses were seized upon by more radical voices as indicative of inequality. Hence any successes the Obama administration would subsequently claim in tackling the bonus culture could arguably be seen as a victory for the political left against the ills of capitalism. Headlines in the trade press certainly presented this as an attack on finance capitalists: 'They're Coming For Your Bonus', read the *Wall Street Journal*; and 'Wall Street Pay Restricted' claimed Bloomberg. In fact though, as I will explain, the goal of state managers was not to reduce overall levels of remuneration and pay, but to ensure that pay was structured in such a way that the short-termist tendencies of financial accumulation did not threaten profitable accumulation in the longer term. As I have argued, this is significantly different from a more *genuinely* radical agenda emphasizing redistribution and a rebalancing of power and wealth. Instead it was primarily concerned with securing the general interest of capital, because it was infused with the liberal goal of saving financialized capitalism from the financiers (Clarke 1988). Put differently, in relation to one big argument of this book remuneration reforms were—paradoxically—measures to protect the financialization of the American economy from the finance capitalists whose conduct threatened to undermine it.

In the drafting of Dodd–Frank in 2009–10, reforming compensation structures for financial institutions came to the fore. On the table, simply put, were a range of complex options that I have sought to simplify: first, Dodd–Frank could potentially give regulators the authority to set the level of pay for executives and other risk-takers (traders, loan officers, investment bankers, brokers, and so on); a second related issue was the possibility of 'clawback', whereby executive remuneration would be repaid in the event of the company restating its financial results in subsequent years; a third issue was the proposal that a portion of each executives compensation be deferred at the time it was earned and invested in cash equivalents to be paid out over the following years. This third option would be contingent upon the company's future performance. The establishment of these three, albeit not mutually exclusive, options was highly significant and framed the following six years of negotiations between the state, the financial services lobby, and civil society.

The first proposal, to limit specific levels of compensation never gained traction. Policymakers, regulators, and firms shared the view that the competitiveness of the market system rested on the ability for individual financial institutions to exercise discretion in setting wages and bonuses. We shall see in Chapter 10 that one result of this was that by the late 2010s bonuses had almost returned to their pre-crisis levels. The undisclosed assumption—largely shared by the political classes—was that wages therefore reflected productivity or value-added; a highly questionable assumption. More importantly though for this book, one significant element of the financialization debate—disproportionately high wages in the finance sector—was immediately removed from the discussion.

In the absence of the first proposal being pursued what followed was a combination of options two and three. With the text of Dodd–Frank simply limiting any bonus incentives that 'encourages inappropriate risks', the details were left to governmental agencies to flesh out (SEC 2016a). One element of this was 'clawback'. Under section 304 of the Sarbanes Oxley Act of 2002, the Securities and Exchange Commission gained powers to recover compensation and stock profits from Chief Executive Officers and Chief Financial Officers of public companies in the event that financial results had to be re-issued following cases of misconduct. Then, in section 954 of the Dodd–Frank act this 'clawback' of executive pay was extended from one year preceding the restatement of financial results to three years preceding the restatement; and also extended to cover all current and former 'executive officers', rather than simply CEOs and CFOs. Further, it also differed from Sarbanes Oxley insofar as the financial restatement triggering the clawback need not necessarily have been caused by misconduct (Latham and Watkins 2010). This constituted a more comprehensive attempt to link pay to performance and impose the consequences for poor conduct on the risk-taker themselves.

Concerning the third issue, the structure of the compensation was also changed. The initial change introduced by Dodd–Frank involved greater executive board oversight of compensation policy. On 18 October 2010 the Securities and Exchange Commission issued proposed rules which would subsequently become section 951 of Dodd–Frank, requiring shareholders to vote on executive compensation (SEC 2010). The implication was that public companies would need a separate non-binding shareholder vote on remuneration and so-called 'golden parachutes'. This raised a separate and controversial issue however, for it assumed that shareholders would seek to act in the best interests of the firm in the long run, thereby reducing the short-termist risk-taking tendencies. In fact however, there was little evidence that these kinds of conflicts—between shareholders thinking longer term and executive boards focused on short-term profits—had played a role in the lead up to the crisis (Forbes 2010). Nonetheless, our main concern here is the *rationale* of state managers (rather than the efficacy of the measures introduced), which clearly reflected an attempt to mitigate the kinds of myopic risk-taking culture that predominated in the lead up to the financial crisis. This was the liberal vision of saving capitalism from the capitalists.

More importantly though, in April 2016 the National Credit Union Administration (NCUA), the Treasury Department, the Federal Reserve, the Federal Deposit Insurance Corporation, the Federal Housing Finance Agency, and the Securities and Exchange Commission jointly issued a proposed rule to implement section 956 of Dodd–Frank. As previously noted, section 956 aimed to: 'prohibit incentive based payment arrangements that encourage inappropriate risks by providing excessive compensation or that could lead to material financial loss'; and for those respective financial institutions 'to disclose information concerning incentive based compensation arrangements to the appropriate federal regulator' (SEC 2016b: 2). At the centre of these proposals were rules requiring top earners at the largest financial institutions to wait up to four years to receive a substantial portion—40, 50, or 60 per cent depending on the size of institution and the role of the individual—of their incentive based pay. In the aftermath of the financial crisis, a number of the largest banks already introduced forms of deferred compensation, in part because they expected this to be a feature of the Dodd–Frank rules (New Yorker 2016). But the final rules issued by US state managers applied to a wider group of employees and extended the bonus deferral period. In particular, the definition of a 'significant risk taker' was not limited to individuals who are senior executive officers (SEC 2016b: 40).

In addition, the 2016 proposed rule explicitly acknowledged that 'the form of incentive based compensation that a senior executive officer or significant risk-taker receives can have an impact on the incentives provided and thus their behavior' (NCUA 2016: 166). The proposed rule therefore demanded compensation in both equity-like instruments and deferred cash payments. It was already widely believed that incentive based compensation in the form of equity-like instruments broadly aligned the interests of the executive officers and risk-takers with the interests of the institutions' shareholders. Since the value of equity like instruments increases or decreases depending on movement in the share price of the covered institution itself, this was seen to tie the performance of the employee to that of the institution itself. More importantly though, incentive based compensation including a substantial cash portion was perceived to be a way of aligning the interests of the employee with wider stakeholders, including creditors and the public (Acharya et al. 2016: 1, Mehran and Tracy 2016: 2). This was because, in the event of resolution or bankruptcy, this cash based compensation would be treated like other unsecured debt and written off; thereby inflicting the losses directly on the employee themselves. Moreover, unlike stock or stock options, deferred cash has 'no upside potential to gain in value' (Mehran and Tracy 2016: 2). Further, deferred cash payments could help to build liquidity buffers that could be drawn upon in the event of the firm experiencing financial stress (Acharya et al. 2016). In other words, the stipulation that the cash portion of the compensation should be increased reflected a recognition on the part of US regulators that too heavy a reliance on 'stock based compensation can lead to excessive risk-taking, and distract from long-term value creation' (NCUA 2016: 167, see also Faulkender et al. 2012, Balanchandarn et al. 2010, Cassell et al. 2012). The main aim of the proposed rule was therefore to establish incentive based compensation arrangements that more appropriately balanced risk and reward (SEC 2016b: 45). The goal was that the 'adverse consequence of investment choices should be internalized [within the firm] as much as possible' (Mehran and Tracy 2016: 6). In line with the arguments of this chapter the proposed rule therefore sought to reinforce the market mechanism, making conduct more socially sustainable. The federal banking agencies found that 'any compensation arrangement would encourage appropriate risks if it did not sufficiently expose the risk-takers to the consequences of their decisions over time' (SEC 2016b: 56).

The key point to note is that both clawback and the structure of compensation were not simply targeted at promoting or rewarding good culture in an abstract way. They were designed to ensure that risk-taking and profitability had a longer time horizon that did not undermine either the legitimacy or functioning of the financial system itself. As the six regulatory agencies explained, 'poorly structured incentive-based compensation arrangements can provide executives and employees with incentives to take inappropriate risks that are not consistent with the long-term health of the institution and, in turn, the long-term health of the U.S. economy' (SEC 2016b: 20). For the bankers, deferral and clawback were not insignificant changes to the structure of their pay; but as one interviewee explained, after the initial three of four year deferral period, little changed in the overall *level* of pay in most cases (Interview 20160131). This was mainly because the more controversial and problematic question of whether finance sector workers deserved disproportionately high wages was not the subject of the political debate over bank culture.

The Soft Approach

The subsection above dealt with new institutions and rules that embodied the more coercive approach of state managers in their attempt to impose the rule of the market and of law, as well as the populist attempt to address the legitimacy crisis. This subsection now examines the *softer* measures introduced by US state managers. As we discussed in Chapter 3, the use of stricter and more punitive measures alongside softer, standard-setting and benchmarking approaches reflects the liberal attempt to protect financialization—by tightening market discipline—and respond to legitimacy challenges; yet both softer and harder approaches reflected the narrower view of bank culture as ethical, socially responsible conduct. The distinction between harder and softer approaches was outlined by Barclays Chairman David Walker in regard to the trustworthiness of financial institutions. He argued that trust depended on three factors: two of them were what he called 'hard ingredients'—the financial soundness of individual institutions and the resilient functioning of operational processes and systems; the third factor though was what he termed a 'soft' factor, namely, how financial institutions 'treat their customers' (Walker 2014: 2). In other words, in line with our argument that state managers were attempting to improve the rule of the market we should not simply expect to witness tougher and more punitive litigation based efforts. The political goal was to combat the distortive behaviours of bank employees, thereby securing the long-term conditions for profitable accumulation. Establishing a set of new norms and expectations about best practices in the banks is therefore an equally important, albeit softer, approach.

Workshops

Arguably the most analytically interesting set of measures introduced to discuss and generate new norms for bank conduct was the range of high profile, annual workshops on promoting 'ethical culture' in the banks (Baxter 2015) hosted by the New York Federal Reserve from 2014 onwards. This can be seen as another feature of the liberal blueprint outlined by the ordo-liberals: educating private actors in the right moral code (Ropke 1957: 98). The first workshop was simply entitled 'Reforming Culture and Behavior in the Financial Services Industry' and took place on 28 October 2014. And, as I have argued, the clue was in the name: good culture was about ethical behaviour. Over one hundred individuals attended this first workshop, and among them were seven participants from academia, thirty-eight participants from regulatory bodies and central banks (including the Swiss and German financial supervisory authorities, the Bank of England, the Dutch National Bank and the European Central Bank), and thirty-nine participants from the financial services sector and banking associations (including UBS, Citigroup, Morgan Stanley, JPMorgan Chase, BNP Paribas, Barclays, Deutsche Bank, Societe Generale, Wells Fargo, BNY Mellon, and AIG) (New York Fed 2014b).

The workshop addressed a number of related themes, including: historical changes in the size and structure of financial services firms; the nature of competition between these firms; how compensation incentivizes particular behaviours; recent initiatives to curb undesirable behaviour; and how law enforcement shapes culture (New York Fed 2014: 1). What was especially noticeable though, was not the discussion of these issues framing bank culture in a particularly narrow vein, but the stated rationale for hosting the workshop in the first place. In his opening remarks, New York Fed President William C. Dudley explained that he had convened the workshop to address an 'apparent lack of respect for law, regulation, and public trust [that] persists within some large financial institutions' (Dudley 2014). Thus the aim was to 'rebuild public trust in the financial services sector' (New York Fed 2014: 1).

This was a particularly illuminating statement, and reflected the fact that Bill Dudley himself had been 'stunned' by the revelations of misconduct the surrounding LIBOR, Forex, and London Whale scandals (Interview 20160419). As Dudley explained, by late 2014 the 'ongoing occurrences of serious professional misbehavior, ethical lapses, and compliance failures' at the largest US financial institutions were leading to a dramatic decline in public confidence (Dudley 2014). LIBOR was, as indicated in Chapter 4, a particularly prominent event for UK and US regulators alike. But around the same time US firms were involved in a series of other high-profile scandals. One of these was the London Whale case. Between March and April 2012 JPMorgan Chase failed to report concerns about its synthetic credit portfolio, which is another way of saying that it mis-stated its financial results and lacked sufficient internal checks to monitor this failure of compliance (*NY Times* 2016). More specifically though, investment officers had sought higher returns by investing excess cash—which would traditionally have been invested in safer government bonds—in credit derivatives and then hedging the risk by shorting their long positions. This complex hedging activity cost the bank $6bn dollars. In effect, the US Senate Permanent Subcommittee on Investigations concluded that JPMorgan Chase had manipulated risk models to reduce capital requirements for higher risk derivatives trading (US Senate 2013, Erturk 2016: x). For Dudley and the Federal Reserve then, the ongoing scandals revealed that 'new laws, regulations, and standards [had] done little to curb banker misconduct' (NY Fed 2015a). Moreover, these scandals suggested that the strategy of responding to the legitimacy crisis by strengthening the market mechanism was insufficient, and an alternative approach, establishing new norms, would need to accompany the tough regulatory and legislative stance.

In November 2015, the New York Fed hosted the second annual workshop, reflecting on 'Progress and Challenges'. This time, there were almost 200 participants in attendance. Over eighty-five of them were industry representatives and a further 105 were regulatory and public agency representatives. But it was not simply the fact that the number of attendees had increased. This time, a far wider range of participants—both in geographic terms and in terms of the range of interests represented—were present. There was a diverse collection of North American financial institutions—including State Street bank, American Express, the Canadian Imperial Bank of Commerce (CIBC), and Bank of America; new foreign institutions such as Rabobank (a Dutch banking firm), Lazard (the world's leading asset management firm), Credit Suisse, HSBC, and RBS; but, equally significantly, participants from the regulatory and public agencies reflected a far wider geographic remit including the Hong Kong Monetary Authority, the Australian Prudential Regulation Authority, the Japanese Ministry of Finance, and the Banco de Mexico (New York Fed 2015). The growing awareness of the scale of the problem and the need to go beyond regulatory and legislative fixes was increasing; as was the capacity for US state managers to join with UK agencies—like the Banking Standards Board and the Parliamentary Commission on Banking Standards (see Chapter 7) in leading the way in the softer, standard-setting agenda. Part of the problem however—from the perspective of this book—was that this widening interest also reflected the growing consensus that the nature of the bank culture problem could be fixed by better ethics and norms.

Indeed, the message that regulation alone would be insufficient to fix the bank culture problem and restore trust was loud and clear. One of the central conclusions of the second workshop was that it is the *banks'* job to restore trust. Of course, framing the problem as one of diminishing trust also depoliticized the underlying structural problems of financialization. In his closing remarks for example, New York Fed Chairman William C. Dudley re-emphasized that 'the private sector must be responsible for changing its culture and curbing misconduct' (New York Fed 2015b: 15). The role of authorities then, was to 'monitor, assess, and encourage the *industry's* efforts' (emphasis added, New York Fed 2015b: 16). Herein lies one of the central dynamics highlighted in this book: bank strategy under financialization had both financial stability and financial credibility threatening impacts, yet it fell to states to restore legitimacy and secure longer-term profitable accumulation. The tightrope they had to walk therefore involved a populist statecraft to appear responsive to mass democratic demands; tightening market discipline to bring into being the idealized market that had been corrupted and distorted; whilst depoliticizing—or deflecting criticism—from the structural conditions which were the real cause of the bank culture problem. The workshops organized by the Federal Reserve were therefore one attempt to address this challenge.

Board Scrutiny

The other area to examine in terms of US state managers' softer approaches to bank culture reform was the increased scrutiny of boards of governors. In particular this was driven primarily by the OCC and the Federal Reserve. As this chapter has been arguing, this was symptomatic of the shift away from the pre-crisis 'lighter touch' approach to banks and their directors, and also a major shift away from the early phase in crisis management (2007–12) when regulators were primarily concerned with issues of financial stability. In the area of board scrutiny then, the goal was to increase regulatory oversight and enforcement of the rule of law by monitoring internal firm culture.

Since 2013, the Fed and other regulators began holding meetings with individual directors at some of the nation's biggest banks. Meetings of this kind had occurred prior to the financial crisis, but their frequency now increased, sometimes even becoming monthly occurrences (Interview 20160419). At these meetings, regulatory officials began demanding detailed minutes and other documentation of board meetings, in a bid to review the level of engagement of bank directors in the actual management of their companies. At Goldman Sachs for example, it was reported that the lead independent director met monthly with the

Fed; at Morgan Stanley and JPMorgan Chase, Fed supervisors were now allowed to sit in on a section of each board meeting. From the perspective of the OCC and the Fed, increased attention to board oversight helped make the banking system safer, by monitoring the build-up of risks (*WSJ* 2015d).

Part of the thinking behind this emphasis on the board of directors in shaping the corporate governance and risk culture of a firm was evident in the 2014 Global Financial Stability report by the IMF, which indicated that firms with an independent Board of Directors were less likely to take on excessive risks, whereas those governed by the bank's CEO tended to be more risk friendly. This message was reinforced though in the wake of subsequent scandals, as was the pressure on regulators to monitor board decision-making. For example, in October 2014 the Federal Reserve's Office of the Inspector General issued a report condemning the failure of the OCC's and New York Fed's supervision of JPMorgan Chase's Chief Investment Office that lead to the London Whale losses of 2012. The report flagged that the Fed had identified trading related risks at JPMorgan Chase in 2008, 2009, and 2010, but had failed to discuss these risks with the OCC and therefore did not act on them, as well as failing to engage decisively with JPMorgan managers once risks were identified (OIG 2014). The OIG therefore pressed the Fed to bolster its supervision of the banks, and its intervention into bank management structures. The implicit assumption though was that closer monitoring could produce a more sustainable approach to risk-taking. But again, this focused attention on the supply-side of bank culture, rather than exploring the structural (demand-side) conditions that made high levels of private debt such an integral part of Anglo-American society.

Closing Remarks

In sum, in their efforts to deal with poor bank culture US state managers focused on improving the rule of the market and the rule of law. Specific measures were taken to enforce the market mechanism and make bank employees more responsible for the consequences of their risk-taking. In addition, softer approaches were applied to bring about changes in norms and values. In all areas though, the goal of state managers was to mitigate the kinds of cultural failure that had threatened profitable accumulation in the longer-term. Even addressing the persistent legitimacy crisis was a function of this deeper goal of restoring and protecting financialized accumulation. This argument is particularly important for two reasons: one is that it challenges accounts of the post-crisis culture response as a leftist victory over the market. Instead, this was a liberal attempt to strengthen the state and enforce the rule of the market. This also, secondly, is a much more apt reading of state managers' efforts to restore the legitimacy of the financial system. Given that we have ruled out a retreat from (neo)liberalism, responding to the legitimacy crisis was important because of the other liberal goal in the US post-2010, that of fiscal consolidation. The underlying public moral outrage at the misconduct in banking was more accurately an outrage at inequality, which was being further exacerbated as the spending cuts kicked in. Getting tough on the bankers—aside from saving capitalism from the capitalists—was therefore a partially successful attempt to deflect attention away from inequality, by ostensibly exposing bankers to the same kinds of market discipline that lower- and middle-income households were experiencing as part of the austerity agenda. As I explain in the Conclusion, the reason it was only partially successful is because it did nothing to solve the underlying inequality problem; it simply bought the political classes some time (Streeck 2014). Chapter 6 will map similar trends in the UK.

6
UK Responses and the First Phase

The aim of this chapter is to begin to analyse UK state managers' responses to the first phase of the culture of banking debate. This immediately poses a problem. For in the US case we were faced with an ostensibly centre-left Obama government whilst in the UK (since 2010) a centre-right Conservative government was at the helm. Yet in both cases we have witnessed a similarly liberal response—tightening the market mechanism and responding to the legitimacy crisis so as to depoliticize and protect the financialization of the respective economies. At one level this is the paradox of neoliberalism, that centre-left governments have also become advocates of the liberal orthodoxy. At a deeper level, as we discussed in Chapter 3, it implies that institutional forms and political parties, though *real* and important, are secondary to the 'social relations which they express' and the social function which the state performs in capitalist society (Clarke 1991: 9). Instead, their function as state managers—if we are to put it rather crudely—is to help establish the conditions for profitable accumulation and to maintain the legitimacy of the incumbent model of capitalism (Gamble 2009). Surface-level differences between political parties become less apparent once this veil is removed.

Together, the broad liberal consensus and the underlying functions required of state managers provide helpful context to the narrowing of the bank culture debate. This is why fiscal consolidation, cuts to social spending and pro-competition labour market policies on the one hand—or an attack on the poor (Radice 2011)—and a pro-market discipline agenda vis-à-vis the banks are not mutually exclusive. Instead they are both part of an overarching liberal project. This is also very important in order to understand the political crisis of the state that the culture of banking problem threatened to provoke, if legitimacy failed to be restored. We return to these big questions in the concluding chapter.

In many respects then the specifics of the US and the UK chapters differ. The regulatory lull of the early 2000s was far more pronounced in the US than in the UK; the foreclosures and emerging social crisis prior to 2007 were then more apparent in the US; likewise the bank collapses of 2007–9 were also more severe in the US than in the UK; although the events surrounding LIBOR did have a noticeable impact on the regulatory agenda, the increased focus on cultural issues was more emphatic post-2012 in the UK; and, equally importantly, by early 2015 the political pressure exerted by central government to target bank culture appeared

The Bank Culture Debate: Ethics, Values, and Financialization in Anglo-America. Huw Macartney, Oxford University Press (2019). © Huw Macartney.
DOI: 10.1093/oso/9780198843764.001.0001

to be waning more in the UK than in the US, despite the late 2016 rhetoric of President Trump. These features point partly to the fact that the crisis unfolded differently in the two economies; in addition the conditions during the 2000s were somewhat different; and, finally, it shows that political agendas and struggles do indeed matter—albeit only to a limited degree.

Yet, though the way in which the two dynamics played out—strengthening the market mechanism and responding to the legitimacy crisis—differed across the two economies, similar challenges (inequality and credibility) and similar goals (protecting financialization and restoring legitimacy) were at work. At the risk of oversimplifying, the centre-left US government was paradoxically even more 'liberal' than the UK centre-right government: the US government emphasized the market mechanism and was less sympathetic to the demands of financial firms (certainly until the Trump administration); whereas the UK government, since 2010, kept attempting to limit their reforms to strengthen the market mechanism, arguably due to their sympathy with the demands of UK finance and the unique position the City of London plays in the UK (Morgan 2012). Though these two strands, the market mechanism and the legitimacy crisis were therefore apparent in both cases, the legitimacy crisis was even more important as a driver in the UK than an attempt to tighten the market mechanism. In the simplest terms possible, Chapters 6 and 7 will now argue that the legitimacy crisis was a problem that simply would not go away in the UK. The result was the repeated need to return to the culture of banking debate even after the Conservative government had hoped it could be laid to rest.

Early Phase

Early 2000s

The first part of this chapter aims to outline the mood of the times and institutional configurations during the early to mid 2000s in the UK. As with the US chapter this serves to show how the mood changed as the global financial crisis unfolded and acts as a backdrop to the regulatory institutions that emerged both in the first phase of the global financial crisis (GFC)—targeting stabilization and resolution—and in the second phase—targeting bank culture. Given that there were no parallels to the Enron and Dot.com crises of the early 2000s that sparked a regulatory push prior to the mid-2000s lull, this chapter begins by addressing the full period 2000–7, examining (i) the institutional set-up (ii), the regulatory mindset, and (iii) the enforcement actions.

Institutional Set-up

In the US we saw that the Enron and Dot.com crises prompted a brief period of tough regulatory action in the early 2000s, only to be followed in the mid-2000s by a regulatory lull. The UK presents a rather different story. Far less affected by crises in the early 2000s the mood in the UK was buoyant until shortly before the collapse of 2007 (FSA 2001: 5, FSA 2006: 6, FSA 2007: 10, HMT 2007: 5). The economic uncertainty and negative impact of the 9/11 terrorist attacks and subsequent collapse of Enron and default of Argentina were noted by the UK authorities. But it was concluded that the lasting impact had been only 'slight' and that the 'recent and lengthening record of macroeconomic and price stability [had] strengthened the fundamentals of [the UK's] financial markets' (FSA 2002: 6, 19).

By June 2007 then, the Treasury was proudly proclaiming that the UK economy had been experiencing its longest unbroken expansion since quarterly records began, with fifty-nine consecutive quarters of economic growth (HMT 2007: 9). This decade of steady economic growth was 'read by many as an endorsement of the UK's principles-based approach to financial regulation and of the tripartite framework established in 1998' comprising The Treasury, the Bank of England, and the Financial Services Authority (HMT 2012a: 5). Under this configuration, the Treasury was responsible for the institutional structure of financial regulation and legislation and, in the event of a crisis, for authorizing particular types of financial intervention; the Bank of England was responsible for rate-setting and ensuring monetary and financial stability, though it relinquished responsibility for banking supervision to the FSA; and the FSA itself was tasked with the regulation and supervision of prudential and conduct of business for all financial services including banks and building societies (HMT 2012a: 16). This is worth noting for two reasons: it placed the regulation of issues related to the culture and conduct of banking institutions firmly in the hands of the FSA itself, making this institution the main focus of the first part of this chapter; and it also sets the context for the changing institutional powers that would occur following the financial crisis.

Most particularly, it was not simply the period of sustained economic growth in the early 2000s in an abstract sense, but the particular 'contribution...to the prosperity of Britain' which the financial services sector was seen to have played (Gordon Brown 2002, 2003). As Gordon Brown, the then UK Chancellor of the Exchequer, emphasized in his 2002 Mansion House speech to City grandees, the financial services sector generated over £50 billion of wealth each year, provided work for over one million people, and accounted for over 5 per cent of UK GDP. Indeed, the ability of the City of London to successfully integrate into the global economy provided a model that the government aspired to achieve for the UK as a whole (ibid.). As the Chancellor would later put it, 'you lead for Britain in the world' (Gordon Brown 2003).

This had important implications for the kind of regulatory trajectory pursued in the UK in the early 2000s. Whereas, as we saw in the previous chapters, between 2000 and 2004 the US introduced sharp stringent new regulations in the form of the Sarbanes–Oxley act, in the UK the authorities resisted pressure for a 'regulatory crackdown' as a response to the US-based Enron and Dot.com scandals. As Gordon Brown explained, 'I believe that we were right not to go down that road which in the United States led to Sarbanes–Oxley... [instead preferring to] build upon our light-touch system of fair, proportionate, predictable, and increasingly risk-based' regulation (Gordon Brown 2006). The deferential approach UK state managers adopted towards the City of London throughout this pre-crisis period was perhaps best characterized by the chancellor in 2007, just prior to the crisis, when he told City grandees, 'I want to continue to work with you in helping you... listening to what you say, recognizing [that] your international success is critical to that of Britain's overall, and considering together the things that we must do—and, just as important, things we should not do—to maintain our competitiveness' (Gordon Brown 2007). In short, the period of New Labour leadership in the UK continued a trend of deferential political treatment of the banking sector; and one in which the confidence in the City's contribution to UK economic prosperity was seemingly unquestioned. In the words of the ordo-liberals though, this was a weakened state, overly concerned with particular private interests.

Regulatory Mindset

This confidence in the City of London and general indifference towards the culture of the banks was also manifest in the institutional and regulatory mindset. The major changes in regulatory institutions and approaches in the UK began in 1997 with the establishment of the Financial Services Authority. Combining the Securities and Investments Board, six other regulatory agencies, and taking responsibility for the prudential and conduct of business regulation from the Supervision and Surveillance Division of the Bank of England, the FSA assumed responsibility for the supervision of banks, building societies, insurance companies, and investment business on 1 June 1998 (FSA 1998).

Setting aside the details of the institutional framework though, our main concern in this section of the chapter is with the regulatory mindset that prevailed within these institutions. It is here that the Financial Services Authority—as the single most important banking regulator—is crucial. Soon after the establishment of the FSA for example, there was a recognition—given the scope of the demands placed on the institution—that emphasis would be placed on firms to 'manage their own risks and thereby reduce the burden of regulation' (FSA 2000: 5). In keeping with the theme of 'pro-cyclical' regulation (discussed in earlier chapters) though, the emphasis on self-regulatory assessment accompanied the prognosis that the UK's financial sector and the economy as a whole had 'been very buoyant over the last couple of years' (ibid.); this created a 'generally reassuring backdrop' (ibid.: 12). Though, as emphasized in the previous chapters, we do not seek to establish causality, there was an unnerving parallel between this growing confidence in the economy and financial system, and the slowdown in regulatory activity. It would be too simplistic an analysis to suggest that regulators were asleep at the wheel. But it would not be inaccurate to claim that the pre-2007 light-touch approach demanded that regulation and supervision (solely) 'minimize the adverse impact on innovation and competition' (FSA 2002: 6) and 'intervene only where the market itself has failed to produce a solution' (FSA 2004: 6, 2005: 6). The FSA itself rejected the notion that it was 'light-touch' on the grounds that the term had pejorative undertones (FSA 2007:6); but it remained clear that the preference of the FSA was to 'work with the grain of the market and facilitate market-led solutions' (FSA 2005: 17). This meant using 'market solutions to effect change rather than adding new areas of rules to the Handbook' (FSA 2007: 10). In other words, the foundations for the later debate on bank culture—that bad culture could not derive from the market itself but from the deviant behaviour of market participants—were readily apparent in the early 2000s.

Light-touch was informed by a regulatory philosophy which believed that: markets were in general self-correcting, meaning that market discipline was a more effective tool than regulation or supervisory oversight; that the primary responsibility for managing risks lay with senior management and the boards of individual firms, who were 'better placed to assess business model risk than bank regulators'; and that consumer protection was best ensured, not by direct intervention, but by ensuring that wholesale markets were as free and as unfettered as possible (FSA 2009: 87). As the G30 highlighted, this was effectively 'market-based supervision' (G30: 12). One major problem was that the institutional architecture—in areas such as resolution and bailouts—meant that the framework did not reinforce the idea of market discipline.

In practice light-touch regulation meant, firstly, that the regulatory approach tended to focus on individual firms, rather than what is known as systemic risk. This was manifest, particularly in banking markets, in a focus on business regulation rather than prudential regulation. It also resulted, secondly, in a focus on ensuring that systems and processes were correctly defined, rather than the regulator probing in greater depth and potentially challenging bank business models. Thirdly and finally, it resulted in regulators simply box-ticking checks on bank employees probity, maintaining an arms-length approach that assumed that senior management had a better grasp of the technical capabilities of their staff (FSA 2009: 88). In all three respects then, ideological assumptions about the benefits of self-regulation and market discipline—coupled with bank lobbying—led to a highly deferential approach on the part of the regulators; and to relatively arms-length scrutiny of culture and conduct issues in the banking sector. But despite all the talk about market discipline, the regulatory structure meant that the costs of bad business strategy would not be borne by the banks as the 2008 crisis unfolded.

Enforcement

The light-touch approach to the banks and bank culture was also apparent in the nature and scale of enforcement action. This too provides some important context to the changed approach as the crisis unfolded. More specifically, the FSA had established a risk-based supervisory programme, whereby the intensity of the regulator's work and the resources allocated to supervising individual firms was in proportion to the size and risk associated with that firm (FSA 2005: 11). This approach included—inter alia—reviews on internal control systems and financial returns, conducted on an annual basis. Yet—as the FSA itself noted—by 2000 there had already 'been a marked decline in the number of these reports', suggesting that banks had resolved risks identified in the initial assessments (FSA 2000: 19). The risk-based approach also involved each larger firm being assigned an FSA relationship manager to highlight issues of concern, and to 'agree mutual expectations from the regulatory relationship' (FSA 2006: 10).

In dealing with issues that would later appear in the culture debate the FSA explained that it would not aim 'to prevent all collapses or misconduct... [but] to seek to minimize the impact of failures on market confidence... when firms collapse or fail to meet expected standards of conduct' (ibid.: 11). Enforcement action was therefore seen as only one of a range of tools to incentivize compliance, and emphasis was placed on giving institutions greater incentives 'to behave in ways which reduce their regulatory burden' (FSA 2001: 8). The burden of responsibility was thus—ostensibly—on the corporation itself, with external regulatory intervention a last resort. In other words, a consensual relationship characterized the interactions between banks and regulatory authorities in the early to mid-2000s. The ordo-liberal conception of a strong, market liberal state was supplanted and weakened by this consensual approach. The FSA clearly specified that it wanted 'firms to understand that failure to meet the required standards is particularly serious' and that, 'where necessary, [it would] take enforcement action in the interests of consumer protection and market confidence' (FSA 2003: 53). But there was also the admission that resources were extremely limited. As a result, much of the FSA's work during this period used 'cease and desist' persuasion tactics, rather than the heavier emphasis on prosecutions and fines that was witnessed after the financial crisis. Fig. 6.1 reveals this trend. The majority of these fines covered cases of market abuse/insider trading, systems controls, fitness and propriety issues, and mis-selling (FSA 2005: 13).

The Financial Services and Markets Act (2000) had introduced a new market abuse regime to complement existing legislation detailing criminal offences, as well as increasing powers to tackle—inter alia—money laundering. This Code of Market Conduct sharpened internal procedures in firms and gave the FSA powers to impose financial penalties and criminal prosecutions (FSA 2002: 5, 23). In principle, the penalties for breaches of market conduct standards became more severe. In practice though, whilst the FSA did indeed bring a series of

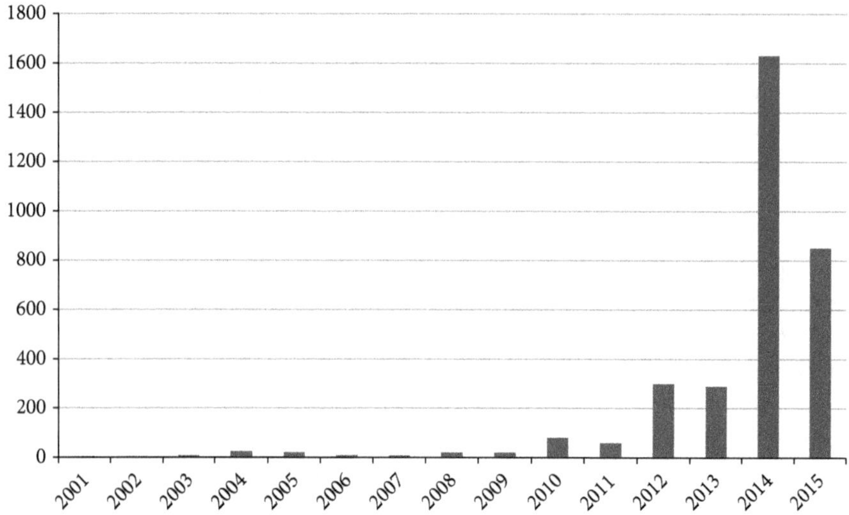

Fig. 6.1 Total UK bank fines (£m), 2001–15
Source: FSA, BoE, FT, authors calculations.

prosecutions during these pre-crisis years, the scale of these activities remained minimal. The FSA focused on three themes: money laundering; fraud and dishonesty; and criminal market conduct, such as insider trading (FSA 2001: 16). Much of the regulatory activity in the early 2000s focused on the mis-selling of pensions and long-term savings products (FSA 2001: 6). By 2003 for example, there was already a recognition of the misleading or complex products—packaged within ISAs—that were being 'aggressively sold' by certain firms (FSA 2003: 35). Moreover, a range of issues associated with the mis-selling of mortgage endowments and pensions had led to falling levels of trust (FSA 2004: 8). Thus, aside from tackling cases of mis-selling by the industry itself, the FSA saw its role as working to restore consumer confidence in financial services (FSA 2004: 7). A kind of embryonic cultural debate was therefore already in gestation, brought about by challenges to the credibility of the banking system; though the form and severity of state intervention changed dramatically as the legitimacy crisis worsened following 2007 and then the LIBOR scandal. But, most importantly, this early iteration of the culture debate already framed the problem as a narrow, conduct issue rather than engaging with the broader, structural features of financialization.

What was particularly interesting as the 2000s progressed was that the FSA argued that the greatest challenges it faced in pursuing the goal of an efficient, orderly, and fair market lay in retail banking, rather than wholesale markets (FSA 2007:7). This is important because many of the later challenges to the culture and credibility of the banking sector were focused on wholesale and investment banking in the City itself. But the FSA rightly highlighted that many of the forward-facing, high-street banking operations were exposing misconduct and leading to declining levels of trust on the part of UK consumers. Part of the issue the FSA highlighted concerned the complexity of some of the financial products involved; in other instances it concerned the difficulty in judging the performance of these products, particularly given the longer timescale involved; and finally, the FSA noted the acute informational asymmetry between providers and consumers, with consumers often lacking the competence to make 'sensible' financial decisions (FSA 2007:7). The conclusion was that 'the frequency with which [the regulator found] examples of poor practice reflect[ed] some inherent and structural difficulties within the retail market' (ibid.: 9). The corollary of this was that it left consumers particularly susceptible to exploitation on the part of a sales-driven culture in retail banking. But, as in the post-2012 period, the solution for authorities was to better inform consumers and improve ethics and accountability for bankers; the root causes of high levels of household debt that encouraged predatory lending for example, were not issues a financial regulator could concern itself with.

The Crisis Hits: 2007–9

As in the US case, the first wave of responses was characterized by a focus on stabilization and then resolution. From our analytical perspective this focus on resolution is significant. The aim, as with certain later measures, was to make banks responsible for the implications of their business strategies. Put differently, the first phase of political responses sought to tighten market discipline, strengthening the state against the need to rescue failing banks in future. Initially though, the emphasis was on stability. Having intervened to provide liquidity support to Northern Rock, the Treasury then announced on 17 September 2007 that it would guarantee all retail and certain other deposits at Northern Rock. Then on 17 February 2008 the Banking (Special Provisions) Act was passed, providing the government with temporary powers to nationalize banks (HMT 2012: 19). Following this, in September 2008 as the global banking system was destabilized by the collapse of Lehman Brothers, a series of British banks and building societies including Halifax Bank of Scotland, Bradford & Bingley, and (in January 2009) Royal Bank of Scotland were either bought up by competitors or part-nationalized. Decisions were made by the Treasury and enacted by the Bank of England to increase the availability of funding under the Special Liquidity Scheme and to establish a Credit Guarantee Scheme. In broad terms then, there were two big peaks of activity during this early period: the recapitalization of banks in autumn 2008; and the establishment of the Asset Protection Scheme in 2009 (HMT 2012: 22). Given our focus in this book on bank culture however, a more comprehensive examination of these measures is beyond the remit of our analysis.

As 2008 unfolded, the bricolage efforts aimed at securing stability shifted into a regulatory drive to establish a framework for orderly resolution of a failing bank without recourse to taxpayer bailouts again. As the government itself would later contend, 'it is right that shareholders should feel the pain if their firm fails' (TSC 2009b: 4). Put differently, there was an acknowledgement that the regulatory framework had in fact come to insulate some of the largest banks from market discipline: 'market discipline must be reintroduced in order to realign the incentives of bank investors and managers' (ibid.). The pristine, idealized vision of the market remained intact; market competition would correct flawed conduct. The Treasury Select Committee proposed a series of measures that would come to shape the next four years of regulatory change. The first was 'a special resolution regime for failing banks' (TSC 2008a: 3). This would involve giving a relevant regulatory institution to gather information about the struggling institution and then to 'take [appropriate] action' to handle this 'failing bank' (ibid.). The second proposal made by the Select Committee was for an expanded depositor protection scheme to ensure that small depositors would continue to be able to withdraw funds in the event of a bank closing (ibid.). Finally, the Select Committee challenged the leadership provided by the Financial Services Authority and proposed a new authority or position be established within the Bank of England charged with financial stability and depositor protection (ibid.: 3) and a reconstitution of the regulatory authority.

By late 2009 this emphasis on improving market discipline and insulating (aggrieved) taxpayers was crystallizing. 'Successful reform' the Treasury committee argued 'would transfer risk away from government and back into the banking sector' (2009b: 3). The government noted that the absence of a resolution mechanism for large complex banks had encouraged complacency within those banks themselves. Thus there was already evidence of the tougher approach towards the banking community, demanding that each bank submit a 'will' for regular evaluation by the Bank of England and indicating that although the 'banks may not like it, [and] may even threaten to domicile elsewhere... this is a reform that is clearly needed' (TSC 2009b: 9).

Ring-fencing

Aside from the special resolution regime, the other major reforms in the UK banking industry initiated in the first phase of the crisis stemmed from the recommendations of the Independent Commission on Banking (ICB) (the Vickers Commission). The Final Report of the ICB, published in September 2011, consisted of two main proposals regarding financial stability: the retail-banking activities of systemically important institutions would need to be placed within a ring-fence; and these retail banking activities would need to be separately capitalized with an equity ratio of at least 10 per cent. The overarching aim was to facilitate the resolution of a failing bank (Interview 20150625 2015); that is, alongside the resolution plans the ring-fence was the missing piece of the market discipline puzzle. It would—if required—allow for a struggling bank to fail; but—aside from that scenario—the *threat* of failure would act as a deterrent on excessive risk-taking and therefore act as a catalyst for good conduct.

Yet, there was also evidence of a second underlying concern animating the ICB: that of addressing the emerging legitimacy crisis surrounding the City. The Chancellor, George Osborne, raised the question 'how can Britain be home to the most successful and global banks in the world, without the British taxpayer being exposed to the most unacceptable of risks?' (Osborne 2010). It was not simply the technical question '[should we] restrict or split the activities of banks?', but that 'millions of people [were] paying the price for what went wrong' (ibid.). In other words, as the Independent Commission on Banking was established there was already a sense that the technical considerations of improved financial stability were filtered through the lens of the taxpayers' questioning of the City's legitimacy (Macartney 2011: 196). As Osborne concluded, the ICB process would—he hoped—establish 'a new settlement between [the] banks and the rest of our society' (Osborne 2010).

Mindset and Culture

Thus there was evidence of a shift in the regulatory mindset with regards to bank culture. Indeed by late 2009 there was a growing scepticism on the part of state managers of the institutional and ideological weakness of the FSA's approach. In a report published November 2009 for example, the UK government noted that 'effective regulation can (and often must) require unpopular decisions in periods of economic growth, which appear at the time immediately to restrain profitable activity' (FSA 2009: 12). The government affirmed this conclusion, noting 'it is easy now for the FSA to promise to be more invasive in its supervision, because public and political opinion has swelled behind such an approach. However we firmly believe that it is not the job of the supervisor to be merely popular and merely follow political fads. The FSA must develop sufficient self-reliance to stick to its guns in the face of criticism from industry or politicians' (TSC 2009a: 2). Starting with the belief that the banking crisis was the result of deviant behaviour that did not conform to the correct market norms, the logical conclusion was that the regulator ought to have been more interventionist in addressing this 'misconduct' prior to the crash of 2007–8.

In addition, and even more specifically in relation to banker conduct, the government noted that the FSA's assessment of whether senior bankers were fit and proper for their posts appeared 'to have been little more than a tick box formality, unless the applicant had a criminal record or gave some other evidence of a shady past' (TSC 2009a: 3). Moreover, the government's desire for the FSA to be more interventionist and stringent was explicitly linked to concerns about costs and credibility. 'It is quite right' the Treasury Committee noted, 'that where the taxpayer is exposed to the risk of bank failure, the regulator should adopt a more proactive approach' (ibid.). In short, whilst the first phase of the response in the UK was primarily devoted to stabilization and then resolution planning, there was also evidence of an awareness of the cultural problems—defined as misconduct problems—within the banking system, and the weaknesses of the regulator in dealing with this cultural deficiency.

Legitimacy Crisis

Though political concerns about culture were evident early in the crisis, the LIBOR scandal was a game-changer in the UK (Interview 20150618). The second half of this chapter will therefore argue that if improving the market mechanism was the main priority in the first phase of the crisis, dealing with the unfolding legitimacy crisis became the priority post-LIBOR. Yet both of these priorities reflected a very narrow definition of the bank culture problem. To understand the legitimacy crisis this section of this chapter again examines three features, as we did in the US case: opinion polls as a proxy for the declining confidence in the banking sector and, importantly, in British politics; fiscal consolidation and austerity measures enacted by the same Conservative government which lead the debate on culture in the banking sector; and the rise of protests not dissimilar to those in the US.

Opinion Polls

Opinion polls in general presented a relatively bleak picture of the declining confidence of the banking industry and politicians. In a survey conducted by Ipsos MORI in 2015 for example, the British public expressed that bankers were the sixth least-trusted profession, with government ministers and politicians in general the second and first least trusted (Fig. 6.2).

Using longitudinal data from the same Veracity Index a picture begins to emerge of the longstanding credibility crisis faced by politicians, government ministers, and bankers which began long before the global financial crisis, but which was significantly worsened by the financial crisis itself. Fig. 6.3 reveals a series of important conclusions when respondents were asked whether they trusted each profession to 'tell the truth'. First, compared to the most trusted

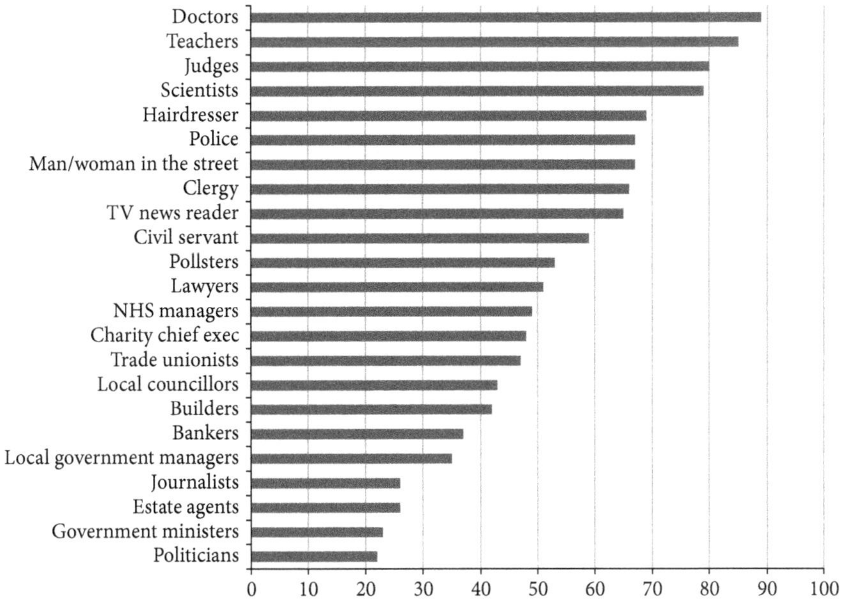

Fig. 6.2 Veracity index 2015 (% trust to tell the truth)
Source: Ipsos MORI 2015.

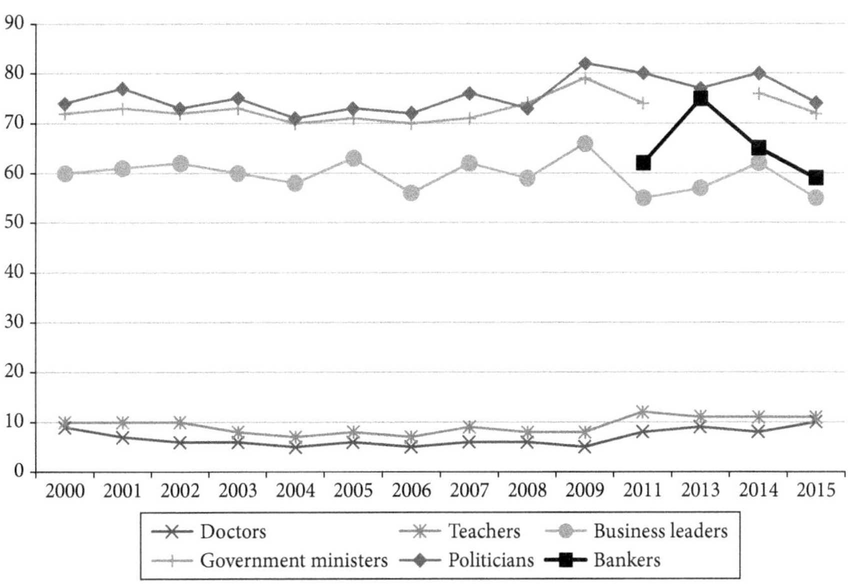

Fig. 6.3 Veracity index (2000–15) (% trust to NOT tell the truth)
Source: Ipsos MORI 2015.

professions (teachers and doctors), levels of confidence in politicians, government ministers, and business leaders had remained extremely low. On average, across the 2000–15 period an average of 69 per cent of respondents doubted the trustworthiness of these least trusted professions. Secondly, although the Veracity Index only recently began to measure trust in bankers, it is noteworthy that confidence in bankers was noticeably lower than other business leaders. On average 65 per cent of respondents doubted bankers, compared to 60 per cent for other business leaders. Finally though, whilst the data on attitudes to bankers is only available for 2011–15, there appeared to be a significant fall in confidence in bankers between 2011–13. We will return to this point below.

There are also a range of ways of showing that confidence in the banking sector declined significantly with the financial crisis. The range of survey data on this topic makes this a robust conclusion in the British case. In 2009, the Institute for Business Ethics and Centrica published their annual 'perceptions of business transparency' report. The research revealed that the proportion of sixteen to thirty-four year olds who believe that companies generally behave ethically had fallen dramatically by 13 percentage points from 64 per cent in 2008 to 51 per cent in 2009 (Ipsos MORI 2009). In particular though, participants were asked whether 'the conduct of banks linked to the financial crisis has damaged my trust in all businesses'? The results are shown in Fig. 6.4. By grouping together respondents who answered either 'Strongly agree' and those who answered 'Tend to agree', 74 per cent of the participants believed that the behaviour of the

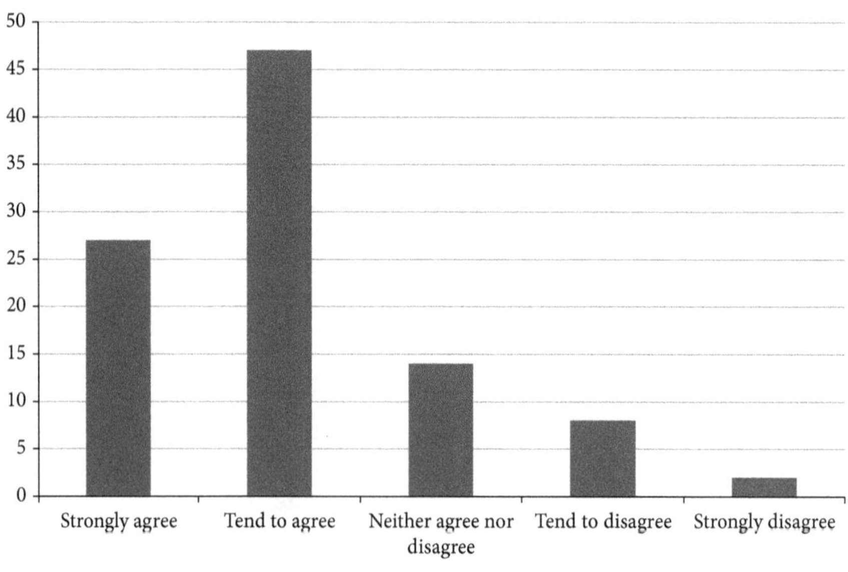

Fig. 6.4 Conduct of the banks damaged my trust in all businesses? (%)
Source: Institute for Business Ethics and Centrica (2009).

bankers—at the early stage of the financial crisis—had had a discernible impact on their confidence in business.

This picture of a fall in confidence in British banking fuelled by the financial crisis was then supported by findings from the Ipsos Global Reputation Centre survey for 2012 (Ipsos MORI 2012). This survey covered twenty-four countries around the world with individuals aged between sixteen and 64 and provides an important comparative snapshot of attitudes towards the banking industry. Two important conclusions can be drawn from this Survey data. Firstly, as Fig. 6.5 shows, the British public in general led the way in thinking that that there was too little regulation of the banking industry. The global average was only 37 per cent whereas in the UK 68 per cent of consumers subscribed to this view. Secondly, even prior to the LIBOR scandal (the survey was completed by February 2012) British attitudes towards the banks were shaped by the financial crisis and the bailouts of these financial institutions. When questioned about which top three issues the British public considered most important for the banks to address, 52 per cent cited responsible lending practices; 42 per cent cited excessive profit; and 41 per cent cited repaying government loans or financial assistance. As an aside, it is therefore interesting to see how state managers sought to capture this underlying public hostility, whilst deflecting criticism of the government bailouts and also depoliticizing the excessive profits in the finance sector.

It is also worth noting, as in the US, that by 2016, richer people trusted the banks more than poorer people; and confidence amongst wealthier individuals had recovered to a greater extent than amongst poorer individuals. In the 2016

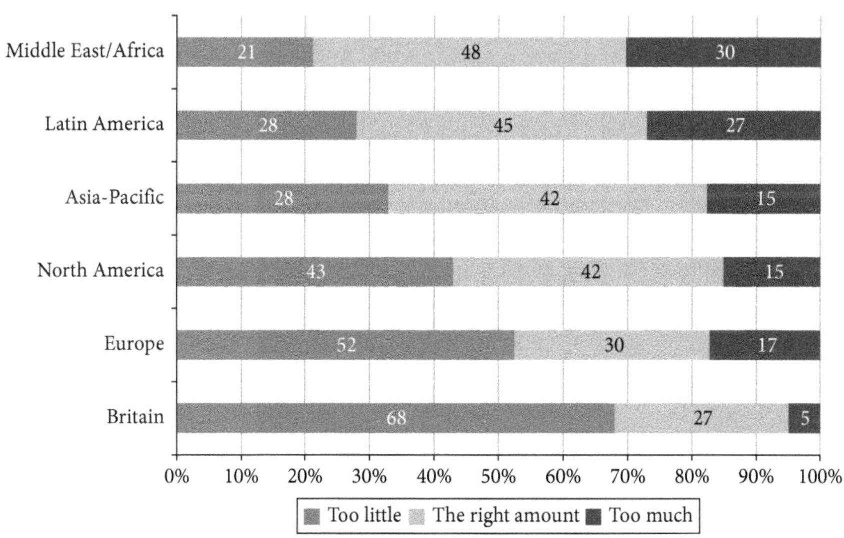

Fig. 6.5 Public perceptions of regulation of the financial sector (%)
Source: Ipsos MORI 2012.

Edelmann Trust Barometer, participants were asked to indicate 'how much trust you have in each of the following industries to do what is right' (Fig. 6.6). Defining the 'informed public' as those between the ages of twenty-five to sixty-four, college educated; in the top 25 per cent of income in their respective country; and reporting significant media consumption and engagement in business news, and the 'mass population' as those not included in the informed public category, the UK recorded the seventh highest disparity between levels of trust of the twenty-eight countries surveyed. What was notable though, and contrasts somewhat with the US, was that levels of trust in the banking sector were lower (amongst both high-income and low-income individuals) in the UK. In the US, 71 per cent of high-income individuals trusted the banks, whereas in the UK only 52 per cent did so; and in the US, 40 per cent of lower income individuals trusted the banks compared to only 33 per cent in the UK.

Relatedly, the recovery in confidence showed evidence of income-related disparity as well. Trust had risen faster amongst higher-income individuals than amongst lower-income individuals. Fig. 6.7 shows this. With a 10 per cent increase in the gap between levels of trust amongst top-earners and lower-income earners between 2012–16, the UK had experienced the second largest change of the countries measured.

Additional survey data is also available to demonstrate the disparity between higher- and lower-income individuals' perceptions of business in Britain (in general) and banks in Britain (in particular). In the previously mentioned survey

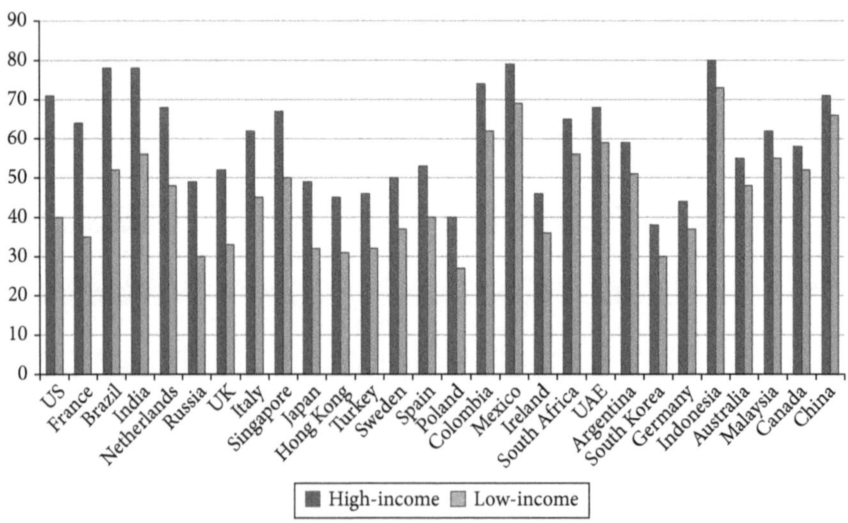

Fig. 6.6 Trust in banking sector by top 25% and bottom 25% of earners
Source: Edelman 2016.

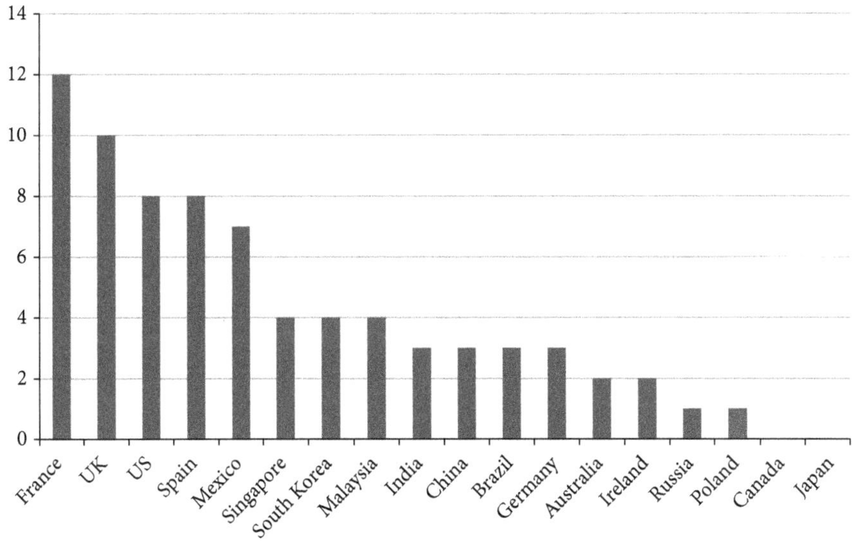

Fig. 6.7 Percentage point increase in trust in banking sector 2012–16
Source: Edelman 2016.

conducted by Ipsos MORI and the Institute for Business Ethics (IBE) for example, participants were asked whether 'company profits in Britain are too high'. Fig. 6.8 shows the responses. Several points should be noted. Those participants with an income less than £17,499 most strongly agreed that profits were too high. In addition, 60 per cent of these same poorest respondents either Strongly agreed or tended to agree, compared to 57 per cent of those with an income between £17,500 and £29,999, and only 43 per cent of those with an income above £30,000. This appears to support the conclusion from another part of the survey which focused on executive pay as the top issue for over 42 per cent of the lower income group, and 44 per cent of the middle income group. Though these questions did not specifically address the banking sector, they appear to reflect a wider concern among lower income social groups about issues related to corporate pay and profits. Indeed, with the question from the 2009 survey examining how 'the conduct of banks linked to the financial crisis had damaged levels of trust', the highest percentage of respondents 'strongly agreeing' were in the £17,499 and under-wage bracket. Amidst the details the point is simply this: the financial crisis damaged confidence in the banking system, and poorer people were most especially concerned about the profits, wages, and bailout packages received by the banking sector (an important feature in Chapter 10). This paves the way for the next subsection which examines the backdrop of austerity and inequality, which in turn fuelled the legitimacy crisis for the state.

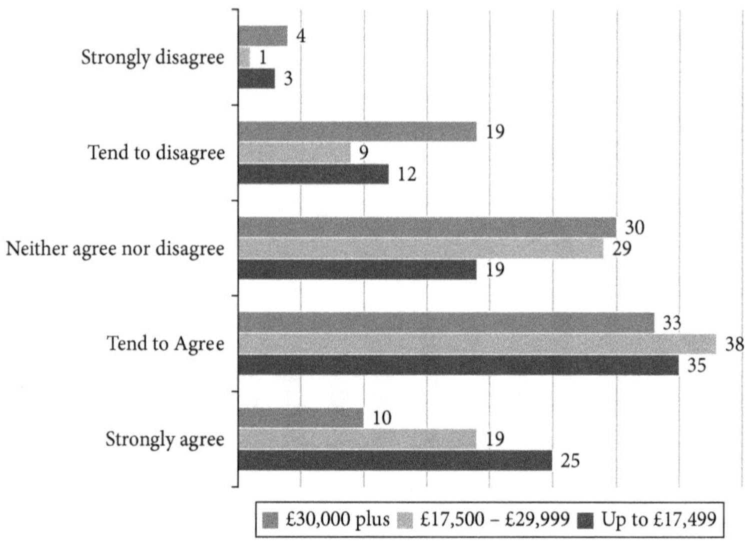

Fig. 6.8 Company profits in the UK are too high (%)
Source: Institute for Business Ethics 2012.

Austerity and Inequality

As Pete Burnham has convincingly argued with regards to the early stages of the financial and debt crises, the political response of state managers was defined by an attempt to reconstitute and strengthen class domination and tighten market-based control over the working classes (2011: 493). This is the underlying logic of austerity and the politics of tight money. As with the US case, these two toxic ingredients—a society divided by inequality and public spending cuts affecting the most vulnerable lower- and lower-middle income households—were present in the UK case. As the OECD noted in 2015, income inequality—measured by the Gini coefficient—in the UK was the sixth largest in the Organization for Economic Co-operation and Development (OECD 2015a: 1). Only Chile, Mexico, Turkey, the United States, and Israel recorded higher levels of inequality between the richest and the poorest members of society. Fig. 6.9 shows this income inequality in terms of the income share of the bottom 40 per cent of society compared to the top 10 per cent of these OECD member countries. In the UK, according to 2015 figures, the top 10 per cent of earners held approximately 28 per cent of the income, whereas the bottom 40 per cent account for only 19.3 per cent of income, and the bottom 10 per cent account for only 2.7 per cent of income. Put differently, 'in the UK the average income of the richest 10% is almost 10 times as for the poorest 10%' (OECD 2015b: 1).

The fact of income inequality is arguably less significant than the message that policies pursued both in the lead-up to and then, in particular, after the financial

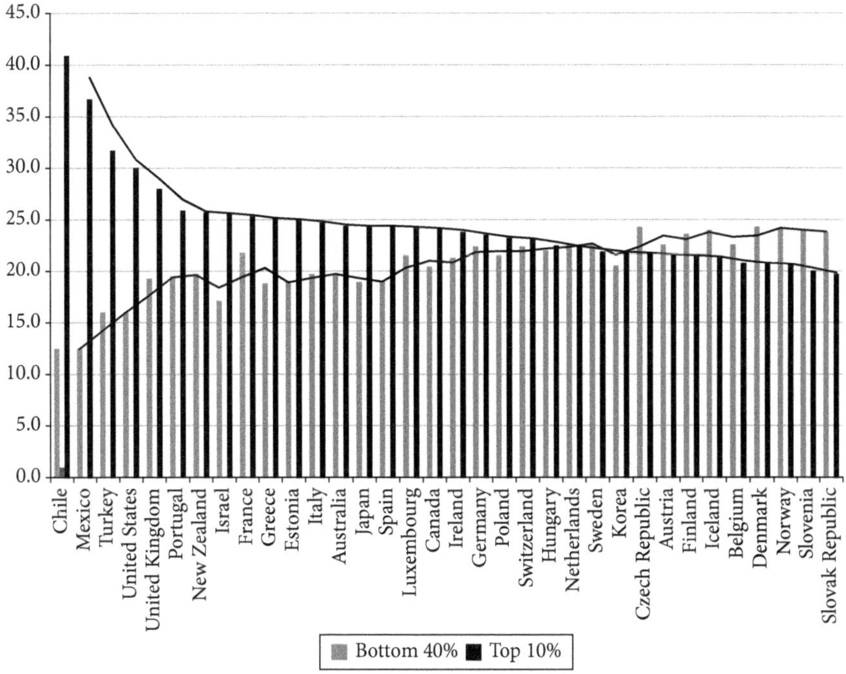

Fig. 6.9 Income share of total income (top 10% of earners vs. bottom 40% of earners)
Source: OECD 2015a.

crisis, significantly increased this inequality. This is the background to the legitimacy crisis faced by British state managers—helping to explain their urgency in addressing the bank culture problem. It is also important because income inequality shaped the populist, point-scoring strategy adopted by the state (the *form* of the response), seeking to position itself as champion of the people against the profligate banks; yet, as I have argued, the *content* of the response was hollow, because it did nothing to address the causes of inequality. In fact the policies made inequality worse, which in turn feeds into the culture of banking problem. The politics of tight money and austerity therefore warrants our attention.

In May 2010, a Coalition Government of the Conservative Party and the Liberal Democrats was formed. Within weeks an 'emergency budget' was introduced with the singular goal of cutting the (ostensibly) bloated spending of the previous Labour government. At various levels though, the austerity measures of this new budget disproportionately targeted more vulnerable members of society and lower income households. Existing programmes designed to reduce economic and educational inequalities—such as the Educational Maintenance Allowance designed to lessen the demands for sixteen-year old pupils to enter the workplace—were scaled back or cut; a new Universal Credit welfare system was introduced, reducing payments and imposing tougher eligibility criteria; and increased consumption taxes (such as VAT) were implemented which are known to affect lower earners—rather than raising taxes on income; all this meant that those more dependent on state support were worst hit (Atkinson et al. 2012: 5). This included savage cuts of between 25 to 40 per cent in unprotected areas. As the 2011 and 2012 budgets were unveiled, similarly regressive fiscal decisions were applied. In key areas such as health, education, and welfare then, the Coalition Government 'launched a radical assault on the nature of the state and its relation to society' (Radice 2011: 134). If bad bank culture is indeed partially a product of reduced disposable income that contributes to heightened household indebtedness, then austerity only made these conditions worse.

As with the US, cutting the public deficit was posited as an economic 'necessity'. In contrast, 'the real reason for the attacks on state borrowing and state expenditure lies not in economics, but in politics, or more specifically in class warfare' (Radice 2011: 132). As the ordo-liberals argued in Chapter 3, a political system characterized by an expanded welfare state reflected a broken society, 'in which disempowered welfare seekers live off the state' (Bonefeld 2014: 2). In the UK, this meant that the public spending cuts were also accompanied by a discourse emphasizing liberalism, empowerment, freedom, and responsibility (Prime Minister David Cameron, cited in the *Daily Telegraph*, 7 February 2011). For the ordo-liberals, the problem with high levels of social spending was not the financial costs per se, but the fact that competition and entrepreneurship were being suppressed by the 'nanny state'— the welfare state. According to the ordo-liberals, this institutionalized 'government organised mass relief' whereby men and women shirked 'their own responsibility' (Ropke 1998: 155). Much as UK state managers therefore also sought to strengthen the British state by inflicting losses incurred through bad behaviour on the financial institutions themselves, the cutting of government social spending was also an attempt to reduce government responsibility for workers. This is what is meant by the state acting to restore financialized accumulation, by establishing a degree of independence from welfare seeking workers and the finance elite. The challenge for the British state however, was that from bailouts to bonuses, and subsequent scandals, state managers were consistently forced to walk a tightrope, seeking to maintain their legitimacy by overcoming the perception that they were overly supportive of finance capital (the banks). State managers were forced to 'intervene in crucial areas to restore profitable accumulation…whilst simultaneously withstanding demands to intervene in other areas to the advantage of particular groups' (low paid workers, the unemployed) (Burnham 2011: 499).

It would therefore be wrong to suggest that UK state managers constructed the culture of banking debate in the expectation that it would fully address the grievances raised by the austerity project. Nonetheless the banking community became a particular focal point for the grievances of subaltern social groups. It also proved to be a suitable (populist) target for embattled politicians themselves fighting for legitimacy. The next subsection will briefly examine the Treasury Select Committee hearings, as an example of the state's efforts to manage the public moral outrage. The Project Merlin lending targets were yet another attempt to construct a new settlement between the banks, the state, and the British electorate (see Macartney 2012 for a more detailed account). Not only did the lending targets fail however, but the subsequent LIBOR and Forex scandals undermined the attempts by the Conservative government to pour water on the fire of the legitimacy crisis. The more formal culture of banking debate that ensued after LIBOR, which we will examine in Chapter 7, therefore came at the end of repeated failed attempts by the British state to quell public hostility towards the banks and restore the legitimacy of the state itself.

The Bonfire of the Bankers

The most obvious early form of protest explicitly targeted at the financial elite was the so-called 'Bonfire of the Bankers'. Starting on 3 November 2008 the Treasury Select Committee (TSC) began holding a series of public inquiries into the banking crisis. Initially the Chancellor of the Exchequer, the Governor of the Bank of England, and the Chairman of the Financial Services Authority were called to give evidence. Then—throughout 2009 and 2010—officials from the failing banks Bradford & Bingley, Northern Rock, and Royal Bank of Scotland as well as the British Bankers Association, the London Investment Banking Association, and the Association of British Insurers, amongst others, were called upon. At face value the Select Committee set about a robust interrogation of the bank failures. At one point for example, the chairman of the TSC asked the chairman of Bradford & Bingley building society to explain exactly why his institution had gone from proclaiming that it was 'a strongly capitalised bank' on 25 September 2008 to announcing that, on 27 September, it was 'no longer able to meet the threshold conditions' that the FSA had placed upon them (TSC 2008b Q 253). The Select Committee tried to ascertain whether blame should be apportioned to the business model of Bradford & Bingley, the underlying economic conditions, or the actions of the regulator (ibid.). In particular, the Committee questioned whether the announcement on that Thursday had been misleading for shareholders and others who may have 'lost money as a result' (ibid.: Q 279). The Committee also asked about how many jobs would be lost as a result of the nationalization of the building society (Q 285), and questioned whether remuneration for executives was appropriate, in spite of the failure of the bank (Q 290–328). Indeed, already at this early stage the Committee began asking whether there had been a conflict between executive remuneration incentivizing short-term gains, whilst the medium and long-term stability of the company had not been prioritized (Q 325).

These two themes of increased public scrutiny and remuneration developed as the Select Committee hearings progressed. When the chief executive of Royal Bank of Scotland, Stephen Hester, was questioned in January 2010 he explained 'I completely understand why banks are of great interest to politics…in terms of the systemic issues arising out of the financial crisis…and I completely understand why a bank such as RBS, which has been very much in the eye of the storm of some of these issues and is in receipt of enormous public support in funding terms should be in that [public] eye as well' (TSC 2010a Q 2). He was then asked more specifically by the chairman of the Select Committee though, 'do you think politicians have a legitimate interest in scrutinizing bankers' bonuses?' (Q 11). Hester's response agreed that public and political interest in bank bonuses was also understandable and that, 'until the banking industry can demonstrate that in times of crisis it does not need public support…the banking industry…has invited on itself this kind of scrutiny and intervention' (ibid.). The Select Committee chairman pressed the issue further however, and asked whether Hester's potential remuneration of £9.7 million 'at a time when the industry has been almost totally bailed out by the taxpayer' was a 'legitimate concern for people?' (Q 12). As was witnessed in the US chapter in the confrontation between Senator Henry Waxman and Lehman CEO Richard Fuld, the Treasury Select Committee specifically targeted remuneration because the financial crisis had helped place it at the very top of the list of public grievances raised by the British electorate (Ipsos MORI 2012).

In the background though, the hearings also became a useful mechanism to channel public moral outrage at specific scapegoats, whilst vindicating the majority of the banking community. The hearings certainly reinforced the culture-as-bad-behaviour trope, deflecting attention from the financialized British economy. Opinion polls early in the Treasury Select Committee process showed that the majority of the public believed there were pathological flaws in the banking system at large, which are actually closer to the version of bank culture proposed by this book: a system predicated on excessive rewards, unbridled risk-taking, and bank executives bent on the search for huge bonuses (Froud et al. 2010: 29), whilst other polls played more explicitly into the narrower framing employed by state managers, emphasizing the culpability of rogue individuals. In an online poll conducted by the Guardian in October 2008 for example, 93 per cent of respondents blamed the bankers for causing the financial crisis, with a further 74 per cent indicating that the bankers now bore the most responsibility for resolving the crisis (*Guardian* 2008a). One function of the Select Committee hearings then, was to shift this focus from wider definitions of culture to a focus on the individual behaviours responsible for the crisis. As the Select Committee admitted, 'this kind of investigation and scrutiny…will help to secure the necessary [popular] support' required to restore confidence in the banking industry as a whole (TSC November 2008a). One aim was therefore to vindicate the pristine vision of the market.

The hearings also served a second depoliticizing function, by reinforcing the impression of independence between the banking community and the state itself (Radice 2011: 9). As we have argued throughout these chapters, the credibility crisis provoked by the bank collapses risked degenerating into a legitimacy crisis for the state, because of the bailouts offered to the banks whilst social spending in other areas was frozen or being cut. At the early stage in the crisis, the 'trial-like' conditions of the Select Committee hearings therefore served as a mechanism to reassert the independence of the state from the banking community (Macartney 2011).

Occupy

The other major form of protest considered in the US chapter was the Occupy movement, which fuelled a parallel movement in the UK. On 15 October 2011 protesters gathered outside St Paul's Cathedral, London, only a month after the New York movement had launched (*WSJ* 2011). Approximately 4000 protesters had expressed their intention to gather in Paternoster Square, outside the London Stock Exchange building (Bloomberg 2011b). Outside of New York the London movement was one of the most high profile and long-lasting of the Occupy protests. The flagship occupation was finally evicted from St Paul's courtyard on 27 February 2012, but activists also occupied a camp in a neighbouring borough until 14 June 2012.

Though the London protest took its name and impetus from the Zucchotti Park initiative, the financial crisis and subsequent austerity measures were not the sole driver of the St Paul's encampment. The fact that it explicitly targeted the banking sector in the UK was undeniable, with banners expressing themes such as 'Bankers got a bailout, we got sold out'. Nonetheless, as with New York, the London Occupy movement also capitalized on the underlying resentment towards inequality in the UK. 'We are the 99%' proclaimed a range of banners; 'Rich, beware, your days are numbered' contended others. As such, it was compared to other global movements for socio-economic justice and alter-globalization (Halvorsen 2012: 428).

Measuring the impact of any of these protests is again both methodologically difficult and arguably unnecessary for this book. Indeed, as an example of grassroots activism, the London Occupy movement was more concerned with protest, asking questions, and exploring and pressing at the 'cracks' in capitalism, than about a programmatic and concrete set of demands (Halvorsen 2012, Holloway 2010). This fits with one key argument of this book, that the legitimacy crisis state managers have been responding to did not originate with the financial crisis and the subsequent credibility crises caused by the banking sector. Instead, the banking crises merely exacerbated deeper social crises within Western advanced economies in general and the financialized Anglo-American economies more acutely, that were typified by rising levels of inequality and declining trust.

What is certainly clear however, was that the London Occupy movement also influenced the political debate as it had in the US. By November 2011 for example, the Liberal Democrat Business Secretary Vince Cable expressed his sympathy for the grievances raised by the protesters. In particular, he emphasized the fact that the crisis had exacerbated divisions between the 'haves' and the 'have nots' in British society: 'I think it does reflect a feeling that a small number of people have done extraordinarily well in the crisis, often undeservedly, and large numbers of other people who have played no part in causing the crisis have been hurt by it' (cited in the *Guardian* 2011). In contrast, David Cameron—the then Prime Minister—was more critical of the movement. He concluded that though people ought to have the right to protest, this right should not be exercised through encampments: 'it's certainly a right that people should have, but I've got this rather quaint view that people shouldn't be able to erect tents all over the place' (cited in the *Telegraph* 2011). Nonetheless, the Occupy movement was symptomatic of the credibility crisis facing the banking sector and the rapidly unfolding legitimacy crisis. It therefore provided an important backdrop to the June 2012 LIBOR scandal, which lead to the narrow culture of banking debate. Occupy's main success was that it reminded state managers on both sides of the political spectrum that the fabric of the neoliberal consensus was coming apart at the seams. A rapid political response would be required, and yet one that sought to quell an alternative debate about the origins of bank culture in the structures of financialization itself.

Closing Remarks

This chapter began with the claim that the first priority of UK state managers as the financial crisis hit was stabilization and then resolution planning. Below this superficial level though, an important shift was taking place. State managers were attempting to strengthen market discipline and thereby distance themselves from the banks. This process is never complete or permanent, since it is always contested and shaped by the ebb and flow of struggle and party politics (Bruff 2008). Neither should this strengthening of the state and market discipline be interpreted as a victory for social democracy. This was a struggle of the liberal state over the weakened state that had been overly deferential to the City. It was however, part of a wider shift—with important implications for bank culture that we shall discuss in Chapter 7—to impose the rule of money and the law on banks, thereby acting in the interests of financialized accumulation. This muddies the waters for an analysis that wishes to lay the blame at the feet of the bankers. For although the banker may be the bearer of the social power of money, he/she 'is no less subject to the power of money [and the market] than is the worker' (Clarke 1993: 100).

The second half of this chapter then began to explain how the credibility crisis facing the banking sector added to a slow-burning legitimacy crisis. Criticism of the banking sector, alongside falling levels of public trust, risked threatening the British state; the economic crisis risked spilling over into a political crisis (Habermas 1973). This was partly the result of a longer-term rise in levels of inequality. It was aggravated even further by austerity measures, which disproportionately affected lower income social groups. Attempts like the Treasury Select Committee hearings and Project Merlin failed to contain the unrest. Chapter 7 will examine how the targeting of bank culture was thus part of this wider attempt to restore legitimacy.

7
UK Responses and the Second Phase

The previous chapter began to explain how the legitimacy crisis and attempts to strengthen the market mechanism shaped the post-crisis reform agenda in the UK. As with the US example, the early phase of the crisis prompted efforts by state managers to address stabilization and resolution. The idealized, liberal vision of the pristine market suggested that in establishing better resolution mechanisms, financial institutions would be more accountable for their own decisions and the problems associated with moral hazard and Too-Big-To-Fail would be reduced; bad culture was reduced to one element of this broader concern. Thus, even at this early stage, resolution measures were driven in part by legitimacy concerns after the bank bailouts. In bailing out the banks, state managers risked being seen as intervening to support the banking sector; this became particularly problematic in the context of austerity and the underlying problems with inequality in the UK.

The current chapter now focuses specifically on the approach taken by the British state to deal with bank culture and legitimacy after the 2012 LIBOR scandal. It also demonstrates similarities between the US and UK responses to the bank culture debate. Harder, legislative and institutional measures, including increased prosecutions and fines, were one approach adopted by UK state authorities. Softer measures, including standard-setting and the establishment of industry bodies to monitor and encourage the dissemination of best practice were also evident in the UK. These strategies were infused with a populist statecraft, seeking to re-assert the appearance of political independence from the embattled banks; the strategies were also infused though with an attempt to depoliticize the financialized economies of Anglo-America, placing them at one remove from public scrutiny and criticism, and presenting the debate about bank culture as a narrow debate about ethical, socially responsible conduct—and rooting out individual and collective instances of malfeasance.

Despite the similarities between US and UK approaches though, there are also important differences as well. In the UK, there was clear evidence of a struggle within the state, particularly between tougher regulatory institutions within the Bank of England and the weaker British Conservative government. Similar struggles were also present between the political left and the political right in the US, but not until the Trump administration did they significantly limit the culture reform agenda. In the UK, in contrast, the Conservative government consistently sought to draw a line under the reform efforts—as early as 2011 with the Project Merlin

The Bank Culture Debate: Ethics, Values, and Financialization in Anglo-America. Huw Macartney, Oxford University Press (2019). © Huw Macartney.
DOI: 10.1093/oso/9780198843764.001.0001

lending targets; but the legitimacy crisis proved to be a problem that simply would not go away, as more and more scandals and ethical issues continued to plague the banking industry.

The Hard Approach

The first section of this chapter explains how the culture of banking problem (first the credibility crisis for the banks and then the legitimacy crisis for the state) prompted a tougher approach to bank culture for UK state managers. Fig. 6.1 (in Chapter 6) has already demonstrated the sheer volume and scale of the fines imposed by UK authorities and how this grew exponentially as the crisis worsened. The prosecutions and fines will be examined in greater detail in later chapters. Instead, this first section looks at new legislation and the bank levies tasked with addressing bank culture.

Legislation

Senior Managers Regime

Without doubt the most important legislation set in place to deal with bank culture in the UK was the Senior Managers and Certified Persons Regime (SMR). It formed the cornerstone of UK state managers' responses after LIBOR. The aim of the legislation was to increase accountability of individuals for both their own activities and those they managed and supervised. It constituted a radical change in the supervisory approach, making individual prosecutions (theoretically) easier. Prosecutions for money laundering, insider dealing, market abuse, and fraud were possible under the previous system. The key difference post-2012 however, was the explicit attempt to target 'standards and culture in banking' by addressing the 'mismanagement and failure of control by *senior* bankers' (emphasis added, PCBS 2013a: 512). Yet—as this book emphasizes—the SMR was still firmly in keeping with the narrow debate about bank culture.

In the immediate aftermath of the LIBOR scandal, the British government set up the Parliamentary Commission on Banking Standards (PCBS) (examined in greater detail later in the chapter) which produced a series of eighty-six 'culture-related' recommended amendments to the banking reform bill in its report 'Changing Banking For Good' (*Guardian* 2013c). As such, of all institutions established after the financial crisis, the PCBS almost certainly had the most significant impact on defining the terms of the bank culture debate. As the Chairman of the PCBS, Andrew Tyrie, indicated, 'Recent scandals have exposed shocking and widespread malpractice. Taxpayers and customers have lost out. The economy has suffered. Trust in banking has fallen to a new low' (cited in

NY Times 2013). Yet the report also noted that 'one of the most striking features of the recent years has been that the failures of the banking sector—including…the near collapse of some major banks [that] required massive taxpayer bailouts, and the conduct failures which lead to large-scale mis-selling—did not lead to action against individuals' (PCBS 2013: 497). The origins of the SMR stemmed from this lack of effective accountability; which in turn stemmed from the liberal view that individual instances of misconduct were the cause of the culture problem. Under the existing Approved Persons regime, enforcement action and sanctions were extremely rare and regulatory authorities 'seemed almost powerless' (ibid.: 509). The Approved Persons Regime essentially meant that certain functions within financial services firms were designated as 'controlled functions', so that only persons approved by the regulator were permitted to perform those functions (HMT 2012b: 9). The main powers available to the Financial Services Authority (FSA)—or the new Prudential Regulation Authority (PRA) and Financial Conduct Authority (FCA) after the Financial Services Bill—were simply to prohibit an individual from performing these functions.

One of the most significant and substantive recommendations made by the PCBS was therefore for greater accountability of senior personnel, which would later become the Senior Managers (or Senior Persons) Regime. This recommendation followed a July 2012 consultation document entitled '*Sanctions for the directors of failed banks*' by the UK Treasury. The government proposals stemmed from the FSA investigation into the failure at RBS. The consultation document highlighted that though the initial measures adopted by the government after the financial crisis were primarily focused on organizational and institutional reform, both the first phase of the crisis and, in particular, the subsequent scandals 'highlighted the important role that individuals—especially bank directors—play in the key decisions taken by banks…which can have far-reaching consequences…for the…government, taxpayers, and the wider economy' (HMT 2012b: 3). *Bad decisions* by *individuals* were therefore the target for concern, rather than structural features of the financialized market itself.

The government therefore considered two reforms in the consultation document, although the wording made clear that it was more favourable towards the former than the latter: the government expressed that it 'favour[ed] legislating to amend FSMA in order to put in place a "rebuttal presumption" that a director of a failed bank is not suitable to be approved by the regulator to hold a position as a senior executive' in future (ibid.: 10); on the other hand though, it was more cautious about proposing increased criminal sanctions, simply saying 'the government is…*considering* the introduction of criminal sanctions for serious misconduct' (emphasis added, ibid.: 13). The government noted that 'the introduction of [this kind of] criminal offence…would send a clear signal that society is not prepared to tolerate conduct of this kind' (ibid.: 14). But it was nonetheless sceptical about the benefits of such reform.

What was clear however was that by 2013 the game had changed. The legitimacy crisis that followed LIBOR demanded a stronger political response. In its June 2013 report, the Parliamentary Commission on Banking Standards provided greater detail on what this kind of new criminal offence might look like. Specifically, it confirmed the need for criminal charges for senior executives in cases of financial mismanagement, the option the government had been reluctant to pursue. The hope was that this would force bankers 'to be less cavalier with risky trading and lending activities' (*NY Times* 2013). The Commission appeared to be sanguine regarding the practical and logistical difficulties of actually securing a conviction. But they nonetheless highlighted that 'the fact that recklessness in carrying out professional responsibilities carries a risk of criminal conviction and a prison sentence would give pause for thought to the senior officers of UK banks' (PCBS 2013: 68). This was unequivocally a measure designed to influence the corporate mentality and behaviour of senior bank personnel—or to strengthen the rule of law—and thereby influence the culture of the institution.[1] But again, the language of 'recklessness' and 'cavalier' captured the sentiment that 'good culture' had been corrupted by a few 'bad apples'.

That said, the details of the recommendations were perhaps the most telling element, and it was here that the tougher approach of the PCBS—compared to that of the government—became more apparent. As we shall see in this chapter, this was symptomatic of the struggle between more radical attempts to strengthen the rule of the market and law, and certain—more conservative—UK state managers' reluctance to go further than was necessary to address the legitimacy crisis. Under the previous regulatory regime one of the main difficulties in holding senior individuals to account stemmed largely from the fact that authorities had to 'be able to show the clear evidential trail from a senior figure, a particular abusive decision, to what actually happened' (Martin Wheatley, cited in PCBS 2013: 503). This meant that prosecutors tended to start at the bottom and work up the accountability chain, searching for those who were 'responsible... and aware' of particular decisions and strategies (Tracey McDermott, FCA, cited in PCBS 2013: 502).

Thus the PCBS proposed two significant changes: firstly and arguably most importantly, it proposed that senior executives and directors of failing banks should be able to 'positively demonstrate that they were active in identifying, arguing against, and seeking to rectify the causes of failure' (PCBS 2013: 511). This would effectively *reverse* the burden of responsibility. This new Senior Persons Regime would mean that particular individuals that held responsibilities in the area 'directly relevant to the subject of the enforcement action' would be considered culpable (ibid.: 511). In effect this would have replaced the traditional

[1] Of course it still subscribed to the view that culture was the product of bad behaviour, that could be remedied by tougher ethical standards and penalties.

'bottom up' prosecution process with a 'top down' one, on the understanding that the senior manager was *automatically* responsible and that protests of ignorance of what was going on within that division of the bank would have no longer held sway. The second major change recommended by the PCBS, was that these executives would not simply be fired by their financial institution but receive an automatic ban from working in the industry itself, preventing them from simply moving horizontally to another financial firm. Given the fact that the former regulator, the FSA, had 'only rarely taken public enforcement action against senior individuals in the large banks' these two proposals constituted a significant step change (PCBS 2013: 511).

In keeping with one of the main arguments of this chapter, that UK state managers were simultaneously looking for a tough enough response whilst also hoping to draw a line under the legitimacy crisis, the British government rapidly accepted many of the even more radical recommendations of the PCBS; popular outrage at LIBOR demanded it. The final report of the PCBS was published on 19 June 2013, and the very same day the Prime Minister agreed to accept the recommendation on introducing criminal sanctions for reckless misconduct (HMT & BIS 2013: 12). If the underlying goal was to diffuse public criticism—by distracting from the structural problems emanating from financialization—then agreeing to criminal sanctions was more than a satisfactory compromise. Less than a month later (on 8 July 2013), the government issued its formal response stating that it 'strongly endorse[d] the principal findings of the report and intend[ed] to implement its main recommendations' (HMT & BIS 2013: 5). Specifically, the government announced that it would implement: the Senior Persons regime, including criminal charges for reckless misconduct; new banking standards rules to cover all bank staff (a licensing regime); and would reverse the burden of proof so that 'Bank bosses are held accountable for breaches within their areas of responsibility' (ibid.: 6). These large, framework changes were then incorporated into the Financial Services (Banking Reform) Act 2013, and the Treasury announced in March 2015 that the Senior Managers and Certified Persons Regime would come into force on 7 March 2016.

As is often the case however, the devil is in the crucial details and as the Financial Conduct Authority took the lead in working out the specifics of the new accountability regimes the struggles between efforts to strengthen the rule of law and addressing the legitimacy crisis became even more apparent. The initial response of the FCA was broadly in line with the governmental statement: senior persons would require regulatory approval before they took up their post; and they would be required to formally accept a written Statement of Responsibilities, helping regulators to hold these individuals to account in the event of failure (FCA 2013: 5–6). The FCA also agreed to extend the period of time between the regulator learning of an offence and taking enforcement action against individuals from the three years to six years. This too would increase the likelihood of enforcement action being taken (ibid.: 7). In July 2014, the FCA and PRA then issued a consultation paper to gather views on: the Senior Managers Regime; a Certification Regime, requiring firms to assess the propriety of certain employees who could pose a significant risk to the firm; and a new set of 'Conduct Rules' (FCA and PRA 2014: 5). Since the best evidence of the struggle between strengthening the rule of law and addressing the legitimacy crisis is provided by the SMR we will focus our attention there. What we will see is that: firstly, in the struggle between more conservative and more radical political agents the final outcome of the SMR swung back towards a more conservative interpretation; secondly however, the struggle between radicals and conservatives still centered around an unhelpfully narrow debate on bank culture.

In the consultation paper, under the SMR, the major features introduced by the Banking Reform Act (2013) remained in place: the requirement for applications for approval as a senior manager, and the potential criminal liability for reckless behaviour. Most importantly though, in the consultation paper, the authorities continued to take the line that 'if a firm contravenes a relevant requirement, the senior manager responsible for the area where the contravention has occurred could be held accountable if they are *unable to satisfy* the regulators that they have taken "reasonable steps"' (emphasis added FCA and PRA 2014: 13). It went on to explain that this new requirement would not establish a strict liability regime, meaning that determining whether the manager had taken 'reasonable steps' would be decided on a case-by-case basis. The authorities did note however that the new requirement would place the evidential burden on those senior managers who 'should have the knowledge and authority to prevent or tackle regulatory failure' (ibid.: 52). It was therefore likened to a 'guilty until proven innocent' approach (Reuters 2015b). The result was that if the Senior Managers Regime was the cornerstone of the regulatory response to the culture problem, then the 'Presumption of Responsibility [was] the most headline grabbing aspect of the new regime' (Allen and Overy 2015).

In the March 2015 summary of the industry responses to the July 2014 consultation it became even more apparent that the 'presumption of responsibility' (reversing the burden of proof) was the most controversial element of the reform bill (FCA and PRA 2015: 7). Yet, despite some clarifications on how the 'presumption' would work in practice, by the July 2015 Regulatory Statement responding to industry concerns, the 'presumption of responsibility' remained intact (PRA 2015: 9, 13–15). Up to this point, both the FCA and the PRA had remained supportive of the clause, stating that it would address 'a key concern…that bankers have not taken their regulatory responsibilities seriously…while, at the same time, making it easier for us to take action against individuals who have not' properly discharged their responsibilities (FCA 2013: 7–8). Again, the value-laden language protecting the pristine market by placing blame firmly at the feet of 'bad bankers' is rather stark.

In the early hours of 15 October 2015 however, press releases began to emerge indicating a dramatic U-turn by the British government. In a draft bill intended to extend the senior managers and certification regime to other areas of the financial services industry, the government shockingly and unilaterally dropped the reverse burden of proof clause and returned to the pre-crisis position that it would be the responsibility of the regulator to prove the indiscretion rather than responsibility lying with the manager him/her self (HMT 2015: 11, *FT* 2015a, Interview 20170511). This was a radical reversal of the initial commitment to cultural reform, which would have made enforcement and prosecutions significantly easier. The reason for the weakened approach was straightforward: with news that the new regime would be extended across all segments of the banking sector, the banking industry itself had lobbied extensively through 2014/15 against the burden of proof clause; and in addition, by late 2015, 'memories of the 2008 banking crisis had started to fade' (Huffington Post 2015).

The FCA, which had favoured a tough approach, was bewildered by the change. In its response to the Treasury announcement, the regulator stated that 'the Government now considers it appropriate to…replace the presumption of responsibility for senior managers with a duty of responsibility' (FCA 2015). Tracy McDermott, the then acting chief executive of the FCA went on to explain the apparent turnaround by highlighting that 'there [had] been significant industry focus on this one, small element of the reforms' (ibid.). It meant however, that 'behind closed doors…the regulators [saw] this U-turn as a setback for their enforcement agendas' (Allen and Overy 2015). Following the announcement—and despite the U-turn, criminal sanctions for the reckless management of a bank were nonetheless incorporated into s.36 of the Financial Services (Banking Reform) Act 2013. But this was clearly a weakened version of the SMR as a result of the political struggles that had influenced it. More conservative forces—coupled with the bank lobby—had triumphed. But the real victim was the broader debate, not on individual instances of *misconduct* which broke from the accepted norms and rules of the industry, but on the accepted norms and rules of the industry itself. These norms—the true *culture* of banking—has far more to do with the structural conditions of financialization, I argue, than could possibly be captured by the narrow political debate that framed the Senior Managers regime.

Electrifying the Ring-fence

As we mentioned in Chapter 6, a major piece of the first wave of responses to the financial crisis in the UK was the ring-fencing recommendations of the Independent Commission on Banking, led by Sir John Vickers. On 14 June 2012 the government published a white paper on the measures it proposed to adopt based on the Final Report of the Independent Commission on Banking (ICB). The manipulation of LIBOR which came to the fore in the summer of 2012 however, lead state managers to revisit the conclusions of the ICB. The 'banks and their employees had suddenly crossed a line. They no longer appeared to be greedy and/or incompetent... [but] "cheats" and "fixers" in ways that most people could intuitively understand as being wrong' (HC Note 2013: 21). The bad behaviour narrative was a particularly compelling explanation of the LIBOR debacle. It was therefore a 'tipping point', requiring a 'strong[er] political response' (ibid.). Parliament thus established the Parliamentary Commission on Banking Standards (PCBS) to examine the 'culture of the UK banking sector' (HM Treasury 2013b: 5). This was a qualitatively new phase in the struggle to manage the so-called British Dilemma—maintaining the City's position as a global financial centre without imposing unreasonable costs on UK taxpayers—since the Vickers Commission had only been required to examine bank structures rather than the root causes of poor professional standards and culture (PCBS 2013a: 170, Interview 20150625 2015).

Here again, there was clear evidence of a struggle between efforts to strengthen the rule of law (tightening the market mechanism) to respond to the legitimacy crisis, and yet to avoid overly stringent measures on the part of the Conservative leadership. Where Vickers had emphasized the structural features of the largest banks that gave rise to the implicit government guarantee and distorted competition, the PCBS was tasked with addressing the pernicious practices that negatively impacted the 'integrity and probity' of the UK's banking system and damaged its reputation as a global financial center (PCBS 2013a: 83).

In its first report, published December 2012, the government had asked the PCBS to conduct pre-legislative scrutiny of the draft Financial Services (Banking Reform) Bill, with a particular focus on the Vickers ring-fence, in light of LIBOR. The PCBS quickly noted that '[t]he separation of deposit-taking from certain investment banking activities can offer benefits not just for financial stability, but also in helping to address the damage done to standards and culture in banking' (PCBS 2012: 5). Highlighting the political struggle underlying these reform efforts though, the Commission argued that the ring-fence risked being eroded over time, due to 'pressure from bank lobbying, possibly supported by politicians' (ibid.). Attempts to address the legitimacy crisis for the state, and the credibility crisis facing the banking sector would be undermined by overly deferential state managers and the bank lobby. The Commission therefore proposed *electrifying* the ring-fence—meaning that banks would face additional disincentives to test the limits of the ring-fence. Three important features of the recommendations are worth noting: if the regulator were to judge that a bank were at risk of breaching the ring-fence, the regulator should have the power to enforce full separation of the bank (a radical option that had been dismissed by the Vickers Commission); a periodic review of the effectiveness of the ring-fence across all banks would be conducted; and these measures would be set out in statutory—rather than secondary—legislation, which would prevent excessive bank lobbying influence over the all-important details (PCBS 2012).

The challenge posed by bank lobbying and overly deferential state managers formed a major theme of this first report. The Commission discussed comments by Sir Mervyn King, who expressed alarm at the lack of independence and resilience of the regulatory authorities in the face of bank lobbying (ibid.: 38); and similar comments were made by Andrew Bailey of the Bank of England (ibid.: 36). The PCBS was particularly persuaded however, by the views of Paul Volcker, the architect of the US proprietary trading rule, who explained that it was the persistent probing at the limits and application of the post-1929 Glass–Steagall Act that had led to the breakdown of the full separation of retail and investment banking activities during the 1980s and 1990s (PCBS 2013a: 5–6). The Commission therefore warned that for any ring-fence framework to be sufficiently robust it would need to resist 'the siren voices of those who contend that structural separation as implemented represents a barrier to financial innovation and growth'. And that 'Politicians need to face up to the possibility that they may prefer those siren voices to the precautionary approach of regulators, particularly if, once again, it appears that banks are performing alchemy', turning base metal into gold (PCBS 2012: 40).

In February 2013 then, the Government published its response to the first report of the PCBS, explaining which recommendations of the PCBS it was incorporating into the Financial Services (Banking Reform) Bill (HMT and BIS 2013). It confirmed that the government would 'amend the Bill to include provisions giving the regulator the power to enforce full separation between retail and wholesale banking in a specified group' (ibid.: 16). It therefore introduced a new section (142K5) into clause 4 of the Banking Reform Bill which was directly lifted from the PCBS recommendation, stipulating that separation of a group would be required if the conduct of the bank 'was having an adverse affect on the regulators advancement of its continuity objective' (HMT 2013b: 3). It also introduced a further three conditions for triggering full separation however, in cases where the banking group had 'repeatedly been able to find creative ways to abide by the letter of the rules while still subverting the purpose' (ibid.: 4).

In short, this was a dramatic change that allowed the regulator to enforce the spirit of the law rather than simply adherence to the details. As George Osborne subsequently explained, this reserve power was possibly 'the most powerful tool' the regulator could have (PCBS 2013a: 8). The 'electrification' of the ring-fence was passed into legislation in December 2013. As with the Senior Managers Regime the changes to the bank ring-fence rules marked an important shift in the emphasis of UK state managers, away from simply focusing on big structural issues of resolution and stability, and towards a focus on bank culture. It was a further example of a compromise between radicals and conservatives—this time closer to the starting position of the radical elites. But, once again, it only served to reinforce that the bank culture debate should be focused on establishing the right market norms for socially responsible conduct.

Bank Levies

Alongside the new legislation and increased emphasis on fines and prosecutions, UK state managers also used a series of bank levies to address the unfolding legitimacy crisis. Once again, these levies were framed by a populist narrative; taxing the banks and forcing them to pay reparations for the financial crisis was perceived to be an appropriate means of re-asserting the autonomy of the state. The first of these was a levy on banks' balance sheets introduced in June 2010. Though the levy itself was introduced prior to LIBOR and the worsening legitimacy crisis, it is discussed in this chapter for two main reasons: one was that aside from being a modest attempt to repay some of the costs of the bank bailouts the structure of the levy also had a culture dimension; the other reason though was that the politics behind the levy, both at the outset and in subsequent years, reveals the struggles in the UK between attempts to address the legitimacy crisis whilst also remaining deferential to the financial sector.

In December 2009, the Labour Chancellor Alistair Darling announced a bank payroll tax: 'a special one off levy of 50% on any individual discretionary bonus above £25,000' (House of Commons 2015: 3). It was anticipated to be only a temporary measure and raise approximately £500 million. But by the time of the March 2010 budget it had become apparent that the payroll tax had yielded approximately £3.5 billion in gross terms (ibid.). In June 2010 the incoming coalition government then announced a new levy which would apply to the balance sheets of UK banks and building societies, and to the UK operations of banks from abroad. It was anticipated to raise approximately £2 billion in annual revenues.

Function 1: Enhancing Legitimacy

At face value, the connection between the bank levy and issues of culture and the legitimacy crisis might not be apparent. But the levy had two functions which support the core argument of this chapter. Firstly, though both the Labour and Coalition government levies were ostensibly designed to raise annual revenues, and repay some costs of the government bailouts of the financial sector, the subtext revealed legitimacy-enhancing objectives. The changing focus of the bank levy also supported the legitimacy enhancing function: initially, the Labour levy was targeted at bonus payments. This reflected the fact that 'public interest in a sort of windfall tax on the banking sector grew...over the year 2009, as some major banks return to profitability, and with this the expectation that several thousand in the City would receive the end of year bonuses of some considerable size' (House of Commons 2015: 6). Indeed the Financial Services Authority consultation paper (March 2009) which preceded the Labour levy, explained the reason for taxing bonuses, noting that 'higher profits translate into higher bonuses...therefore losses are born by long-term shareholders and society, but only to a small extent by employees and short-term shareholders' (FSA 2009: 21). The ground swell of public opinion in favour of a tax on bankers' bonuses quickly gathered momentum in the second half of 2009 (*FT* 2009a, *Guardian* 2009). Martin Wolf, *Financial Times* columnist, captured this by explaining that 'ordinary people can accept that risk-takers receive huge rewards. But such rewards for those who have been rescued by the state and bear substantial responsibility for the crisis are surely intolerable.' Thus 'windfall support', referring to the state bailouts of the banking sector, 'should be matched by windfall taxes'. He went on to explain that 'the time has come for some carefully judged populism. A one-off windfall tax on bonuses would make the pain ahead for society so very much more bearable' (*FT* 2009b). The size of the levy in financial terms was arguably less important than the political message which the levy was intended to send.

By the time the coalition government took office the objective of the second round of bank levies had altered somewhat. This time, rather than taxing bonuses, the levy was applied to the balance sheets of the banks. As we shall see, this was a not insignificant change, since it placed less emphasis on the salaries of individual bankers, and it became a more traditional fiscal instrument. Unsurprisingly, it also captured the conservative classes' attempt to shift attention away from high wages in the finance sector. The balance sheet levy had been the original position of the Liberal Democrat business secretary Vince Cable—an otherwise quite radical challenger to the banks—when Alistair Darling had announced the Labour levy. Cable had contended that it made no sense 'to try to tax bankers separately from other high earners, but to have a levy on bank profits because the banks depend on a taxpayer guarantee' (Vince Cable, House of Commons 2009, c.376). The reason that it appealed to the new Conservative leadership was that it represented a workable compromise: on the one hand it gave the impression of equity, with the state distributing the cost burden onto both the banks and taxpayers; whilst on the other hand it allowed bonuses to return to normal, a far more sensitive issue for the bank lobby. As the Chancellor of the Exchequer explained to the Treasury Select Committee, 'asking the general population to accept a VAT rise, asking them to accept that there were going to be changes to welfare eligibility and the like, doing these things is a difficult thing for any government to do but I thought it would be totally inappropriate not to ask the banking sector to make a contribution as well' (TSC 2010b, Q270). Beyond the benefits to annual revenue then, the objective of the levy was to ensure 'that banks make a fair contribution in respect of the potential risks they posed to the UK financial system and the wider economy' (ibid.). This language was lifted directly from a parallel IMF report which also spoke of 'the financial sector [making] a fairer and substantial contribution towards paying for any burden associated with government interventions to repair the banking system' (IMF 2010: 4). Alongside measures such as the Project Merlin lending targets, the levy was an attempt to redress the impression that—having been saved by the government—the British banking sector was refusing to aid the economic recovery. Indeed the budget report which accompanied the announcement of the levy explained that it was intended to rebalance 'the burden of taxation between banking and other sectors' (House of Commons 2010a: 26).

Function 2: Influencing Culture

The second function of the levy was ostensibly to promote a change of behaviour and strategy on the part of the banks. This culture-related objective was apparent in both the original Labour levy and that of the subsequent coalition government. As Alistair Darling explained the aim of the Labour levy to the Treasury Select Committee, he noted that 'the reason we have introduced this measure—and it is not a great revenue raiser; it does not bring in that much—is to send a clear signal that *we need to change behaviour*...That means if you want yourselves off the front pages...show the sort of restraint that the general public would want you to' (emphasis added , TSC 2009a, Q 243). Again, Darling saw this as an attempt to discourage conduct that deviated from proper market norms. Though he repeatedly emphasized that this was a one off charge—meaning that it would not subsequently be used to punish misconduct or non-compliance—it was an early warning shot.

When it came to the Coalition government levy however, the tax was structured in such a way as to encourage banks to move to less risky funding profiles, and encourage the banks 'to lend more' (David Gauke, Treasury Minister, House of Commons 2010b c.725). The government explained that a tax simply based on profits—such as the corporation tax—is not related to risk and would 'not create the behavioural effect' that the bank levy could (ibid.), whereas 'the intention [of this particular levy was] to find a means of discouraging risk' (ibid.). This goal would be achieved through the targeted exemption of certain funding sources from the levy. For example, insured deposits would not be included in the taxes for the bank levy, whereas wholesale funding would be. As was discussed in Chapter 2, large exposures to wholesale funding markets tended to be a cause of instability during the financial crisis, when these funding markets dried up. As such, by taxing the banks' reliance on shorter term wholesale funding, the coalition government aimed to 'encourage banks to move to a less risky, longer term funding', shifting from short term interbank (wholesale) loans to longer term debt and equity (*Tax Journal* 2012).

Beyond the two stated functions of the levy however, there was once again evidence of the struggles between managing the legitimacy crisis and protecting financialization and City interests which form the basis for this chapter. This was particularly apparent in two further details of the Conservative-led levy. Firstly, as noted above, the shift from a levy on bonuses to a levy on balance sheets was a particularly important and telling change. Even as the Coalition government levy was being introduced in 2010/11 it was accompanied by a staged reduction in the main rate of corporation tax from 28 per cent to 24 per cent over the course of four financial years from April 2011. This was projected to cost £2.7 billion by 2014/15, whereas the new levy itself was projected to raise only £2.4 billion by 2014/15 (House of Commons 2010a: 3, 40). In other words, the levy introduced by the new coalition government was ultimately a point-scoring, populist exercise, since—on balance—it actually produced no overall positive gains to the annual revenue.

Secondly, once the Liberal Democrats were no longer part of the coalition government, the Conservative government quickly scaled back the levy. This was partly due to mounting criticism that the levy was proving less and less effective and a consensus amongst analysts at the banks that the levy was poorly structured. For example, including foreign banks' and UK banks' foreign operations was a major source of criticism; as was the fact that particular banks were unequally targeted. This applied most especially to HSBC, which despite having a large part of its balance sheet overseas and having received no direct government supports during the financial crisis, continued to pay a disproportionately high share (one-third) of the levy (*FT* 2015c). But, as we will argue towards the end of this chapter, the phased reduction of the bank levy rate—from 0.21 per cent in 2015 to 0.10 per cent by January 2021—also reflected a change in approach of the Tory government to the banking sector.

Put simply, the first part of this chapter has examined a range of 'harder' approaches employed by British state managers to tackle the culture of banking debate. The bank levy was one particularly important example of this, as were increased prosecutions (the focus of later chapters) and new legislation such as the Senior Managers Regime. The chapter has argued thus far that these tough approaches were shaped by two goals: improving the market mechanism as a means to influence banker conduct; and addressing the nascent legitimacy crisis. But it has also pointed to the fact that at various points along the way Conservative leadership sought to draw a line under the reform process and stop the so-called banker-bashing. In the next section we will examine some of the softer approaches employed by these same state managers, before returning to this theme of a more diluted conservative approach to the banks at the end of this chapter.

The Soft Approach

As was the case in the United States, British state managers pursued two overlapping yet relatively distinct strategies: a 'harder' approach focused on legislation and prosecutions; and a 'softer' approach based on standard and norm-setting that will now be discussed in this section of the chapter. Beyond tightening market discipline this was part of what the ordo-liberals described as constructing the economic constitution, educating bankers in the right market ethics. For our purposes, it also marked the final step to narrow the bank culture debate and deflect scrutiny away from financialization.

Standard-setting

Parliamentary Commission on Banking Standards

The Parliamentary Commission on Banking Standards has already appeared earlier in this chapter in the discussion of bank ring-fencing and the Senior Managers Regime. On 2 July 2012, immediately following the LIBOR revelations, the government announced that a review would be undertaken to ensure that the UK had the 'toughest and most transparent rules of any major financial sector' (Cameron 2012). Beyond considering the specifics of LIBOR and whether it should be more tightly regulated, the aim was to examine 'the adequacy of the UK's current civil and criminal sanctioning powers, with respect to financial misconduct and market abuse' (TSC 2012: 10). More specifically though, in relation to the big theme of this book, there was an explicit focus on 'professional standards and of the culture of the financial services industry that was allowed to grow up in the years before the crisis and which still needs to change' (ibid.: 11). Then, on 16 July, the House of Commons also instigated a review, initiated by the newly formed Parliamentary Commission on Banking Standards.

Similar reviews had been initiated at earlier stages in the crisis (the Turner Review, the Walker Review, and the private Bischoff Report). Yet the scandals surrounding LIBOR made the legitimacy crisis significantly more problematic than it had been in earlier years. Evidence of this can be seen in how the British government responded. During the first phase of the financial crisis, the Labour government had refused to establish a public commission to review the banking industry and its standards. So great was the public outcry over the LIBOR scandal however, that the prime minister, David Cameron, agreed to 'support Parliament in setting up the Parliamentary Commission on Banking Standards' (HMT & BIS 2013: 3). The goal of the Commission was explicitly to restore 'society's faith in the banking system' (ibid.). As I noted earlier though, no single institution was as influential as the PCBS in explicitly defining the terms of the bank culture debate. It was almost entirely responsible for spearheading the UK's ethical campaign to improve conduct; it crystallized the view that problems lay in bad behaviour rather than the financialized market itself; and it proved to be the role model for the New York Federal Reserve's later culture agenda.

Banking Standards Board

As noted, the PCBS proceeded to make important (hard) legislative recommendations. In terms of softer, standard-setting measures however, the PCBS also recommended, as part of its final report, creating a professional body, funded by the industry, to promote higher professional standards. Initially titled the Banking Standards Review Council before changing to the Banking Standards Board (BSB), the body was established and funded by six of the UK's largest banks, including Barclays, HSBC, Santander, Lloyds, RBS, and Standard Chartered (Interview 20150618). Each of the member organizations would submit a range of information on an annual basis covering, for example, customer complaints, banker conduct, and bank culture. The data would then be included in an annual report that would show how well members were performing against the body's standards. In comparison to the US case, this was a relatively original approach to the idea that reforming bank culture was more than simply abiding by the letter of the law.[2] As the first chairman of the Board explained, 'regulators [were supportive of the body because] they want us to be in a world—which some of the banks don't want to be in—where just following the letter of the rulebook is not enough' (Richard Lambert, cited in *WSJ* 2014b). In reality though, most UK banks were more than happy to collaborate with the BSB because it constituted a relatively weak, non-binding agency with no enforcement powers. Though—as I will show in Chapter 9—values and ethics have indeed improved somewhat as a result of the normative, standard-setting agenda, if the BSB was the culmination of the narrow bank culture debate then it simply reinforced how far removed the political classes had become from the underlying structural causes of bad bank culture.

From 2014 the Board was then lead by Dame Collette Bowe, a former regulator and chairwoman of a private equity firm. It set about its work in two stages: Firstly determining a set of appropriate standards; and then secondly monitoring compliance on an annual basis. The target for the first round of their analysis would be the corporate governance boards of the banks themselves. The BSB therefore saw its function as more of a 'mirror' asking board members 'what have you been doing to improve behaviour, culture, capability? And what evidence do you have that it is working?' (Interview 20150618). Rather than a process of naming and shaming however, the BSB described its function as 'aspirational', stating that it was 'trying to go above and beyond the [regulatory] rules' (ibid.). The strategy was to examine existing ethics, values and practices, and then to suggest modifications in order to bring outliers better in line with proper market conduct.

Starting in August 2015, the BSB conducted an initial qualitative assessment of its six founding member firms, plus Nationwide and an additional three member firms, Metro Bank, Citibank, and Morgan Stanley. The Board conducted a

[2] In the case of the US, as we saw, banking ethics and culture were primarily part of the remit of the New York Federal reserve; whilst in Malaysia, a new industry lead body called the Financial vices Professional Board in 2014 to improve the professionalism and ethical behaviour.

high-level review in three parts: the first part focused on the board-level and asked 'what is your purpose; what do you stand for? And how do embed that into your culture?'; the second part focused on executives and asked how they rewarded and disciplined employees; finally, the BSB ran a series of employee focus groups to gather their views on culture and values within the ten firms. The results were then compiled into individual reports which were presented to the boards of the banks (Interview 20160601). As we demonstrated in Chapter 2, the assumption was that if values and strategies could be better aligned, then culture would be improved. By implication, most market participants intuitively knew the right kind of market behaviours, but their strategies were often at odds with their values.

Then in 2016, working alongside London Business School and the London School of Economics, the BSB disseminated 75,000 employee surveys across a wider range of firms. The aim was to be able to present to the firms a comparative analysis of where particular divisions of their bank sat in comparison to culture, ethics, and values in similar divisions of other banks. The BSB also ran board level interviews and focus groups again, as well as introducing a series of interviews with the remuneration committees (Interview 20160601). From the outset however, many of the issues we have focused on in this chapter were evident in the establishment and working of the Banking Standards Board. One of the main concerns was that the board remained completely independent of the regulatory process and lacked any formal disciplinary measures for those firms lagging behind cultural reform standards. In other words, some critics claimed that the BSB was merely 'a nod to public opinion'—that is, a populist attempt to address the credibility crisis—rather than 'a serious attempt to improve standards' (Mark Garnier, Conservative member of the PCBS, cited in *WSJ* 2014b, Interview 20150703). Indeed, the main aim of the annual review process was arguably targeted at boosting the banks' reputational standing with the public (*Guardian* 2015b). As with much of the bank culture debate, the workings of the BSB had a highly performative dimension aimed at showing that both the political classes and the banks were actively focusing on bank culture—without requiring substantive structural changes.

Fair and Effective Markets Review

A second strand of the 'softer' response to the legitimacy crisis was the Fair and Effective Markets Review (FEMR). It was established by the British Chancellor in 2014 to examine measures to restore trust in the wholesale financial markets. If the PCBS was a direct response to the LIBOR debacle and aimed at fixing banking more specifically, then the FEMR was a response to the foreign exchange scandal and considered trust in financial markets more broadly. The Forex scandal came to light in February 2014 when the Financial Conduct Authority, the Hong Kong Markets Authority, and the New York Department of Financial Services requested further information from the banks in response to allegations of alleged manipulation of the FX benchmark (CityAM 2014a). This was not just another case of a scandal harming the credibility of the banking system; claims quickly emerged that a Bank of England staff member had either encouraged or ignored traders' attempts to manipulate the benchmark (CityAM 2014b). The reputational damage therefore spread to the Bank of England itself with the Governor, Mark Carney, vowing to 'ruthlessly, relentlessly follow through with the investigation' (ibid.).

The FEMR was conducted by the Treasury, the Financial Conduct Authority, and the Bank of England, and examined fixed income, currency, and commodity (FICC) markets that are at the heart of the financial system. These markets affect the borrowing costs of households, companies, and governments, as well as affecting exchange rates and the cost of everyday commodities (Minouche Shafik, cited in *FT* 2014c). In particular though, the fact that the UK was a market leader in foreign exchange transactions once again meant that the credibility crisis (this time provoked by the Forex scandal) had an international dimension to it; as George Osborne himself explained when discussing the FEMR, 'the integrity of the City matters to the British economy just as much as it does to London's status as an international banking and markets hub' (cited in *FT* 2014d). The political response was therefore heavily shaped by an attempt to restore credibility, for both the City and the state.

One of the major recommendations of the FEMR was an extension of the Senior Managers and Certification Regime beyond banking, to cover insurers, investment firms, and consumer credit firms; the range of financial instruments that would carry prison sentences if they were rigged was extended; and the maximum jail sentence was also extended from seven to ten years (BoE 2015). By October 2015, the government had responded to these demands, given the gravity of the Forex case (HMT 2015: 9). Yet the FEMR was a prime example of the fact that the legitimacy crisis facing the City and UK state managers was a problem that refused to go away. This sentiment—of the need for a stronger state and public legitimacy—was reflected by Mark Carney as he prepared to unveil the FEMR. Firstly, he noted that 'though markets can be powerful drivers of prosperity, markets can go wrong. Left unattended, they are prone to instability, excess and abuse' (cited in the *Telegraph* 2015), explaining the rationale for tougher sanctions. Interestingly though, the focus of the political response was on the latter two dimensions—excess and abuse—in keeping with the liberal confidence in 'the market' itself; human weakness was the problem, rather than an inherent flaw in the market mechanism itself—or, more specifically, the structure of the financialized markets of Anglo-America. Secondly, Carney also noted though that 'markets are not ends in themselves, but powerful means for prosperity and security for all. As such they need to retain the consent of society—a social licence—to be allowed to operate, innovate and grow' (ibid.). Any potential confusion in his first comments, which might have implied a fault in the market, was discarded. Instead, his main concern—aside from regulating excess—was to restore public trust that was required for the efficient functioning and longevity of the market. Hence the FEMR had a dual function in strengthening the state and restoring legitimacy.

Remuneration Changes

A third and final strand to the softer responses of UK state managers involved changes to remuneration policy. Once again, as was the case in the US, the connections between remuneration (annual pay and bonuses) and conduct was clear to UK state managers early in the financial crisis. In the Turner review for example, the FSA noted that 'higher apparent profits and higher bonuses…reinforced management and traders' certainty that they were pursuing sensible strategies' (FSA 2009b: 25). More specifically, 'illusory profits were…used as the basis for bonus decisions, and created incentives for traders and management to take further risks' (ibid.: 48). The review explained that other factors, such as dominant personalities, also played a significant role in the strategies of financial institutions and that proving a direct causal link between remuneration and risk-taking was problematic. But the key point, according to a FSA consultation paper, was that 'the balance of risk and reward offered by poor remuneration policies is unequal. Employees have the incentive of substantial and immediate reward if risky strategies are successful and remuneration is not deferred. If the strategies are unsuccessful, the loss to the employee is limited' (FSA 2009c: 160). Simply put, 'the design of bonus schemes and the banking sector were…not aligned with the interests of shareholders and the long-term sustainability of the banks' (TSC 2009d: 15). Once again, probing questions about *why* exactly bonuses in the banking were so high (in aggregate terms) and whether pay in the financial sector genuinely reflected the contribution of the banks to the economy, were avoided. Instead the emphasis was placed on promoting more socially sustainable bonus policy, to reduce *excessive* risk-taking. On this reading, excessive was implicitly defined as stability-threatening. Again the aim was to protect financialization from the financiers.

The fact that the crisis had created a political opening (read necessity) for state managers to intervene was also therefore a significant shift from the 2005–6 regulatory culture (TSC 2009d: 19). Indeed, the Treasury Select Committee was critical of the FSA's approach to remuneration, questioning whether the regulator had 'attached sufficient priority to tackling remuneration in the City' (TSC 2009d: 3). Importantly though, divisions (momentarily) emerged amongst state managers over whether or not the regulator should play a role in determining the actual *level* of the remuneration, or simply the *structure* of the pay. For its part, the FSA emphasized a focus only on the structure of remuneration (FSA 2009b: 28); whereas the Select Committee clearly stated that 'it should be the FSA's function to regulate levels or the amount of pay within the banking sector' (TSC 2009d: 22). This was one of those rare instances where more radical voices asserted themselves and sought to broaden the debate a little. In due course the bonus debate gathered some steam, assisted by impending EU initiatives.

By early 2010, as the bailed out banks began to return to (a degree of) stability the legitimacy crisis proved to be one driver for the debate on bonuses. Though bonuses had dropped marginally in 2009, a survey in February 2010 revealed that bankers working in London had received average bonus increases of 40 per cent (Reuters 2010). Around the same time, a YouGov poll revealed the growing popular resentment towards these pay increases, indicating that 76 per cent of respondents supported a cap on bankers bonuses (*Guardian* 2010). Despite the Labour government's one-off tax on bonuses however and minor amendments to remuneration in the Financial Services Act 2010, the first *major* changes to the UK Remuneration Code (in December 2010) came as a result of the Principles for Sound Compensation Practices issued by the Financial Stability Board (2009), the EU Capital Requirements Directive (CRD3), and the tougher new rules introduced by the Committee of European Banking Supervisors (CEBS), rather than from the UK government (*Telegraph* 2010). The new EU guidelines also began with the conclusion that 'excessive remuneration in the financial sector fuelled a risk appetite that was disproportionate to the loss-absorption capacity of institutions and of the financial sector as a whole' (CEBS 2010: 7). This was not a debate about the root causes of high pay in the finance sector, but it nonetheless presented more of a challenge to the bonus culture than conservative state managers would have desired.

The FSA's existing Remuneration Code applied to the largest banks, building societies, and broker dealers and was intended to require firms to apply 'remuneration policies . . . that are consistent with and promote effective risk management' (FSA 2006: 12). There was little evidence though in the lead up to the financial crisis that the FSA Code had been effective. With the CRD3 the proportion of remuneration paid in shares increased; this variable remuneration paid in shares was made subject to a 'retention period'; and the Code was extended to a larger group of firms. This meant that, importantly, at least 50 per cent of the variable remuneration (the bonus) should be paid in shares or equivalent ownership interests, thereby reducing the amount of cash-like instruments in the bonus package (CEBS 2010: 61); and at least 70 per cent of the remuneration should be deferred (ibid.: 65). The main aim of these first two revisions to the Code—increased remuneration in shares, and the retention period—was to more closely align remuneration with the performance of the firm as a whole, and to dilute the emphasis on short-term profits. The measures were also intended to act as an antidote to the pre-crisis culture of bankers threatening to join rival firms unless bonus demands were met; any such decision would mean potentially forfeiting up to four years of deferred payment (ibid.: 38, Interview 20161107).

Equally importantly, the FCA adopted the definitions of the European Union, extending the Remuneration Code from senior managers and the board of directors to cover senior traders—defined as Material Risk Takers. Material Risk Takers were 'staff including senior management, risk takers, staff engaged in control functions and any employee receiving total remuneration that takes them into the same remuneration bracket as senior management and risk takers, whose professional activities have a material impact on the firm's risk profile' (FCA, SYSC: 19A.3.4).

As the banks entered 2011 it became clear that the Conservative-led coalition government wanted to adopt a more sympathetic stance on bonuses than the spirit of the CRD III rules demanded. This was also evidence of a truce on bank bonuses between the Conservative government and the largest five British banks. Public anger demanded greater transparency over bank bonuses, hence the largest banks agreed to publish the pay of their five highest paid executives below board level; but they secured a deal with the government whereby top-earning traders without managerial responsibility would avoid this requirement. The banks explained that this was a response to 'the public mood' (Project Merlin 2011:4). By the end of 2011, the government released a proposal for disclosure of the remuneration of the eight most senior executives in order to 'enhance the transparency of the relationship between risk and reward... in the largest banking institutions' (HMT 2011: 9).

By 2012, bonuses were back on the agenda, as public outrage spiralled out of control following the LIBOR revelations. In total, remuneration appeared 373 times in the 500-page report produced by the PCBS. In keeping with the argument about the heightened legitimacy crisis sparked by LIBOR, the PCBS duly noted that the 'public perception of bankers' remuneration, and particularly their bonuses, remain drivers of anger against banks and bankers' (PCBS 2013a: 102). As emphasized above, it was not simply the high salaries in an abstract sense that fuelled this outrage but the perception that the 'salaries, bonuses, and remuneration packages of very senior bankers... have not been visibly affected by the financial crisis which has brought austerity to the doorstep of most families' (ibid.). The PCBS therefore recommended introducing a new statutory code which would give regulators new powers over remuneration.

In its response (July 2013), the government also confirmed this view that 'at the root of the financial crisis was the development of fundamentally improper risk appetite within financial institutions, driven by inappropriate incentive structures for individual bankers' (HMT 2013 & BIS : 13). The government however rejected the PCBS's calls for a new Code, arguing that it could achieve the desired objectives through the existing Remuneration Code which had recently been amended in the UK. Indeed, the British government had already rejected other, international, challenges to its revised remuneration standards. In the negotiations over the EU Capital Requirements Directive (CRD4) for example, European authorities had concluded that bonuses would be limited to no more than 100 per cent of fixed pay. The British government had challenged this, raising concerns that this may only lead to increases in fixed pay. This would be problematic in the sense that fixed pay could not be called back in instances of malpractice, nor was it performance related. It would also mean that banks could not reduce remuneration quickly during financial difficulties, since fixed pay is harder to cut. The government therefore stipulated that its own amended Remuneration Code—revised in 2011 to incorporate the CRD3—was already sufficiently robust. It applied to senior management, risk-takers, and staffing control functions; required at least 40 per cent of the bonus to be deferred for at least three years; in the case of individuals whose bonus was more than £500,000, it required that at least 60 per cent be deferred; and the UK remuneration code also stipulated that at least 50 per cent of any bonus must be made in shares or other equivalent of non-cash instruments (FCA 2015c).

The position of the UK government on further amendments to the revised Remuneration Code was—at one level—simply a pragmatic and logical response. In their view, though incentive structures were an important determinant of bank behaviour and culture, the changes already introduced had remedied the misalignment of incentives present in the pre-crisis period. Despite the quasi-populist outrage following LIBOR there was therefore no need for further tampering. Beyond the pragmatic stance of the Conservative leadership however, a more disturbing shift was taking place. It was evident in the Merlin negotiations (2011); it had been challenged by the LIBOR revelations (2012); but by early 2014 it had returned, as Conservative state managers sought to draw a line under reform efforts and the bank culture debate and—once again—the British state tried to return to a deferential approach to the financial elite. The financialized UK economy had been saved; the worst of the public outrage at austerity had arguably passed; and it was now time to return to business as usual. It was time to lay the (narrow) bank culture debate to rest.

Closing Remarks and 2015 Weakening

One of the main aims of this chapter has been to map the contours of the struggle between attempts to strengthen the rule of law on the part of certain state agencies (variably, the FCA, the Select Committee and Commission on Banking Standards, and the Bank of England); attempts to deal with the legitimacy crisis whilst wishing to remain deferential to the City (on the part of the Conservative government and the Treasury); and the financial elite itself, challenged by its own credibility deficit but ultimately still reliant upon and empowered by the profit-making openings of the financialized British economy. In a similar fashion to what was witnessed in the US, UK authorities sought to strengthen the market mechanism as a means of placing the burden of responsibility for the investment decisions of the banks on their own shoulders. The assumption was that the lack of effective market discipline had allowed bad conduct to proliferate, in turn giving rise to the bank culture problem. The previous chapter discussed this in relation to framework regulations such as resolution. But the same thinking lay behind many of the measures discussed in this chapter, ranging from the Senior Managers Regime, to the electrification of the ring-fence, and the increasing prosecutions and fines.

Equally importantly though, this chapter has also highlighted the pivotal role that the legitimacy crisis played. Against the background of increased austerity, the credibility crisis facing the banking sector threatened to transform into a political crisis of legitimacy for the British state. Under the coalition government (2010–15), the inclusion of more radical, Liberal Democrat voices (in particular, MP Vince Cable), also translated into a tougher response towards the banks. Following the 2015 general election win for the Conservative government however, it quickly became apparent—with the legitimacy crisis subsiding—that UK state managers would also weaken their approach towards the banks. As one City law firm explained in 2015, 'there [were] already... indications that under the new Conservative government, HM Treasury [was] keen to move away from the harsh enforcement approach that the regulators [had been] taking in relation to the banks over the past few years' (Allen and Overy 2015). The need for populist statecraft had apparently subsided. This new approach to banking reform became even more apparent in the Chancellors Mansion House speech (June 2015). An aide to George Osborne was quoted in the lead up to the speech, for example, as saying 'we are in a stable position... [and hence] there is a sense that this is a settlement' between the government and the City of London (cited in *FT* 2015). From the perspective of the bankers, the argument was that 'a chancellor interested in growth should be less tough on them with structural reform' (*Guardian* 2015).

Setting aside the change to the Presumption of Responsibility in the Senior Managers Regime, the other prominent example of the softening approach of UK state managers was the resignation of the FCA's chief Executive, Martin Wheatley, in July 2015, following the decision by the Chancellor George Osborne not to renew his contract. Wheatley was known for his tough approach to banking reform and was clearly surprised by the Chancellor's decision (Interview 20170511 2017). At the FCA's headquarters just days after his resignation, Wheatley explained 'frankly, I'm disappointed to be moving on with a sense of unfinished business' (cited in CityAM 2015).

In short, the main message to take away from the UK and the US cases is that in the midst of (1) the political struggle between radicals and conservatives, concerning (2) tightening market discipline and improving market ethics, and (3) the invocation of populist tactics to pacify the public, the culture of banking debate moved further and further away from a broad-based discussion of the influence of financialization on banking. The results were twofold: firstly, ethics and values become buzzwords in the new world of banking, and compliance-monitoring provided increased levels of scrutiny in a bid to improve market conduct; but, secondly and far more importantly, the structural determinants of bad bank culture were allowed to continue virtually unchecked. Part III of the book now begins to examine the extent of the changes that occurred in banking as a result of the political agenda.

PART III
BANK CHANGES

8
Fines as a Mechanism for Culture Change?

Part II of the book argued that aside from pursuing the liberal project of tightening the market mechanism, US and UK state managers had pursued a secondary objective: addressing a legitimacy crisis. Not only did this lead to a narrowing of the bank culture debate, but allowed the continuation of financialization as a process. Ultimately, this book argues that the legitimacy crisis stems—at least in part—from the inability and unwillingness of US and UK state managers to overcome the financialization of their respective economies. Financialization leads to financial instability; but financialization also leads to socio-economic inequality, contributing to declining levels of trust in the political establishment.

Part III of the book now focuses on the banks. The main aim is to show the limited extent of change in banking culture, despite the extensive resources that have been invested at improving (relatively superficial) matters like ethics, values, and conduct. The present chapter therefore sits somewhere between Part II and Part III of the book. It examines the massive financial penalties levelled against the Anglo-American banks. Judging by the rhetoric state managers attach to these fines, the penalties are clearly meant to have a significant cultural impact. As I will explain in the present chapter and the following Chapter 9, one of these cultural effects is via increased compliance monitoring—to avoid future misconduct. But the main argument of this chapter is that the effect of the fines was significantly more limited than state managers wished to suggest. Instead, in keeping with the argument of Part II of the book, one major purpose of the fines was to address the legitimacy crisis. Big monetary penalties made great headlines and gave the impression that state managers had applied the heavy hand of the law to the offending banks; the reality however is much less black and white.

I focus on the fines in particular because they were perhaps the most striking example of populist statecraft used by radical and conservative elites in both the US and the UK. The fines reflect the fact that state managers were concerned to send a political message to their respective electorates. The intended message was that the political classes were distancing themselves from the embattled banks. But the fines were also somewhat puzzling, because if the only goal was to send a strong political message then alternative measures—such as the prison sentences used in Iceland after the global financial crisis, or after the 1980s Savings and

The Bank Culture Debate: Ethics, Values, and Financialization in Anglo-America. Huw Macartney, Oxford University Press (2019).
DOI: 10.1093/oso/9780198843764.001.0001

Loans Crisis in the US—would arguably have been even better. Why did state managers therefore choose fines rather than prosecutions?

The answer—I argue—is apparent in the subtle details of the fines. Essentially, state managers had a secondary motivation in the fines, to diffuse criticisms of their financialized economies and, to an extent, to protect their biggest banks. I say this, because behind the hard-hitting rhetoric attached to the fines (the political message) the substance of the fines had far less economic impact on the banks, particularly their domestic banks. In fact, the evidence in this chapter suggests that state managers were far less concerned with what happened in the banks—in terms of culture change—than with the political message. In other words, of the two priorities behind the fines—(1) protecting financialization and the banks, and (2) sending a populist message to their electorates—the former was more important than the latter.

The chapter unfolds as follows: firstly, I briefly outline the scale of the fines themselves and the rhetoric state managers used in relation to them; in the second section I explain that if one mechanism for promoting culture change was (purportedly) via an impact on the profitability of the banks, the evidence was not compelling; in the third section I explain how the bank fines simply became a cost of doing business; whilst in the fourth section I explain that via charitable donations and so-called consumer relief a large portion of these fines was written off; then in the sixth and final section I show that even some of the compliance-related conditions attached to the fines were weak and poorly enforced.

Big Fines, Big Impact?

Since the global financial crisis, the banking industry has paid out over $326 billion in financial penalties, with over $150 billion paid by the US financial institutions alone (*FT* 2017) and UK banks paid £66 billion between 2010–14 (*Guardian* 2016b). Bank of America paid more than one-third of that total, with $56 billion in settlements to state and federal regulators and the Department of Justice; and JPMorgan Chase paid out $27 billion in fines. In total, banks paid $42 billion dollars in 2016, a 68 per cent rise on the previous year though lower than the peak of $76 billion in 2014 (Bloomberg 2017a, see Fig. 8.1). The majority of these fines stemmed from money laundering, market manipulation, and terrorist financing, as I explained in the introductory chapter. The bulk of the $150 billion paid by US institutions though—$89 billion—related to allegations of mis-selling mortgage-backed securities.

What was clear, judging by their rhetoric at least, was that Anglo-American state managers also repeatedly contended that these large financial penalties were intended to have a positive impact on bank culture. In the UK, in 2008 the director of enforcement at the UK Financial Services Authority stated, 'it's great

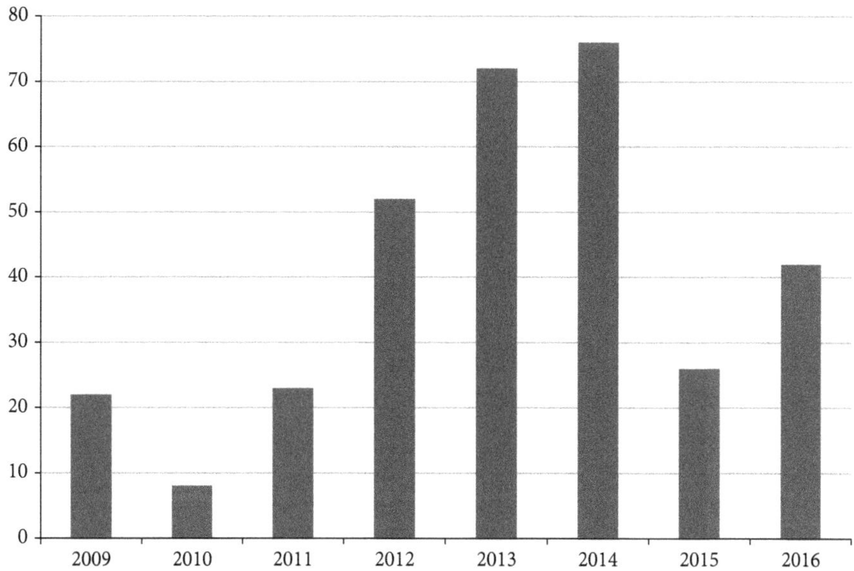

Fig. 8.1 Total financial penalties paid by all banks, 2009–16 (US$ bn)
Source: Author's own calculations, various sources.

to see the FSA hitting companies where it hurts. This record PPI fine should send out a clear message to other companies that mis-selling will be severely punished' (*Guardian* 2008a). In 2010, concerning JPMorgan the FSA again stated 'This penalty sends out a strong message to firms of all sizes... Firms need to sit up and take notice of this action—we have several more cases in the pipeline' (*Guardian* 2010b). Then in 2013, speaking about the fines against RBS, George Osborne stated, 'What happened at RBS and other banks is totally unacceptable. At my insistence, the bankers, not the taxpayers, will pick up the bill' (*Guardian* 2013b). Whilst in 2014, concerning the fines for the Forex scandal, the head of the Financial Conduct Authority (FCA) noted 'The FCA does not tolerate conduct which imperils market integrity or the wider UK financial system. Today's record fines mark the gravity of the failings we found, and firms need to take responsibility for putting it right' (cited in CityAM 2014). In 2015, Tracy McDermott—then head of FCA enforcement explained 'We don't set ourselves targets for the number of fines we will issue in a given period—what we look at is whether the sanctions we do impose are having an impact on behavior' (*Guardian* 2015c). Whilst again in 2017, the new director of enforcement at the FCA stated 'The size of the fine reflects the seriousness of [the bank's] failings' (*Financial Planning Today* 2017). This latter point is worth emphasizing, because it implied that state managers believed that the size of the penalty itself was meant to be a disincentive for misconduct, by affecting profit margins. This is important, because we will argue later in the chapter that the relationship between the size of the penalty and the performance of the firm is not clear. At the very least however, the populist rhetoric reflected the narrow culture definition focused on conduct which deviated from proper market norms.

Similarly, in the US in 2009 the Justice Department noted 'Today's agreement is but one milestone in an ongoing law enforcement effort to reassure hard-working and law-abiding taxpayers who pay their fair share of taxes that those who don't will pay a heavy price' (Finextra 2009). In 2012, the SEC contended that 'Today's actions involving RMBS securities are a continuation of the SEC's strong efforts to pursue wrongdoing committed in connection with the financial crisis' (SEC 2012). Concerning another JPMorgan fine, attorney general Eric Holder stated in 2013, 'The size and scope of this resolution should send a clear signal that the Justice Department's financial fraud investigations are far from over. No firm, no matter how profitable, is above the law, and the passage of time is no shield from accountability' (DoJ 2013). Whilst in 2014, Holder again emphasized that 'The significant financial penalties...send a powerful deterrent message to any company that places its profits ahead of its adherence to the law' (DoJ 2014). Then in 2015, the head of the New York DFS stated 'Financial institutions must heed this message: banks that operate in the United States must comply with our laws, and banks that ignore the warnings of those charged with compliance will pay a very steep price' (*NY Post* 2015). Whilst Attorney General Loretta Lynch concluded that the sizeable penalties over LIBOR allegations 'should deter competitors in the future from chasing profits without regard to fairness, to the law, or to the public welfare' (DoJ 2015). And again in 2016, the DFS emphasized 'Today's settlement is another example of the department's resolve to hold accountable those whose illegal conduct resulted in the financial crisis of 2008' (DoJ 2016). Meanwhile in 2017, Christy Goldsmith Romero, the inspector General of Sigtarp, the federal agency overseeing government bailout funds, contended that 'our nation cannot afford to take our eye off the ball when it comes to crime or other legal practices inside banks...they should not be able to buy themselves out of accountability. The [fines] are important because there must be a cost' (cited in *FT* 2017). The message should therefore be clear that both US and UK state managers attached a great deal of importance to these financial penalties. They spoke consistently of sending a clear message; and they asserted that the size of the penalty was important because it emphasized the degree of seriousness authorities would attach to misconduct.

It is also important to note however, how the financial penalties were seen to be related to the culture reform agenda. The mechanism for promoting culture change was essentially twofold: firstly, the fines were obviously intended to make misconduct financially costly; whilst secondly, the intention was that improved checks and balances (what is understood in the industry as *compliance*) would promote better, and more ethical decision-making. Compliance comprises the formal regulatory compliance—with official legal requirements—as well as internal compliance—where the banks establish their own norms and standards which are not necessarily enforced by law. In this way, both the regulatory emphasis on compliance and the firms' internal reforms were further examples of the good culture as ethical, socially responsible behaviour trope. As I will show in Chapter 9, there was certainly a change in the compliance and risk-taking culture. This did not however, overcome the problematic cultural tendencies which are symptoms of financialization. In fact, the financial penalties were another attempt to depoliticize bank culture reform and focus public attention on the surface level, behavioural changes. This present chapter will start to explain how and why.

This book is not the first account to take issue with the idea of financial penalties promoting cultural change. At stake, as we shall see, is the relationship between fines, performance, and culture change, which has been the subject of extensive study in the corporate reputation literature (see Barnett and Pollock eds, 2012). Specifically concerning bank fines, a number of critics also argued that 'the threat of fines has proved laughably inadequate at producing better behaviour' (*The Times*, cited in Karpoff 2012: 361). US Securities Commissioners for New York and Colorado shared the view that 'regulatory slaps on the wrist and high-priced legal counsel become a cost of doing business for securities violators' (Stern and Schifrin 1987). Indeed, studies during the 1970s and 1980s seeking to establish a correlation between financial performance variables and corporate social responsibility variables found mixed evidence (see Wood and Jones 1995 for an overview). That is, it was not clear whether firms that were less socially responsible performed worse, or that bad behaviour hit profit margins. We discussed this contention in Chapter 2 in relation to bonuses, but that same academic research also pointed to the tenuous relationship between financial penalties and behavioural reform. Instead, critics argued that if the pain of the financial penalty was diluted, 'future deterrence of corporate wrongdoing is weakened' (USPIRG 2015a: 6). As Brandon Garrett, Professor of Corporate Crime, remarked, 'these billions of dollars in fines imposed in recent years are not all that they appear' (Garrett 2016: 39). Whilst the Washington-based Better Markets group concluded 'these settlements . . . are more about headlines than accountability or deterrence' (2017: 82). The argument of this chapter contributes to these findings.

Fines and Profitability

The big claim of this chapter can be stated simply: the view that fines are an effective method for promoting culture change because they impose a financial disincentive for bad behaviour is very dubious. The sub-claim of this first section can be framed as a hypothesis: if there were a direct, linear relationship between fines and financial performance we would have expected the banks hit by the biggest fines to have performed the worst financially. The conclusion of this first section is that this simply was not the case. This subsection will firstly examine the effects of fines on the share price of the largest UK and US banks. Over recent years I have collected and analysed data on all the financial penalties imposed by UK and US authorities on banks of all sizes. Here I shall simply focus on the largest US and UK banks hit by the largest fines.

We will begin by looking at share prices. The reason is that share price performance can be used as a proxy indicator for the reputational damage to a bank. In a sense this is a means of (almost) isolating the direct influence of the financial penalty itself, from the (secondary) effect of increased spending on the compliance function (new systems and staff costs). We might expect to see the impact of compliance costs on *profitability* (the second measure used below) as costs rise over time, whereas share prices are often a more immediate gauge of market reactions. But as I shall demonstrate, in both instances—more immediate share price performance and medium term profitability—there is not a clear relationship to the penalties.

Beginning with share prices, there is a body of academic research which suggests that something relatively nebulous such as reputation can have very concrete, tangible effects. So-called 'reputational capital' may not be readily apparent on a firm's balance sheet, but there is plenty of evidence that it is nonetheless significant. The corporate culture literature discussed in Chapter 2—and the idea that firms might attempt to improve ethical behaviour as a means to improve financial performance—points to the influence of reputational capital. The obvious anecdotal example that sellers with higher reputational scores achieve higher prices has been supported by research findings (Resnick et al. 2006). You only have to think of eBay as an example of this. Similarly, other studies have confirmed that investment banks with high reputations are able to charge higher fees. More specifically though, announcements of regulatory investigations have been found to be associated with up to a 50 per cent decline in the average share price of an initial public offering (IPO); and that daily stock returns can be significantly more volatile following these regulatory announcements (Beatty, Bunsis, and Hand 1998). Similarly, another set of studies also concluded that it is logical for firms to act in socially responsible and lawful ways as a matter of enlightened self-interest: that failure to do so has a statistically significant impact on shareholder wealth (Frooman 1997: 222, Ross, Westerfield, and Jaffe 1996). In the case of banks more specifically, the predominant mechanism through which reputational loss can manifest is through a reduction in credit ratings and a lower share price (Karpoff 2012: 364). Share prices reflect the opinion of market participants regarding a firm's future cash flows. 'If participants believe that the future cash flows of a firm will decrease due to some behavior of the firm, demand for the stock will decrease, thus lowering the value of the stock' (Frooman 1997: 225).

The aim of the first part of this chapter is not to comprehensively refute this body of existing research. Instead I will argue though that the financial penalties provide a very limited explanation for what has been going on in terms of share price and profitability. That is, a whole range of other factors, including the rate of recovery of their respective economies and the structure of the bank bailout packages themselves (Woll 2014), provide a much more substantive explanation for the financial condition of the banks.

In relation to share prices, consider the examples of Barclays and Bank of America as two of the banks hit by the largest fines. As Tables 8.1 and 8.2 show, these two banks were hit by severe financial penalties from *both* US and UK authorities. Figs 8.2 and 8.3 track the share price of these two banks. The date of the fines being announced has been marked on Figs 8.2 and 8.3 and the largest fines have a numerical value attached to them. An important methodological note should also be added though. In most cases we would not expect to see a significant fall in the share price on the day of the regulatory announcement itself. This is because, of course, the announcement follows months or even years of investigations by regulatory authorities; and the exact starting point for these

Table 8.1 Barclays fines (2007–16)

	Date	Amount	Description
1	2007-05-30	$10.9m	US—charges for insider trading
2	2009-08-19	£2.45m	UK—fined Barclays Capital for transaction reporting failures
3	2010-08-18	$298m	US—sanctions violations charges for dealings with Cuba, Iran, Sudan
4	2011-01-18	£7.7m	UK—failure to provide adequate information in relation to the sale of two major funds
5	2011-01-26	£1.13m	UK—fined Barclays Capital for failure in protecting customers' money
6	2012-06-27	£59.5m	UK—for LIBOR and Euribor manipulation
7	2012-06-27	$360m	US—for LIBOR manipulation
8	2012-08-18	$176m	US—settled sanctions violations for dealings with Cuba, Iran, Burma, Sudan
9	2013-07-16	$435m	US—charges for energy market manipulation
10	2013-09-10	$36m	US—settlement over mortgage-backed securities
11	2014-04-24	$280m	US—misleading investors over mortgage-backed securities
12	2014-05-23	£26m	UK—mis-selling and conflicts of interest
13	2014-09-23	£38m	UK—failure to protect customer's assets
14	2015-05-20	$992m	US—price-fixing in Forex markets
15	2015-05-20	£284	UK—price-fixing in Forex markets
16	2015-05-20	$60m	US—additional fine for LIBOR manipulation
17	2015-11-26	£72m	UK—failure to minimize risk in transactions open to financial crime

Source: author's own calculations, various sources.

Table 8.2 Bank of America fines (2007–16)

	Date	Amount	Description
1	2008-10-08	$50m	US—manipulation of securities auction rate
2	2010-02-04	$150m	US—failure to disclose bonuses and losses before merger
3	2010-12-07	$137m	US—bid rigging in derivatives markets
4	2010-12-31	$1350m	US—sale of faulty mortgages
5	2011-01-03	$1520m	US—sale of faulty mortgages
6	2011-05-26	$20m	US—foreclosure relief to military borrowers
7	2011-11-10	$20m	US—foreclosure relief to military borrowers
8	2011-12-21	$335	US—discrimination claims against minority borrowers
9	2012-02-01	$200m	US—LIBOR rate-rigging
10	2012-02-09	$11,820	US—National Mortgage Settlement charges
11	2012-09-13	$370m	US—discrimination against disability recipients
12	2013-01-07	$2886	US—Independent Foreclosure Review settlement.
13	2013-01-07	$11,600	US—settlement over faulty mortgage sales
14	2013-03-29	$165m	US—sales of poor MBS securities to credit unions
15	2013-12-12	$131m	US—fine for insider dealing
16	2014-03-26	$9330m	US—misleading investors over mortgage backed securities
17	2014-04-09	$772m	US—misleading customers on credit card protection
18	2014-08-06	$16650m	US—mis-selling mortgage backed securities
19	2014-11-12	$250m	US—unsound practices on foreign exchange trading business
20	2015-05-20	$205m	US—rigging foreign exchange markets and LIBOR manipulation.
21	2016-03-23	$430m	US—misusing client funds to finance trading activity
22	2016-09-16	$15.5m	US—risk control failures on trading activities

Source: author's own calculations, various sources.

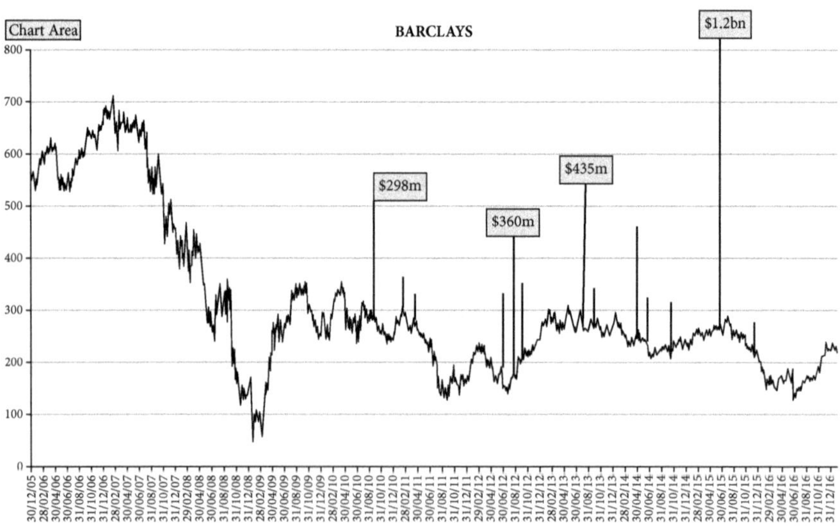

Fig. 8.2 Barclays share price 2006–16 (Sterling pence)

Source: Datastream.

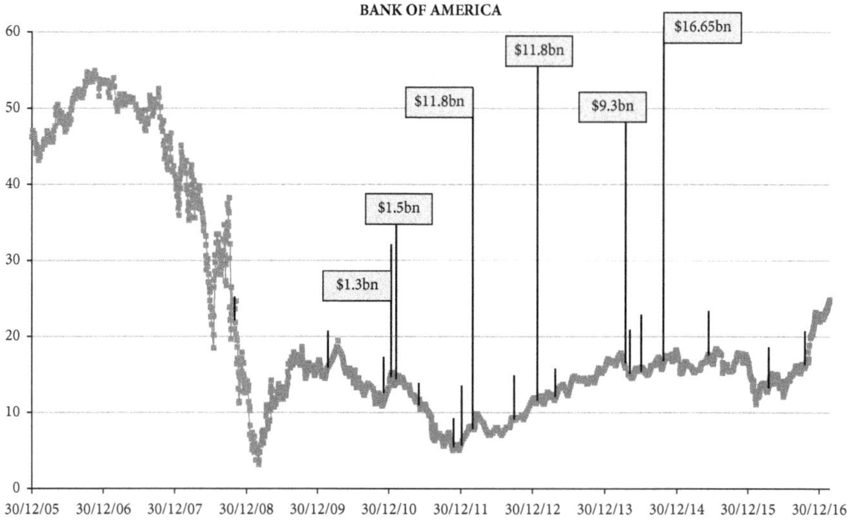

Fig. 8.3 Bank of America share price (USD)
Source: Datastream.

investigations is often hard to discern. In most instances markets are aware of these pending settlements. This conclusion is confirmed by existing research, where identifying the precise 'event' we would expect markets to be responding to has traditionally proven extremely problematic (Karpoff et al. 2013). Thus, if anything, we might expect to see a slight rise in the share price immediately after the announcement, as uncertainty about the size of the penalty is resolved. However, as per the existing literature above, over a given period—if our hypothesis that banks hit by the largest fines also suffer the biggest decline in share price is correct—we would still expect to notice a relationship.

Instead, if anything, the data suggests that after the initial crisis period (2007–9), markets became increasingly less responsive to announcements of further penalties. As I will explain further later in this chapter, it is as if markets rapidly priced in the likelihood of fines—thereby reducing their pain and effectiveness. In this sense, the case of the bank fines following the financial crisis perhaps challenges the findings of earlier research in one important respect: the sheer volume of fines, the size of each penalty, and the vast range of financial institutions to be hit, was unprecedented. Thus the data suggests a case of overload; the extent of the fines may actually have worked to undermine their effectiveness, by inadvertently desensitizing markets to their impact.

Three points should be noted then: first, it was not unusual for share prices to be inflated in the 2005–7 period, which distorts the subsequent fall as the financial crisis hits. Secondly, all banks in our survey did indeed experience a fall in their share price since 2009. Thirdly though, the fall in share prices appears to bear little relationship to the fines themselves. This is particularly evident in the case of *all* the US banks. Though the size of their fines were in orders of magnitude greater than the UK counterparts, US bank share prices recovered significantly more than their UK counterparts.

The argument that neither the fines nor the associated increase in compliance costs are an accurate indicator of the financial performance of the banks can also be demonstrated in another way. Compliance laws, rules, and standards generally cover issues ranging from correct market conduct, managing conflicts of interests, and ensuring that clients and customers are treated fairly (BIS 2005: 7, Interview 20170627). Compliance is aimed at regulating banks' behaviour towards their shareholders, customers, employees, and the markets (International Compliance Association, 2017). The banks unequivocally highlighted the rise in compliance costs in the post-crisis regulatory environment. According to the Global Accenture Survey of Executives for example, approximately 89 per cent of financial services industry executives expected continued cost increases in compliance due to 'an explosion in digital data, a finite talent pool of compliance professionals to draw from and a more-complex risk ecosystem' (Accenture, 2017), with costs having already risen anywhere between 20–59 per cent for the largest US and UK banks alike, between 2008–16 (Thomson Reuters 2016: 23).

Fig. 8.4 shows the financial performance of the largest British and American banks however and helps to capture the secondary effect—after the initial financial penalty—by showing that despite the increased compliance spending, profits for US banks recovered dramatically and even for UK banks improved from their

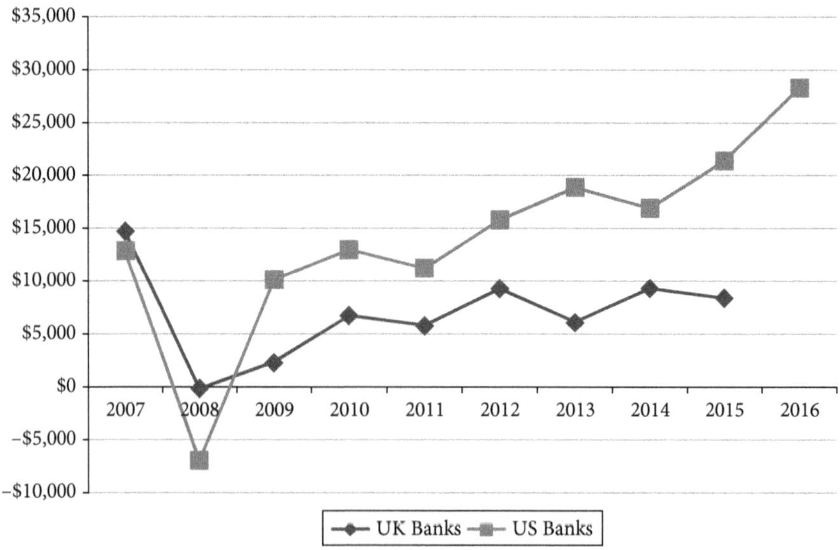

Fig. 8.4 Average operating profits of US and UK banks (US $ millions)
Source: Fitch Connect.

2008 low. A graph of this type cannot explain the content or impact of the compliance reforms brought into being as a result of the fines; we will discuss this in due course. What the graph does do however, is to begin to problematize the view that either in the immediate or medium-term the fines imposed an inexorable economic imperative to reform conduct as state managers had claimed. In other words, it begins to highlight the disjuncture between the rhetoric attached to the fines (their stated objective), and the reality (or real objective).

The message is clear: though the American banks were hit by larger fines, they continued to experience a growth in profitability far in excess of their UK counterparts. Put differently, the largest US banks experienced fines in orders of magnitude greater than those of UK banks, but UK banks experienced more prolonged stagnation in their share price and profits whereas US banks showed marked improvement by the tail-end of 2016. This is not, of course, to suggest that reputational damage to the bank does not influence financial performance. The academic studies referenced earlier have shown that it does. But this first section has begun to problematize the simplistic notion that 'big fines = big financial impact on the banks = big incentive to address culture'. This leads towards our central claim that the bank fines were motivated by another concern: the guiding priority was the populist message sent by the fines, rather than the impact on conduct and culture that the fines would have. And the populist message itself was a veiled attempt to deflect criticism away from financialization.

A Cost of Doing Business

Having begun to show that the impact of the fines on financial performance is highly questionable, the remainder of this chapter unpacks the finer details of the penalties. In so doing I will show that, behind the hard-hitting rhetoric, the fines were structured so as to be relatively benign. That may sound rather odd, because the sums involved were still large—even after tax deductability and charitable write-offs (see section 'Tax Deductions and Surcharges' below)—and the compliance conditions brought about by the fines were indeed onerous. But I will show that, in reality, the fines were primarily designed to make the headlines, whilst paradoxically protecting the banks from more savage structural reform or individual jail sentences.

In sum, the remainder of this chapter will show how the fines became normalized. As one industry insider noted, the fines went 'from being unthinkable, to being a grave existential threat, to being a cost of doing business' (Levine 2017). Indeed, another account suggested 'the threat of fines is [now] seen as a footling expense, just another cost of doing business, no different from paying the quarterly phone bill' (The *Times* 2009). Or as one senior Wall Street lawyer put it, 'I look at the major banks in the world who've paid humongous fines and they just continue as usual...it's just a matter of business and if you're lucky you get that deducted as an expense for taxes...It's an expense of doing business' (Interview 20160421). This subsection will therefore briefly examine these two related features: the tax deductibility of the penalties; and the size of the fine in relation to the size of the profits from the relevant activity.

Tax Deductions and Surcharges

Arguably the most important component was the tax deductibility of the fines. As one report by the US Public Interest Research Group noted, when large companies cause harm they rarely pay a financial penalty as other citizens might. Instead, 'these companies negotiate out-of-court settlements that resolve the charges in return for stipulated payments or promised remedies' (USPIRSG 2015a: 1). At stake is the fact that 'the pain of penalties from improper activities can be significantly reduced when the penalties are tax deductible' (Forbes 2016b). In the UK, tax deductibility was highly controversial. In fact, by 2016, a highly publicized political debate was unfolding over whether the costs of fines incurred as a result of misconduct would be able to be offset against corporation tax bills. In February 2016, the Treasury Committee Chairman Andrew Tyrie wrote to the then Chancellor of the Exchequer asking for clarification on this issue. In the letter, which he published in the press, he contended that 'it is important to ensure that, when a UK bank reaches a settlement with a foreign regulator, any fines cannot be structured to permit UK tax deductibility' (FT 2015d). A similar clause had been introduced into the Finance Act 2015 to ensure that banks would not be entitled to any tax relief for compensation payments made to customers. According to Tyrie, the idea that the costs for misconduct could be covered as 'legitimate business costs' under the HMRC's Business Income code was unacceptable, as it would mean that taxpayers were 'required to be a part of the burden of any payment imposed by the FCA or overseas regulators' (Treasury Committee 2016a).

The Conservative Chancellor, George Osborne, replied confirming that 'fines imposed as a punishment by regulators are non-deductible for UK corporation tax purposes' (HM Treasury 2016). Andrew Tyrie subsequently responded that if certain payments to regulators might be considered to be general compensation—to people other than customers—then they might be considered deductible, which was again 'unacceptable'. This was a not insignificant technical point. In almost all cases, the financial penalties comprised of different segments: in both the UK and the US a relatively limited amount would return to the central budget (the Treasury in the UK; the respective regulators; or federal or state budgets in the US); other elements of the fine comprised commitments to increase lending to particular communities, or charitable donations. In Tyrie's view this created a grey area whereby compensatory payments to customers were not tax-deductible and neither were fines; but compensation payments to the regulator could still be offset against the tax bill of a firm (Treasury Committee 2016b). Tyrie therefore urged that 'any payments required from banks for misconduct are either compensation to customers...or are clearly set out as fines' (ibid.). Yet the Chancellor failed to respond to the final line of criticism and the issue slowly faded from view.

In reality then, it remained largely unclear in the case of the UK the extent to which the largest banks were able to offset portions of the penalties against their tax bill. Moreover, these tax data are obviously not publicly accessible. Yet, as some commentators have argued, the fact that finance ministry officials in the US and the UK did not make every effort to promote transparency in this area was suggestive of a desire to depoliticize the tax issue and to conceal it from public scrutiny. Moreover, if developments in the US were indicative of the tax loopholes the largest banks were able to exploit in relation to the fines, they raise significant concerns about the UK case.

In the US a similar political struggle was taking place. In September 2015 Senator Elizabeth Warren had sponsored the Truth in Settlements Act, making it a requirement for regulatory authorities to publicly disclose the 'amount the settling party is obligated to pay that has been expressly specified as a civil or criminal penalty or fine and any amount expressly specified as not deductible for tax purposes' (US Congress 2015). As with the UK case, the US tax code prohibited 'any fine or similar penalty paid to the government for the violation of any law' from being tax deductible (Tax Code section 162f). But, on the other hand, *civil* settlements may be tax deductible (USPIRG 2015). This lead the Inland Revenue Service (IRS) to conclude that unless enforcement agencies explicitly forbade a corporation from doing so '*almost every defendant* deducts the entire amount' of the settlement as a business expense (emphasis added IRS 2013).

Because of the opacity of the issue almost no systematic studies were conducted. The United States Public Interest Group, a non-profit advocacy group, did however conduct a study examining the ten largest settlements by five government regulators since 2012: the Department of Justice, the Securities and Exchange Commission, the Environmental Protection Agency, the Department of Health and Human Services, and the Consumer Financial Protection Bureau. Admittedly, the study was not limited to financial penalties paid by banks themselves but the conclusions were noteworthy. In that time, the firms in question were required to pay nearly $80 billion in fines, but the analysis found that they were able to write off at least $48 billion. As noted above, the study found that this stemmed from a 'grey area' in the tax code. Whilst corporations were not permitted to deduct penalties or fines, many of the largest settlements were structured in such a way as to address some form of liability connected to alleged misconduct. In relation to banks more specifically though, Frontline noted that the civil penalty imposed by the Department of Justice on JPMorgan in 2013 for its mis-selling of mortgages totalled $13 billion. Yet, of that amount, $11 billion was eligible for tax deduction. Similarly, in 2012 the Department of Justice reached a $25 billion mortgage settlement with Ally Financial, Bank of America, JPMorgan and Wells Fargo. Yet $20 billion of that amount was eligible for tax deduction (PBS 2015).

What is equally important however, is that in explaining the rationale behind these large fines and the tax adaptability issue, the US PIRG drew a very similar conclusion to the key argument of the first half of this book. The report described it as 'a compromise' because 'the corporation gets to ultimately deduct these huge amounts of payments, the government agency gets to advertise these huge topline numbers saying that they are holding the corporation accountable for its behaviour, but the bottom line is that taxpayers are the ones who are losing' (cited in PBS 2015). In other words, the key purpose of the penalties was a populist and performative attempt to redress the legitimacy crisis. The fines were indeed a slap on the wrist for the banks, but little more.

Beyond tax deductibility though, the fines were also simply a surcharge on an otherwise highly lucrative business activity. Once again, determining precisely how much banks profited from illegal or unethical activity is an impossible task, not least because this data is not publicly accessible. As the Better Markets Group noted however, if a prosecution is concluded with a $10 billion settlement, but investor losses (or bank gains) total $100 billion, then the fine is simply a small percentage of the profit. The National Mortgage Settlement levelled by the forty-nine state attorneys general, the District of Columbia, and the federal government, against the country's five largest mortgage providers (GMAC, Bank of America, Citibank, JPMorgan, and Wells Fargo) in February 2012 is a prime example. The $50 billion settlement involved relief to distressed borrowers and direct payments to the relevant states and Federal government. The Department of Justice emphasized that this was the 'largest consumer financial protection settlement in US history' (NMSS 2018). Of the lenders involved, the largest portion of the penalty was paid by Bank of America ($16.65bn).

In response to the settlement however, BoA chief executive Brian Moynihan simply stated that 'We believe this settlement, which resolves significant remaining mortgage-related exposures, is in the best interests of our shareholders, and allows us to continue to focus on the future' (BoA 2014). There are three reasons for believing the sentiment expressed by Moynihan: firstly, the $16.65bn settlement was estimated to reduce pre-tax earnings for 2014 by only $5.3 billion, due largely to the structure of the penalty which will be examined below; secondly, and much more importantly, Bank of America had made significantly more than $16.65 billion from its original investment. In fact, BoA made approximately $57.5bn on the bonds it sold to Fannie Mae and Freddie Mac alone. The settlement was therefore only—effectively—an 8.5 per cent surcharge on a very lucrative business deal (Bloomberg 2015b). Thirdly and finally though, as with many other parts of the mortgage mis-selling penalties, approximately one-third of the settlement involved repurchasing troubled mortgage bonds that BoA had sold to Fannie Mae and Freddie Mac. The catch was that the regulatory agency—the Federal Housing Finance Authority—did not force BoA to repay the original sums Fannie and Freddie had paid for the defective bonds. Instead BoA were allowed to purchase them at the (then) current market price, which was approximately 20 per cent of their original face value. The point was that as the economy and housing market recovered, these distressed mortgage bonds became a hot investment. As a result it was estimated that the group of bonds BoA had bought in the settlement had already earned the bank $138 million in only two months (Fortune 2014). The implication was that the costs were hardly sufficient to make the activity itself less attractive. Or as the above Fortune article concluded, 'The way post-financial crisis justice is doled out for Wall Street banks is a head-scratcher' (ibid.).

Charities and Consumer Relief

The second reason for thinking that the guiding priority of the fines was as a populist strategy, rather than a severe challenge to the banks, was evident in the structure of the penalties themselves. Two features stand out: the first was that a large portion of the fines—in both the US and the UK—came in the form of charitable donations; the second was that, in the US, a further portion of the penalty was structured as a requirement to increase lending to poorer communities.

In the US, with data taken from 2015 when the size of the penalties totalled $110bn: $44.68bn went to consumer relief; $5.35bn went to states; $14.49bn to the Treasury; and $38.99bn to Fannie Mae and Freddie Mac for housing provision (*WSJ* 2015e). Of the settlements with the three largest banks then, over 35 per cent went to consumer relief, 29 per cent to the Treasury, 20 per cent to other agencies, 5 per cent to states, and 0.3 per cent to harmed investors and whistleblowers. Labelling this as 'consumer relief' however, was rather disingenuous. As the *Wall Street Journal* proclaimed: 'Imagine if the president of the United States forced America's biggest banks to funnel hundreds of millions—and potentially billions—of dollars to the corporations and lobbyists who supported his agenda, all while calling it "Main Street Relief." The public outcry would rightly be deafening. Yet the Obama administration has used a similar strategy to enrich its political allies, advance leftist pet projects, and protect its legacy—and hardly anyone has noticed' (*WSJ* 2016a). The agency responsible for collecting these particular penalties was the Residential Mortgage-Backed Securities Working Group, a coalition of federal and state regulators and prosecutors established in 2012 and working alongside the Justice Department. Ostensibly, this consumer relief portion of the penalties was supposed to benefit homeowners harmed after the financial crisis. Yet, in reality, large portions were allocated to organizations on a federally approved list. At one level this fact was neither surprising nor unusual. Yet our aim in this chapter is simply to show that the stated intention behind the fines—of penalizing bad conduct—needs to be qualified by the less widely publicized political motivations that shaped the content of the fines, behind the headline figures.

Simply, large portions of the funds raised via bank fines were used to serve the political agenda of federal or state authorities. Many of the groups benefitting from so-called Main Street Relief were overtly political, liberal allies of the Obama administration. These groups include La Raza, the National Urban League, and the National Community Reinvestment Coalition. Further, members of the Residential Mortgage-Backed Securities (RMBS) Working Group were also directing money to their supporters and states. Beyond that, other state officials used bank fines to raise funds for their respective constituencies, jumping on the 'banker-bashing bandwagon' (so to speak) to serve their populist agenda. Lisa Madigan, the Democrat attorney general for Illinois, announced that she had negotiated $422.5 million of a Morgan Stanley settlement to channel to Illinois pension schemes (Madigan 2016). In New York, Governor Cuomo used the proceeds to replace the Tappan Zee Bridge and renovate the Port of Albany, as well as providing horse stables for its annual state fair (*WSJ* 2016b, Fortune 2016). Again, the point was not that this political statecraft was new or isolated to post-crisis fines. But it provides an important qualifier to the claim that the size of the fines was directly correlated to the size of the crime; and that state managers were only, or even primarily, using the fines as a mechanism to promote changed conduct. In keeping with our description of populism in Chapter 2, radical and more conservative state managers (of the left and right) saw the opportunity to use financial penalties to present themselves as champions of the people against the profligate banks. This claim is relatively easy to substantiate. More important for this book is the idea that in so doing the political classes were deliberately or inadvertently—depending on their ideological stance—deflecting attention away from the more necessary debate about financialization.

The second issue revealing how populism rendered the fines relatively benign was that the details of the consumer relief element considerably diluted the penalty banks would face. One component of this was the fact that most of the deals with the banks gave 'double credit or more against the settlement amount for every dollar in "donations"' (*WSJ* 2016b). An analysis of the Bank of America's donation list showed that $1.15 million 'donated' to the National Urban League counted as if it were $2.6 million against the banks settlement; and $1.5 million to La Raza took $3.5 million off the total amount of consumer relief owed by the bank. In the case of a Goldman Sachs settlement, for example, the bank was called to spend $240 million on affordable housing. But an appendix to the deal explained that the bank would have to pay—at most—only 30 per cent of that total to actually fulfil the terms of the deal (DoJ 2016: 4). A conservative estimate was that this could save the bank as much as $1bn from the total of the overall fine (*NY Times* 2016b). As one Justice Department official explained, banks were given extra credit for activities that the government wanted to encourage since the final terms of the deals had been significantly influenced by bank lobbying (cited in *NY Times* 2016a).

Arguably even more perplexing though was that some of the banks that incurred consumer relief as part of their US mortgage settlement packages never had a consumer mortgage business. Goldman Sachs Group earmarked $1.8bn for consumer relief even though it had no consumer mortgages to speak of; it bought up other firms' mortgages, repackaged them as securities and then sold them on to investors. As part of the mortgage relief settlement then it opted to buy up other banks' mortgages at a discount, and then modify them. But the stock of busted subprime loans a decade after the crisis was minimal. So some of the larger banks developed an alternative strategy: indirectly funding new loans to subprime borrowers. Deutsche Bank, which had a small US mortgage business, agreed to provide $4.1bn in relief to borrowers. The bank would lend to companies offering government-backed mortgages to persons with weaker credit scores. These include Federal Housing Administration mortgages which allowed for a down payment as low as 3.5 per cent (Bloomberg 2017a). The result was that—paradoxically—financial penalties for the original subprime mortgage crisis were structured in such a way as to potentially contribute to a second subprime lending spree.

Similarly, in October 2017 it was reported that JPMorgan had been engaged in equally unscrupulous practices. As part of the $25bn National Mortgage Settlement, JPMorgan was fined $5.3 billion, but only $1.1 billion had to be paid in cash. The other $4.2 billion came in the form of financial relief for homeowners in danger of losing their homes to foreclosure. In reality though, JPMorgan set about forgiving loans on properties it no longer owned. Several years earlier it had sold the outstanding mortgages to twenty-one third-party investors when these loan portfolios were virtually valueless. And then, at a later date when it was required to provide consumer relief under the settlements, the bank fraudulently created paperwork indicating that it still owned the properties (*The Nation* 2017). Not only was the bank therefore attempting to deceive investors and Federal authorities, but it also defrauded homeowners, who were informed that their mortgages had been forgiven only to receive subsequent notification that this was not the case because JPMorgan did not own their mortgages to be able to forgive them (Levine 2017). It was yet another example of the ability of banks to exploit the technical details for writing off large portions of their financial penalties. It was also evidence of the type of culture bred by financialization and the search for yield. Ethical reform to inculcate socially responsible behaviour only goes so far. The coercive pressures of competition under financialization drive behaviours that will consistently operate at the edges of what can be considered ethically justifiable; and drive a business model that preys on weakness in the economy, a morally objectionable strategy.

The conclusion of a number of commentators was that the government agencies 'appear[ed] to have grossly inflated the settlement amount for P.R. purposes to mislead the public, while in the fine print, enabling [the banks] to pay 50 to 75 percent less' (Dennis Kelleher, founder of Better Markets, cited in *NY Times* 2016b). On this reading, the bank settlements were 'carefully crafted to conceal more than reveal to the American public' (ibid.). As a senior lawyer involved in negotiating one major US misconduct case phrased it, 'we used the banking system as a political tool' (Interview 20160421).

The claim that the financial penalties levelled against the banks had an ulterior, performative function, was equally evident in the UK. In particular, from 2012 the Chancellor George Osborne committed to allocate a portion of the fines to military charities. This process began with an amendment to the Financial Services Bill on 2 July 2012. The amendment meant that fines would go to the Exchequer, rather than remaining in the hands of the regulator (Osborne 2012). Up until that point, funds retrieved through fines allowed the FCA to keep membership fees for financial institutions artificially low. As Osborne argued, this created the situation where fines actually served to benefit other banks (ibid.). In October 2013 the Treasury announced it would allocate £35m to the armed forces community, including Help for Heroes, Royal Marines Families, and Veterans Centres (BBC 2013). In 2014 that figure rose to £45m (Osborne 2014); and in the 2015 Budget a further £75m was committed to these charitable causes (Osborne 2015). Over and again, in the annual and summer budget speeches, Osborne emphasized 'We're using the money raised from fines on those who demonstrated the very worst values in our society to support those who demonstrate the very best' (Osborne 2013, 2014, 2015). Peculiar rhetoric coming from the mouth of the Chancellor presiding over the most dramatic cuts to social spending and the welfare state in recorded history; unless of course we grasp that the bank fines were a populist attempt to legitimize the savage austerity budget. With the new Conservative leadership in place in 2016, the charitable donations continued, with Phillip Hammond—the new Chancellor—committing £102m in donations.

Together, the diversion of funds towards political agendas in the US, and towards charitable causes in the UK challenges the idea that the financial penalties were *simply* aimed at penalizing misconduct and promoting cultural reform. Instead, as this chapter has argued, the large financial penalties were intended to serve another purpose, as an extension of the populist point-scoring tactics by UK and US state managers, and an attempt to respond to the legitimacy crisis outlined in Chapters 4–7.

Compliance Conditions

A third and final reason for thinking that state managers attached greater importance to the headlines surrounding the financial penalties than the impact they had on corporate conduct, were the legal terms attached to the penalties themselves. Here we risk straying into the territory covered more fully in Chapters 9 and 10, where we will examine the extent of the compliance-related changes that have taken place within the banks themselves. Instead though, here we can briefly address the conditions *attached* to the penalties, in a narrower sense. What we will see is that the demands state managers placed upon offending banks were extremely limited, with the result that many of these banks were repeat offenders.

This is not the place for a lengthy discussion about whether or not prosecutions of specific individuals ought to have been pursued, though the fact that they were not supports our argument that state managers could have pursued a tougher response. Certainly there has been an extensive body of thought arguing that only individual prosecutions cannot effectively remedy culture (see Rakoff 2014 for an overview). Other accounts have pointed to the historical parallels between corporate misconduct during the Savings and Loans crisis of the 1980s and the financial crisis 2007–9, highlighting the conspicuous absence of individual prosecutions in the most recent period compared to the 1980s (Better Markets 2016). In a similar vein, other academic accounts contended that the explanation for the lack of prosecutions lies in the weakness of, in particular, the US Department of Justice in the face of the overweening power of the largest banks. Certainly, as we explained in Chapter 7, there was evidence that the UK was moving towards this kind of individual accountability with the Senior Managers Regime (Cullen 2016). Though, as we also explained, the absence of the reversed burden of responsibility was disconcerting; just as other legal experts explained that they doubted whether the powers given the FCA under the SMR would actually ever be deployed (Interview 20170511).

Instead, setting aside the individual accountability question, in this brief final section I will present the evidence that the terms attached to the financial penalties were weak at best. The UK case can be dealt with swiftly, for the British legal system does not have a mechanism for attaching (cultural reform) conditions to financial penalties (Interview 20170511). In sharp contrast, the US legal system has an extensive history of applying Non-Prosecution Agreements (NPAs) and Deferred Prosecution Agreements (DPAs) to fines, as was briefly discussed in Chapters 4 and 5. Essentially, NPA and DPA's 'trade criminal charges for promised reforms and criminal fines' (Garrett 2015b). The terms of non-prosecution deals usually specify that banks must not engage in additional criminal activity for two or three years; but the caveat is that the subsequent wrongdoing must not be a *similar* offence. This important caveat contributed to the inability and unwillingness of prosecutors to follow through on the punitive action specified in the terms of an original penalty in cases where banks (and indeed other large corporations) failed to abide by the original terms. The point is that although the US legal system *does* have a mechanism for promoting cultural reform attached to financial penalties, it was highly ineffective (Eisinger 2017).

One of the most telling features of the Forex manipulation penalties when considering the use of fines and compliance conditions, for example, was that the involvement of a number of banks breached the terms of earlier non-prosecution agreements. In fact there was a pattern of 'repeat offending' or *recidivism* following compliance monitoring attached to prosecution agreements: Credit Suisse entered a deferred prosecution agreement in 2009 only to re-offend and sign a plea agreement in 2014; HSBC faced a non-prosecution agreement from 2001 and then a deferred prosecution agreement in 2012; JPMorgan faced a non-prosecution agreement in 2011, a deferred prosecution agreement in 2014 and a further plea agreement in 2017; Lloyds faced a deferred prosecution agreement in 2009 and another deferred prosecution agreement in 2014; RBS a deferred prosecution agreement in 2013, a guilt plea in 2013, and another guilty plea in 2017; and there are numerous other examples (see Garrett 2014: 42). Yet the largest banks had 'almost without exception avoided convictions and sentences entirely' (ibid).

Barclays was arguably one of the best examples however, because its series of misconduct-related charges happened in a particularly short space of time and highlighted the unwillingness of US authorities to take a stronger stance, preferring instead the eye-catching use of big fines. In 2010 the bank entered a DPA for violations of economic sanctions against Burma, Cuba, and Iran. The bank avoided conviction but paid a $300 million fine. It was warned not to violate any Federal laws for two years. Two years later though Barclays was being prosecuted over the LIBOR rate, but received a more lenient NPA for its 'extraordinary cooperation'. Then in 2015 however, the bank admitted that its FX trading and sales practices and its collusive conduct violated a principal term of the June 2012 NPA following the LIBOR manipulation (DoJ 2015a). The Justice Department specifically explained that 'some of that [Forex] conduct occurred during the pendency of the [LIBOR] NPA', which had 'prohibited the defendant from committing any United States crime during that term' (DoJ 2015b: 9). The result of this criminal activity though was a $60 million fine. The fine was minimal because, once again, Barclays had agreed to plead guilty to the Forex allegations and had again agreed to 'specific remediation with respect to the conduct' that led to Forex (ibid.: 10). This involved strengthening its compliance and internal controls, including 'thorough reviews of the activities and decision-making by employees of the defendant's legal and compliance functions' (ibid.:12).

At face value, the banks' promises to introduce new checks and balances and thoroughly review its practices sounds honourable. Indeed, in Chapter 9 I will chart the rise of the so-called compliance culture that emerged, in large part, due to the penalties and increased regulatory scrutiny. In Chapter 10 however, I will show some of the limitations to this compliance culture. I will show that whilst compliance works—to an extent—at the level of risk-taking and socially responsible conduct, it does not address the underlying pressures and incentives of financialization in Anglo-America.

Closing Remarks

To conclude, this chapter has argued that despite the claims of US and UK state managers that financial penalties were intended to make misconduct financially injudicious, the reality is far less black and white. The notion that the fines significantly impacted profitability is dubious: markets adapted to a new normal, where fines were anticipated; large portions of the fines were tax deductible; and the structure of the fines either allowed for substantial write-offs via charitable donations or, even more paradoxically, allowed banks to *profit* via the terms of the deals. In line with the argument of the first half of this book the fines were examples of a populist strategy to appear to be hitting the banks hard, whilst depoliticizing the underlying structural conditions of financialized accumulation in Anglo-America. In line with the argument in the second half of this book, the fact that the fines were weak and diluted characterizes the narrow bank culture debate that was satisfied with seeing only relatively superficial reforms.

9
What Has Changed

'It's a completely different world now'; 'everything has changed'. These were the sentiments expressed by countless interviewees. And yet we began this book by arguing that the culture of banking had actually changed very little. Put differently, at the core of Chapters 9–10 lies a puzzle: how could so much and yet so little have changed? The aim of this chapter is to show why, from the perspective of bank employees, culture change after the global financial crisis was quite dramatic; working in a bank, and certainly the largest banks in our study, was a very different experience a decade after the financial crisis. The answer which this chapter provides is that the narrower bank culture debate did indeed produce some results. Despite the hollow populist rhetoric and the weak enforcement—outlined in Chapter 8—new rules and compliance measures introduced by banks did produce some 'cultural' change. In Chapter 10 however, we return to the main argument of this book, that the underlying, structural drivers of bad bank culture had changed very little by the time of writing. In answer to the above puzzle then, this is why *everything* and *nothing* have changed.

CSR and the Culture Puzzle

The critical literature on Corporate Social Responsibility (CSR) provides a way to reconcile the arguments of Chapters 9 and 10. Though not examined in any depth earlier, the CSR movement springs from the same tensions—between profitability and ethical conduct—highlighted in Chapters 2 and 3. Though traces of the CSR movement can be seen in social auditing in the 1970s, the movement itself was largely a product of the anti-globalization critique and corporate failures of the late 1990s. In response, big corporations began developing and/or advertising their philanthropic endeavours and ethical conscience: 'Most large companies now issue a voluntary social and environmental report alongside their regular annual financial report; meanwhile the amount of money being poured into socially responsible investing (SRI) funds has been growing at an exponential rate, year over year' (Doane 2005).

One assumption by proponents of the CSR movement is that business outcomes and social objectives can be more or less aligned; that the market can deliver (short-term) financial returns and (long-term) social benefits (see Kurucz et al. 2008,

The Bank Culture Debate: Ethics, Values, and Financialization in Anglo-America. Huw Macartney, Oxford University Press (2019).
DOI: 10.1093/oso/9780198843764.001.0001

see also Crane et al. 2008). Indeed this assumption underpinned the writings of Smith and the ordo-liberals, provided that the correct form of political intervention was put in place. A critical reading of CSR argues however, that, ultimately, when trade-offs must be made between profits and ethical principles, profits will triumph. The (albeit simplistic) distinction employed in this book between narrower ethical and socially responsible conduct, and the underlying, structural pressures and incentives under financialization (delimiting the range of opportunities for profit) reflects a similar profit-versus-ethics dilemma.

In the narrower bank culture debate the right measure and form of accountability, the right financial and non-financial incentives, and deeply embedding the right market ethics, act as a counterweight to outright profiteering and malfeasance. The assumption is that genuine market competition will engender proper market conduct and therefore the right kind of bank culture; if a culture problem emerges it is that (1) participants are distorting competition, (2) the state has not fulfilled its role in maintaining proper market conduct, or that (3) participants have not internalized the right market norms. The virtue of the market is beyond question; the problem lies in the behaviour of participants.

But the broader view of bank culture adopts a more critical view of the structure of the market itself; not simply in an abstract sense, but in the very concrete manifestation of the market evidenced in the economies of Anglo-America. For reasons I explained in Chapter 2, these economies underwent crises of profitability that now skew the world of financial services in general, and banking in particular. Returns from (*redistributive*) financial activities now far outstrip returns from *creative* work in their respective non-financial economies, producing a seismic shift in bank models away from the so-called real economy (Bootle 2012). Remuneration and bonuses in the financial sector therefore now reflect this redistributive activity more than they do the value-added of the financial institutions themselves. Meanwhile for workers in the majority of other sectors wages fell with the profitability crises, and consumption became an ever more important part of government economic strategy; the result was heightened household indebtedness, greater income inequality, and bank models that prey on the indebted and were prone to excessive risk-taking in their search for yield.

These features reveal that there is something very fundamentally wrong with the financialized markets of Anglo-America, which no amount of ethical training and checks and balances can remedy. The narrow version of the bank culture debate is akin to applying a fresh coat of wax to your otherwise fully functioning car; whilst the broader version of the bank culture debate considers that exercise either ridiculous or ignorant, in view of the fact that the car itself is on fire and rolling off a cliff. This chapter therefore seeks to show that ethical and conduct-related reform was reasonably dramatic; in Chapter 10 this will be juxtaposed against the actual profit-making strategies of these same banks.

Structure and Methodological Concerns

The chapter is divided into four sections, examining values and ethical codes, compliance, risk, and pay. The tone of this chapter is somewhat different however, to that of Chapter 8 and Chapter 10. The aim is to demystify culture change, and to explain why culture might have 'felt' very different to bank employees, whilst still having severe limitations—the main argument of Part III of this book. Three methodological points must therefore be noted: firstly, the wide range of interviews conducted in researching this book provide a significant resource for this chapter. It is problematic however, to place too much weight on subjective interview material (Hycner 1985). I respond to this challenge in two ways: by triangulating the interview material with annual reports and financial data to support the claim that the perceptions of dramatic changes (by bank employees) were also manifest in some tangible changes in, for example, risk-taking and compliance; yet, I would also remind the reader of the main argument of this book, which is that despite employee perceptions the *real* culture of banking had changed very little. In other words, I do not *need* to attach too much weight to the perceptions of bank employees, because the core argument is that regardless of their impressions change was very limited.

A second methodological consideration is that culture change is a moving target. Risk-taking is a prime example. Following financial losses and increased compliance monitoring risk-taking became more conservative in the period immediately following the global financial crisis. This might have signalled a culture change. By late 2016 however, risk-taking was increasing again. As Hyman Mynsky would have argued, this is typical of the financial cycle which moves from conservative to excessive and then repeats (Mynsky 1977: 24–5). In this chapter I track some of these changes. But again, my underlying argument—linking the arguments of Parts II and III of the book—extends beyond Mynsky's contention that excessive risk-taking is bad but somewhat inevitable. Mynsky's arguments describe the financial cycle, but they tell us little about the politics. Inserting the distributional questions—of inequality—and the role of the state in reproducing the financialized mode of accumulation, takes us beyond Mynsky. And this is my aim in this book, because a broader debate on bank culture should expose both the political and the economic imperatives that determine the structures of financialization itself.

What does that mean for this chapter? Essentially, the fact that risk profiles are always fluctuating can also be said of discourses, compliance measures, and pay. This means that although they are useful heuristic devices for measuring cultural change in this chapter, they are not definitive or permanent. But, once again, this only supports the central claim of this book. Indeed the fact that risk and pay fluctuate only confirms the fact that we need to look beyond these surface-level issues to understand the real culture of banking. To put it rather bluntly—and at the risk of oversimplifying a complex issue—the fact that a $30m dollar bonus might now be structured differently and paid over a longer time horizon to promote better risk appetite, says nothing about why individuals are paid $30m for dubious contributions to society and the economy whilst 39.7 million people in the US live in poverty and the bottom 40 per cent of the population earn only 11.4 per cent of the total income (US Census 2017: 8,11). Instead—to understand the relationship of the banking sector to these underlying problems—I emphasize the exploitative and rent-seeking elements of financialization that remain, regardless of superficial cultural or behavioural changes.

Thirdly, as with earlier chapters, both as part of the organizational structure—to make the project more manageable—and because the scandals and subsequent regulatory focus were most targeted at the largest UK and US banks, they will provide the substance for much of the analysis of this chapter. Interviews were conducted however, with approximately 150 employees of financial institutions, and these range from the largest US and UK banks to smaller bank and non-bank financial firms. For disclosure reasons only a small sample of these interviews have been referenced in this book. But based on this wider research a similar story could be told for many of these other banking institutions.

Values and Ethical Codes

This first section examines high-level ethical codes. As a simple heuristic to highlight the increased emphasis on culture Fig. 9.1 shows the number of times the term 'culture' was mentioned in the annual reports of RBS, Barclays, Lloyds, Citigroup, Bank of America, JPMorgan, Goldman Sachs, and Wells Fargo between 2005–16. The sharp rise post-2011 is obvious.

Moreover, a similar search for other key terms is suggestive of the *kind* of discursive change that took place within the banks between 2005–16. Fig. 9.2 shows the number of times that customers, values, and ethics were mentioned in the annual reports of the banks in question. As was indicated in Chapter 2, the cultural problems within the banking system were oftentimes defined as the banks prioritizing their own profit margins and sales targets ahead of the customers and clients' interests. As Wells Fargo (2013: 28) suggested, 'across the industry, mistakes clearly were made leading up to the financial crisis of 2008, as some competitors put profits before their customers interests'. On the basis of the annual reports, the first conclusion we can draw is that there was certainly evidence of a discursive shift emphasizing customers, values, and ethics to a greater extent than in the 2000s.

It is not simply the fact that customers, values, and culture received a greater number of mentions in the annual reports of the banks, but a closer reading of the annual reports provides a more nuanced account of the discursive shift. The UK-based Lloyds bank noted in 2013 for example, that: 'we recognise that the biggest shift we need to make is cultural; we need responsible business to become business as usual for colleagues', before indicating that 'The shift in culture is

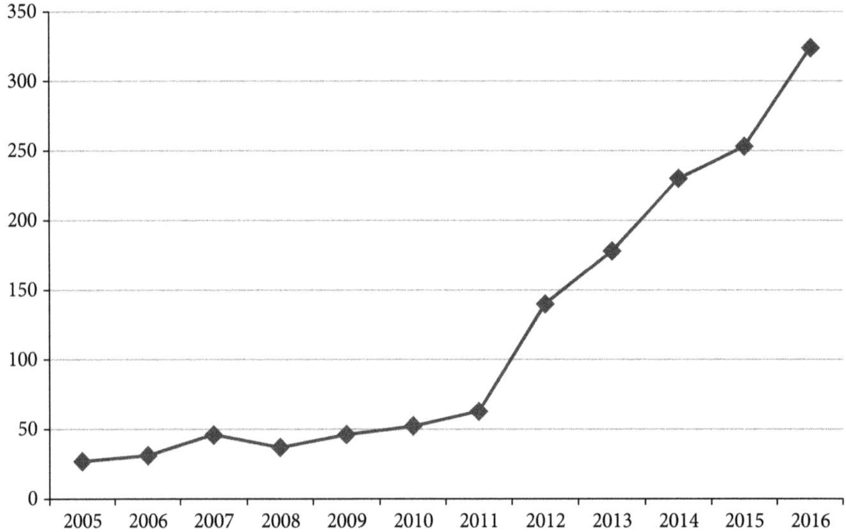

Fig. 9.1 Culture mentions in annual reports (2005–16)
Source: Annual reports of all UK and US banks surveyed in Part III of the book.

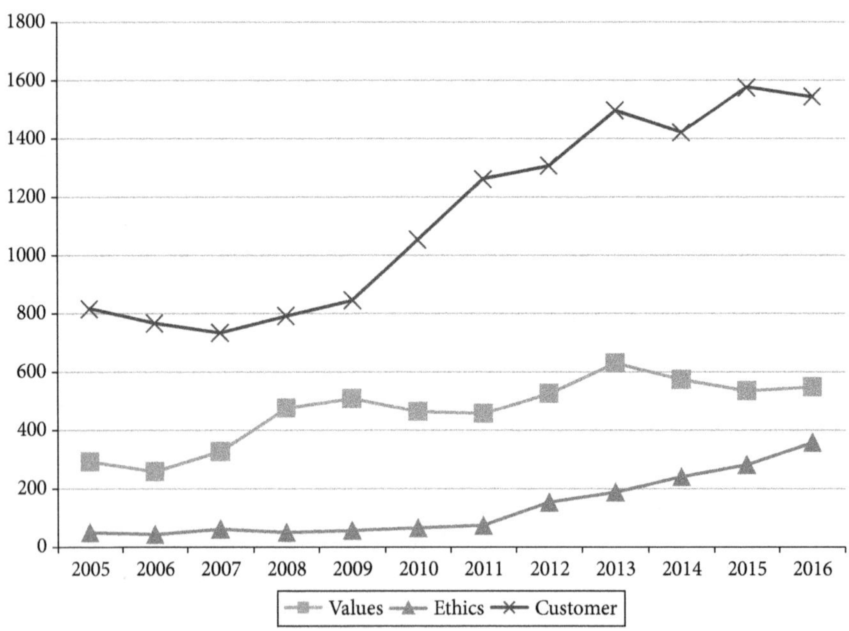

Fig. 9.2 Mentions of values, ethics, customers in annual reports (2005–16)
Source: Annual Reports.

already underway' (2013: xx). Yet—and in line with the key argument of this book—beneath the discourse of culture change the message was essentially of continuity rather than radical overhaul; of the need to remind deviants of the appropriate market conduct (and culture) that they had seemingly forgotten. Though a greater focus on culture therefore emerged, much of the discussion emphasized the need to better embed existing values rather than root and branch reform. As we shall see in later sections of this chapter, the big value statements were indeed accompanied by changes in performance management. But the purpose of this first section is simply to show that though values were discussed more frequently, this should not necessarily be read as a complete U-turn on the pre-crisis strategy. Here we will focus on five of the Anglo-American banks to demonstrate this point.

In the case of Citigroup, culture made an appearance in the 2007 annual report, but was reduced to a particular approach to risk: 'we are aggressively building a new risk management culture' (2007: xx), claimed the report. Again in 2008 the focus was still on risk culture, with the bank emphasizing their policy of 'taking intelligent risk with shared responsibility' (2008: xx). And again in 2011–12 the emphasis was still on a culture of responsible value creation: 'At Citi, we aim to conduct business in a manner that creates value for our clients, shareholders, people and communities. We understand that being a good corporate citizen starts with operating responsibly. This philosophy is ingrained in every aspect of [...] our culture' (2011: xx). 2011–13 then appeared to be a (discursive) turning point for Citi, with the discussions of ethics becoming increasingly pronounced in the parlance of the annual reports. Indeed, the pivotal moment seems to have been the financial results for 2013: the relevant annual report highlighted that 'our 2013 results also surprised us with a damaging example of how ethical failures can jeopardize everything we work for' (2013: xx). In line with the argument of the previous chapter though, the change in tone in Citi's culture statements did not emanate from a particular financial penalty itself, but rather from the write downs the bank faced as a result of fraudulent dealings in Mexico. 'I know that Citi's culture is robust and that the overwhelming majority of our people know right from wrong and strive to do the right thing every day, in all aspects of our work', proclaimed the chairman. 'But I also know that it takes only one person to jeopardize our credibility' (2013: xx). Indeed, having consistently received five to seven mentions between 2005–2013, ethics and ethical behaviour were discussed thirteen to fifteen times in each of the 2014–2016 annual reports. And by 2015 the association between ethical behaviour and risk management was explicit: 'risk management must be built on a foundation of ethical culture' (2015: xx) noted the report. The framing was significant though: when the chairman spoke of what was 'right', he was not appealing to some abstract notion of what was morally virtuous but rather the proper market conduct and norms. But what if those market norms themselves are flawed?

A similar message could be seen in the annual reports of the Bank of America. In 2006 for example, the bank noted that 'our history and culture of superior execution enables us to get things done right: on schedule [and] on budget' (2007: xx). Yet through each annual report from the mid-2000s, the same message—in fact, exactly the same wording—was used to describe culture and ethics. The annual reports repeated 'Corporate culture and the actions of our associates are also critical to effective risk management. Through our Code of Ethics, we set a high standard for our associates. The Code of Ethics provides a framework for all of our associates to conduct themselves with the highest integrity in the delivery of our products or services to our customers' (2005: 46, 2006: 59, 2007: 65, 2008: 54, 2009: 58, 2010: 65).

In 2008, the bank acknowledged that 'corporate culture and the actions of our associates are also critical to effective risk management'; and that their 'Code of Ethics provides a framework for all of [their] associates to conduct themselves with the highest integrity' (2008: xx). Indeed, exactly the same language was still being used in regard to corporate culture in 2013, reflecting the idea that continuity rather than change was the order of the day for BoA. By 2015, a similar message was still being disseminated: 'our culture emphasizes that we are one team, and we have a shared responsibility to manage risk, act responsibly, [and] have an ownership mindset' (2015: xx). Likewise in 2016, the culture was described as one of a hunger for improvement, by 'identifying areas for greater effectiveness and efficiency and driving change one step at a time' (2016: xx). Throughout this time, the bank did indeed repeat a message that 'we are transforming our company, making Bank of America simpler, more transparent, easier to do business with and focused on serving the needs of our customers and clients' (BoA 2011: 1). But, to use a distinction discussed in earlier chapters, this was less about the 'softer' normative changes to ethics and values, and more to do with the 'harder', structural changes to the bank to meet the financial and business needs of customers. As the bank proceeded to highlight, 'we listen to our customers...learn what their needs are, and to do all we can to provide the advice, services, and products that respond to those needs' (BoA 2011: 3). As was argued in Chapter 8, the pressures to reform bank culture—in spite of the scandals and financial penalties—was somewhat diluted by the emphasis on risk reduction and the return to profitability. Overall, the conclusion to be drawn from the Bank of America was that appropriate market conduct had never been disputed, but that some fine-tuning and reminding was necessary in the aftermath of the financial crisis.

For Wells Fargo, a dominant theme of early (2005–8) reports was that of 'caring' for customers: 'The way our team partners together, cares about each other, cares about customers and solves their financial needs is rare in any company. "Culture" makes it happen' (2005: 12); 'A "culture of caring" for our communities—at Wells Fargo, community involvement is [...] central to our vision' (2008: 24);

and 'our vision puts our customers first. It's the heart of our culture' (2009: 1). In fact, throughout the 2008–15 period the message remained fairly consistent. In 2010 the bank stated that 'every decision we make is guided by our vision... and our values: people, ethics, "what's right for our customers", diversity and leadership' (2010: 9); in 2011 the message was the same, 'living our vision and values is about trust, personal responsibility... and making things right for our customers' (2011: 7); in 2013, the annual report noted 'our vision and values set us apart from our competitors. They form the basis of our culture and define who we are' (2013: 8). The implication seemed to be that in contrast to other banks which had been involved in major scandals in 2012 and 2013, Wells Fargo prided itself on being an ethical bank and an exemplar of good market conduct.

As was the case with Citibank, a major scandal involving fraudulent behaviour by Wells Fargo employees prompted a restatement of the core values and an attempt to re-embed them. The chairman noted in the 2016 report for example: 'my fellow Board and I were deeply troubled that Wells Fargo violated [customers'] trust by opening accounts for certain retail banking customers that they did not request or in some cases even know about... We recognize that these events signaled a need for fundamental changes in Wells Fargo's culture, management systems, and executive leadership' (2016: 3). The report then proceeded to explain that in 2017, 'every Wells Fargo team member will be invited to provide feedback about our culture through a review conducted by an independent third party' (2016: 6). This had proven to be a common strategy—employing independent agencies to review what went wrong—amongst a number of other scandal-ridden banks. But, again, the message was of needing to return to existing market values.

For the British bank Barclays, a major change was clearly associated with the arrival of Antony Jenkins, the new CEO in 2012. In 2005 the bank spoke of 'using rewards to drive a high-performance culture' (2005: xx). As with many of the other banks however, there was a recognition even as early as 2005 of the need for a conscientious ethic: 'Corporate responsibility is, first and foremost, about responsible business conduct. For us, it is founded on the principles, ethics and values that Barclays has embodied for over 300 years' (2005: xx). The point is that, in most cases the banks responded to the financial crisis and subsequent cases of misconduct not by fully reworking their values; that is because these values, the correct norms appropriate for market competition, were well-established and widely accepted. As I explained in Chapter 2, the liberal vision of the pristine and idealized market has a long heritage. Instead, the banks conceived of the crisis as evidence of the need to re-embed and monitor existing values that had perhaps been forgotten. The 2006 annual report said 'responsible banking means making informed, reasoned and ethical decisions in our business dealings. Our Guiding Principles of Winning Together, Customer Focus, The Best People, Pioneering and Trusted describe how we expect our employees to behave' (2006: xx). Yet Barclays' involvement in the subsequent LIBOR scandal revealed quite different priorities. Barclays was another bank which subsequently employed an external agency—the Salz committee—to review its culture. Thus, by 2012, the process of re-embedding values had begun: 'The Council has also delivered training on reputation risk to senior executives across the bank to ensure the knowledge and culture is embedded' (2012: 97). Similarly in 2013, the focus was on '*embedding* our Purpose and Values throughout the organisation' (emphasis added 2013: 2).

In the case of the British bank RBS, the group stated in 2010 that 'the culture which allowed the old RBS to fail has changed and changed for good' (2010: 17). As with other banks, the problem was defined as a risk management problem, so that the change ensured that the bank now 'manage[d] reputational risk with sound controls and a strong risk culture' (ibid.: 17). But by 2013 the bank was also talking about 'new values', which 'focus on serving customers, working together, doing the right thing and thinking long term' (2013: 20). In the case of RBS it seemed that the bank had underestimated the importance of ethics and valuing customers to appropriate market conduct; market competition and accumulation itself falter if conduct undermines trust in either the particular financial institution or the market mechanism. As one of the worst offenders in the UK it seemed that this message had begun to sink in. By 2016 RBS was then able to assert that based on a survey of 63,000 staff, 'we are changing the culture of RBS for the better' (2016: 28). The thinking that good culture promotes sustainable returns then seemed to be more apparent by the 2015–16 reports: 'We believe the focus on culture and encouraging good behaviours will, in time, make a significant contribution to driving sustainable returns for shareholders' stated the 2015 report (2015: 65). Again, the order and rationale were very revealing: returns and profitability depended on not jeopardizing the foundation of the market economy, a point that Mark Carney alluded to at the start of this book.

In summary, the picture which emerges from the culture statements made by the banks tends to highlight three common features: firstly, most of the banks believed that their core values, which existed prior to any scandals and prior to the onset of the financial crisis, were sufficient. What followed from this, secondly, was the conclusion that it was not that the values themselves needed reworking, but they were not deeply embedded enough in the daily running of the bank or the mindset of the employees. In broad, discursive terms, they had always agreed on valuing customers, being ethical, and acting in socially responsible ways. These were relatively uncontested market norms. And in keeping with the narrow version of the culture debate, the banks agreed that the root cause of the problem was with the application of these market norms, rather than the norms itself. These norms allowed for high bonuses and skewed business models, and so banks accepted that behaviours which threatened the stability or credibility of these norms should be avoided. Thirdly, systematic efforts were then made to introduce new programmes to repackage and embed the right culture and values. Put simply, it was not that the values themselves changed dramatically but the banks began talking about them much more. One could therefore conclude that understanding culture change using big value statements is meaningless; the annual reports are too vague and abstract. But this would be to miss a more subtle point: one major purpose of good culture—as highlighted by the corporate social responsibility literature—is to promote the right external image: banks were not unaware of this prior to the financial crisis; and they simply renewed their efforts at achieving this purpose once crises and scandals unfolded. The remainder of this chapter now turns to examining the (more) substantive changes made in light of these value statements.

Risk

The previous section highlighted the fact that discussions of culture, ethics, and values were increasingly prevalent in all of the major Anglo-American banks after the financial crisis. One of the most prominent aspects highlighted by the qualitative survey of the annual reports however, was the increased focus on risk management. The aim of this section is to examine what changed within the banks with regards to their risk culture, in part because this takes us beyond rather more abstract discussions of ethics and values. This section therefore leads into the third section of this chapter which discusses the rise of the compliance culture more broadly. Using the banks' annual reports, two simple word cloud diagrams from 2005 and 2016 point to one interesting conclusion: risk—risk profile, risk management and so forth—was certainly more prominent in the language of the world's largest banks by 2016 (Fig. 9.3).

This conclusion is supported by Fig. 9.4, which shows the rise in the mentions of risk in the annual reports themselves.

Providing a comprehensive overview of all the changes to risk culture would be impracticable. Instead, this short section examines some of the most important

Annual Reports 2005 Annual Reports 2016

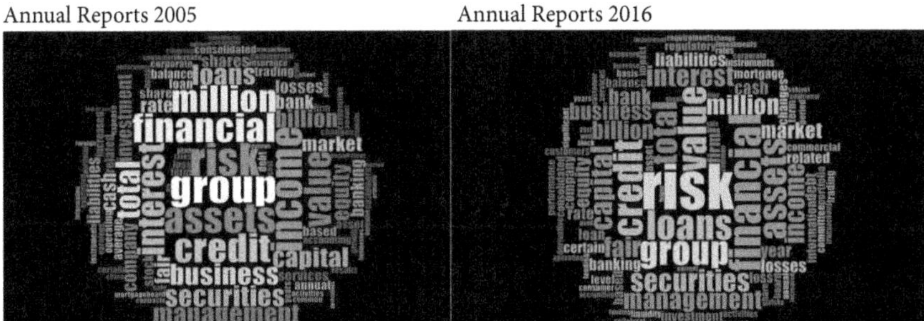

Fig. 9.3 Word cloud showing usage of all terms in annual reports 2005 & 2016
Source: Annual reports.

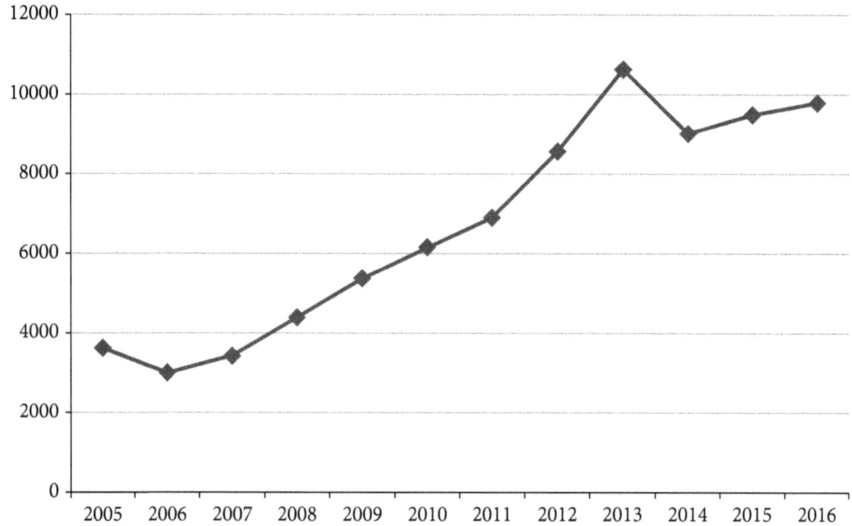

Fig. 9.4 Mentions of risk in annual reports 2005–16
Source: Annual reports.

trends across the industry. One could easily be forgiven however, for assuming that risk management, and conduct and compliance, were mere technical and mundane aspects with little implication for culture and values. But risk profile is one of the major, 'hard' ways in which culture shifted following the financial crisis. The business studies literature informs us that 'risk management refers to the processes by which risk is identified, analyzed, included in strategic planning, and either reduced through risk control or accepted as inherent in activities that the organization wishes to conduct' (Miller 2017: 21). Put simply, it is a very good place to start our study of what culture looked like inside the biggest Anglo-American banks by 2017–18.

That said, given the arguments about the limited extent of the changes; the emphasis on the structural conditions of financialization that are more influential to bank culture than behavioural reforms; and the simple point that risk appetite increases as the economy improves and confidence returns; risk culture too does not necessarily provide a good basis for assessing long-term processes of cultural change. It is understandable that, in light of defaults and new regulation, risk appetite was more conservative in the early 2010s. We will show this point in the present section. But by late 2016, both in terms of lending and trading, risk appetite was returning. The Office of the Comptroller of the Currency's (OCC) annual Survey of Credit Underwriting Practices explained for example, that the main cause of the increase in lending to Private Non-Financial Corporations (PNFCs) by 2016 was that banks had continued 'to ease underwriting practices in response to competitive pressures, expanding credit risk appetites, and a desire for loan growth'. They concluded that 'credit risk has increased since 2015 in commercial and retail lending activities' (OCC 2016: 3). The OCC report was only moderately concerned about this trend, indicating that this was broadly consistent with a credit cycle theory, whereby banks generally tighten underwriting practices when the economy contracts and ease underwriting practices when the economy expands' (ibid.). The same was true in trading, with low yields on safe assets and slow returns, combined with excess liquidity, encouraging 'investors to put money into riskier asset classes' (*FT* 2013, Haldane et al. 2016: 8). We will return to this claim in Chapter 10. For now, let us consider the (albeit relatively transient) shifts in risk culture.

Early chapters of this book discussed ways in which the dominant culture in many areas of the banks became one of increased risk-taking in the early 2000s. This was in part attributed to lower interest rates and a slowdown in economic growth, making traditional, safer banking less profitable. The economic downturn from 2007, and the need to stabilize the banks, led to a more risk-averse culture across almost all areas of the banks. In grand terms, a 2014 Forbes article concluded 'deleveraging, or shedding assets, has become a global obsession in the [banking] industry. Proprietary trading is gone, investment banking departments have shrunk, mortgage servicing is not worth the capital and far-flung operations are being sold off' (Forbes 2014). By 2016 then, when describing the changes that their bank had undergone, a number described themselves as 'smaller, safer…less leveraged, and better capitalized' (Barclays 2016: 02). The key aim in the mid-2010s then, across most of these larger banks, was to 'reduce the balance sheet and simplify the organization' (Citigroup 2008: 8): 'simpler, smaller, safer, stronger' (Citigroup 2016: 2), making a 'smaller and more humble financial services industry' (BoA 2008: 3). Reduce and simplify; reduce and simplify.

Risk Exposure

In relation to risk, this meant a more cautious approach to risk exposure (Goldman 2011: 2). Perhaps ironically, Bank of America reiterated the message 'we instill a risk-conscious culture through communications, training, policies, procedures, and organizational roles and responsibilities' right up until the financial crisis hit (2005: 46, 2006: 59, 2007: 65, 2008: 54, 2009: 58). It then changed the phraseology slightly in 2010, to 'We instill *a strong and comprehensive* risk management culture' (emphasis added 2010: 65, 2011: 66, 2012: 66), recognizing that the previous model had been found wanting. The bank then explained that it had 'taken a number of steps to strengthen and sustain a strong risk management culture. We have developed a clear understanding of our risk appetite across all businesses' (2011: 7). More tangible and specific than the rather nebulous emphasis on customers and values, the emphasis on a more moderate risk appetite reflected a greater awareness of the fact that poorly calculated risk-taking could be existence-threatening. The primary goal of profit-making had to be tempered by a desire to preserve the market itself.

One interviewee explained the mechanism by which a tighter risk profile might manifest. Typically, they explained, these risk profile decisions would be made at the executive board level before being passed down to division and line managers throughout the different arms of the business. Strengthening risk management might focus on placing very specific, tighter limits: for example, it might involve stricter rules about the types and levels of a particular product that would be sold, or reducing exposure to a particular client base (Interview 20170629). Similarly, Barclays noted that it had 'reduced its credit risk appetite in the most severely affected segments of the economy' (2010: 12); whilst RBS also stated that it had 'reduced its risk appetite in the higher-risk sectors of leisure, media, commercial real estate, construction, automotive and airlines' (2011: 135). Likewise in the US banks, they made extensive efforts to 'reduce [their] exposures in certain high-risk... markets' (BoA 2008: 14). This also included deleveraging, with Barclays reducing its leverage ratios from fifty-six times its balance sheet in 2008 to twenty-one times by 2016 (2016: 3); and Goldman reducing from twenty-six times to ten times its balance sheet by 2014 (2014: 2, 25).

Cost-cutting

It also meant that the expansionary mindset of growth by mergers, with megabanks buying out smaller firms to expand their footprint, had significantly diminished. As the Citigroup CEO Michael Corbat explained in 2012, 'one thing is certain: there is no appetite among regulators for us—or any large bank—to grow inorganically' (2012: 5), meaning that US regulators were opposed to the culture of big acquisitions and mega-mergers. At the time of the Bank of America merger with Merrill Lynch for example, the global markets (investment banking) business had assets of nearly $1 trillion; by the end of the year this had been reduced to $600 billion (BoA 2014: 2). This was evidence of a culture shift. In the past, many of these banks, Bank of America, Citibank, Barclays, RBS (and even some of the smaller banks) had operated under the mentality that 'bigger is better'. Now the goal was to 'produce higher quality revenue and profits', rather than needing to be 'the largest in the business' (BoA 2014: 2, Interview 20170718); and to 'build revenues organically in...core business areas' (BoA 2014: 5). This meant that 'success depend[ed] on investing [their] resources in the right places, in the right businesses, at the right time' (2012: 6). Again though, all of these culture changes were of the same type: the aim was to preserve the market, so that socially responsible conduct was defined as anything which did not undermine the credibility and sustainability of the market itself.

A number of interviewees explained what this more risk conscious approach looked like from inside the banks. One human resources manager explained that the message from the top at their firm had been 'We need to drive profit still [but] we're not making much margin on our products; therefore the only other factor we can deal with is our cost base and try and shrink that' (Interview 20161109). What that meant in practice was that, from the human resources perspective, 'they went through a lot of redundancy programs, cost cutting, chipping away' (ibid.). In relation to investment decisions, another employee explained that prior to the financial crisis the view tended to be 'take the risk, and the costs will work themselves out'. Whereas the focus had become, 'at least in the retail sector... how can we reduce costs?' (Interview 20161107).

Similarly another employee working in the finance function (another name for the back office staff tasked with structuring and costing out products and deals) explained that when they had joined their firm in the late 1990s that their finance team 'had a voice' and could be 'heard', because even though the bank was relatively large the finance team, the operations team, and the trading floor were closely integrated. In effect, this meant that risk-taking was moderated by the influence of more conservative divisions of the bank. They explained that this had changed significantly after a major acquisition: 'it got so big and bigger things are hard to control' (Interview 20161216). In their experience too, the ethos had then changed to 'nobody care[s] about the cost of capital', in the mid 2000s; whereas by the late 2010s the message from senior management was '[we] don't want to end up with a deal that's not going to work or cost too much in capital terms' (ibid.). The interviewee explained that 'things like leverage ratios, capital requirements are so much more focused on'. In the past it would be 'we're coming up to year end how can we reduce our capital? Now it's throughout the year. How much capital is this going to cost? How can we do it? Does it make sense?' (ibid.). Another senior manager at a large firm confirmed this changed approach. They explained that 'one of the big changes that occurred is the way performance is measured... in the past there was a very heavy focus on targeting the business to earn more revenue. It was all around the top line. Whereas now... it's very much about... profit as a return on capital... so not just the revenue generators, but also the support costs that go with that business line... the cost of capital, the cost of potential bad debts and so forth' (Interview 20170313). In short, across a range of the Anglo-American banks there was a palpable emphasis on cost-cutting and cost-monitoring as a means to reduce risk.

Trading

Arguably however, one of the most noticeable changes was in the trading divisions within the largest banks. As I will explain in Chapter 10, this change should not be overstated. Nor should we ignore the cultural problems in other non-banks firms engaged in trading, though they do not form part of our study. But, there was nonetheless evidence of a change in risk culture in trading activities during the 2010s. Across most of the banks then, this meant that they reduced the size of their global markets (investment banking) sales and trading operations. In large part this was a response to the new regulatory requirements attached to trading activity. For example, the new Basel II and Basel III capital rules approximately tripled the amount of regulatory capital for trading portfolios including market-making and hedging activities, acting as a major disincentive (JPMorgan 2010: 23). As JP Morgan noted, 'exotic products are small in size and more transparent, and trading books [now] require far more liquidity to support' (2010: 22).

Perhaps one of the most important areas of de-risking was that of proprietary trading. Essentially, this was trading conducted solely for the profit of the bank itself (Hardie and Macartney 2016, see also Chapter 4). Trading activity is typically defined as one of three types: facilitating clients transactions, taking proprietary positions, or as a means of risk management (Goldman Sachs 2006: 67). Put differently, proprietary trading was defined in distinction to market-making activity, which was 'buying and selling on behalf of clients' (Goldman Sachs 2010: 5, see also Wells Fargo 2006: 74, 2011: 40). The scale of the activity was significantly larger in the US than in the European banks, and the cutting back or closing down of propriety trading desks was primarily driven by new regulation (the Volcker rule in the US and the Liikanen proposals in the EU) (see Barclays 2013: 57, Hardie and Macartney 2016).

Focusing on the Volcker rule, in December 2013, the relevant US authorities (the Federal Reserve Board, the FDIC, the SEC, and the CFTC) finalized the rules implementing section 619 of the Dodd–Frank Act prohibiting banks and their subsidiaries from undertaking certain proprietary trading. The rules still permitted certain activities however, such as underwriting, market-making, and risk mitigation hedging (Barclays 2013: 136). As a result, and even prior to the final ratification of Dodd–Frank, many of the banks had already begun to wind down their proprietary trading line of business, 'In anticipation of the adoption of the final regulations' (BoA 2010: 61, Citigroup 2011: 77, JPMorgan 2010: 22, Wells Fargo 2011: 83). By 2011 for example, BoA stated that its proprietary trading business was $434 million for the first six months of 2011, compared to $1.4bn dollars for 2010 (2011: 27).

Raw numbers can be somewhat opaque, and one aim of this book is to demystify the culture and practice of banking. What did the change in attitude towards trading look like inside the bank? A large number of employees working on the sales and trading side of the business explained that the most obvious way in which this new, more conservative attitude affected the trading culture was in the willingness to take a risk on a particular transaction. They explained that they typically made their money for the firm by finding a particular stock or commodity that, in their estimations, the market had under- or over-priced. They would subsequently purchase that stock or commodity, or short the market—a way of saying that they would bet against that particular stock and commodity, expecting it to fall in price—via a range of derivative or synthetic products. In this scenario, the transaction itself of course involved an element of risk, but the real test was in how long their firm would be willing to hold that position if the rise or fall in price did not transpire under a given (short) time horizon. Countless employees explained that, not necessarily because of increased regulatory oversight, but their firms became increasingly reticent about 'holding a position' for a longer period (various interviews).

Part of the issue here is that 'market-makers' would typically purchase assets and then sell them on to clients. Under the new conditions of the Volcker rule however, one implication was that market-makers should only purchase these assets if they knew that there was already a market available for them. This was due to strict speculative position limits (*CFTC* 2016). Further, the implication would be that if no markets were found for these assets in a relatively short space of time, a decision would have to be made over whether to continue to hold that position or unwind it, potentially at a loss. As Goldman Sachs (2011:6) noted, 'we need to know that we can carry this inventory for the optimal time, not a minimal time, and have judgments made by people who are trying to determine an appropriately effective manner in which to dispose of this position; if restricted from doing this, market-makers will provide less liquidity and at worse prices.' Similarly, JPMorgan contended that 'market making requires that traders, in order to facilitate client business, take positions in inventory that they hope to sell later' (2011: 36). This shift in risk culture led Jamie Dimon—CEO of JPMorgan—to quip that 'if you want to be trading nowadays, you have to have a lawyer and a psychiatrist sitting next to you determining what was your intent every time you did something' (cited in *NY Times* 2012e). There was certainly evidence then that during the early to mid-2010s, risk culture in trading had changed to a degree.

Compliance

It should be recalled that our aim in this chapter is not to provide a comprehensive list of all the ways in which bank culture had changed; particularly given the fact that the main argument of this book is that the structural drivers of culture had changed very little. Neither do we wish to simply list the changes to leverage or capital ratios for example, though these had important cultural implications. Instead, from a variety of different angles, our aim is to go beyond big value statements in annual reports, and explain why culture in the largest Anglo-American banks certainly 'felt' quite different to employees. This third subsection therefore examines one of the largest areas of change, compliance. Indeed, in our interviews with bank employees (from lower ranked staff to managers), almost all referred to the new environment of compliance when asked what key issues were shaping their organizations' culture. BoE Chief Economist Andy Haldane even called this 'the age of the compliance officer', estimating that 70,000 new compliance jobs would have to be created in 2012 simply to deal with implementing Basel III (*Telegraph* 2012). In a certain sense, compliance is simply another aspect of the risk culture that was discussed in the previous subsection. But, there is enough of a distinction to warrant considering the compliance culture separately, with risk often referring to risk appetite and compliance referring to 'the processes by which an organization polices *its own behavior* to ensure that it conforms to the applicable rules' (emphasis added Miller 2017: 54).

One interviewee expressed that 'compliance has moved to center stage' (Interview 20170130). Several interviewees explained that 'compliance is the new game in town' (various interviews). This is not altogether true however, since compliance in financial services had an extensive history. There was certainly a qualitative and quantitative shift in compliance culture after the financial crisis however. Leading accountancy and consultancy firms defined the financial crisis as a 'Darwinian process of selection', whereby banks 'whose appetite for growth and risk exceeded their ability to handle it' suffered the most (PWC 2009: 5). In part, this was perceived as a failure of systems and models designed to manage risk, which had led to a false sense of security. More importantly though, there was the view that in the pursuit of profits compliance departments had faced 'intense pressures...to approve increasingly risky transactions' (PWC 2009: 6). In other words, alongside the increasingly risk-conscious culture (the previous section) a major component of the compliance culture was an attempt to (re) empower compliance and risk officers of various kinds (BCBS 2015, European Commission 2010). Again, in keeping with the narrower bank culture debate, the re-emergence of compliance officers reflected a belief that greed and recklessness could be tempered, and the pristine market saved from existence-threatening risk-taking.

Compliance laws, rules, and standards generally cover issues ranging from correct market conduct, managing conflicts of interests, and ensuring that clients and customers are treated fairly (BIS 2005: 7, Interview 20170627). Compliance is aimed at regulating banks' behaviour towards their shareholders, customers, employees, and the markets (International Compliance Association, 2017). The types of activity therefore covered by compliance can range from market misconduct to conflicts of interest, customer mistreatment, unfair customer advice, as well as money laundering, terrorist financing, tax avoidance, and failure to meet regulatory or financial reporting requirements (Basel Committee on Banking Supervision, 2005). And as a result of the bank culture debate, compliance risk became one of the most significant concerns for banking executives following the financial crisis (McKinsey 2016).

As a microcosm for understanding the scope and nature of the changes that took place, we will focus on the three-lines-of-defence model. Prior to the financial crisis, the compliance model was designed to function predominantly in an *advisory* capacity. Post-financial crisis however, there was a renewed focus on the so-called three lines model, empowering compliance officers and protocols. The three lines model itself was developed during the 1990s, and particularly following the Dot.com demise, which showed 'the sheer breadth and depth of the risk landscape' (KPMG 2016: 1). Since the financial crisis however, it became 'the most common benchmark for assigning control and risk management responsibilities to business functions in a [banking] organization' (BIS 2015: 4). Under this model, management control was the first line of defence in risk management; secondly came the various risk control and compliance oversight functions; and thirdly, there was the internal auditing process. The first line was intended to 'own and manage risks', the second line to 'oversee risks', and the third to 'provide independent assurance' (IIA 2013: 3). At the first stage, operational (senior) managers were meant to identify, assess, and control risks, whilst mid-level managers then designed detailed processes to control and supervise these risks for lower level employees. The second stage was then comprised of risk management structures—to facilitate and manage the implementation of effective risk management practices—and compliance teams—to ensure compliance with specific laws and regulations. Finally, internal auditors were meant to provide comprehensive and independent assurance of governance, risk management, and internal controls (ibid.: 5–6).

A series of deficiencies became apparent over the course of the financial crisis however, prompting revision to the model. One was the misaligned interests for risk-takers in the first line of defence. Though, in a sense, the entire compliance and risk culture of an organization was determined by senior management (the first line), this responsibility was seen to conflict with their main objective which was to generate profits and revenue (BIS 2015: 5). A second problem was that the effectiveness of the control function (the second line of defence) was also compromised by their lack of independence. A further problem was that, even if the control function was sufficiently independent, it often lacked the skills and expertise to challenge management. Similarly, a final problem identified was that the internal audit assessment (the third line) was often inadequate or subjective (ibid.). This type of diagnosis of conflicts of interests and weak accountability mechanisms was a standard feature of the bank culture debate.

What followed was that all of the major Anglo-American banks began investing heavily in improving their compliance function. Early annual reports (2006–10) often contained a generic message about the importance of *regulatory* compliance. Barclays for example, stated 'Non-compliance could lead to fines, public reprimands, damage to reputation, enforced suspension of operations or, in extreme cases, withdrawal of authorizations to operate' (2009: 11, see also

2008: 13, 2007: 8, 2006: 6). By 2010 however, the bank noted that it was 'taking steps to enhance its compliance programmes'. It also began emphasizing 'significant additional compliance costs' (2011: 12). Then, by 2012, it explained that in response to the restructuring of the FSA, to 'go beyond the previous focus on compliance with rules, on process and on treating customers fairly, to embrace a holistic approach of how a firm organizes itself and does business in order to ensure good customer outcomes', that Barclays was establishing a Board Conduct, Reputation, and Operational Risks Committee (2012: 98). The result was that by 2013, the group noted that whilst 'Intensified regulatory and government intervention ensures a sound operating environment;...it does lead to increased cost of compliance and complexity of doing business' (2013: 27). Similarly, JPMorgan released a memo to staff in November 2013 stating that they had hired an additional 4000 compliance team members and spent an additional $1 billion on controls in 2013. In April 2015, Citigroup noted that approximately 59 per cent of the bank's $3.4bn efficiency savings would be 'consumed by additional investments...in regulatory and compliance activities'. Another interviewee explained that banks such as HSBC had gone from a compliance team of ten people to approximately '10% of their organization' working in the different compliance functions (Interview 20170627).

Moreover, at the time of writing the expectation from industry insiders was that these costs would only continue to increase. According to the 2017 Global Accenture Survey of Executives for example, approximately 89 per cent of financial services industry executives expected continued cost increases in compliance due to 'an explosion in digital data, a finite talent pool of compliance professionals to draw from and a more-complex risk ecosystem' (Accenture 2017). According to Accenture's fourth annual compliance risk report, 'Dare to be Different', 48 per cent of the executives expected compliance costs to increase by 10–20 per cent in the coming year or two. The same survey reported that banks believed fraud and financial crime risk, business risk, and cyber risk to be the top three compliance risks that would be the most challenging. Similarly, as stated in the Thomson Reuters Global Cost of Compliance 2016 Survey, 83 per cent of global systemically important financial institutions (G-SIFIs) expected costs related to compliance staff to increase in 2016. This increase in costs was supported by US and UK banks' cost-to-income ratio data, which spiked moderately in 2008—due to a smaller revenue base—and in 2014—due to rising expenses (Figs 9.5 and 9.6).

In relation to the *range* of activities, this too was indicative of the ways in which compliance progressively influenced the day-to-day running of most (and especially the largest) banks. Once again, anecdotal examples are a useful heuristic device. In an interview with Joris Luyendjik (a columnist for the *Guardian* newspaper), a former compliance officer discussed the pressure he experienced when one trader approached him two minutes before markets closed, asking him to sign off a multi-million dollar deal. Such a large deal so close to end of day

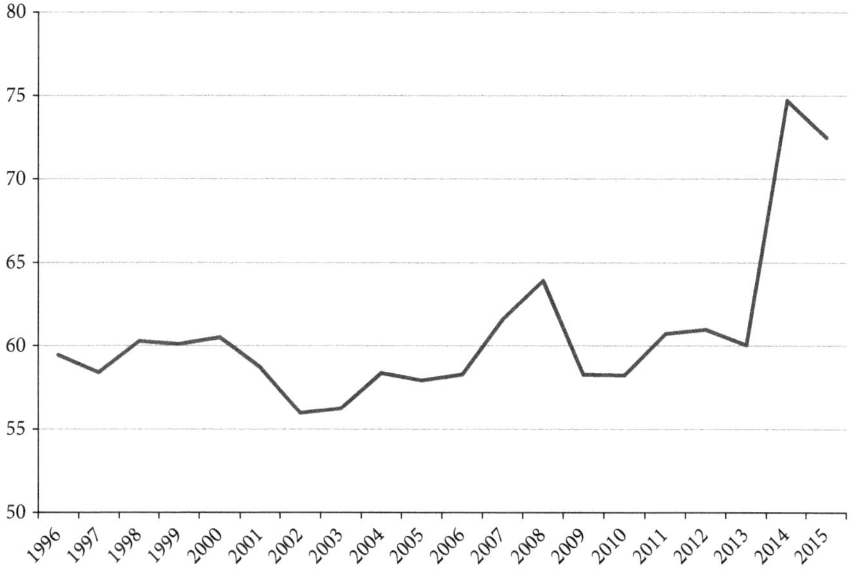

Fig. 9.5 Cost-to-income ratio for US banks (%, annual, not seasonally adjusted), 1996–2015

Source: St Louis Federal Reserve.

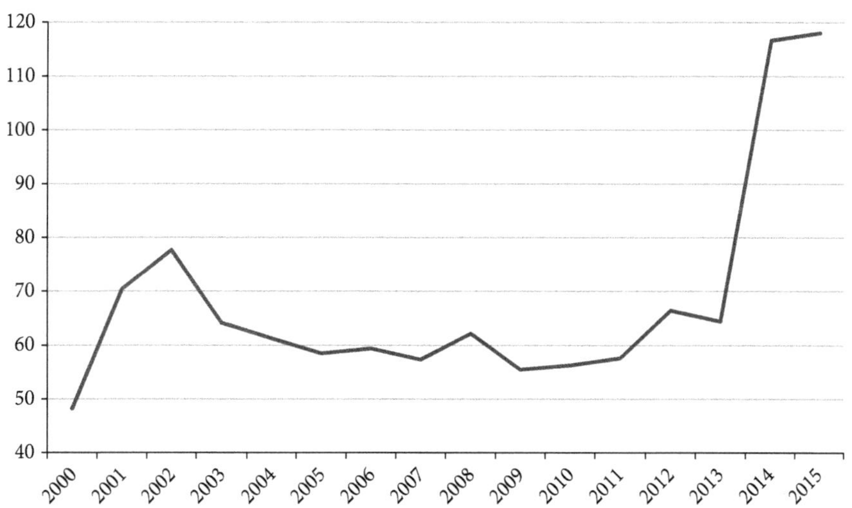

Fig. 9.6 Cost-to-income ratio for UK banks (%, annual, not seasonally adjusted), 2000–15

Source: St Louis Federal Reserve.

might have raised suspicions of insider trading, he explained. The compliance officer rapidly conducted his due diligence, confirming that the prices for the deal were publicly listed, and that there was a telephone recording of the interactions between the dealer and the client in case of future regulatory investigation (Luyendijk 2015: 46). In this way compliance imposed an extra layer of checks on trading activity, with the aim of promoting caution (Interview 20170629).

Compliance also impacted on data handling and behavioural anomalies. One of the big issues to emerge with the financial crisis was the treatment of sensitive information, both inside and outside of the workplace. In the case of the LIBOR and Forex scandals, online chat rooms were used to discuss confidential information between traders. Due to internal reforms and heightened regulatory scrutiny compliance divisions therefore began monitoring all email traffic. As one interviewee explained, compliance teams were concerned with 'capturing any potential misdemeanour or any malfeasance from anyone on the trading desk, sales desk, [or were] aggressively monitoring electronic communication, traffic, capturing oddities in the trading patterns' (Interview 20161123). Indeed, many of the larger banks also introduced CCTV to monitor the behaviour of employees on the trading floor, just as one would in a casino. Again though, the rationale behind these compliance efforts was important: the aim was to bring any abnormal behaviour back in line with market norms. Establishing good culture meant reinforcing stricter parameters to ensure that participants behaved as the market dictated. Even the term 'compliance' was indicative of the assumption that if participants adhered to the proper rules for market conduct then adverse outcomes could be avoided.

Once again though, to speak of a compliance culture or the empowering of compliance officers risks sounding incredibly dry and technical. In a sense, nothing could be further from the truth. What it signified, according to industry insiders, was—in certain areas—tantamount to an identity crisis in banking (Levine 2016). The rise of the compliance function typified a struggle between a more explicitly profit-oriented, discretionary culture and a more rules-based culture. In our analysis, we have characterized the two layers of struggle over bank culture: that which is taking place at the level of ethical, socially responsible conduct; and the underlying, structural pressures and incentives derived from financialization. Within the narrower debate the compliance culture might be considered the most important influence on changed behaviours. As we noted, risk-taking fluctuates with the business cycle. The influence of compliance officers over risk strategy may also therefore have been only a temporary change. Yet many of the compliance reforms discussed here have become permanent features of banking and so we would expect them to have a certain longevity. Yet as we will explain in Chapter 10, even the most profound compliance changes barely scratched the surface of the culture-from-financialization problematique.

That said, it is easy to see why—during the late 2010s—bank employees viewed compliance reform as a game-changer. When Barclays held its 'town hall' (the name given to a general forum meeting) whilst the Dodd–Frank act was being put in place, compliance executives shared images of how each group viewed the other: to represent bankers, compliance executives showed an image from the Wild West, of Cowboys on horses with guns; whilst on the other side, to show how bankers view compliance officers, the executives revealed a picture of nuns carrying guns, an indicator that the group was seen as 'ultraconservative but still dangerous' (*WSJ* 2016c). To bank employees this was a clash of tribes and cultures.

Discussing the environment in their particular firm, one director in the investment banking area explained that during the late 1990s whilst the focus was on 'growing the business rapidly and rapid expansion of the business', there was little emphasis on what they described as 'control processes' (Interview 20161123). Another banker from the wealth management division expressed that 'financial services as an industry was under-regulated prior to 2008 [but] the scrutiny which we are under now from the regulator for compliance . . . it has gone too far the other way I think' (Interview 20161101). Another interviewee explained how the compliance culture—alongside greater personal accountability—had led to a slower, committee-led decision-making process. They noted that the 'shift towards more personal accountability has brought a desire for people to make decisions via committee rather than someone take a decision as a kind of senior leader would in the business, and that naturally will slow down the speed at which we can respond to clients' (Interview 20161101–08). They concluded that 'it is orders of magnitude more difficult now to do business than it was before' (ibid).

Finally, one other interviewee explained that the new compliance culture had 'created a fear factor' that was both 'good and bad' (Interview 20161018). In part this stemmed from a perceived lack of clarity about expectations placed on firms by regulators. A compliance expert explained that when the five US federal regulators established the Federal Financial Institutions Examinations Council and produced the FFIEC Manual, the hope amongst firms was that this 400-page textbook would clarify the regulatory requirements. Instead, the manual 'raised more questions than answers' (Interview 20170627). This meant that despite the appearance of a flurry of new regulations and compliance initiatives, firms still remained uncertain about what was expected of them, yet clear about the implication that 'if you don't do what is *generally* expected, you're going to get whacked again' (original emphasis, ibid.). Indeed, this goes a long way to explain the frustration most interviewees expressed about the purpose of such intensive compliance monitoring; whilst also helping to explain another feature of many interview responses, that employees felt that their banks were 'trying to cover their backs' (various interviews). In short, compliance was strengthened in order to reinforce and enforce proper market conduct. But the new environment felt almost stifling to bank employees in *many* divisions of *most* banks.

Remuneration

> 'Before, we had people coming in on motorbikes and shorts and T-shirts, unshaven and saying, "Let's make some money guys!" ... It's not like that at all anymore. It's a lot more stuffy. It's a lot more of a framework. There's just ... a lot less money to be earned.'
>
> (Interview 20170213)

This final section examines the issue of remuneration or, as it is euphemistically labelled, *compensation*. The short version is that much had changed in the area of remuneration during the 2010s as was discussed at length in Chapters 4–7; bank employees repeatedly confirmed this during interviews. And yet, as I explain at length in Chapter 10, remuneration in the banking sector was still entirely disproportionate to either the value-added of the sector or wages in other parts of the economy. It was therefore one of the most important economic and political factors at the core of the culture of banking debate.

As noted in earlier chapters, pay does not *determine* culture, but it is an important *determinant* of behaviour—risk-taking, ethical decisions, and so forth. Much has already been written in the academic literature about two aspects of changes in banker pay: deferral, and lower overall levels (Chon 2013). Here a simple overview will suffice. Deferral refers to the delaying of a portion of the variable part of remuneration to allow time for any financial results to be revised. This was because, as we discussed in Chapters 5 and 7, 'compensation systems ... too often rewarded the quick deal, the short-term gain—without proper consideration of long-term consequences' (Financial Crisis Enquiry Report 2010, xix). Deferral was therefore seen as the 'primary risk adjustment mechanism to align rewards with sustainable performance' (Walker Review 2009: 21). In 2009 the Financial Stability Forum (FSF) called for a 'substantial portion ... such as 40 to 60%' of bank bonuses to be subject to deferral (2009: 3); whilst in the UK the minimum deferral period for senior managers was set at 3–5 years (FCA and PRA 2015: 13–14). Certainly, deferral was central to state managers' efforts, though its effect on culture was hard to assess. One interviewee simply noted that 'actually once we got through the first three years of transition, you are kind of back to receiving effectively a full year's bonus in a year albeit some of it will be shares that are vesting from prior years' (Interview 20161101). In other words, the impact of deferral was questionable.

On the second issue, there was also clear evidence that average pay in the banking sector had fallen for most staff (I will return to this point in Chapter 10)

(Interview 20161101). As one interviewee explained, 'the actual value of the financial performance bonus that you can earn I think it would be fair to say, is quite substantially less than it used to be... The days of earning big mega bonuses even at relatively junior or less influential levels I think have just gone. You just wouldn't expect to be seeing that now' (20161130). Once again though, the impact that lower bonuses had on culture was hard to determine. From the perspective of bank employees, it certainly *felt* as though the bonus culture had changed. But the culture of banking problem is always a relative and relational problem, because it is—in the area of remuneration—a form of inequality. In other words, more objective indicators of pay and the perspective from outsiders are arguably more informative than the view of bank staff themselves.

Instead though, this final section focuses on an aspect of pay which was less discussed in the post-crisis literature, but arguably had a greater impact on culture: how *performance reviews* were structured. Indeed, this might have been one of the most influential mechanisms for translating abstract value statements into daily activities of bank staff. In examining the impact that values and ethics had on remuneration by the late 2010s, there were, of course, important differences both between firms and between different divisions within the same firm. Across the industry however, there was now a far greater focus on the 'how's' (how did you treat the clients and your colleagues? And how well did you apply the regulatory rules) as well as the 'what's' (did you hit your targets?). The big picture was that in both retail and commercial banking in the UK and the US there was a significant increase in focus on ethical performance indicators as a component in performance-related pay. As one interviewee explained, 'there's been a huge change in how people are performance managed' (Interview 20161101).

Changes in performance reviews were not limited to the banking industry. A whole range of other large global firms—from Microsoft to GE, and Gap to Accenture—had been shifting from annual evaluations to continual feedback mechanisms (*New Yorker* 2015, FastCompany 2015). Research psychologists had suggested that there were two driving factors behind these changes: one was that, for a variety of reasons, annual performance reviews were ineffective. For example, biases and prejudices on the part of the reviewer made the review process highly subjective, whilst negative feedback during annual performance reviews, rather than motivating employees, was found to have the opposite affect (Culbertson, Henning and Payne 2013). The second explanation lay with the demographics and zeitgeist of the millennial generation. The suggestion was that this generation demanded personalized and timely feedback (Levine 2017). The banking industry was therefore following this wider corporate trend. That did not make the changes in banker remuneration any less important though.

Pay and performance are, predictably, opaque areas. One insider described the practice at his firm as follows: 'basically, it's a bunch of guys in a room going over a list of names and accounts and saying "OK, so how much do we give this guy?"'

(cited in the *Guardian* 2013b). Nonetheless, whereas remuneration was previously linked to a more 'objective set of [financial] measures' in many areas of banking, the review process was now more 'tied in with the [firms'] values' (Interview 20161216). Another interviewee explained that '60 percent of our performance is now rated around our behaviors, so *how* we do things rather than *what* we do. So an individual could be the highest performing person in terms of lending money in the whole country, but if they are deemed to have done that in an unacceptable way or treated their colleagues or customers or just behaved inappropriately, then that would wipe out any variable pay they might get' (Interview 20161101). At least this was the view in one major global bank. Performance reviews and pay therefore became an increasingly relevant means to promote conformity and good behaviour amongst employees.

Arguably the most obvious changes were within the retail banking divisions though. This was important because whereas investment banking had always prioritized a trading and sales culture, many criticisms after the financial crisis focused on the emergence of this sales culture in retail banking. Beyond compliance then, the incorporation of values and ethics into performance reviews in retail banking was arguably the second most significant mechanism for addressing culture-as-good-conduct. This shift in retail banking meant, of course, a far greater focus on metrics of customer satisfaction. One of the most important, industry-wide sources for gauging customer service became the Net Promoter Score (NPS). The NPS represents the percentage of customers who say that they would definitely recommend the bank to a friend or colleague, using a ten-point scale. It was significant for example that by 2012 a wide range of both British and US banks—from RBS and Lloyds, to JPMorgan and Citi—were referring to their NPS rankings in their annual reports (various annual reports); other firms had also begun to use independent agencies to conduct customer satisfaction surveys (Interview 20161101); whilst there were also now outcomes testing agencies, that would audit clients to ascertain 'Did the manager discuss with you the interest rates, the type of products? Did they explain to you how the product works? And they'll grade that as to whether it was sold appropriately' (Interview 20161101). These customer surveys were therefore a direct response to the fallout from mis-selling scandals.

Relatedly, less emphasis was also placed on sales targets. Once again, the Wells Fargo example—of falsely opening millions of customer accounts during the 2010s—is an important reminder of the limits to these changes. Nonetheless, almost all firms operating in the retail banking space began placing less emphasis on sales targets. In the UK, TSB became a prominent market-leader in this regard. In 2013 the bank piloted a scheme in two Birmingham (UK) branches whereby they initially removed all sales targets, subsequently replacing them with appointment targets, rather than account opening, credit card, or mortgage approval targets. The thinking was that the former (financial) sales 'could potentially drive wrong behaviour' (Interview 20161123). Indeed, it was not simply that sales targets carried with them the potential for big bonuses. In many cases the staff pushing these products were on relatively low pay. Often the incentive was simply 'peer group pressure; and people would get called out if they were the bottom of the sales list' (Interview 20170511, also Interview 20170504).

Another major bank explained that they too had abolished all product-specific targets. They noted that 'there are no product-related targets any more anywhere...You cannot say to someone, "I need you to do more of x type of loan or x type credit cards." It just doesn't happen' (Interview 20161101). Instead 'there are targets around growth of specific areas, like growing our overall lending', but these will not be achieved 'by pushing certain products' (ibid.). Yet another manager explained that they were 'not allowed to know how many customer needs we have met, or sales, [to ensure that] our sales data won't be used in performance benefit' (Interview 20161114). They also expressed how frustrating this made their role as a manager.

In investment banking and asset management divisions of the largest banks, change was more ambiguous. A senior employee who had worked within the asset management division of their bank for nearly two decades, for example, explained that they had essentially 'cut-and-pasted' large sections of a management appraisal form for the last ten years, because 'it doesn't make any difference'; they were 'remunerated on the performance of our funds and my personal contribution to that performance, which is purely mathematical' (Interview 20170215). Yet within other investment banking divisions, employees spoke of an increased focus on behaviours, attitudes, and values in performance reviews. One director within an investment bank explained that in the annual appraisal, they had witnessed a change in recent years: 'you have to rate people's collaborative type of behaviours; did they show that team player kind of attitude? Which wasn't there before' (Interview 20161128). In this particular bank, right conduct did not effect the *level* of remuneration; but bad conduct would almost certainly guarantee *no* or reduced variable remuneration: 'In other words, you'll get your bonus...as long as you've achieved what you were meant to achieve—targets or whatever—and you've done it in the correct manner, correct depending on whatever business line you're in; then you're eligible for a bonus. If you've done something wrong, you can probably assume you will not get one' (Interview 20161128).

Closing Remarks

Of course, our argument here is not that a set of anecdotal examples from bank employees provides a comprehensive assessment of culture change. In fact, the opposite is true: the argument of this book is that culture change was very limited. Instead, the purpose of this chapter was to show that (1) by the late 2010s bank culture certainly *felt* very different to employees, and that (2) this perception was also supported by some substantive changes in—inter alia—remuneration, performance management, risk appetite, and compliance. But this conclusion also raised a tension, because a core argument of this book is that bank culture has actually changed very little. Our twofold framing of culture—as concerning good, ethical conduct on the one hand, versus being determined by the structural pressures of financialization—helps to address this paradox.

It is clear that by the late 2010s large areas of banking felt very different to employees. Pay was oftentimes lower, compliance teams made business more conservative and complex, and risk management was, at least for a time, tighter. The conclusion that we should draw is that the narrower bank culture agenda had worked, to a degree. Earlier chapters reflected my scepticism about the underlying motivations behind this narrower culture debate. State managers employed a populist statecraft that was more concerned with vote-winning than promoting big structural changes to the banks. Yet, at the same time, these earlier chapters also argued that a mix of tightened market discipline and softer, normative changes were deployed. This present chapter has shown the results of this approach to the bank culture problem. Chapter 10 now returns to the financialization argument however, in order to show the underlying drivers of bank culture and therefore the limitations of the narrower culture debate.

10
What Has Not Changed

At the start of this book we defined the cultural problems in banking as both economic and political. In economic terms they refer to—inter alia—banking practices in Anglo-America that exploit the indebted, risk-taking which tends towards excessive levels due to a bloodthirsty search for yield, and the finance premium that is disproportionate to either the value-added of the finance sector or wages in other parts of the economy. These factors also pointed to political or legitimacy problems, with high bonuses and the privileged access of banks to policymaking in Anglo-America being a target for popular criticism, particularly against the backdrop of government spending cutbacks and wage stagnation. Can these cultural problems be remedied by the narrower approach to bank culture that state managers and the banks themselves adopted? Chapter 9 showed that to a certain extent they can be alleviated, yes. Demanding that bonuses are better tied to long-term performance alleviates certain excesses. Increasing compliance monitoring of email and chat-room traffic might catch suspicious behaviour; it certainly makes employees more aware of the risks of being caught. Moreover, increasing personal accountability might promote caution. And reducing the emphasis on sales targets might limit retail bank staff from pressurizing customers.

The core argument of this book however, is that remedies solely aimed at promoting ethical, socially responsible conduct were superficial responses. More importantly, they reflected a deep liberal faith in the market, so that the practical aim of policy was to make participants conform to purportedly healthy market norms; the belief was that if this goal was achieved, the market would produce benign, socially optimal outcomes. As with bank fines these remedies also served a secondary legitimacy-enhancing purpose. What they failed to tackle, in any meaningful way, were the underlying structural imperatives of financialization in Anglo-America. In contrast to the orthodox liberal assumptions, it would appear that the financialized markets of Anglo-America produce anything but benign, socially optimal outcomes. In fact, these financialized markets are a driver of inequality, instability, and socially useless (redistributive) activity in the financial sector.

Ultimately, I argue, it is these imperatives that give rise to the more fundamental cultural problems in banking. Another way of framing this argument is that conduct-related reform and regulation is predominantly supply-side focused,

The Bank Culture Debate: Ethics, Values, and Financialization in Anglo-America. Huw Macartney, Oxford University Press (2019). © Huw Macartney.
DOI: 10.1093/oso/9780198843764.001.0001

whereas financialization creates overwhelming demand-side pressures, particularly among increasingly indebted households. If this diagnosis is right, we would expect to see these cultural problems continue to proliferate within the banking sector; or alternatively, the regulatory squeeze on the banking sector might lead to other parts of the financial system—the shadow banking sector, or high-cost credit providers—moving into the space vacated by banks and yet displaying some of the same cultural traits. This book does not deal with the latter claim in a systematic way, though I will discuss it briefly in the Concluding chapter. But this final chapter examines the former claim—about financialization and persistent cultural problems.

This chapter develops in three stages: firstly, I explain that the global financial crisis did not disrupt the financialization of Anglo-America. I do this by examining pay, the continued emphasis on non-interest income in the largest Anglo-American banks, and Quantitative Easing. Secondly, we examine the exploitative lending practices that banks continued to employ. This was certainly not the only example of remaining cultural problems. But since it relates to wage stagnation and indebtedness, key issues that we highlighted in Chapter 2 and which worsened since the financial crisis, it was one of the most important considerations. Moreover, as we shall argue, since wage stagnation is deeply rooted in the crisis of accumulation that drives financialization, it is also one of the most problematic issues for state managers to address. Simply, it sits at the apex of the political and economic challenges associated with bank culture in Anglo-America. Thirdly and finally, we examine one of the other most important cultural issues, that of disproportionately high pay. We argue that despite certain changes (see Chapter 9) remuneration was also an economic and political (legitimacy-threatening) challenge.

Financialization

As was argued in Chapter 2, the process of financialization refers to a broad shift in the pattern of accumulation in Anglo-America. In Chapter 2 we highlighted that a useful proxy for examining financialization was to consider 'where profits are generated in an economy', indicative of the 'growing weight of finance' (Krippner 2005: 175, 174). The point was that the rise in importance of stock market performance fuelled the capacity for profits from financial activity to become increasingly detached from the non-financial economy. Roger Bootle described this as gains from *distributive* activity, and juxtaposed it against *creative* work in the non-financial sector (2012). Non-financial corporations are also obviously imbricated in the emphasis on profits from financial activities and focus on shareholder returns. Yet our concern in this chapter is to show how financialization plays into the hands of the banks.

Pay

We will return to the issue of pay in the third section of this chapter. We begin this first section on financialization by briefly showing that, (1) compared to the benchmark of the European Union and (2) compared to their own respective economies in the 2000s, both the US and the UK continued to have a disproportionate emphasis on the services sector—dominated by financial services—relative to their industrial sectors. Figs 10.1 and 10.2 show the levels of employee compensation by sector, measured as a percentage of gross value-added (GVA). To reiterate, the figures show two important issues: firstly, that—compared to the EU average—the US and the UK economies are outliers. And secondly, the graphs show that whilst the pay in the services sector remained fairly consistent at around 43–45 per cent of gross value-added between 2005–16, remuneration in industry fell by 1–2 per cent over the same period.

A comprehensive examination of the Anglo-American, services-driven economies is unnecessary for our purposes here. The data is Figs 10.1 and 10.2 does however, provide a useful reminder of the argument outlined in Chapter 2 concerning the changing patterns of accumulation in these two economies. It also serves to show that despite the language of 'rebalancing the economy' (IEA 2017) both the US and the UK remained firmly services economies with consumption-led growth (*Washington Post* 2014b). In the US employment in financial services had risen well above the 2008 peak by 2018, to 6.3 million individuals (BLS 2018); whilst in the UK, employment in financial services had also returned to its 2007

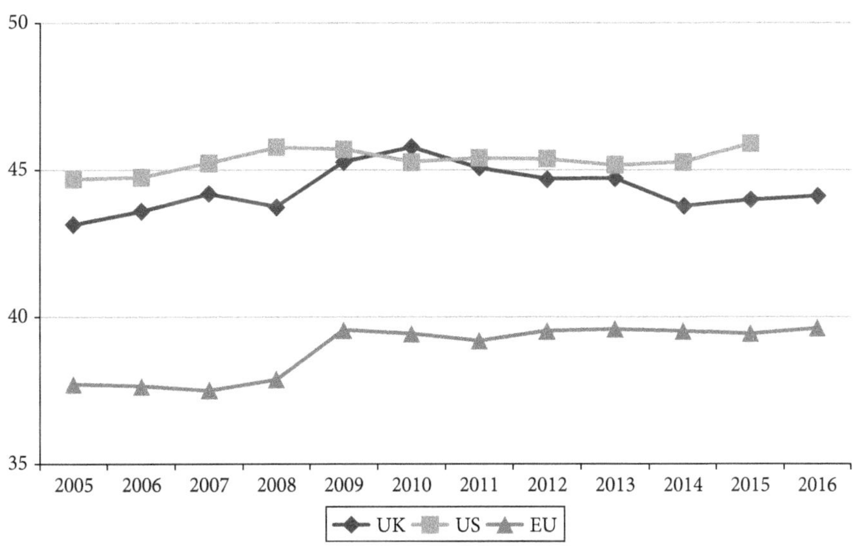

Fig. 10.1 Employee compensation in services sector (% of gross value added)
Source: OECD statistics.

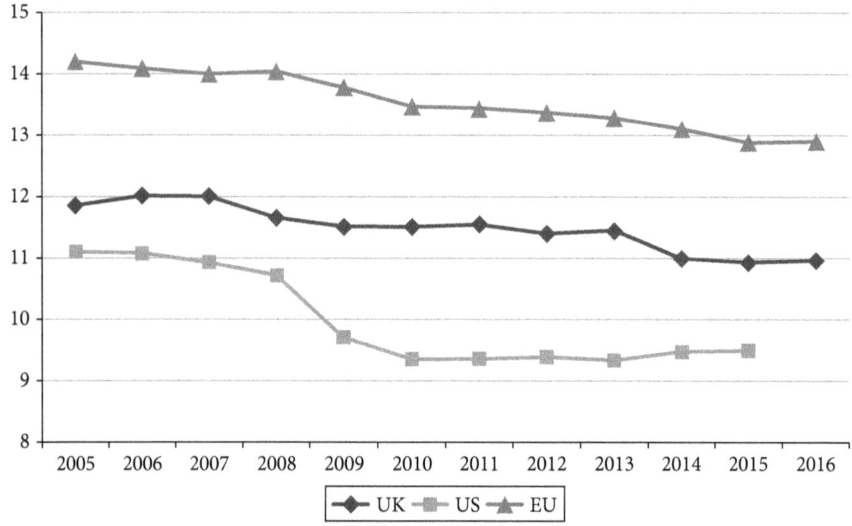

Fig. 10.2 Employee compensation in industry (% of gross value added)
Source: OECD statistics.

peak, employing 2.2 million individuals by 2017 (CityUK 2017: 2). Yet the relative size of the financial services sector to other sectors is far less important to our argument than the fact that the role and business strategies of the largest banks remained deeply financialized in spite of the narrow bank culture reform agenda.

In other words, the purpose of this chapter is not to provide an exhaustive examination of post-crisis financialization in Anglo-America. That said, a brief overview of a key indicator of financialization—non-interest income in the banks—confirms that relatively little had changed by the late 2010s.

Non-interest Income

As Engelen et al (2011: 115) argued, the traditional model of banking in the past—with banks acting as intermediaries channelling investment—meant that the major source of income derived from interest earned on the spread between interest paid to depositors and the interest charged to borrowers. One major feature of Market-Based Banking (MBB) was the shift away from interest-income towards non-interest income, including retail banking fees and commissions from selling financial products such as mortgages, and wholesale banking earnings from various kinds of trading activity (Uppal 2011). As noted, certain studies are ambiguous on the costs and benefits attached to greater diversification of activities within the larger universal, commercial banks: Canals (1993) found that diversification improves revenue; whilst Smith, Staikouras, and Wood (2003) argued that non-interest income reduces bank risk. Yet in their study of non-interest income and financial performance, DeYoung and Roland (2001) found that fee-based income increased the volatility of bank revenues; this finding was also supported by Stiroh (2004) and Stiroh and Rumble (2006).

The sustained financialization of the US and UK has not necessarily meant that banks simply reverted to pre-crisis patterns and practices. In particular, both US and UK banks made lower profits from non-interest income in the late 2010s than in the lead up to the financial crisis. This was partly driven by lower volatility post 2011–12, a prerequisite for higher profits. It was also driven by lower risk appetite, partly as a result of new regulations, including capital requirements and leverage ratios, and partly as a result of the more conservative approaches within the banks (Jaffer 2014b: 203). Yet Figs 10.3–10.7 show the continued importance of both non-interest income and fee income to the bank structures of some of the largest Anglo-American firms examined in Part III of this book.

A few points are worth highlighting. Comparing sources of revenue across the 2008–17 period can be misleading: several of these banks underwent significant sell-offs or mergers, including the Lloyds divestiture of TSB, Barclays selling off BarCap, and Bank of America's acquisition of Merrill Lynch, to name but a few. This distorts the size of revenue from particular activities in particular years.

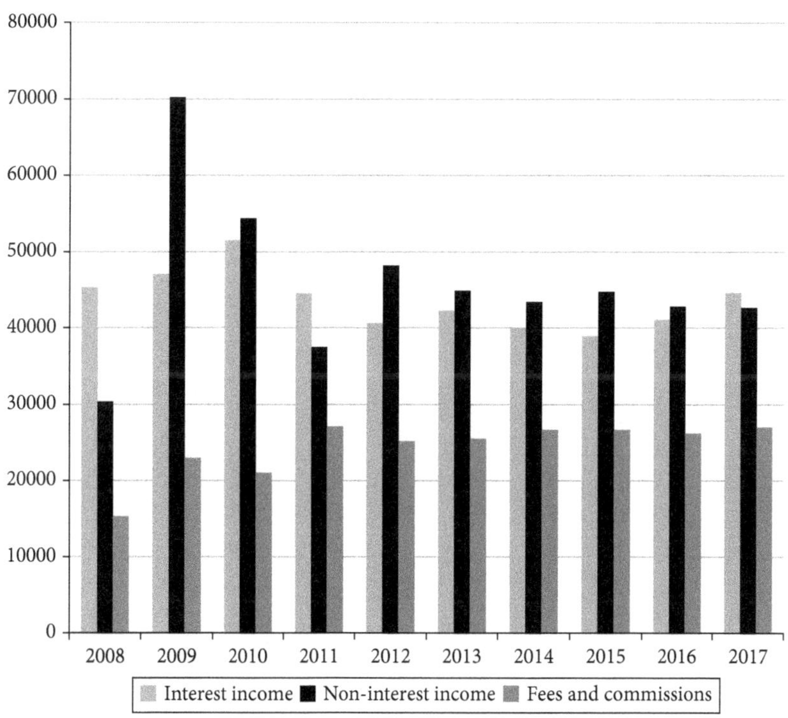

Fig. 10.3 Bank of America revenue streams, 2008–17 (US $ millions)
Source: Fitch Connect.

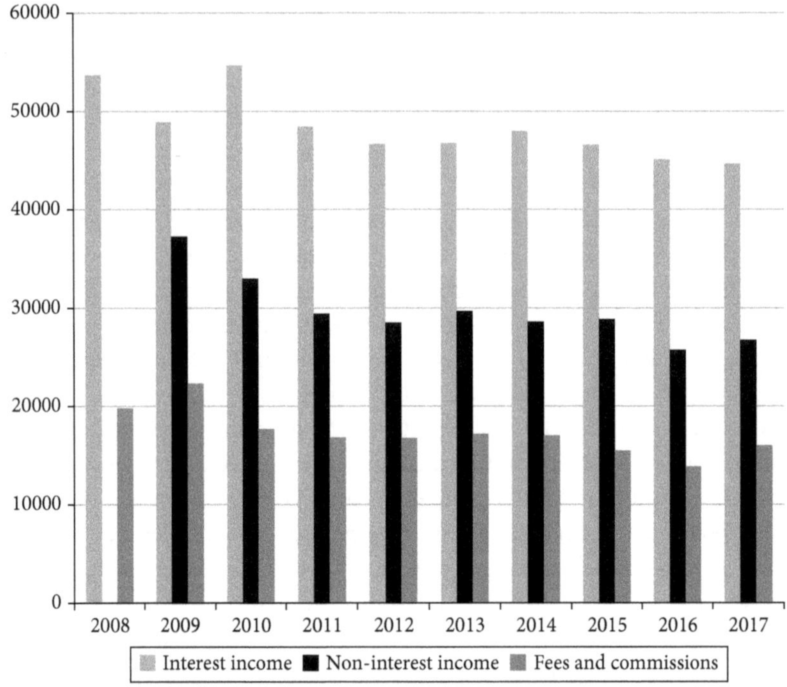

Fig. 10.4 Citigroup revenue streams, 2008–17 (US $ millions)
Source: Fitch Connect.

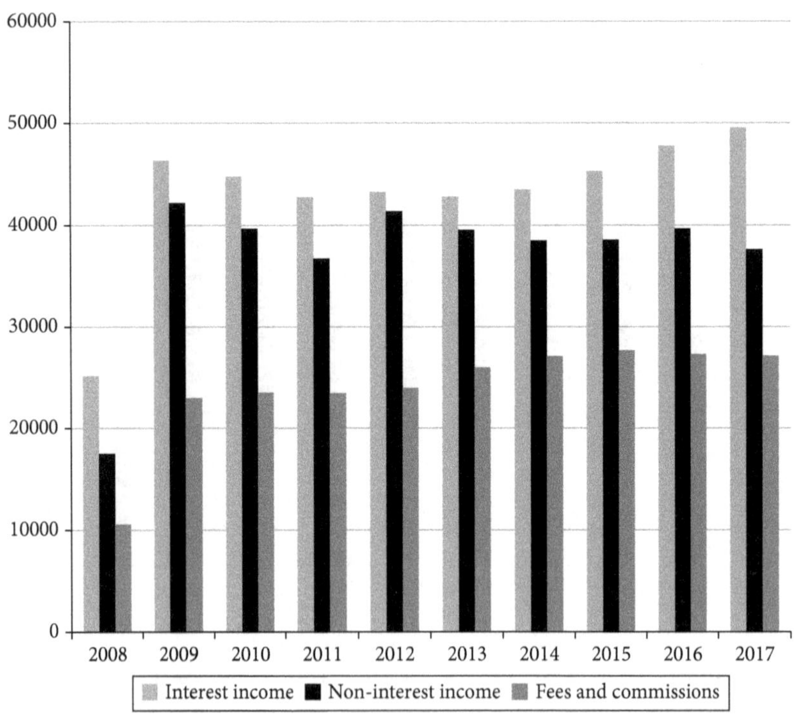

Fig. 10.5 Wells Fargo revenue streams, 2008–17 (US $ millions)
Source: Fitch Connect.

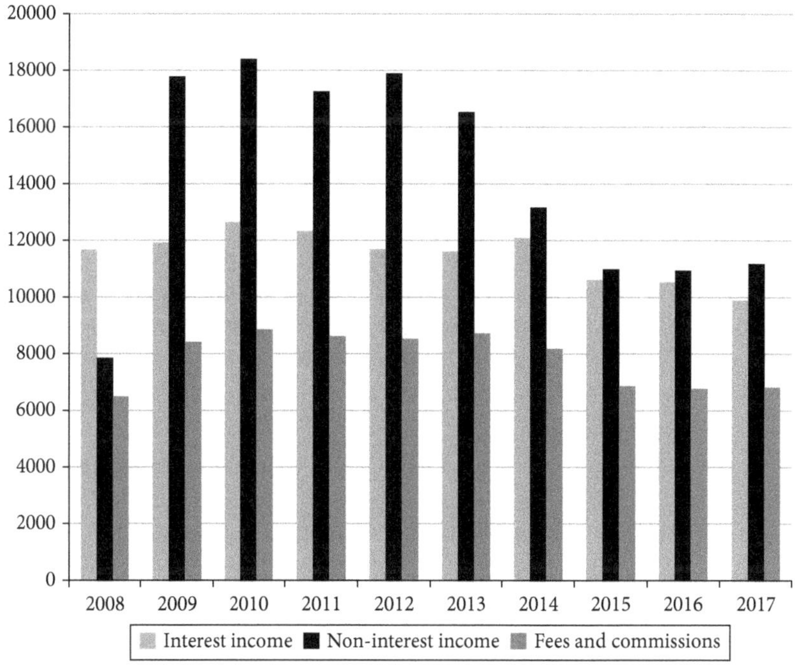

Fig. 10.6 Barclays revenue streams, 2008–17 (£ millions)
Source: Fitch Connect.

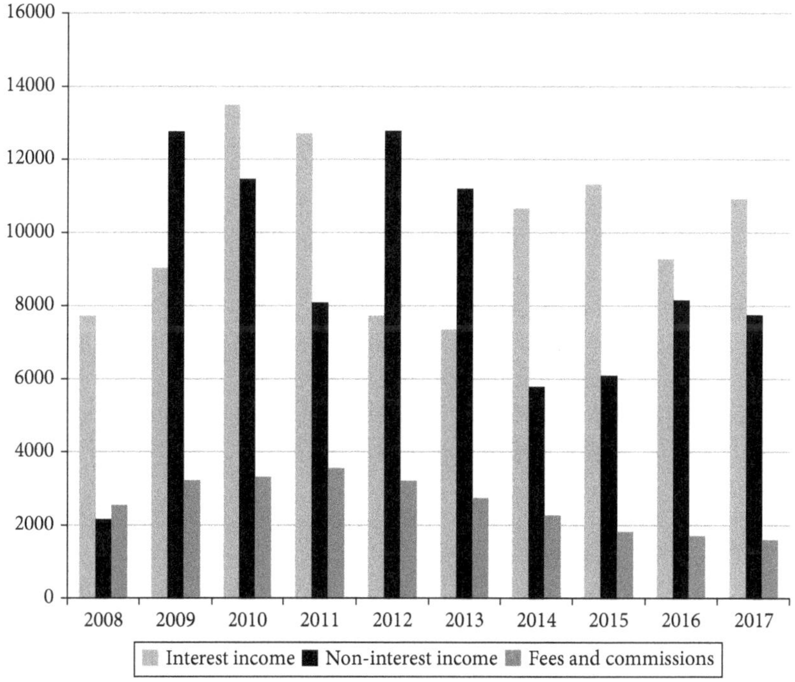

Fig. 10.7 Lloyds revenue streams, 2008–17 (US $ millions)
Source: Fitch Connect.

Also, the revenues derived from interest income on loans—particularly in the UK—was arguably unusually low during this period, though this is not necessarily reflective of skewed business strategies, but was also influenced by the slow recovery of the UK economy and low demand amongst non-financial corporations (Macartney 2014). Of course, this latter point is also an important factor in understanding the financialization of the Anglo-American economies, where slow growth in the non-financial economy is a driver of the shift towards financial activities. I will examine this more fully in the 'Quantitative Easing' section. But the most significant point—at this stage—is that, certainly on the evidence of these large five Anglo-American banks, fee revenue and non-interest income remained particularly significant.

As noted, certain academic accounts suggest that these business models pose stability risks though this argument is not pursued further in this chapter. Instead the aim here in this first section is simply to show that, based on a range of indicators—from employment in financial services through to an emphasis on non-interest income—neither the financial crisis nor, more particularly, the reform agenda had changed some integral features of bank business models. What we labelled Market-Based Banking in Chapter 2 remained a central feature of Anglo-American banks (Maxfield et al. 2017). Again, this is not a dry and abstract claim. As I will show as the chapter unfolds, the lack of change in business structures was central to the continuation of—inter alia—exploitative lending patterns.

Quantitative Easing

Before we explore these exploitative lending practices and remuneration we will briefly examine one other (cultural) feature of financialization discussed in Chapter 2. In that chapter we explained how the slowdown in the non-financial economy, alongside increased access to cheap credit, had reshaped both financial and non-financial corporations. Buoyant stock markets became a guiding light at the core of the shareholder value revolution (Froud et al. 2006). But this further reinforced the decline in relative profitability and output in the non-financial sector, reflecting a degree of detachment between profits in finance and the health of the economy.

In the aftermath of the global financial crisis loose monetary policy and quantitative easing (QE) only exacerbated these tendencies under financialization. Again, this is not an immanent critique of trading and investment banking activity per se; but neither is it an insignificant vignette to be glossed over. In particular, as we shall see in the third section of this chapter, it is arguably one major cause of the fact that profits and pay in the Anglo-American finance sector bear so little relationship to those in other sectors. And high pay, I will argue, is pivotal to the economic and political aspects of the bank culture problematique.

It is also worth emphasizing from the outset though, that these extraordinary monetary policy measures derived from state managers' decisions to abdicate responsibility for promoting economic recovery in the 2010s (Wren Lewis 2015). In Chapter 2 we showed how financialization was exacerbated by the politics of tight money—fiscal restraint. The preferred policy response to the global financial crisis by Anglo-American state managers was once again to pursue fiscal conservatism and a deferral to central bank-led stimulus. This too is an important point, for banks simply benefit from and exploit conditions not of their own creation; state managers are again complicit in the reproduction of financialization.

As interest rates in the US and the UK were cut—the first step in the monetary policy response—the Federal Reserve and the Bank of England (alongside the European Central Bank) extended their range of policy instruments to various different asset and bond purchasing schemes, or Quantitative Easing—the second stage of the monetary policy programme. Under these schemes, the central bank essentially prints money to buy government or corporate bonds; the aim was to increase the ability for banks and financial institutions to borrow in order to lend to non-financial corporations, by effectively lowering the market-implied interest rate. The newly created money—used to buy banks' assets—is thought to put that money into general circulation, further encouraging spending and investment and fighting off deflation. By 2017, approximately $15 trillion in assets had been purchased by all central banks since the financial crisis (*Telegraph* 2017c).

There is little evidence however, in either the UK or the US economy, that the QE schemes worked. Analysis by the St Louis Federal Reserve found that in comparison to other economies that had not engaged in QE, there was little difference in levels of economic output. The conclusion was that QE had been largely ineffective in stimulating economic (value-adding) activity (Williamson 2017). The symptoms of the malaise were threefold: anaemic economic growth, low inflation, and weak levels of lending to non-financial corporations (*FT* 2015e). The theory holds that all three of these features—growth, healthy inflation, and lending to the economy—would benefit from QE. In other words, the theory suggested that QE would be an effective means to boost asset prices, aggregate demand, and inflation. In particular, banks would receive additional funding through these asset purchases, thereby improving the condition of their balance sheets. Proponents therefore contended that increases in deposit funding caused by these purchases might, potentially, lead to increased bank lending through what is known as the Bank Lending Channel (BLC) (Charkaborty et al. 2017: 2).

In the US, the Federal Reserve purchased both mortgage-backed securities and Treasury securities in three rounds of QE. Studies found that banks benefiting from MBS purchases increased their mortgage lending whilst reducing their commercial lending. There was little to no positive impact from Treasury securities purchases (Chakraborty 2017: 1). Similarly, in the UK, analysis by the Bank of England found 'no evidence to suggest that QE operated by a traditional bank lending channel' (Butt et al. 2014: I). It was *hoped* that there might be positive effects via an alternative—asset price—channel, but evidence was limited. As noted, all of this depended however, on an (optimistic) assumption regarding what banks would do under conditions of rising asset prices and a further (optimistic) assumption about the possibilities of profitable investment opportunities—evidenced in an increase in demand. Yet all evidence indicated that demand from non-financial corporations in the UK was subdued, making this second assumption highly questionable.

So, if funds generated through QE did not fuel lending to non-financial corporates and economic growth, how were they put to use? One conclusion was that—much as with the early 2000s—low yields on safe assets and slow returns from stagnant economies, combined with excess liquidity, 'encouraged investors to put money into riskier asset classes' (*FT* 2013, Haldane et al. 2016: 8). There was certainly strong evidence that QE boosted the stock market. Indeed, as Stiglitz noted QE 'can increase the value of "unproductive" fixed assets—an increase in the value of wealth that is unaccompanied by any increase in the flow of goods and services' (2012: 9). In the US, three rounds of QE saw the S&P 500 gain approximately 140 per cent (*CNBC* 2017). Indeed, on the mere suggestion—in 2013—that the Federal Reserve would begin to scale back its $85bn a month government and mortgage bond buying programme, asset prices and currency markets tumbled—so great was their dependence on accommodative monetary policy (*FT* 2013), whilst QE also kept long-term borrowing costs down, allowing US and UK governments to fund their deficits more cheaply, as well as benefiting asset owners—or the rich—disproportionately. In the US this 'asset price channel' benefited the 4 per cent of the population who owned stocks and other financial products, without helping the 96 per cent who receive their income through wage labour (Forbes 2015a). Put simply, the evidence that QE boosted growth through the (1) Bank Lending Channel is limited; whilst the evidence that (2) asset prices rose benefiting asset class owners but not leading to boosted lending to the real economy, is robust.

In short, this is why reducing the bank culture problem to one of 'misconduct' is entirely misleading; because matters such as 'high risk' trading activity, asset price inflation, and anaemic growth in the productive sector are results of the financialized economies of Anglo-America. Simply re-embedding the market norms is an exercise in futility if those market norms produce malign and regressive outcomes. Most importantly, the product of these policies therefore only reinforces the real and perceived divide between the finance sector and everyone else (non-financial corporations and households); an impression that is also affirmed by exploitative practices and disproportionately high pay.

We have therefore begun this chapter by showing that the financial crisis did not disrupt the financialization of Anglo-America. This claim is a necessary precondition to the broader argument of this chapter, that bank culture has not changed to the degree that bank employees implied in Chapter 9.

Pernicious Lending

The second section of this chapter examines exploitative lending practices as one of the most important economic and political issues surrounding bank culture in Anglo-America. Chapter 2 explained that Anglo-American banks had developed structures to promote non-interest income (see also Figs 10.3–10.7); one of these sources of income was via fees and charges; and one major area of fees and charges focused on exploiting heavily indebted individuals (Montgomerie 2009). It was also highlighted that states had exacerbated the problem by promoting wage repression to tackle the profitability crisis facing US and UK economies (Brenner 2003). Wage stagnation had contributed to indebtedness, particularly in consumption-driven economies, giving the banks new opportunities for pernicious lending practices. Moreover, states had been slow to tackle these practices, focusing only on the more extreme forms—such as payday lending, where new regulations were introduced during the 2010s. This section of the chapter therefore examines wage stagnation since the financial crisis, consumer indebtedness, and bank strategies targeting revolving debtors.

Wage Stagnation

In the UK, the period since the global financial crisis was described as the 'lost decade' for earnings growth—the first since the 1860s (*Telegraph* 2016). In fact, average earnings remained below their 2008 levels (*FT* 2016) and fell in real terms, lagging behind inflation (*Independent* 2017). Fig. 10.8 shows this. The Institute for Fiscal Studies explained that real wages were likely to remain below their pre-crisis peak beyond 2021, describing this as 'extraordinary and dreadful' (*FT* 2016).

In the US Americans had also waited years for wage gains, and hourly earnings growth slowed dramatically following the global financial crisis before returning to their pre-crisis level in late 2015 (Bureau of Labour Statistics 2018). Fig. 10.9 shows this.

The debate over the causes of wage stagnation tended to focus on two key issues: unemployment and productivity. What puzzled economists was that both the US and the UK had historically low levels of spare capacity—or unemployment—which is usually seen as a driver of wage increases. In the US the official unemployment rate rose from 5.3 per cent in January 2005 to a high of 10 per cent in October 2009, before falling to 4.1 per cent in January 2018 (Bureau of Labour Statistics 2018). Similarly, in the UK unemployment stood at 4.7 per cent in January 2005 and though it rose to a peak of 8.5 per cent in the third quarter of 2011 it fell again to 4.3 per cent by the final quarter of 2017 (ONS 2018). The fact

Fig. 10.8 Average weekly earnings total pay (UK): real wages, whole economy, seasonally adjusted (Index 2015 = 100)
Source: ONS 2017.

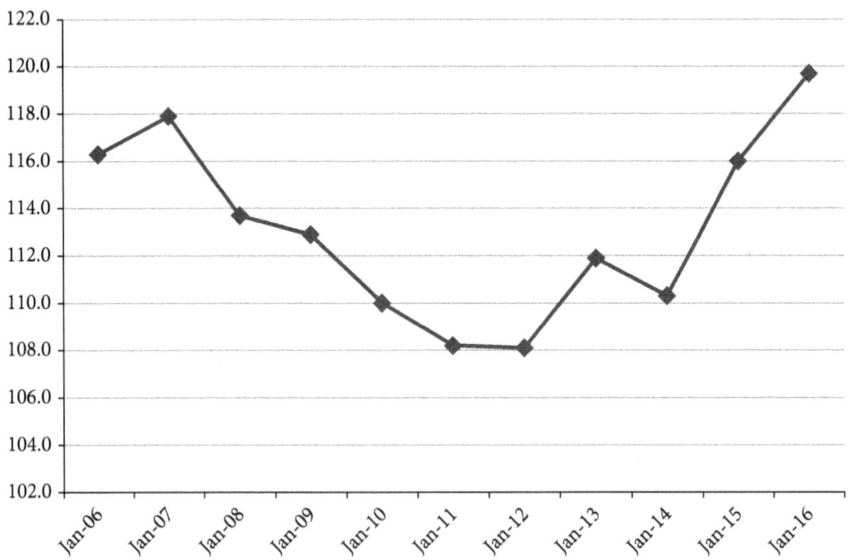

Fig. 10.9 Real median household income (US): annual, not seasonally adjusted (Index 1984 = 100)
Source: St Louis Fed 2017.

that anticipated wage gains had not been forthcoming, despite the relatively low levels of unemployment in both the US and the UK led economists to wonder whether there was excess slack—such as *underemployment*—in the labour market not reflected by the headline unemployment figures (Blanchflower and Machin 2016: 3, *FT* 2017c). In short though, economists remained unclear over the extent to which employment was the root cause of slow wage growth.

The other major set of explanations for low wage growth focused on productivity. As discussed in Chapter 2, the long-term slowdown in total factor productivity (TFP)—a measure of how quickly output is growing relative to the growth of labour and capital inputs—is a reasonable proxy for the crisis of accumulation that drives the shift towards financialization (Krugman 1994: 11, Gordon 2016: 2). In its simplest sense, for workers to experience rising living standards labour productivity—or the value of a workers economic output—must also increase (Shambaugh, Nunn, Liu, and Nantz 2017: iii). Though slow productivity growth is by no means the *only* reason for low wage gains, it certainly acts as a drag on income growth. In the US, productivity growth since 1970 was barely a third of the rate achieved between 1920 and 1970 (Gordon 2016: 22). And, despite a slight spike in 2009 and 2010, productivity growth declined sharply since 2004 (Bureau of Labor Statistics 2018). Over the decade 2004–14 growth averaged 1.2 per cent and fell to an average of 0.6 per cent since 2011. Indeed quarter over quarter productivity growth in the business sector fell to negative figures between the end of 2015 and the first half of 2016 (McKinsey 2017: 2). Similarly, in the UK the situation was even more extreme. Having grown by an average of (only) 2.1 per cent since the 1970s, productivity had been flat since 2011. Indeed, the Office for Budgetary Responsibility (OBR) showed that productivity was 20 per cent lower than the pre-crisis trend (OBR 2017: 7). Despite questions over the precise relationship between wages and productivity in Anglo-America, the fact that wages had been low and that growth in the economy was relatively anaemic are indisputable. And this is what matters for our analysis of bank culture because it fuelled indebtedness.

Consumption-led Growth

Slow earnings growth—driven at least in part by the prolonged slowdown in profitability in the Anglo-American economies—was just one driver of increased indebtedness however. Cuts to working age benefits, and rising private sector rents also led to a prolonged squeeze on disposable incomes. But one thing is clear, low wage gains and cuts in disposable income, and the propensity towards a consumption-driven recovery in Anglo-America, drove heightened indebtedness that US and UK banks continued to exploit.

Again, just as not all debt is *bad* debt (Graeber 2013), a high emphasis on consumer spending as a driver of an economy is not inherently problematic, and is not atypical of net importer, demand-driven growth models (Hope and Soskice 2016: 4–5). But here the problem which confronts us is that state managers' reliance on a consumption-driven recovery whilst wages stagnate will, all things being equal, lead to heightened indebtedness accompanied by lower disposable income. This might not have been immediately apparent, as the low interest rates of the post-2008 period resulted—in the short-term—in slightly above-average levels of disposable income for—inter alia—homeowners with low fixed-rate mortgages or on variable rate products. Lower income individuals and non-homeowners would not necessarily have experienced the upside to lower interest rates. But as interest rates rise, even these middle and upper-middle income households would experience squeezed living standards (Resolution Foundation 2018). For our purposes in this section we are only concerned with these wider macroeconomic issues as context to the strategies deployed by Anglo-American banks to exploit heightened indebtedness.

Table 10.1 is adapted from the Bank for International Settlements (BIS) (2017). It shows that consumption-led recoveries were a common feature amongst a wide-range of economies following the global financial crisis; and that the number of economies relying on consumption as a driver was on the increase. The BIS defines periods of consumption-led expansions as periods during which private consumption grows more quickly than GDP, either in nominal terms, so that the consumption-to-GDP ratio increases over time, or in real terms, so that real

Table 10.1 Number of countries experiencing consumption-led growth*

	2010	2011	2012	2013	2014	2015	2016
Brazil		x	x	x	x		
Canada	x		x	x	x	x	x
China		x	x		x	x	x
France					x	x	x
Germany			x	x		x	
India		x		x			x
Italy					x	x	x
Japan			x	x			
Russia	x	x	x	x	x		
South Africa	x	x	x			x	x
United Kingdom			x			x	x
United States		x			x	x	x
TOTAL	3	6	8	6	7	8	8

Note: * Growth is defined as consumption led when the real rate of growth rate of private consumption in a given year is higher than that of real GDP.

Sources: OECD, Economic Outlook; World Bank; CEIC; national data. Adapted from BIS (2017).

consumption growth exceeds real GDP growth. There are a number of problems associated with consumption-led growth highlighted by recent research. Jorda et al. (2015) and Lombardi et al. (2017) found that where consumption-led growth is driven by credit growth (heightened indebtedness) this can hinder economic growth in future; either through a financial crisis or because agents have over-borrowed and need to deleverage. Also, consumption-led growth can be driven by the wealth effects of house price rises, where households use capital gains to increase consumption. Yet if incomes fail to increase in line with house prices households have to cut back on consumption (BIS 2017: 30). These are far broader discussions than are necessary for our purposes in this book though. Most importantly, we have already presented the evidence of wage stagnation, which means that the emphasis on consumption was not driven primarily by wage gains. The remainder of this subsection will show instead that consumer debt was the key instrument for consumption-led growth in Anglo-America. This is obviously important because one of our main arguments regarding the culture of banking problem is that banks exploit revolving debtors.

It should also be added that the big picture of consumption-led recoveries fails to convey the ways in which reduced disposable income—the result of wage stagnation, austerity, and inflation—affects individuals at the lower end of the income distribution more acutely. And this too is an important element of financialization and the culture of banking problem; for it means that higher penalty charges for indebtedness for example, and the accompanying impact on disposable income, are likely to have a greater impact on the quality of life of poorer families. In the UK for example, in a 2016–17 review the FCA noted that high cost credit users 'may need credit to make ends meet and avoid wider financial difficulties (e.g. default on household bills or priority debts). They may also have very limited options for obtaining essential goods or for managing other larger purchases or bills' (FCA 2018: 9). Financial providers had therefore developed—inter alia—rent-to-own schemes. The merits and flaws of these schemes are beyond the remit of this chapter. But the reality was that rent-to-own consumers had an annual median income of £16,100 and had seen an increase in their outstanding debt from £2000 to £4300 between 2014–16. This meant that their debt repayments had increased at a far faster rate than any wage gains they may have experienced (FCA 2018: 10). Similarly in the US, 'Households with below-median income are buying more cars and bigger houses' (Bloomberg 2017c). In essence, this is the paradox at the heart of Anglo-America: 'Even as lower-income pay has officially stagnated since the 1970s, consumption has climbed' (ibid). This is the reality of tighter spending conditions and consumption-led growth in Anglo-America. And this is one reason why banks' heavy dependence on revenue from personal-debt related fees and charges is so exploitative and pernicious.

Heightened Indebtedness

We have run ahead of ourselves though. Before we can begin to examine the exploitative practices in the banks, we must first show the rise in consumer indebtedness that followed wage stagnation and the consumption-led growth. Fig. 10.10 shows the rise in household indebtedness in the US, by its composition. The composition is largely unsurprising, with mortgages comprising the vast majority of household debt. Moreover, by some standards the composition of debt was more sustainable and conservative than in earlier periods. By November 2017 $2.8 trillion of the overall $3.827 trillion was non-revolving debt—personal loans, car loans, mortgages, and home loans. This meant that non-revolving debt had risen from 62 per cent of the total in 2008 to 73 per cent by 2017; likewise credit card debt had fallen from 38 per cent of the total in 2008 to only 26.7 per cent by 2017 (Federal Reserve 2017). Moreover, household debt service payments as a percentage of disposable income had fallen from a high of 13 per cent in Q4 2007 to around 10 per cent by mid-2017 (St Louis Fed 2018) and delinquency rates on all loans had fallen: in Q1 of 2010 delinquency rates on all household debt rose to 7.4 per cent, then falling to 1.8 per cent by Q3 of 2017 (Federal

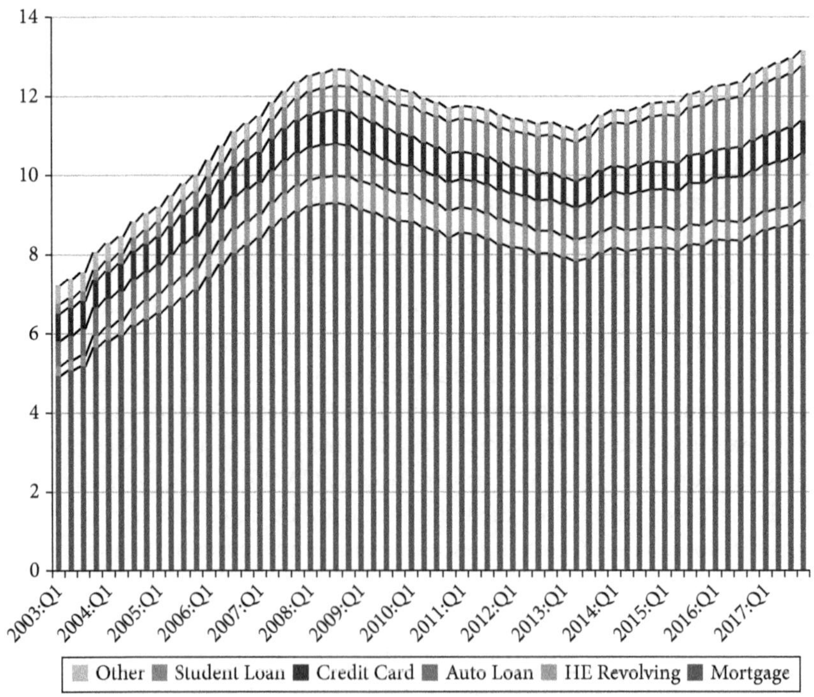

Fig. 10.10 Total US debt balance by composition (US $trillions)
Source: Federal Reserve 2017.

Reserve 2018). Nonetheless, the fact that in some segments debt ratios had fallen from their 2007–8 levels did not negate the fact that—overall—debt levels were high and rising again by the second half of 2017: in fact, *total* household debt reached a new peak in the fourth quarter of 2017, rising $193bn to $13.15 trillion (New York Fed 2018). And, most importantly for our analysis in this chapter, these high levels fuelled opportunities for the banks.

Fig. 10.11 shows the rise in household indebtedness in the UK. By Q2 of 2017 the total stockpile of UK household debt was £1.6 trillion, comprising £1.3 trillion in mortgage debt, £0.2 trillion in consumer debt, and £0.1 trillion in student loans (FPC 2017: 13). That meant that, in terms of the breakdown, approximately 43 per cent of debt took the form of secured lending, 25 per cent was credit card debt, and a further 21 per cent hire purchase debt (IFS 2018: 11). The rate of growth in household indebtedness had slowed during the financial crisis, but by the mid-2010s consumer indebtedness in particular was rising rapidly. In fact, as the BoE Financial Policy Committee (FPC) began sounding alarm bells about the sustainability of the debt bubble late in 2017, it was estimated that there were 8.3 million people in the UK with debt problems (*Guardian* 2017c). Poorer households were, of course, the worst affected. By January 2018 the Institute of Fiscal Studies concluded for example that one in four of Britain's poorest

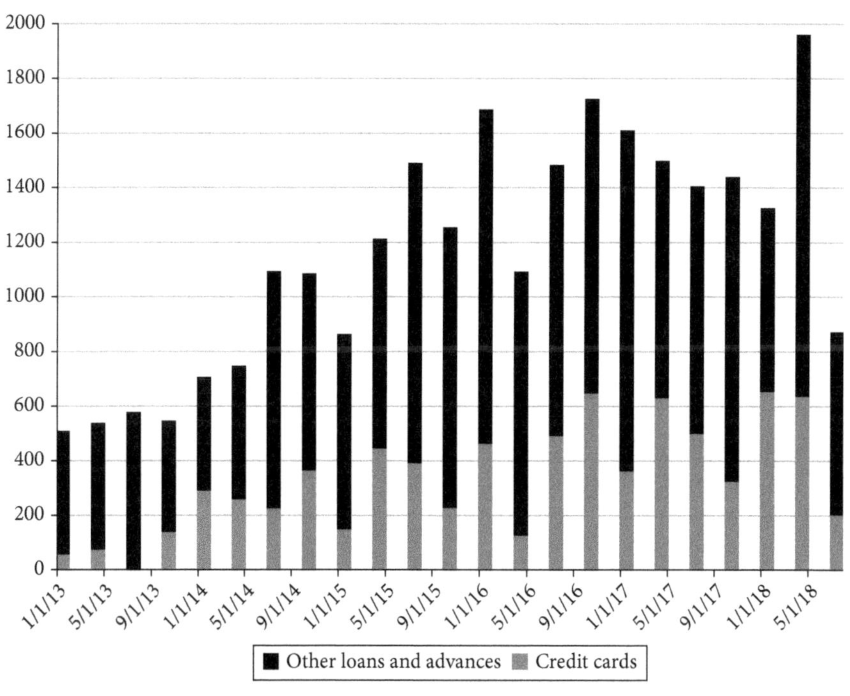

Fig. 10.11 UK consumer credit flows (£millions)

Source: BoE 2018.

households were either falling behind with debt payments or spending more than a quarter of their monthly income on repayments. In fact, 35 per cent of households in the poorest decile had debts of greater value than their financial assets (IFS 2018: 25).

Fig. 10.12 also shows that whilst household debt to income levels as a percentage of disposable income in both the UK and the US had fallen from a 2007 peak and—in the case of the US—was slightly below the G7 average by 2016, the levels had increased quite substantially since the mid-1990s and were, for most of this period, significantly higher than the G7 average. Arguably the most concerning feature though was that the moderation of debt-to-income ratios in the 2010s in large part reflected the period of low interest rates, making 'the debt burden more affordable for households' (UK Parliament 2017: 4), yet diluting the full impact of the heightened indebtedness.

As noted above, the purpose of this subsection is not to argue that increased indebtedness is inherently problematic. Indeed, one argument is that increased indebtedness is consistent with economic recovery. As the FPC highlighted, 'debt provides benefits to the economy by allowing people to make purchases that they otherwise would not be able to pay for in one go, smoothing their consumption over time' (2017: 13). Consumer sentiment increases, leading to greater consumption (spending), so the argument goes; and the upturn in the business cycle leads banks to increase lending, as credit scores improve. In contrast, there is robust evidence that high debt to disposable income levels are suggestive of

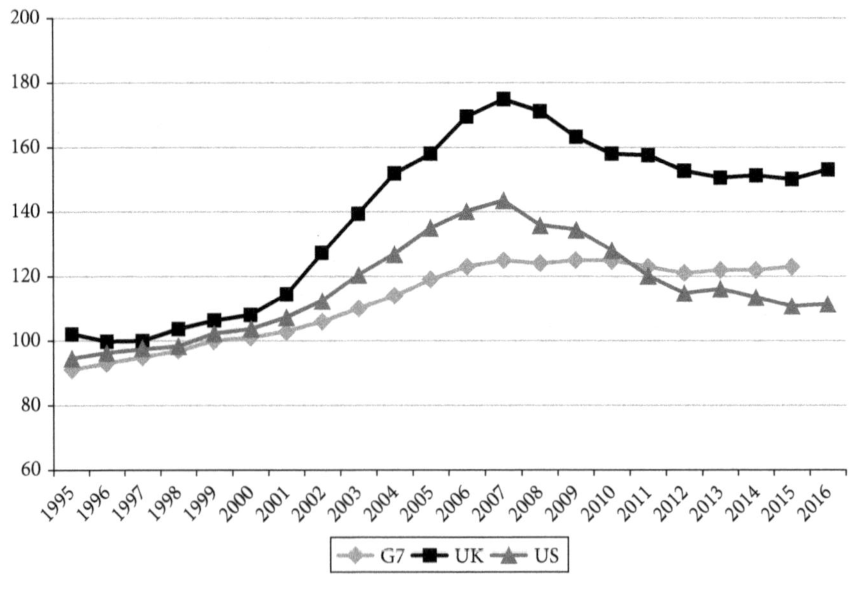

Fig. 10.12 Household debt to disposable income ratio, % 1995–2016
Source: OECD statistics.

squeezed incomes; and these squeezed incomes bring with them a range of social and psychological pathologies ranging from depression to suicide, or what has been called 'financial melancholia' (PERC 2015). And whilst it is beyond the remit of this chapter to examine these themes in greater depth it should be noted that these are just some of the human costs to the culture of banking problem.

Instead the argument of this section, simply stated, is that reduced disposable income, consumption driven growth, and heightened indebtedness placed UK and US households in an increasingly precarious position. This is not the fault of the banks per se. But it makes their exploitative strategies even more objectionable. Indeed, the fact is that increased household indebtedness was not simply a symptom of healthy optimism in Anglo-America. One liberal think tank commented on the rising debt post-2008: 'this is not a marker we should be super excited to get back to' they contended. 'In the abstract, more debt signals optimism. But in reality, families are using debt as a mechanism to pay for things their incomes don't support' (Heather Boushey, chief economist at Washington Center for Equitable Growth, cited in *NY Times* 2017a). Likewise in the UK, a YouGov poll found that 14 per cent of respondents would have been unable to pay an unexpected £100 bill without borrowing, with a further 31 per cent unable to pay a £500 bill without borrowing (*YouGov* 2016). In the following subsection we will examine the strategies of US and UK banks that prey on this indebtedness.

Revolving Debtors

Behind all the new value statements (see Chapter 9), the largest Anglo-American banks therefore still exploited a model that targeted heavily indebted individuals and households. As Johnna Montgomerie pointed out, 'targeting existing revolving debtors became central to new marketing strategies. Extensive market research found that the more often people used their credit cards, the more likely they were to overspend and not pay their full balance. The desire for a larger proportion of revolving debtors meant new marketing strategies focused on luring individuals with existing debts' (2009: 8). By the late 2010s, a new generation of debt products targeting the (already) heavily indebted had emerged. Payday lending—though not strictly part of the mainstream banking system explored in this book—was one obvious example of this. By 2017 there were almost as many payday lenders as Starbucks and McDonalds in the US, and 12 million Americans used them each year, paying more than $7bn in loan fees (CFPB 2017, *Washington Post* 2017).

Focusing on the large banks again, in the US a range of examples pointed to the fact that their business models continued to exploit opportunities amongst indebted middle and lower income individuals. As one former JPMorgan executive explained 'commercial bankers tend to see consumers as customers who can be "exploited" by layering on more fees' (cited in ThinkProgress 2011). Most of the largest US and UK banks operate with a 'free-if-in-credit' bank account model, but a number of studies in recent years highlighted the high revenues generated by penalty charges. In 2016 for example, the FCA and CMA concluded that approximately a third of UK bank revenues came from overdraft charges (2016: ix). In the US, data collected by the Federal Financial Institutions Examination Council (FFIEC) required banks with more than $1 billion in assets to report revenue from overdraft-related service charges, a category that also includes non-sufficient funds (NSF) charges (or fees for cheques which failed to clear). In the first three quarters of 2016, 626 large banks reported collecting $8.4bn from overdraft and NSF charges. Two other points are worth noting though: the top ten largest banks—including several of those we have focused on in this book—represented over 67 per cent of the total in charges; and for 2016, this fee revenue accounted for an average of 8.1 per cent of reporting banks' net income, making it an essential source of income for them (USPIRG 2016: 8).

Many current or checking accounts are labelled free-at-the-point-of-access, though there has been a longstanding discussion in both the US and the UK over the introduction of monthly fees (Financial Ombudsman 2017). In 2011, over 300,000 Bank of America customers signed an online petition against the introduction of a $5 a month, prompting not only BoA but also Wells Fargo, Chase, and Suntrust to abandon the introduction of the fees (*Washington Post* 2011b). Meanwhile however, Bank of America had signed an agreement with various states to administer unemployment benefits and established prepaid card programmes for welfare recipients and charged them for the use of these cards at non-BoA cash machines. In this particular case, banks were responding to new federal laws that limited the amounts that banks could charge retail merchants each time one of their cards was swiped. One estimate suggested that this new law would cut Bank of America revenues by up to $2bn in 2011 (*Huffington Post* 2011). The new federal limits did not apply to prepaid debit cards though, making them an attractive line of business for the banks: by 2009 these prepaid cards had risen from 9 per cent of all card payments to approximately 22 per cent, compensating for some of the losses incurred under the new law (St Louis Fed 2011). The point is that in spite of the narrow culture debate and the conduct-related reform agenda, US banks remained deeply dependent on business models that exploited heavily indebted and more susceptible individuals; and as a result had responded to federal limits and popular protests by diverting their strategies into less conspicuous but nonetheless exploitative areas, like prepaid cards.

Likewise in the UK, the Competition and Markets Authority estimated that income from personal current accounts (PCA) totalled £8.7bn in 2014 (CMA 2015). This compared to revenues of £2.7bn and £2.9bn in corporate and SME lending markets, making personal accounts the most important income source. But of the £8.7bn it was estimated that total fees and charges on overdrafts paid by PCA totalled £2.9bn (or approximately 30 per cent of revenue), with £1.7bn accounted for by arranged overdraft charges and £1.2bn in unarranged overdraft charges (CMA 2016: 350). Fig. 10.13 shows the importance of overdraft fees to the PCA revenue of UK banks in percentages. Beyond PCAs, credit cards were another area in which financialization and exploitation continued to reflect the culture of banking problem with a further 3.3 million UK customers in persistent credit card debt (FCA 2017). Indeed 'because these customers remain profitable, [banks] have few incentives to intervene' to lighten the (additional) financial burden fees and charges placed upon them (FCA 2017).

Moreover, in the UK the issue of punitive fees and charges for the heavily indebted is compounded by the lack of effective competition, a lack of transparency over which accounts are most competitive, and difficulties of account portability (CMA 2016: 13).

In the UK the Financial Services Consumer Panel published a report in 2017 indicating that barriers to account-switching meant that 'Financial services firms exploit their customers' inertia and misplaced loyalty' (FSCP 2017a). Over 75 per cent of respondents had at one least one additional product from their bank aside from their bank account; the main explanation was *convenience* and the perception of a *lack of difference* between providers. Yet the evidence clearly showed that the largest banks were not providing value for money for customers. A total of £665bn was held in easy-access accounts where the average interest rate

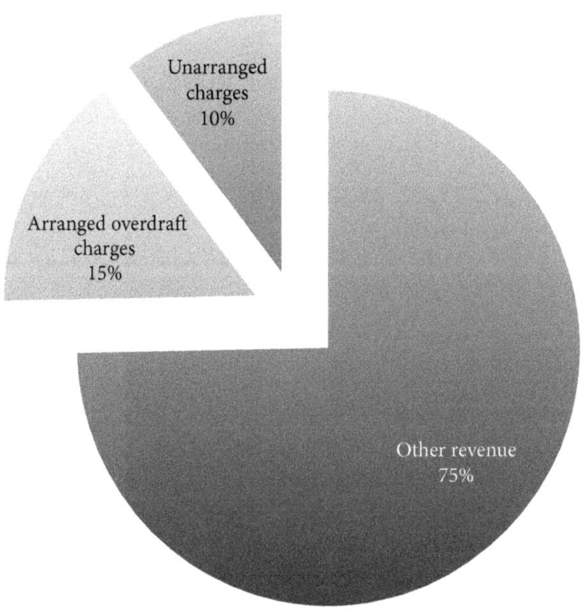

Fig. 10.13 Different types of overdraft revenue for UK banks (% 2014)
Source: CMA 2016.

was only 0.4 per cent; this meant that banks paid out only £2.66 billion in interest a year. In contrast, if customers had used the top paying accounts available, with interest rates of around 1 per cent, this would have earned approximately £6.65 billion in interest—an increase of nearly £4 billion (ThisIsMoney 2018). Data compiled from two price comparison websites, displayed in Table 10.2, confirms that by late 2017 only a small number of the largest UK banks offered rates as competitive as those of smaller, challenger banks.

Yet, as the FSCP report highlighted, this was not simply the product of exploitative behaviour within the banks, but a failure of regulation. The FSCP concluded that 'competition authorities' emphasis on traditional demand-side remedies does not work for consumers. Relying on consumers to take action has had only limited effectiveness' (2017b: 1). As a result, the FSCP demanded that regulatory 'authorities…take robust and effective action to tackle supply-side problems like firms' exploitation of consumers' behavioural biases and "monopolistic competition" where products, prices and information are complex and sometimes misleading' (FSCP 2017b: 5).

It is therefore also important to emphasize the failure of regulation to tackle these business practices because this too confirms our argument that the underlying structural conditions of financialization create overwhelming demand-side pressures that—despite the aforementioned assertions by the FSCP—neither the narrow bank culture debate nor supply-side reform can remedy. On the supply-side, in both the US and the UK there was some evidence that increased regulatory activity was having a modest impact on punitive fee regimes. In the US, since 2011 a total of 94 US banks had come under the supervision of the CFSB allowing consumers to complain over unfair overdraft fees; the result was a reduction in the average overdraft revenue generated by those ninety-four banks (USPIRG

Table 10.2 UK banks ranked by competitiveness of savings and current accounts

Rank	Savings account	Current account
1	Nationwide	Santander
2	First Direct	Tesco
3	HSBC	Nationwide
4	M&S Bank	TSB
5	Santander	Halifax
6	Saffron Building Society	Leeds Building Society
7	Kent Reliance	Virgin Money
8	Lloyds	Ulster Bank
9	Hanley Building society	Bank of Cyprus
10	Ipswich Building society	
11	Swansea Building society	
12	First Trust bank	

Sources: MoneySavingExpert and Moneywise data.

2016). This suggested that the complaints process strengthened by the CFSB was producing results, or that supply-side measures could indeed be effective by monitoring and intervening in more extreme cases that pushed beyond accepted market norms. Similarly, in 2009 the Federal Reserve introduced a new rule that meant that customers had to opt-in to the overdraft scheme before they would be charged fees; this was intended to prevent banks *automatically* charging fees. Initially, overdraft-fee revenue fell in response to the new rule. In short, aside from the risk-taking and compliance measures outlined in Chapter 9, there was also evidence that certain regulatory initiatives—all products of the narrow culture debate—were improving exploitative practices stemming from financialization. But my argument in this book is that unless the root causes of the changes in bank business models and the propensity towards high levels of private and household debt are tackled, the exploitative culture of banking will not change.

To support this argument, we might look to the rising revenue earned from overdraft charges by mid-2015. Indeed revenue from overdraft fees and nonsufficient funds (NSF) in the first three quarters of 2016 had increased 2.6 per cent over the same period in 2015 (ibid., Fig. 10.14) representing a 5.4 per cent rise since 2011 (WSJ 2017). Likewise Fig. 10.15 shows the increase in overdraft fee revenue for three of the banks from our survey sample. In the US case this is hugely significant, because there was little evidence that the increase was due to banks circumventing the regulation; supply-side mechanisms may even have been moderately effective. Instead, the increase was driven by increased demand amongst US consumers where indebtedness does not necessarily reflect optimism, but tougher living conditions (FFIEC 2016).

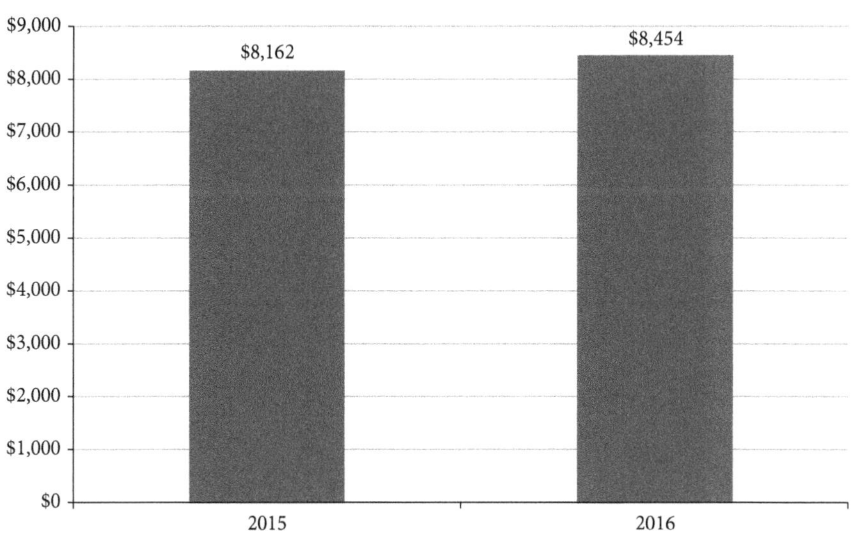

Fig. 10.14 Overdraft and NSF revenue (US$ millions)
Source: FFIEC 2016, cited in USPIRG 2016.

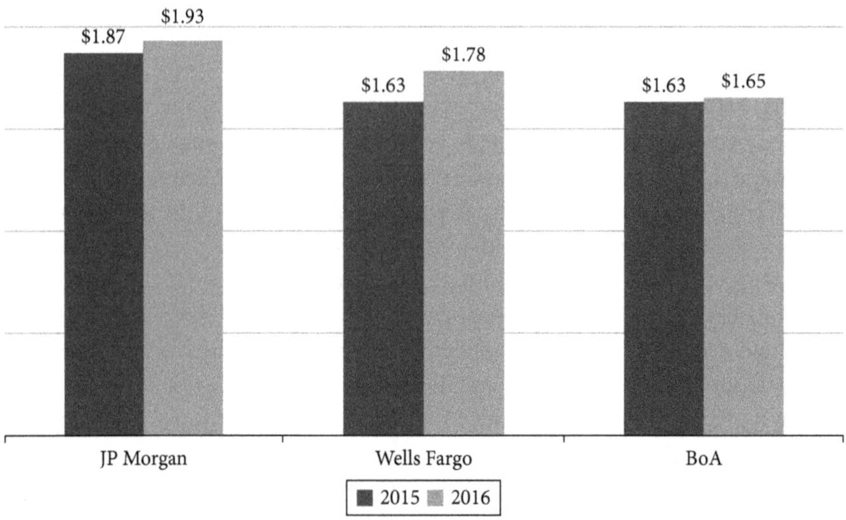

Fig. 10.15 Overdraft revenue at three large US retail banks ($US billions)
Source: S&P Global Market Intelligence, cited in *WSJ* 2017b.

In short, the second section of this chapter has sought to map out the pressures that financialization generates through wage stagnation, consumption-led growth, and heightened indebtedness. The main aim though has been to show that the Anglo-American banks examined in Part III of this book continued to employ exploitative practices targeting the heavily indebted. As a Member of the UK Treasury Select Committee argued, 'Banks are sending many people deeper into debt…They should have a responsibility to help people out of debt, rather than adding to their problems' (Rachel Reeves MP, cited in the *Guardian* 2017a). This is why supply-side and behavioural reforms are surface-level and superficial, for they do not address the underlying (demand-side) conditions that banks exploit.

Banker Pay

The third and final section of this chapter examines banker pay as both an economic and political cultural problem. Chapter 2 explained that whilst high pay is neither unique to the Anglo-American banking sectors nor inherently problematic, high pay against the backdrop of stagnant economic growth, weak to moderate profitability for the financial firm itself, and stagnant or declining wages for the average worker should be seen as evidence of rent-seeking behaviour and the cause of further legitimacy challenges. Indeed, the defining issue in Anglo-America—for both economic and ideological reasons—is inequality (Gill 2002). And disproportionately high pay for bankers is simply an extreme example of the cultural problem associated with inequality. In other words, as was argued in Chapter 2, there are two related problems associated with high pay and bonuses: one concerns the correlation between pay and performance; and the other concerns their legitimacy-threatening impact.

Disproportionately High Pay

The aim of this first subsection is to show the state of banking remuneration in Anglo-America in the post-crisis period. In the US, the Securities and Exchange Commission (SEC) requires registered banks to publish summary compensation tables for the top five highest paid executives. Using Proxy Statements for all of the major US banks we have surveyed in the second half of this book, Fig. 10.16 was compiled. The base salary comprises the gross salary total for the CEO and the four other most highly compensated executive officers. The upper line comprises the total compensation for these same five executives: this includes their base salary, their bonus, any other annual compensation, restricted stock options, and securities underlying options. It was not atypical to find base salaries at around 8 per cent, with cash and deferred cash bonuses at around 30 per cent, and deferred equity and long-term compensation (in various forms) at around

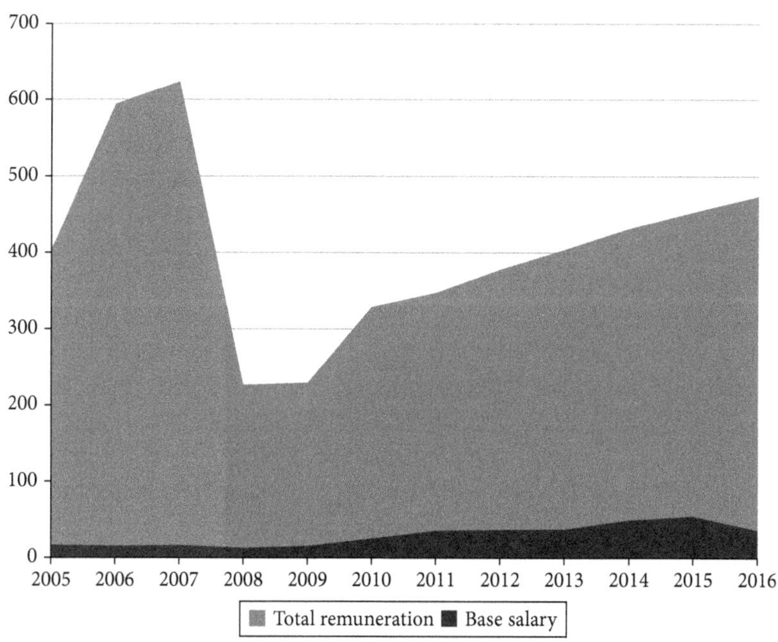

Fig. 10.16 Total top five executives' remuneration, five US banks (2005–16) (US $millions)

Sources: Proxy Statements Bank of America, Citigroup, Goldman Sachs, JPMorgan, Morgan Stanley.

62 per cent (see for example Morgan Stanley 2014: 30). Two important points are worth noting: over the period there was a moderate rise in base salaries, often driven by regulatory shifts limiting the amount of cash bonuses that could be paid; more importantly though, after a drop in 2008–9 bonuses rose back to levels higher than those of the early-mid 2000s. This meant that total remuneration for each of these five executives by 2016 ranged between $15–30 million per annum. Indeed, by 2018 average bonuses for *all* US bank employees (that is, not just senior executives) had risen to almost their 2006–7 levels (*FT* 2018).

Data on bonuses is not publicly available for the individual UK banks we have surveyed. Instead though, data from the Office for National Statistics (ONS) points to a similar conclusion (see Fig. 10.17): (1) that pay in the financial sector was rising again, and that (2) it was rising at a faster rate than pay in all other sectors of the economy.

Rent-seeking

The previous subsection clearly demonstrated the continued prevalence of (disproportionately) high salaries in the finance sector. In Chapter 2 we challenged the view that this pay is correlated to either merit and performance or social utility. One industry insider defended banker pay as follows: 'For a normal person the salaries are very high and the bonuses seem even higher. But in this world [of financial services] you get a top bonus for top performance, a medium bonus for mediocre performance and a much smaller bonus if you don't do so well' (*Guardian* 2008c). Put differently, pay reflects the contribution or value-added by the individual. This is underpinned by the orthodox view of executive compensation, which assumes that 'pay arrangements are the product of arms-length bargaining—bargaining between executives attempting to get the best possible deal for themselves and boards seeking to get the best possible deal for shareholders' (Bebchuk and Fried 2004: 2).

Yet, as we noted, disproportionately high pay in the finance sector is hard to explain in either meritocratic or value-added terms. As discussed in Chapter 2 a range of studies concluded that neither higher cognitive skills, higher education levels, differences in job characteristics, nor technological change could explain the *finance sector premium* (Lindley and McIntosh 2014: 20). A systematic examination of the value-added of the banking and finance sector, and the degree to which this explains disproportionate wages is beyond the remit of this chapter. Instead I provide two simple indicators which problematize the claim that an *increase* in the contribution of the finance sector explains the fact that remuneration continued to rise so far and so fast: the evidence of the financial crisis in the US, and the value-added by financial services in the UK.

First, the financial crisis itself, which imposed significant costs on both the US and the UK in slowed output, debt repayments, and austerity cuts, challenged the claim that high pay was justified in light of long-term performance (Better Markets Report 2015). The New York State Attorney General's Office conducted a review of compensation practices in the American banking system and concluded that there was 'no clear rhyme or reason to the way banks compensate and reward employees'; and that 'compensation for bank employees [had] become unmoored from the banks' financial performance' (Cuomo 2009: 1). In terms of evidence, the report noted that in 2008 Citigroup and Merrill Lynch had suffered losses of more than $27 billion but had paid out $5.3 billion and $3.6 billion respectively in bonuses (ibid.). Three other firms, Goldman Sachs, Morgan Stanley, and JPMorgan Chase also paid out bonuses substantially greater than the banks' net income: in total the three firms earned $9.6 billion in 2008 but had paid bonuses of nearly $18 million. One response was that pay was high in order to retain talent. This is not disputed here; competition between financial firms is fierce. That does not negate the fact however, that defending high pay as performance-related is misleading. And this claim is important, for it points to the detachment between profits and pay in the financial sector and the health of the economy, which is politically and economically problematic.

Secondly, the gross value added to the UK economy by the finance sector as a percentage of GDP is a useful proxy indicator of the contribution made by financial services. The data does not provide conclusive evidence of rent-seeking behaviour; that is, 'a level of pay in financial services... out of all proportion to their contribution to society' (Bootle 2012: 13). Nonetheless, if there were a direct correlation between (disproportionately) rising pay (see Fig. 10.17) and value-added to the UK economy, we would expect to witness a parallel increase in the GVA of the finance sector. Fig. 10. 18 shows however, that this was not the case. In fact, the GVA of finance fell from a peak of 9.1 per cent in 2009 to only 7.2 per cent in 2016. Put differently, the UK finance sector was contributing relatively less to the UK economy and yet—as Fig. 10.17 showed—reaping higher financial rewards.

Again, as we discussed in Chapter 8 the performance of—inter alia—UK banks and the UK economy has lagged behind that of their US peers. This was almost certainly a driver of the reduction in GVA on the part of financial services. Profits were lower and hence the net contribution fell. Yet the ONS data (Fig. 10.17) provides conclusive evidence that despite these factors—lower GVA, slowed performance by UK banks, and a sluggish economic recovery—the finance premium continued to grow, exacerbating the divide between wages in finance and those in the rest of the economy (see also Erturk et al. 2011).

As I highlighted, the aim here is not to definitely *prove* that wages in the banking and financial sectors are completely detached from the social utility of financial activity. But the point is that the narrow bank culture debate focused on a very different, and less contentious issue: tying remuneration (pay) to long-term performance. This debate was certainly contentious for the bankers whose pay was affected. But it barely even touched the surface of the much broader and arguably more important question of whether such high pay was warranted,

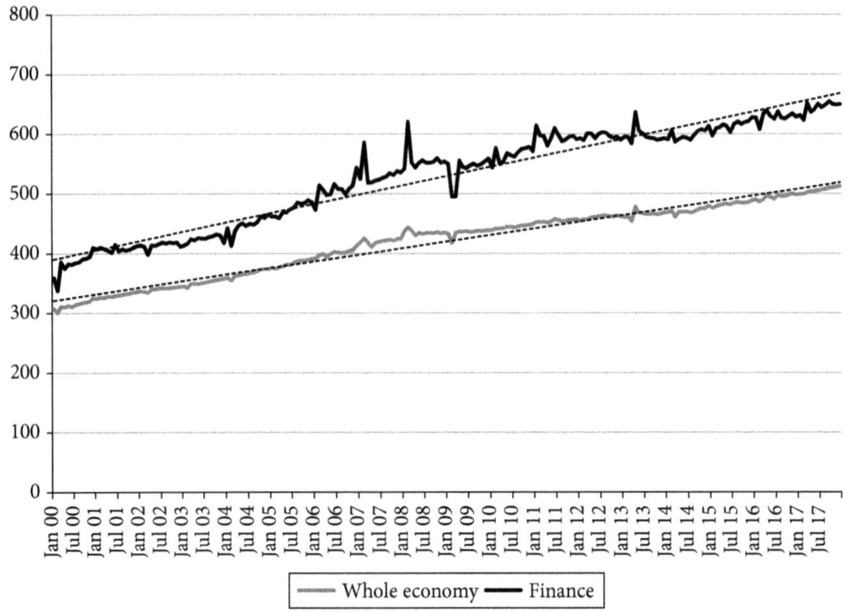

Fig. 10.17 UK average weekly wages for whole economy (not excluding finance) & finance sector (2000–17) (£ sterling) seasonally adjusted

Source: ONS 2018.

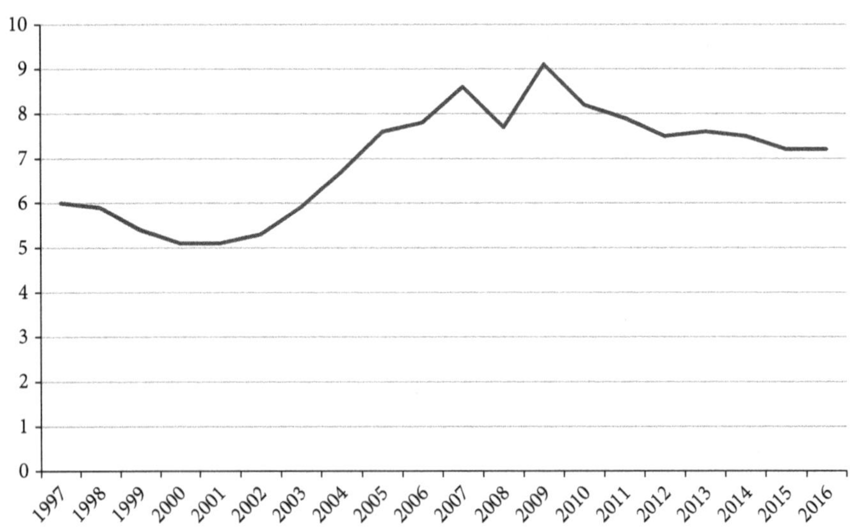

Fig. 10.18 Gross value-added by finance sector (% of UK GDP)

Source: House of Commons 2017.

given the function which the banks fulfil. My main contention is that a more robust and wide-ranging debate on this aspect of bank culture is still required.

Closing Remarks

Bonuses as a Legitimacy Threat

For our purposes we therefore need only highlight the paradox of rising pay out of proportion to either value-added or performance, rather than comprehensively explaining the anomaly. This is because our aim is only to highlight the continued prevalence of cultural problems in both economic and political terms. We can therefore close this chapter by pointing to the ongoing legitimacy challenges associated with the bonus culture.

'How much pay is too much?' is a question that cannot be answered in objective terms. Instead, as US Representative Henry Waxman noted in Chapter 4, the more appropriate question that we should be asking—against the backdrop of indebtedness and wage stagnation—is 'is this fair?' This is because, as was noted in earlier chapters, wage inequality is always a relative and a relational phenomenon (Brosnan and de Waal 2003). The puzzle which confronts us in closing this chapter is that despite rising pay in the financial sector and the return of the bonus culture[1] public interest in banker remuneration appeared to have subsided somewhat by the late 2010s. Fig. 10.19 is adapted from Google Trends, and

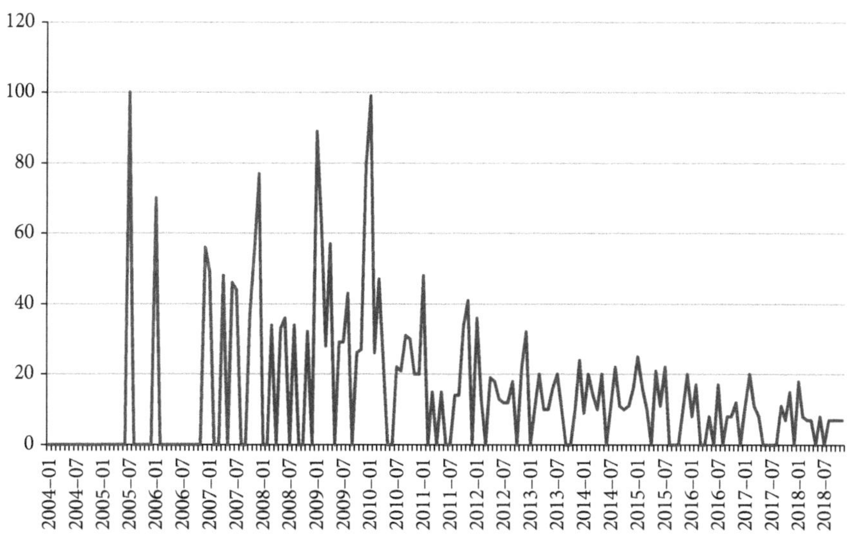

Fig. 10.19 Google trends: mentions for 'banker bonuses' (2004–18)
Source: Google Trends

[1] Certainly in the US, and there is evidence that once Brexit is negotiated in the UK the EU-imposed bonus cap will be lifted.

indicates that mentions of 'banker bonuses' in search engines, as well as social media, and news publications had subsided since 2011–12. Should this be read as a popular acceptance of high pay in the financial sector?

In closing, our argument is definitively no. The fact that there was a steady but silent decline in public interest in banker pay is by no means proof that the legitimacy-threat of bank bonuses has dissipated. In April 2014 for example, shareholders and protesters gathered in London for Barclays' annual general meeting. Their concern was that the bank had announced a 10 per cent increase in bonuses despite a dramatic fall in profits and plans to cut 12,000 jobs that year (*Guardian* 2014). By 2017 it was shareholders rather than the general public that protested against the lowering of targets attached to Standard Chartered chief executives' bonus package (CityAM 2017). A similar shareholder revolt unfolded at Credit Suisse in 2017, though the Swiss bank is not part of our Anglo-American study. These were however, the exceptions rather than the norm by the late 2010s. It appeared that the public moral outrage that had sparked the Occupy movements had subsided.

But as I will argue in Chapter 11, the fact that protests had declined should in no way be interpreted as an acceptance of high and rising wages and bonuses in the banking sector. It is better explained by arguing that the general public had forgotten rather than forgiven; and that the narrow bank culture debate had worked, in so far as it had temporarily diffused criticism and bought both state managers and the banks time. But, I will argue, the anti-establishment sentiment reflected in the (US) Trump and (UK) Brexit vote, were simply an extension of the same legitimacy crisis that had developed around the bank culture problem. And if this is true, the wages issue will re-emerge, because it is a very visible manifestation of the inequality at the heart of financialization.

Thus the evidence presented through Chapters 4–10 suggests that state managers' attempts to depoliticize the bank culture problem had proven to be moderately successful. The legitimacy crisis was deferred rather than resolved; anti-establishment protest votes for Donald Trump and Brexit were embedded in the same populist politics that had shaped state managers responses to the post-2012 banking scandals (Blyth 2016). But the emphasis on supply-side measures and conduct-related reform by the state and within the banks would also seem to have deflected popular criticism away from the largest Anglo-American banks, judging by the relative decline in protests over remuneration. The central argument of this chapter is that the deeper, structural causes of the bank cultural problems have not been remedied. And, as a result, the legitimacy crisis that was ratcheted up by bank culture problems was only shifted to the backburner. It too is a problem that has not gone away.

So where does this leave us? The culture of banking problem—which, I argue, is ultimately a culture of financialization problem—spilled over with the bank failures and bailouts of 2008, and again with the scandals of 2012. Yet our core argument contends that state managers and the banks have fought tooth and nail to protect the neoliberal, financialized status quo. The question we must address in Chapter 11 is, have we—at the time of writing in 2018—reached a tipping point? Put differently, if the attempt to contain and neutralize the seismic political and economic forces that gave rise to the bank culture problem is an exercise in futility, are we reaching a watershed moment in Anglo-American capitalism? Are Trump and Brexit the answer to challenges exposed by the culture of banking problematique? I will turn to these questions in Chapter 11.

11
Conclusion
Finance, Trump, and Brexit

I began this book by arguing that the *culture* of banking was the most pressing issue facing Western financial systems in the mid-2010s, and yet the problems around bank culture remained unresolved. Many informed readers would balk at this claim. Since 2015–16 much of the regulatory and political pressure to reform bank culture in the UK and the US has subsided. The departure of Martin Wheatley from the FCA and the sluggish rate of the economic recovery in the UK added weight to the view that authorities needed to pursue a more lenient approach towards the banks, and Brexit proved to be a further distraction. Whilst in the US, the deregulatory rhetoric of Donald Trump, the more robust economic recovery, and the improved financial performance of the largest banks seemed to imply that the post-crisis reform agenda had met its objective of improving both the stability and the conduct of the banks. The fraudulent account-opening revelations surrounding Wells Fargo in 2016–17 were therefore deemed to be the last remnants of the bad sales culture that had been so pervasive in the pre-crisis years. As a result, the regulatory focus in the UK and the US shifted towards the fintech industry and high-cost credit. One might therefore conclude that the bank culture debate could be laid to rest in these two countries.

But the opening premise of this book is that the culture of banking problematique is far from resolved. Informed readers who think otherwise have, I would argue, accepted the misleading, narrower definition of bank culture. As a result of the misdiagnosis their conclusions are also misinformed. They have also, I would argue, accepted that some of the more disturbing features of Anglo-American capitalism, from its instability to its high levels of inequality, are beyond the realm of the culture of banking debate.

The main argument of this book is that the narrow culture of banking debate that unfolded in the political realm largely ignored the more important structural drivers of bank culture in Anglo-America. The debate focused instead on improving the conduct and behaviour of bankers. Regulatory politics focused on improving market discipline, structuring incentives to promote longer-term strategies, and encouraging better market values and ethics in firms. The assumption was that participants had evidently forgotten or ignored the rules of the game. The effective, efficient, and benign market had been distorted. Good culture had been undermined by the 'misconduct' of participants.

The Bank Culture Debate: Ethics, Values, and Financialization in Anglo-America. Huw Macartney, Oxford University Press (2019). © Huw Macartney.
DOI: 10.1093/oso/9780198843764.001.0001

In contrast this book has argued that the financialized markets of Anglo-America were and still are the more significant drivers of banking culture. And these markets are anything but benign and distributionally-neutral. The orthodox liberal dogma that believes that the free market mechanism is the most efficient and socially robust means of organizing political and economic relations is incorrect. The structure of these markets actually promotes bad culture in banks. This is because these markets fuel economic inequality and instability, as well as engendering rent-seeking behaviour and empowering the financiers, which also distorts democratic politics. The simple message of this concluding chapter is that a broader debate is urgently needed. This broader debate needs to explore a wider range of causes of banking culture; but it therefore also needs to call into question some widely accepted but nonetheless disturbing features of the financialized economies of Anglo-America.

The Argument

Let me briefly unpack the range of issues that this book has drawn attention to. On inequality, this book has clearly shown that compared to relatively stagnant wages in many other sectors wages in the finance sector were disproportionately high again by the late 2010s. As I noted in Chapter 9, this is not the sentiment expressed by bank staff; but the data presented in Chapter 10 speaks for itself. We should perhaps conclude that many higher paid bank employees have lost touch with the chronic problems of underemployment and low paid labour that characterize their respective economies.

On instability, conceptually and empirically this book has defended the claim that market-based banking and the bloodthirsty search for yield at the heart of financialization drive what Hyman Minsky would have described as a cyclical pattern of financial instability. Heavily indebted, consumption-led recoveries move swiftly through the credit cycle from cautious to overly-exuberant risk-taking. Market-based banking feeds non-interest revenue streams that bring few benefits to the non-financial economy.

On rent-seeking, these same market-based banking structures adjust for low wage gains and low growth rates in the non-financial sector by re-distributing fee and commission income within the financial sector. There is little to no value-creating work generated by these activities, contrary to the protestations of the financiers. Profits in the banking sector reflect huge distributive gains but reinforce the disconnection between the finance sector and the non-financial economies of Anglo-America.

Meanwhile, lastly, the shift in gravity towards financial activities in the US and the UK has strengthened the influence of the financiers, and continues to do so. In the US this became particularly apparent with the appointment of Goldman

Sachs grandees to the Trump administration; whilst in the UK the same influence exerted by the City elite prompted the Conservative government to adopt a more deferential approach towards the banks post-2016.

The Everyday Life of Banking Culture

What we require is a much broader-based discussion of the causes and effects of banking culture. One major concern that animated both the research and writing of this book was to re-connect the debate about bank culture with the lived experiences of millions of British and North American citizens. In my opinion, one unfortunate consequence of the narrowing of the political debate about bank culture was that it all but ignored the broader questions of what—inter alia—income inequality felt like to these individuals and households. For them, bank culture was not solely a matter of fraudulent account-opening or the 'pushy' sales techniques they encountered upon entering their local bank branch. Financialization placed strong downward pressures on their wages, driving them into vicious debt cycles, and bad bank culture then compounded these circumstances at every turn. Bank culture affected the punitive charges they incurred every time they exceeded their overdraft limits; bank culture led to the threatening, debt-related letters that appeared in their mail; bank culture drove the fees they encountered every time they applied for a personal loan or mortgage; and bank culture shaped the wages and bonuses which they saw bank executives being paid.

Frankly I doubt whether most of the US and UK public know or care about ring-fencing, proprietary trading bans, or deferred bonus payments. Their experiences of bank culture (and financialization) were far more pervasive and personal. The legitimacy crisis I pointed to in Part II and the challenges associated with stagnant wages, heightened indebtedness, and the predatory practices of banks (in Part III) were an attempt to redress this imbalance in the political debate. The bank culture debate that took place in the political realm—with its questions of compliance monitoring and tax deductions—risks sounding esoteric and technical. In economic jargon, this is arguably a product of the focus on supply-side reforms. But financialization is also, equally, a demand-side process. And its impacts on mental and physical wellbeing, and—by extension—on families and relationships, are very real components of a broader bank culture discussion (PERC 2016).

Is it Really About Financialization?

To launch a broader debate however, we must first be convinced that the culture of banking problem is indeed a culture of *financialization* problem. Despite the protestations of some practitioners I remain convinced that it is. In Chapter 10 for example, the observant reader will have noted that in a number of ways it is almost impossible to distinguish between the two: for example, the disconnect between the banks and the economy is also largely true for a wider range of financial institutions; and disproportionately high pay in the banking sector is true for the finance sector as a whole.

As I highlighted in the Introduction chapter, a major obstacle to recognizing the underlying causes of the bank culture problem is that financialization is now considered part of the natural order of things. It is so deeply embedded in the spending patterns of households and the commercial strategies of almost all corporations that we can no longer see where it begins or ends. Yet the first step towards a broader debate begins with the recognition that there is something wrong with the status quo. As I noted in the Introduction some non-academic authors have sought to make this claim on historical grounds; once upon a time banking was simpler and fairer. Others would seek to make the same claim on comparative grounds; there are economies with more stable financial systems and a more equitable distribution of wealth and resources. My main concern is that whether we invoke historical or comparative cases as a point of reference, we need to dismantle certain unquestioned assumptions about the financialized markets of Anglo-America.

A second step towards the claim that financialization is the root cause of the problem is to look at what has happened in the *financial* and *regulatory* spaces in the UK and the US in parallel to the focus on bank culture. In the financial space, there is growing evidence that the space vacated by banks—now operating under stricter rules—is being occupied by other financial institutions, such as shadow banks and high-cost credit providers. Put differently, the actors may have changed but the problems—of exploitative practices and instability—have not. One result of the post-crisis reform of the banking sector—the cultural agenda and the wider tightening of banking regulation and supervision—was that the shape of the financial sector changed. Embattled domestic banks, still adapting to the new regulatory environment, withdrew from certain, higher-risk lending markets. In the US, racial minorities and less creditworthy households were the worst affected. As further proof that the cultural problems affecting banking are rooted in demand-side, structural conditions other non-bank providers moved into the space vacated by the banks. In particular, less tightly regulated shadow banks were the major winners.

On the upside, recent studies have shown that these shadow banks tend to be three to five basis points cheaper than traditional banks. In that sense there may be gains for lower income households. On the downside however, these same studies have shown that borrowers from shadow banks are more likely to default (Buchak et al. 2017: 26). This is hardly surprising given that shadow banks have been shown to *target* higher risk borrowers (ibid.). The result however, is that in key markets—like mortgage lending—the market share of shadow banks has nearly tripled from 14 per cent to 38 per cent; whilst in the Federal Housing Administration mortgage market, which serves less creditworthy borrowers, 'the market share of shadow banks increased from 20% to 75%' between 2007–2015 (ibid.: 4).

In other words, the regulatory focus on bank conduct has simply squeezed risk into other parts of the financial system. This is because demand for cheap credit amongst lower income households has not declined. Of course, the point is not that lending to less creditworthy households is problematic in abstract terms. Rather the point is that solving the problem of maintaining effective demand via expansion of the credit economy—rather than through rising wages—has been shown to be far less economically stable and to further exacerbate all kinds of income inequality (Crouch 2009).

This requires us to challenge the trite liberal economics mantra that an increase in the supply of credit in an economy is a sign of recovery and prosperity. A central message of this book is that this is simply not the case for large segments of the US and UK populations; credit—or debt—expands because of *problems* that their stagnant wages cannot fix. In the case of shadow banks and mortgages, inflated property prices, unaffordable rental markets, and the neoliberal aspiration of homeownership drive prospective buyers towards higher risk providers. Ironically then, the regulatory focus on banks has actually made the culture of financialization problem even worse.

Aside from shadow banks, perhaps the best evidence of a culture of financialization problem lies in the area of high-cost credit. Since the bank culture debate became less of a priority, state managers have—in both the US and the UK—shifted their attention to other areas. High-cost credit has therefore been a major area of focus for both the CFPB in the US and the FCA in the UK. Yet once again, despite the regulatory focus on curbing the worst excesses of these markets, here is another problem that cannot be solved via a supply-side strategy. For example, in 2014 the UK Financial Conduct Authority introduced price caps intended to protect vulnerable borrowers. The idea was to prevent 'spiralling payday debts' (FCA 2014). Yet by 2017 complaints about payday loans had increased by 64 per cent (*Guardian* 2018a), with over 3.1 million lower income households forced to turn to high cost credit providers during 2017–18 (*Guardian* 2018b). Indeed some of the rent-to-own providers that catered explicitly for less creditworthy borrowers, charged interest rates as high as 1557 per cent (ibid).

In other words, the punitive fees on credit cards and overdrafts for traditional banks were actually dwarfed by the charges imposed by high-cost credit providers. State managers were not unaware of this problem. But they employed the same supply-side strategy in their approach to high-cost credit as they had in relation to the big banks. Making high levels of debt more sustainable by placing stricter levels on penalty charges and interest rates was the main objective of US and UK authorities. The underlying structural causes of unsustainable levels of household indebtedness were largely ignored. Household indebtedness is then categorized as a financial stability concern that macro-prudential regulators within the central bank should oversee. State managers have again abdicated responsibility by reproducing the logic of tight money and fiscal discipline.

On Financial Instability

But one final point should be noted on this matter. Throughout the book I have argued that we need to engage in a debate about the structural determinants of bank culture. If the main feature of that bad bank culture was simply excessive risk-taking and instability then the work of Hyman Mynsky might be appropriate. Mynsky provides a critical perspective of the financial cycle, which moves from hedging to speculative to excessive risk-taking (1977). And this theory certainly captures some of the structural dynamics highlighted in this present book.

But the debate I am advocating for is more far-reaching than Mynsky's theory would allow, because we need more than a theory of the economy, but a theory of statecraft too. In this vein, throughout this book I have sought to emphasize the *class politics* of financialization. I did so because an alternative debate on bank culture should be particularly critical of the role that the state plays in maintaining and reproducing class relations.

I developed this argument in three key ways: one is via the emphasis on politics within the state apparatus. My focus on state managers' attempts to fight the legitimacy crisis highlighted a political move to depoliticize the asymmetrical distribution of wealth and power that occurs under financialization. This is because, as I explained in Chapter 3, the financialized markets of Anglo-America are forms of exploitation. Secondly though, I have also emphasized a class politics that is a stretch for Mynsky by showing the exploitative relationships between the banks and large segments of society. This is one reason why I did not concern myself with mapping the credit cycle in Chapters 9 and 10 for example, for exploitation and class politics permeates a far broader range of banking activities—from remuneration to punitive fees and charges. Thirdly though, rather than settle for a Mynsky-esque critique that would imply that the financialization of Anglo-America is simply and primarily a result of the shift to financial activities in the 1970s, I argued in earlier chapters that *class politics* shaped this shift from the outset. For instance, the crisis of accumulation and profitability (see Chapter 2) that gave rise to financialization was an attempt by capital in general to place downward pressure on wage growth; and these efforts were facilitated by state managers and central bankers.

In other words, a broader debate on the structural determinants of bank culture needs to go beyond an economic theory of financial cycles. It must also shine light on the role that the state has played, through action and inaction, in establishing and reproducing the forms of exploitation highlighted in this book. This debate therefore needs to go beyond a superficial focus on party politics and the differences in a party's stated manifesto. It needs to begin with the assertion that the state itself is a manifestation of class forces and therefore deeply imbricated in the class politics that shape financialization.

The Way Forward?

In closing though, I would argue that the abdication of responsibility by state managers has a limited lifespan. The culture of financialization problematique has both stability and legitimacy-threatening outcomes. On the one hand, in dealing with the culture of banking problem state managers bought themselves a little more time. In allowing shadow banks to fill the mortgage market space and by targeting high-cost credit providers state managers have, perhaps, delayed the day of reckoning. And in the election of Trump and the promise of a better post-Brexit future state managers may believe that they have provided a sufficiently robust response to the legitimacy crisis. On the other hand however, in the politics of tight money and the turn towards Quantitative Easing (QE), financialization has actually worsened. I would argue that the symptoms of inequality—lower levels of disposable income, homelessness, and debt-related disorders, amongst other things—will return to haunt the political classes. The culture of banking issue was just the tip of the iceberg.

What is to be done? There are no easy answers. But that does not mean that we should simply accept the status quo. As John Holloway once argued, 'we do not need to have a picture of what a true world would be like in order to feel that there is something radically wrong with the world that exists. Feeling that the world is wrong does not necessarily mean that we have a picture of a utopia to put in its place' (2002: 3). The broad debate I have called for requires us, as critical observers, to question and probe the contradictions in our respective economies. 'That is our starting point: rejection of a world that we feel to be wrong, negation of a world we feel to be negative' (ibid.). The pathologies of Anglo-American capitalism are very visible. We can no longer turn a blind eye to them. At the very least we must acknowledge that the post-crisis attempt to invoke fiscal discipline and loose monetary policy do not offer the required solutions.

In the Introduction I dismissed the claim that 'the episode marked by financialization is coming to a close' (Krippner 2012: 139). But I would agree that the financialized economies of Anglo-America bear a close resemblance to the zombies of Hollywood B-movies. Anglo-America is in a seemingly permanent state of terminal decline: where expansion of the credit economy—rather than being a symptom of health, wealth, and prosperity—compensates for wage stagnation and dilutes popular resistance; and where the buoyancy of stock markets promotes the recycling of capital within the financial sector, rather than reflecting value-creating activity in the non-financial economy. The words of Antonio Gramsci come to mind: 'The crisis consists precisely in the fact that the old is dying and the new cannot be born; in this interregnum a great variety of morbid symptoms appear' (1971: 276). The economies of Anglo-America are economies on life-support.

Over the course of writing this book I have regularly walked the streets of London and New York and this is what has struck me. These are cities where affluence and abject poverty sit side by side. In Tower Hamlets—the London borough where the financial district of Canary Wharf is located—the average life expectancy of the rich is eleven years longer than that of the poor (Tower Hamlets 2018). In New York City, 43 per cent of the population live at or near the poverty line (NYC Mayor's Office 2018). But these cities are simply microcosms of their respective financialized economies. Even the founder of liberal economics, Adam Smith, recognized that the 'affluence of the few supposes the indigence of the many' (2008: 408). It is time to stop accepting that the financialization of Anglo-America is a given. It is time to question the justifications of inequality. And it is time to re-engage with the debate on banking culture.

Bibliography

Accenture (2017) 'Compliance Costs for Financial Institutions Will Continue to Increase Over the Next Two Years Driven by Regulations and Emerging Risks, According to Global Accenture Survey of Executives', News Release, 10 April 2017.

Achyrya, V. et al. (2010) *Regulating Wall Street: The Dodd–Frank Act and the New Architecture of Global Finance.* John Wiley.

Acharya, V. et al. (2014) 'The end of market discipline? Investor expectations of implicit government guarantees', https://papers.ssrn.com/sol3/papers.cfm?abstract_id=1961656

Acharya, V. et al. (2015) 'Whatever it Takes: The Real Effects of Unconventional Monetary Policy', Paper presented at the 16th Jacques Polak Annual Research Conference Hosted by the International Monetary Fund Washington, DC, 5–6 November 2015, https://www.imf.org/external/np/res/seminars/2015/arc/pdf/Eisert.pdf

Acharya, V. et al. (2016) 'Cash Holdings and Bank Compensation', *Federal Reserve Bank of New York Economic Policy Review* 22: 1.

Admati, A. and M. Hellwig (2014) *The Bankers' New Clothes: What's Wrong with Banking and What to Do about It.* Princeton University Press.

Afonso, G. et al. (2014) 'Do "Too-Big-to-Fail" Banks Take On More Risk?' *Federal Reserve Bank of New York Economic Policy Review* 20(2): 41–58.

Akerlof, G. A., and R. E. Kranton (2010) *Identity Economics: How Our Identities Shape Our Work, Wages, and Well-Being.*, Princeton, NJ: Princeton University Press.

Albert, M. (1991) *Capitalism against Capitalism.* London: Wiley-Blackwell.

Alessandri, P. and A. Haldane (2009) 'Banking on the state', Paper by Andrew G. Haldane, Executive Director, Financial Stability, Bank of England, and Piergiorgio Alessandri, based on a presentation delivered at the Federal Reserve Bank of Chicago twelfth annual International Banking Conference on 'The International Financial Crisis: Have the Rules of Finance Changed?', Chicago, 25 September 2009.

Allen and Overy (2015a) 'Proposed "u-turn" on the Presumption of Responsibility?' Allen and Overy Investigations Insight, http://www.aoinvestigationsinsight.com/proposed-u-turn-on-the-presumption-of-responsibility/

Altunbas, Y. et al. (2010) 'Does monetary policy affect bank risk-taking?' ECB Working Paper series 1166.

American Banker (2015a) 'Bank Culture Can't Be Measured in Scorecards', 29 June 2015; http://www.americanbanker.com/bankthink/bank-culture-cant-be-measured-in-scorecards-1075131-1.html

American Banker (2015b) 'Obsessing about rules won't improve culture', 22 December 2015, http://www.americanbanker.com/bankthink/obsessing-about-rules-wont-improve-culture-1078412-1.html

Anderson, S. (2015) 'Off the deep end: the Wall Street bonus pool', 11 March 2015, Institute for Policy Studies http://www.ips-dc.org/deep-end-wall-street/

Andries, A. M. et al. (2015) 'Low interest rates and bank risk-taking: has the crisis changed anything?' *Review of Economic and Business Studies* 8(1): 125–48.

Armous, J. et al. (2017) 'Regulatory Sanctions and Reputational Damage in Financial Markets', *Journal of Financial and Quantitative Analysis* 52(4): 1429–48.

Armstrong, A. (2012) Restoring Trust in Banking, *National Institute Economic Review* 221, July 2012.

Armstrong, J. et al. (1991) *Capitalism since 1945*. Oxford: Blackwell.

Atkinson, W. et al. (2012) *Class Inequality in Austerity Britain: Power, Difference and Suffering*. Palgrave Macmillan.

Aupperle, K., A. Carroll. and J. Hatfield (1985) 'An empirical examination of the relationship between corporate social responsibility and profitability', *Academy of Management Journal* 28: 446–63.

Avgouleas, Emilios (2009) 'The Global Financial Crisis, Behavioural Finance and Financial Regulation: In Search of a New Orthodoxy', *Journal of Corporate Law Studies* 9(1): 23–59.

Awrey, Dan and David Kershaw (2014) 'Toward a more ethical culture in finance: regulatory and governance strategies'. In: Nicholas Morris and David Vines (eds) *Capital Failure: Rebuilding Trust in Financial Services*. Oxford: Oxford University Press, pp. 277–304.

Bagehot, W. (1873) *Lombard Street, a Description of the Money Market*. Henry S. King and Co. Publishers.

Bailey, Andrew (2017) 'Culture in financial institutions: everywhere and nowhere', Speech by Andrew Bailey, Chief Executive of the FCA, at the HKMA Annual Conference for Independent Non-Executive Directors, 16 March 2017.

Balachandran, K. et al. (2010) 'The Probability of Default, Excess Risk and Executive Compensation: A Study of Financial Service Firms from 1995 to 2008', working paper (June 2010), available at: http://www.insead.edu/facultyresearch/areas/accounting/events/documents/excess_risk_bank_revi sedjune21bk.pdf (last accessed 15 March 2019).

Balasubramnian, B. and K. B. Cyree (2011) 'Market discipline of banks: why are yield spreads on bank-issued subordinated notes and debentures not sensitive to bank risks?' *Journal of Banking and Finance* 35: 21–35.

Bale, T. et al. (2009) 'Thrown around with abandon? Popular understandings of populism as conveyed by the print media: A UK case study', *Acta Politica* 46(2): 111–31.

Bank of America (2006–17) Annual Reports, 2006–17.

Bank of America (2006–17) Proxy Statements, 2006–17.

Bank of England (2003) Financial Stability Review, December 2003.

Bank of England (2007) Financial Stability Report April 2007, BoE London.

Bank of England (2009a) Credit Conditions Survey, 2009 Q3, BoE London.

Bank of England (2009b) Financial Stability Report December 2009, BoE London.

Bank of England (2010a) Trends in Lending June 2010, BoE London.

Bank of England (2010b) Credit Conditions Survey 2010 Q4, BoE London.

Bank of England (2017) Financial Policy Committee statement, 20 September 2017.

Bank of England (2018) Financial Stability Report, December 2018, BoE London.

Banktech (2014) 3 Compliance Trends Community Banks Should Watch in 2015, http://www.banktech.com/compliance/3-compliance-trends-community-banks-should-watch-in-2015/a/d-id/1318291

Barclays (2012) Barclays Bank PLC Settlement with Authorities, http://www.newsroom.barclays.com/r/2305/barclays_bank_plc_settlement_with_authorities

Barclays (2013) Barclays Response to Salz Review, https://www.home.barclays/content/dam/barclayspublic/documents/news/471-392-250413-salz-response.pdf

Barclays Bank (2006–17) Annual Reports, 2006–17.

Barclays Bank (2006–17) Proxy Statements, 2006–17.

Barnett, M. and T. Pollock, eds (2012) *The Oxford Handbook of Corporate Reputation*. Oxford University Press.

Barney, J. B. (1986) 'Organizational culture: can it be a source of sustained competitive advantage?' *The Academy of Management Review* 11(3): 656–65.

Baxter, T. (2014) 'Reflections on the new compliance landscape', remarks by Mr Thomas C. Baxter, Jr, Executive Vice President and General Counsel of the Federal Reserve Bank of New York, at 'The New Compliance Landscape: Increasing Roles—Increasing Risks' Conference, New York City, 23 July 2014.

Baxter, Thomas C. (2015) 'The rewards of an ethical culture', Remarks at the Bank of England by Thomas Baxter, Executive Vice President and General Counsel, 20 January 2015.

BBC (2007a) 'Mis-selling is rife at Barclays\, http://news.bbc.co.uk/1/hi/business/6476155.stm

BBC (2007b) 'Barclays sells sub-prime business', http://news.bbc.co.uk/1/hi/business/6528655.stm

BBC (2007c) 'Barclays profits hit record level', http://news.bbc.co.uk/1/hi/business/6377801.stm

BBC (2013) 'Bank fines go to good causes after rule change', http://www.bbc.co.uk/news/business-25214567

BCBS (2015) 'Corporate Governance Principles for Banks', http://www.bis.org/bcbs/publ/d328.pdf

Beatty, Randolph P., Howard Bunsis, and John R.M. Hand (1998) 'The indirect economic penalties in SEC investigations of underwriters', *Journal of Financial Economics*, Elsevier 50(2): 151–86.

Bebchuk, L. (2009) 'Fixing Bankers' Pay', *Economists' Voice* 6(11): Article 7.

Bebchuk, L. and J. Fried (2004) *Pay Without Performance: the Unfulfilled Promise of Executive Compensation*. Harvard University Press.

Beck, T. et al. (2014) 'Is More Finance Better? Disentangling Intermediation and Size Effects of Financial Systems', *Journal of Financial Stability* 10: 50–64.

Bell, B. and J. van Reenen (2013) 'Extreme Wage Inequality: Pay at the Very Top', Centre for Economic Performance, February 2013.

Bell, S. and A. Hindmoor (2018) 'Are the major global banks now safer? Structural continuities and change in banking and finance since the 2008 crisis', *Review of International Political Economy* 25(1): 1–27.

Bernanke, B. (2017) 'The Fed and fiscal policy', Brookings blog, 13 January 2017, https://www.brookings.edu/blog/ben-bernanke/2017/01/13/the-fed-and-fiscal-policy/

Bernanke, B. and C. Lown (1991) 'The Credit Crunch', *Brookings Papers on Economic Activity* 22(2): 205–48.

Best, J. (2005) *The Limits of Transparency: Ambiguity and the History of International Finance*. Ithaca: Cornell UP.

Best, J. and M. Patterson (2009) *Cultural Political Economy*. Routledge.

Better Markets (2015) *The Cost of the Crisis: $20 trillion and Counting*. Washington: Better Markets Report.

Bhattacharya, S. and A. Thakor (1993) 'Contemporary banking theory', *Journal of Financial Intermediation* 3: 2–50.

Bhattacharya, S., et al. (1998) 'The economics of bank regulation', *Journal of Money, Credit, and Banking* 30: 745–70.

Bieler, A. and A. Morton (2008) The Deficits of Discourse in IPE: turning base metal into gold? *International Studies Quarterly* 52(1): 103–28.

Bikker, J. and T. VerVliet (2017) 'Bank profitability and risk-taking under low interest rates', DNB Working Paper 560, July 2017.

BIS (2005) 'Compliance and the compliance function in banks', BCBS Working Paper 113.

BIS (2008) *Quarterly Review*, March 2008.

BIS (2012) 'Shareholder value and stability in banking: is there a conflict?', Speech by Jaime Caruana, General Manager, Bank for International Settlements, Morgan Stanley European Financials Conference London, 27 March 2012.

BIS (2015) 'The "four lines of defence model" for financial institutions', Occasional Paper 11, Financial Stability Institute.

BIS (2017) 'Consumption-led expansions', *BIS Quarterly Review*, March 2017.

Blackburn, Robin (2008) 'The Subprime Crisis', *New Left Review* 50.

Blanchflower, D. and S. Machin (2016) 'The Current 2% UK Wage Growth Norm', Centre for Economic Performance working paper, March 2016.

Block, F. (1977) *The Origins of International Economic Disorder: A Study of United States International Monetary Policy from World War II to the Present*. University of California Press.

Bloom, N. and J. van Reenen (2007) 'Measuring and Explaining Management Practices Across Firms and Countries', *The Quarterly Journal of Economics* 122(4): 1341–408.

Bloomberg (2011a) 'Lawsky Juggles Conflicting Roles as Financial Cop in N.Y.', 20 October 2011.

Bloomberg (2011b) 'Protesters to "Occupy" London Exchange After Wall Street', 13 October 2011.

Bloomberg (2012) 'HSBC to Pay $1.92 Billion in U.S. Money-Laundering Probe', 11 December 2012.

Bloomberg (2013a) 'Obama Fraud Task Force Takes on the Big Banks', 9 August 2013.

Bloomberg (2013b) 'Where Bank Regulators Go to Get Rich', 7 April 2013.

Bloomberg (2014) 'Wall Street Bonuses Grew 15% in New York', DiNapoli Says, 12 March 2014.

Bloomberg (2015a) 'Time for bankers to start swearing', 1 April 2015.

Bloomberg (2015b) 'Bank of America Said Selling $1.2 Billion in Home Loans', 6 August 2015.

Bloomberg (2017a) 'Deutsche Bank said to eye new home lending for settlement', 29 March 2017.

Bloomberg (2017b) 'World's Biggest Banks Fined $321 Billion Since Financial Crisis', 2 March 2017.

Bloomberg (2017c) 'Wage Stagnation in the U.S. Might Not Be As Bad as You Think', 4 April 2017.

Bloomberg (2018a) 'UBS Boosts Compensation for CEO and Staff After Profit Rises', 9 March 2018.

Bloomberg (2018b) 'Bankers Bonuses: culture of risk', 30 January 2018, http://www.bloombergview.com/quicktake/banker-bonuses, [last accessed 9 July 2018].

BLS (2018) 'Employment, Hours, and Earnings from the Current Employment Statistics survey', United States Bureau of Labor Statistics.

Blyth, M. (2013) *Austerity: The History of a Dangerous Idea*. Oxford.

Blyth, M. (2016) 'Global Trumpism: Why Trump's Victory Was 30 Years in the Making and Why It Won't Stop Here', *Foreign Affairs*, 15 November 2016.

BNA (1991) 'BNA's Banking Report', 56: 18, Bureau of National Affairs, Washington DC.

BoA (2008) Annual Report.

BoA (2010) Annual Report.

BoA (2011) Annual Report.

BoA (2014) 'BoA reaches comprehensive settlement with US Department of Justice and State Attorney's General to Resolve mortgage-related litigations and investigations', Financial Release, 21 August 2014.

BoE (2015) 'Fair and Effective Markets Review: Final Report', June 2015, Bank of England.
Bolton, P. et al. (2010) 'Executive Compensation and Risk Taking', Federal Reserve Bank of New York Staff Report 456.
Bonefeld, W. (1996) 'Monetarism and Crisis', in Werner Bonefeld and John Holloway, eds, *Global Capital, National State and the Politics of Money*. Basingstoke: Macmillan, pp. 35–68.
Bonefeld, W. (2010) 'Free Economy and the Strong State: some notes on the state', *Capital and Class* 34(1): 1524.
Bonefeld, Werner (2014) 'Big society and political state', *British Politics* 20(4): 413–28.
Bonefeld, W. (2015) 'Big Society and political state', *British Politics* 10(4): 413–28.
Bootle, R. (2012) *The Trouble with Markets: Saving Capitalism from Itself*. London: Nicholas Brealey.
Bouwman, C. (2013) 'The Role of Corporate Culture in Mergers and Acquisitions.' In: E. Perrault, ed., *Mergers and Acquisitions: Practices, Performance, and Perspectives*. New York: Nova Science Publishers, Inc.
Boyd, J. and G. De Nicolo (2005) 'The theory of bank risk-taking and competition revisited', *The Journal of Finance* 60(3): 1329–43.
Bradnao, Marques et al. (2013) 'International Evidence on Government Support and Risk Taking in the Banking Sector', FRB International Finance Discussion Paper No. 1086 (no page numbers).
Bregman, R. (2017) 'No, wealth isn't created at the top. It is merely devoured there', *Guardian* 30 March 2017.
Brei, M. and B. Gadanecz (2012) 'Have Public Bailouts Made Banks' Loan Books Safer?' *BIS Quarterly Review* (no page numbers).
Brenner, Robert (2003) *The Boom and the Bubble: The Us in the World Economy*. London: Verso.
Brenner, N. and N. Theodore (2012) *Spaces of Neoliberalism: Urban Restructuring in North America and Western Europe*. London: Blackwell.
Brittan, S. (1977) *The Economic Consequences of Democracy*. London: Temple Smith.
Brittan, S. (1989) 'The "Economic Contradictions of Democracy" Revisited', *Political Quarterly* 60(2): 190–203.
Brosnan, S. and F. de Waal (2003) 'Monkeys reject unequal pay', *Nature* 425: 297–9.
Brown, Gordon (2002) Mansion House speech, http://www.theguardian.com/politics/2002/jun/27/economy.uk
Brown, Gordon (2003) Mansion House, http://www.theguardian.com/politics/2003/jun/19/economy.uk
Brown, Gordon (2006) Mansion House, https://www.theguardian.com/business/2006/jun/22/politics.economicpolicy
Brown, Gordon (2007) Mansion House, http://webarchive.nationalarchives.gov.uk/+/http:/www.hm-treasury.gov.uk/2014.htm
Bruff, I. (2008) *Culture and Consensus in European Varieties of Capitalism*. Basingstoke: Palgrave Macmillan.
Bruff, I. (2014) 'The Rise of Authoritarian Neoliberalism', *Rethinking Marxism* 26(1): 113–29.
Brunnermeier, M. K., et al. (2009) *The Fundamental Principles of Financial Regulation*. Geneva and London: International Centre for Monetary and Banking Studies; Centre for Economic Policy Research.
Buchak, Greg et al. (2018) 'Fintech, Regulatory Arbitrage, and the Rise of Shadow Banks', *Journal of Financial Economics* 130(3): 453–83.
Bureau of Labor Statistics (2018) 'Productivity Data', https://data.bls.gov/timeseries/PRS85006092

Burnham, P. (1994) 'Open Marxism and vulgar international political economy', *Review of International Political Economy* 1(2): 221–31.

Burnham, Peter (2011) 'Towards a political theory of crisis', *New Political Science* 33(4): 493–507.

BusinessInsider (2016a) 'Something startling is going on with antidepressant use around the world', 4 February 2016.

BusinessInsider (2016b) 'Analysts are losing sleep over what's happening at US banks right now', 10 March 2016.

Butt, N. et al. (2014) 'QE and the bank lending channel in the United Kingdom', Working Paper 511.

Cameron, David (2012) 'David Cameron announces banking sector inquiry', 2 July 2012.

Cameron, K. S., et al. (2014) *Competing Values Leadership.* Northampton, MA: Edward Elgar Publishing.

Campbell-Verduyn, Malcolm (2017) 'Capturing the Moment? Crisis, Market Accountability, and the Limits of Legitimation', *New Political Science* 39(3): 350–68.

Canals, J. (1993) *Competitive strategies in European banking*. Oxford: Oxford University Press.

Carlson, M. (2006) *A Brief History of the 1987 Stock Market Crash,* Finance and Economics Discussion Series, Divisions of Research and Statistics and Monetary Affairs, Federal Reserve Board, Washington, DC.

Carney, M. (2017) 'Policy Panel: investment and growth in advanced economies', remarks by Mark Carney given at the 2017 ECB Forum on Central Banking, Sintra.

Cassell, C. et al. (2012) 'Seeking safety: The relation between CEO inside debt holdings and the riskiness of firm investment and financial policies', *Journal of Financial Economics* 103(3): 588–610.

CBO (2015) 'The 2015 Long-Term Budget Outlook Analysis', Congressional Budget Office, 16 June 2015.

CBS (2011) 'Poll: 43 percent agree with views of "Occupy Wall Street", http://www.cbsnews.com/news/poll-43-percent-agree-with-views-of-occupy-wall-street/

CEBS (2010) 'Guidelines on Remuneration Policies and Practices', Committee of European Banking Supervisors, London.

Cecchetti, S.G. and E. Kharkroubi (2012) 'Reassessing the Impact of Finance on Growth', Working Paper no. 381, Bank for International Settlement, Geneva.

Ceresney, A. (2015) Speech by Director, Division of Enforcement, 2015 National Society of Compliance Professionals, National Conference: Keynote Address.

CFPB (2017) 'CFPB Finalizes Rule to Stop Payday Debt Traps', Consumer Financial Protection Bureau ruling, 5 October 2017.

CFTC (2016) 'Fact Sheet: Reproposal of Regulations on Position Limits for Derivatives and Final Regulations on Aggregation of Positions', Commodity Futures Trading Commission Office of Public Affairs, 5 December 2016.

Chakraborty, I. et al. (2017) 'Monetary Stimulus and Bank Lending', 20 December 2017, http://finance.wharton.upenn.edu/~itayg/Files/qebanklending.pdf

Chon, G. (2013) 'Why investment bankers will be depressed next week', *Quartz Magazine,* 1 February 2013.

Citibank (2006–17) Annual Reports, 2006–17.

Citibank (2006–17) Proxy Statements, 2006–17.

CityAM (2014a) 'Forex rate-rigging scandal 2015 probe: Foreign exchange crisis engulfs London', 6 February 2014.

CityAM (2014b) 'Bank of England plans shake-up to tackle forex probe', 12 March 2014.

CityAM (2014c) 'FCA hits RBS, HSBC, UBS, JPMorgan and Citi with record £1.1bn fine in Forex rigging scandal', 12 November 2014.

CityAM (2015) 'FCA boss Martin Wheatley: disappointed to be leaving with "unfinished business"', City AM 22 July 2015.
CityAM (2017) 'Standard Chartered becomes latest firm to be caught up in exec pay row, as shareholders protest targets for Bill Winter's pay are too easy', 26 March 2017.
CityUK (2017) https://www.thecityuk.com/assets/2017/Reports-PDF/Key-facts-about-the-UK-as-an-International-financial-centre-2017.pdf
Citigroup (2008) Annual Report.
Citigroup (2011) Annual Report.
Citigroup (2016) Annual Report.
Citywire (2011) 'How excessive derivatives trading turned investment banks into bookies that contribute little to the economy', 28 February 2011.
Clarke, S. (1988) *Keynesianism, Monetarism and the Crisis of the State*. Palgrave.
Clarke, S (1991) *The State Debate*. Palgrave.
Clarke, S. (1994) *Marx's Theory of Crisis*. Basingstoke: Palgrave.
CMA (2015) 'Retail banking market investigation: updated issues statement', 21 May 2015.
CMA (2016) *Retail banking market investigation: Provisional decision on remedies*. Competition and Markets Authority, London.
CNBC (2017) 'Fed economist: "No evidence that QE works" as central bank starts unwinding program', 19 September 2017.
CNN (2017) 'Big banks rack up $6.4 billion in ATM and overdraft fees', 22 February 2017.
Coates, D. (1995) *The Question of UK Decline*. Brighton: Harvester.
Coffee, J. (2011) cited in: 'Lawsky Juggles Conflicting Roles as Financial Cop in N.Y.', Bloomberg 20 October 2011.
Committee on Government Affairs (2002) 'Financial Oversight of Enron: the SEC and Private-Sector Watchdogs', Report by the Committee on Governmental Affairs United States Senate, 7 October 2002.
Congressional Budget Office (2011) 'Report: Reducing the Deficit', CBO 112th Congress 2011–12.
Congressional Budget Office (2015) 'Report: Updated Budget Projections', 114th Congress 2015–16.
Congressional Oversight Panel (2011) 'Final Report of the Congressional Oversight Panel', 16 March 2011.
Connor, J. M. (2014) 'Big bad banks: bid-rigging and multilateral market manipulation', working paper.
Crane, A. et al., eds (2008) *The Oxford Handbook of Corporate Social Responsibility*. Oxford: Oxford University Press.
Crémer, Jacques (1993) 'Corporate Culture and Shared Knowledge', *Industrial and Corporate Change* 2(3): 351–86.
Crotty, J. (2011) 'The great austerity war: What caused the deficit crisis and who should pay to fix it?' EconStor Working Paper, 2011–17.
Crouch, C. (2011) 'Privatised Keynesianism: An Unacknowledged Policy Regime', *British Journal of Politics and International Relations* 11(3): 382–99.
CSJ (2015) 'Future Finance: a new approach to financial capability', Centre for Social Justice June 2015.
Culbertson, S. et al. (2013) 'Performance appraisal satisfaction: the role of feedback and goal orientation', *Journal of Personnel Psychology* 12(4): 189–95.
Cullen, J. (2016) 'A Culture Beyond Repair? The Nexus Between Ethics and Sanctions in Finance', In: *Just Financial Markets: Finance in a Just Society*. Oxford University Press, ed. Herzog, 2017.

Cuomo, A. (2009) 'No rhyme or reason: The heads I win, tails you lose bonus culture', Andrew M. Cuomo, Attorney General, State of New York, http://workplacebullying.org/multi/pdf/Cuomo.pdf

Cuomo, A. (2014) 'Governor Cuomo Announces Plan to Provide More Than $2 Billion in Tax Relief to New York's Families and Businesses', New York State Governor Cuomo website, available at https://www.governor.ny.gov/news/governor-cuomo-announces-plan-provide-more-2-billion-tax-relief-new-yorks-families-and (last accessed 15 March 2019).

Dahlgren, S. (2014) 'The New Era of Supervision: Progress to Date and the Road Ahead', Remarks at the New York Bankers Association's Annual Meeting, New York City, 5 November 2014.

Davies, H. (2010) The Financial Crisis: Who is to Blame? Polity Press.

Davis, A. and C. Walsh (2016) 'The Role of the State in the Financialisation of the UK Economy', *Political Studies* 64(3): 666–82.

Dayen, D. (2016) 'Why the Goldman Sachs settlement is a sham', *The New Republic*, 13 April, 2016. https://newrepublic.com/article/132628/goldman-sachs-settlement-5-billion-sham

Deaton, A. (2017) 'Where in the world is the world heading?', *Journal of Policy Modeling* 39(4): 603–7.

De Bondt, W. and R. Thaler (1995) 'Financial Decision-Making in Markets and Firms: A Behavioral Perspective', ch.13 in R. Jarrow et al., eds, *Finance: Handbooks in Operations Research and Management Science*, Vol. 9, Elsevier.

Deegan-Krause, K. and T. Haughton (2009) 'Towards a More Useful Conceptualization of Populism: types and degrees of populist appeals in the case of Slovakia', *Policy and Politics* 37(4): 821–41.

De Goede, M. (2004) 'Repoliticizing financial risk', *Economy & Society* 33(2): 197–217.

Delis, M. and G. Kouretas (2011) 'Interest rates and bank risk-taking', *Journal of Banking and Finance* 35: 840–55.

Demirguc-Kunt, A. and E. Detragiache (2011) 'Basel Core Principles and bank soundness: Does compliance matter?' *Journal of Financial Stability* 7(4): 179–90.

Demirguc-Kunt, A., and E. J. Kane (2002) 'Deposit insurance around the world: Where does it work?' *Journal of Economic Perspectives* 16: 175–95.

Denison, D. and A. Mishra (1995) 'Toward a Theory of Organizational Culture and Effectiveness', *Organizational Science* 6(2): 204–23.

Department of Business Innovation and Skills (2010) Access to Finance, 2010.

Department of Justice (2014) 'BNP Paribas Agrees to Plead Guilty and to Pay $8.9 Billion for Illegally Processing Financial Transactions for Countries Subject to U.S. Economic Sanctions', https://www.justice.gov/opa/pr/bnp-paribas-agrees-plead-guilty-and-pay-89-billion-illegally-processing-financial

DeYoung, R., and T. Rice (2004) 'How do banks make money? The fallacies of fee income', *Economic Perspectives: Federal Reserve Bank of Chicago* 28(4): 34.

DeYoung, R. and K. P. Roland (2001) 'Product mix and earnings volatility at commercial banks: evidence from a degree of total leverage model', *Journal of Financial Intermediation* 10: 54–84.

Di Tella, R. and R. MacCulloch (2014) 'Culture, Beliefs and Economic Performance', MOTU working paper No. 14-06.

DFS (2012) 'Consent Order against Standard Chartered Bank,' http://www.dfs.ny.gov/about/ea/ea120921.pdf

DFS (2013) Annual Report, New York State Department of Financial Services, http://www.dfs.ny.gov/reportpub/annual/dfs_annualrpt_2012.pdf

DFS (2014) Enforcement Action: Consent Order to Standard Chartered Bank, New York State Department of Financial Services http://www.dfs.ny.gov/about/ea/ea140819.pdf

Doane, D. (2005) 'The Myth of CSR', Stanford Social Innovation Review, Fall 2005.

DoJ (2013) 'Justice Department, Federal and State Partners Secure Record $13 Billion Global Settlement with JPMorgan for Misleading Investors About Securities Containing Toxic Mortgages', Department of Justice 19 November 2013, https://www.justice.gov/opa/pr/justice-department-federal-and-state-partners-secure-record-13-billion-global-settlement

DoJ (2014) 'Justice Department, Federal and State Partners Secure Record $7 Billion Global Settlement with Citigroup for Misleading Investors About Securities Containing Toxic Mortgages', 14 July 2014, https://www.justice.gov/opa/pr/justice-department-federal-and-state-partners-secure-record-7-billion-global-settlement

DoJ (2015a) 'Five Major Banks Agree to Parent-Level Guilty Pleas', 20 May 2015, https://www.justice.gov/opa/pr/five-major-banks-agree-parent-level-guilty-pleas

DoJ (2015b) 'Attorney General Lynch Delivers Remarks at a Press Conference on Foreign Exchange Spot Market Manipulation', 20 March 2015.

DoJ (2015c) 'Plea Agreement with Barclays Bank Plc', United States District Court, District of Connecticut, https://www.justice.gov/file/440481/download

DoJ (2015d) 'Plea Agreement: United States and Barclays PLC', 20 May 2015.

DoJ (2016a) 'Consumer Relief, Annex to Goldman Sachs settlement with DoJ', https://www.justice.gov/opa/file/839906/download

DoJ (2016b) 'Goldman Sachs Agrees to Pay More than $5 Billion in Connection with Its Sale of Residential Mortgage Backed Securities', 11 April 2016, https://www.justice.gov/opa/pr/goldman-sachs-agrees-pay-more-5-billion-connection-its-sale-residential-mortgage-backed

Dudley, W. C. (2014) 'Enhancing Financial Stability by Improving Culture in the Financial Services Industry', Remarks at the Workshop on Reforming Culture and Behavior in the Financial Services Industry, Federal Reserve Bank of New York, New York City, 20 October 2014.

Dugan, A. (2015) 'Confidence in US banks low but rising', Gallup, 22 June 2015, http://www.gallup.com/poll/183749/confidence-banks-low-rising.aspx?g_source=position2&g_medium=related&g_campaign=tiles

The Economist (2012) 'Blessing or bureaucracy: The firestorm over the appointment of a new regulator is just beginning', 6 January 2012.

The Economist (2014) 'What macroprudential regulation is, and why it matters', 5 August 2014.

Edelman (2015) Edelman Trust Barometer Archive.

Edmans, A. and Q. Liu (2010) 'Inside Debt', *Review of Finance* 15: 75–102.

Eisinger, Jesse (2017) *The Chickenshit Club: Why the Justice Department Fails to Prosecute Executives*. Simon & Schuster.

Eissa, N. and H. Hoynes (2005) 'Behavioral Responses to Taxes: Lessons from the EITC and Labor Supply', NBER Working Paper No. 11729.

Ekpu, V. and A. Paloni (2015) 'Financialisation, Business Lending and Profitability in the UK', https://www.gla.ac.uk/media/media_424705_en.pdf

Emmenegger, Patrick (2015) 'The long arm of justice: U.S. structural power and international banking', *Business and Politics* 17(3): 473–93.

Engelen, E. et al. (2011) *After the Great Complacence: Financial Crisis and the Politics of Reform*. Oxford University Press.

Epstein, R. (2017) *Banking on Markets: The Transformation of Bank–State Ties in Europe and Beyond*. Oxford University Press.

Erturk, I. (2016) 'Financialization, Bank Business Models and the Limits of Post-crisis Bank Regulation', *Journal of Banking Regulation* 17(1).

Erturk, I. et al. (2011) 'City State against national settlement UK economic policy and politics after the financial crisis', CRESC Working Paper Series No. 101.

Eucken, W. (2004) *Grundsätze der Wirtschaftspolitik*, 7th edn, Tübingen: Mohr Siebert.

European Commission (2010) 'Corporate governance in financial institutions and remuneration policies', Green Paper, Section 3.4, 2010.

EU Commission (2015) 'European Financial Stability and Integration Review', Commission Staff Working Document, April 2015, Brussels.

FastCompany (2015) 'Why the Annual Performance Review is Going Extinct', 20 October 2015.

Fatouh, M. (2015) 'The Impact of Quantitative Easing on Bank Lending in the UK', https://www1.essex.ac.uk/economics/documents/paper-fatouh.pdf

Faulkender, M. et al. (2012) 'Cash flows and leverage adjustments', *Journal of Financial Economics* 103(3): 632–46.

FBI (2014) 'Bank Guilty of Violating U.S. Economic Sanctions: Record Penalties Levied Against Global Financial Institution', https://www.fbi.gov/news/stories/bank-guilty-of-violating-us-economic-sanctions

FCA (2013) 'The FCA's Response to the PCBS', October 2013, Financial Conduct Authority: London. https://www.fca.org.uk/publication/corporate/pcbs-response.pdf

FCA (2014) 'FCA confirms price cap rule for payday lenders', https://www.fca.org.uk/news/press-releases/fca-confirms-price-cap-rules-payday-lenders

FCA (2015a) 'FCA Handbook', Financial Conduct Authority: London, https://www.handbook.fca.org.uk/handbook

FCA (2015b) Statement from the Financial Conduct Authority following the announcement by HM Treasury of changes to the Senior Managers' Regime, Financial Conduct Authority: London, https://www.fca.org.uk/news/statements/statement-financial-conduct-authority-following-announcement-hm-treasury-changes

FCA (2015c) FCA Remuneration Code 2015, London.

FCA (2017) 'FCA proposes new rules for credit card firms to help millions of customers get out of persistent debt', 3 April 2017, Financial Conduct Authority: London.

FCA (2018a) 'High Cost Credit review: update', January 2018, Financial Conduct Authority: London.

FCA and PRA (2014) 'Strengthening accountability in banking: a new regulatory framework for individuals', FCA CP14/13/PRA CP14/14, https://www.fca.org.uk/publication/consultation/cp14-13.pdf

FCA and PRA (2015) 'Strengthening accountability and banking: a new regulatory framework for individuals: feedback on FCA CP14/13/PRA CP14/14 and consultation on additional guidance', https://www.fca.org.uk/publication/consultation/cp15-09.pdf

FCIC (2011) 'Final Report of the National Commission on the Causes of the Financial and Economic Crisis in the United States', https://www.gpo.gov/fdsys/pkg/GPO-FCIC/pdf/GPO-FCIC.pdf

FDIC (1987) *Mandate for Change: Restructuring the Banking Industry* 112. Washington: Federal Deposit Insurance Corporation.

FDIC (1989) 'Financial Institutions Reform, Recovery, and Enforcement Act', https://www.fdic.gov/regulations/laws/rules/8000-3100.html

Federal Reserve (2015) 'Statement on Prudent Risk Management for Commercial Real Estate Lending', Federal Reserve Board of Governors, https://www.federalreserve.gov/newsevents/pressreleases/files/bcreg20151218a1.pdf

Federal Reserve (2018) 'Charge-Off and Delinquency Rates on Loans and Leases at Commercial Banks', Federal Reserve Board of Governors, https://www.federalreserve.gov/releases/chargeoff/delallsa.htm
Federal Reserve (2018) 'Household Debt Overview', Board of Governors of the Federal Reserve System.
Feldman, R. and J. Schmidt (1999) 'Noninterest income: A potential for profits, risk reduction and some exaggerated claims', Federal Reserve Bank of Minneapolis, Fedgazette October 1999.
FESSUD (2011) 'Description of Work.' In Grant Agreement no: 266800 for Collaborative Project Under Framework Programme 7 of the European Union, Financialisation Economy Society and Sustainable Development (FESSUD).
FFETF (2016) Financial Fraud Enforcement Task Force website, http://www.stopfraud.gov/members.html
FFIEC (2016) 'Federal Financial Institutions Examination Council: Instructions for Preparation of Consolidated Reports of Condition and Income' (FFIEC 031 and 041), September 2016.
Financial Ombudsman (2017) 'Packaged Bank Accounts', technical notes, Financial Ombudsman Service: London.
Financial Planning Today (2017) 'Deutsche Bank hit with record £163m fine for money laundering failings', 31 January 2017.
Fine, B. and D. Milonakis (2009) *From Economics Imperialism to Freakonomics: the Shifting Boundaries Between Economics and Other Social Sciences.* Routledge.
Finextra (2009) 'UBS to pay $780 million fine over secret bank accounts', 19 February 2009.
Fisher, J. (2015) Risk, recklessness and policing the financial markets. In: Nicholas Ryder, Umut Turksen, and Sabine Hassler eds, *Fighting Financial Crime in the Global Economic Crisis.* London: Routledge.
Fitch Ratings (2013) 'More Banks Facing U.S. Anti-Money Laundering Scrutiny', 5 April 2013, https://www.fitchratings.com/gws/en/fitchwire/fitchwirearticle/More-Banks-Facing?pr_id=787636
Forbes (2009) 'Why Ken Lewis Destroyed Bank Of America', 3 March 2009.
Forbes (2010) 'No Need to Over-Regulate Banker Compensation', 25 August 2010.
Forbes (2013) 'Online Gambling: A Pastime Whose Time Has Come', 30 June 2013.
Forbes (2014) 'Brian Moynihan's Grand Plan for Bank Of America', 28 March 2014.
Forbes (2015a) 'How Federal Reserve Quantitative Easing Expanded Wealth Inequality', 25 June 2015.
Forbes (2015b) 'A Small Barracuda in a Big Pond: New York's Department of Financial Services', 26 February 2015.
Forbes (2016a) 'Goldman Sachs' Historic $5 Billion Settlement Has Silver Lining: Tax Deduction', 19 January 2016.
Forbes (2016b) 'When Penalties are Punitive They are not Tax Deductible', 23 May 2016.
Forbes (2017) 'Liquidity Transfer Pricing is Now a Key Element in Banks' Success', 12 September 2013.
Fortune (2014) 'Bank of America is making money on its financial crisis settlement', 23 May 2014.
Fortune (2016) 'Here's where the $110bn in Wall Street fines went', 10 March 2016.
Foster JB (2007) 'The Financialization of Capitalism', *Monthly Review* 58(11).
FPC (2016) 'Financial Stability Policy Statement', 18 November 2016, Financial Policy Committee: London.

FPC (2017) 'Financial Stability report No. 42', November 2017, Financial Policy Committee: London.
Freeman E. (1984) *Strategic Management: A Stakeholder Approach*. Boston: Pitman.
French, S. et al. (2011) 'Financializing space, spacing financialization', *Progress in Human Geography* 36(6): 798–819.
Friedman, M. (1962) *Capitalism and Freedom*. Chicago: University of Chicago Press.
Frooman, J. (1997) 'Socially Irresponsible and Illegal Behaviour and Shareholder Wealth: a meta-analysis of event studies', *Business and Society* 36(3): 221–49.
Froud, Julie et al. (2002) 'Financialisation and the coupon pool', *Capital & Class* 26(3): 119–51.
Froud, J. et al. (2006) *Financialization and Strategy: Narrative and Numbers*. London: Routledge.
Froud, J et al. (2010) 'Wasting a crisis? Democracy and markets in Britain after 2007', *The Political Quarterly* 81(1): 25–38.
Froud, J. et al. (2011) 'Groundhog Day Elite power, democratic disconnects and the failure of financial reform in the UK', CRESC Working Paper Series No. 108.
FSA (1998) Annual Report 1998, Financial Services Authority: London, http://www.fsa.gov.uk/static/pubs/annual/ar1997_98.pdf
FSA (2000) Annual Report 2000, Financial Services Authority: London, http://www.fsa.gov.uk/static/pubs/annual/ar1999_00.pdf
FSA (2001) Annual Report 2001, Financial Services Authority: London, http://www.fsa.gov.uk/static/pubs/annual/ar00_01.pdf
FSA (2002) Annual Report 2002, Financial Services Authority: London, http://www.fsa.gov.uk/static/pubs/annual/ar01_02.pdf
FSA (2003) Annual Report 2003, Financial Services Authority: London, http://www.fsa.gov.uk/static/pubs/annual/ar02_03/ar02_03.pdf
FSA (2004) Annual Report 2004, Financial Services Authority: London, http://www.fsa.gov.uk/pubs/annual/ar03_04/ar03_04.pdf
FSA (2005) Annual Report 2005, Financial Services Authority: London, http://www.fsa.gov.uk/static/pubs/annual/ar04_05/ar04_05.pdf
FSA (2006) Annual Report 2006, Financial Services Authority: London, http://www.fsa.gov.uk/pubs/annual/ar05_06/ar05_06.pdf
FSA (2007) Annual Report 2007, Financial Services Authority: London, http://www.fsa.gov.uk/static/pubs/annual/ar06_07/ar06_07.pdf
FSA (2008) 'Financial Capability: a behavioural economics perspective', Financial Services Authority: London, https://www.fca.org.uk/publication/research/fsa-crpr69.pdf
FSA (2009a) 'Reforming remuneration practices in financial services, consultation paper (CP09/10)', Financial Services Authority: London, www.fsa.gov.uk/pubs/cp/cp09_10.pdf
FSA (2009b) 'The Turner Review: a regulatory response to the global financial crisis', Financial Services Authority: London, http://www.fsa.gov.uk/pubs/other/turner_review.pdf
FSA (2009c) 'A regulatory response to the global banking crisis, Discussion Paper 09/2', Financial Services Authority: London, http://www.fsa.gov.uk/pubs/discussion/dp09_02.pdf
FSB (2012a) 'Intensity and Effectiveness of SIFI Supervision: Progress Report to the G20 Ministers and Governors', Financial Services Authority: London, http://www.financialstabilityboard.org/publications/r_121031ab.pdf
FSB (2012b) 'Recovery and Resolution Planning', Financial Services Authority: London, http://www.fsb.org/wp-content/uploads/r_121102.pdf?page_moved=1

FSCP (2017a) 'Press Release: Don't rely on consumers to boost competition says Panel', Financial Services Consumer Panel, https://www.fs-cp.org.uk/press-release-dont-rely-consumers-boost-competition-says-panel

FSCP (2017b) 'Position Paper: Consumers and Competition', 11 July 2017, Financial Services Consumer Panel https://fs-cp.org.uk/sites/default/files/fscp_consumers_and_competition_position_paper.pdf

FSF (2009) 'Financial Stability Forum: Principles for Sound Compensation Practices', 2 April 2009.

FT (2008) 'Barclays shares hit by Mideast move', 1 November 2008.

FT (2009a) 'Editorial: the bonus points in Darling's plans', 8 December 2009.

FT (2009b) 'Tax the windfall banking bonuses', 19 November 2009.

FT (2010a) 'Barclays profits almost double to £11.6bn', 16 February 2010.

FT (2010b) 'UK unveils dramatic austerity measures', 20 October 2010.

FT (2011) 'Enron's fall raised the bar in regulation', 1 December 2011.

FT (2012) 'StanChart settles NY claims for $340bn', 15 August 2012.

FT (2013) 'Hunt for yield: Unconventional asset classes widen their appeal', 29 April 2013.

FT (2014a) 'NY regulator probing Barclays and Deutsche over Forex algorithms', 11 December 2014.

FT (2014b) 'Credit Suisse woes go beyond $2.6bn fine', 20 May 2014.

FT (2014c) 'City facing more than "a few bad apples"', 27 October 2014.

FT (2014d) 'George Osborne to toughen rules on market abuse', 11 June 2014.

FT (2015a) Treasury abandons senior bankers' accountability rule, 14 October 2015.

FT (2015b) George Osborne to signal end to 'banker bashing', 2 June 2015.

FT (2015c) 'Bank levy is ripe for reform as lenders cannot be villified forever', 11 May 2015.

FT (2015d) 'Tyrie demands FCA settlements are scrutinized', 3 March 2015.

FT (2015e) 'UK bank lending to business grows for first time since crisis', 24 December 2015.

FT (2016) 'UK facing "dreadful" wage stagnation: 3 charts from the IFS', 24 November 2016.

FT (2017) 'US haul from credit crisis bank fines hits $150bn', 6 August 2017.*

FT (2018) 'Wall Street bonuses rise 17% to pre-crisis levels', 26 March 2018.

FT Alphaville (2011) 'Barclays: Too big for Britain', 29 March 2011.

Gallup (2011) 'Americans confidence in banks falls to record low', 27 June 2012.

Gallup (2015) 'Ratings of U.S. Banking Industry Level Off', 28 August 2015.

Gamble, A. (1988) *The Free Economy and the Strong State*. London: Macmillan.

Gamble, A. (1994) *Britain in Decline: Economic Policy, Political Strategy and the British State*. Palgrave.

Gamble, A. (2009) *The Spectre at the Feast: Capitalist Crisis and the Politics of Recession*. Basingstoke: Palgrave Macmillan.

Garrett, B. (2014) *Too Big to Jail: How Prosecutors Compromise with Corporations*. Harvard University Press.

Garrett, B. (2015a) 'The Corporate Criminal as Scapegoat', *Virginia Law Review* 101(7): 1790–849.

Garrett, B. (2015b) 'Time to crack down on recidivist banks instead of slapping wrists', *The Conversation*, 26 March 2015.

Garrett, B. (2016) 'The Rise of Bank Prosecutions', *Yale Law Review Forum* 126(33).

Germain, Randall (2016) 'Locating authority: Resolution regimes, SIFIs and the enduring significance of financial great powers', *Journal of Banking Regulation* 17(1).

Gill, Stephen (2002) 'Constitutionalizing Inequality and the Clash of Globalizations', *International Studies Review* 4(2): 47–65.

Glavas, A. and L. Godwin (2012) 'Is the Perception of "Goodness" Good Enough? Exploring the Relationship Between Perceived Corporate Social Responsibility and Employee Organizational Identification', *Journal of Business Ethics* 114(1): 15–27.

Goldman Sachs (2006–17) Annual Reports, 2006–17.

Goldman Sachs (2006–17) Proxy Statements, 2006–17.

Gonzalez, F. (2005) 'Bank regulation and risk-taking incentives: an international comparison of bank risk', *Journal of Banking and Finance* 29: 1153–84.

Goodhart, C. and E. Perotti (2015) 'Maturity mismatch stretching: Banking has taken a wrong turn', Centre for Economic Policy Research, Policy Insight No. 81.

Gordon, R. J. (2016) *The Rise and Fall of American Growth: the US Standard of Living Since the Civil War*. Princeton University Press.

Grabel, J. (1997) 'Savings, investment, and functional efficiency: A comparative examination of national financial complexes.' In: I. Grabel, J. Tobin, and J. K. Galbraith (eds), *The Macroeconomics of Saving: Finance and Investment* (pp. 251–97). Ann Arbor, MI: University of Michigan Press.

Graeber, D. (2013) *Debt: The First 5,000 Years*. London: Melville House.

Graham, J. et al. (2015) *Corporate Culture: Evidence from the Field*. New York Federal Reserve, https://www.newyorkfed.org/medialibrary/media/research/conference/2015/econ_culture/Graham_Harvey_Popadak_Rajgopal.pdf

Gregg, P. et al. (2012) 'Executive Pay and Performance: did bankers' bonuses cause the crisis?' *International Review of Finance* 12(1): 89–122.

Griffin, J. and J. Mahon (1997) 'The corporate social performance and corporate financial performance debate: 25 years of incomparable research', *Business and Society* 36: 5–31.

Gropp, R. et al. (2011) 'The Impact of Public Guarantees on Bank Risk-Taking: Evidence from a Natural Experiment', *Review of Finance* 18(2): 457–88.

Group of Thirty (2015) 'Banking Conduct and Culture: A Call for Sustained and Comprehensive Reform', G30 Working Group, Washington DC.

Guiso, L. et al. (2006) 'Does Culture Affect Economic Outcomes?' *Journal of Economic Perspectives* 20(2): 23–48.

Guiso, L. et al. (2015) 'The Value of Corporate Culture', *Journal of Financial Economics* 117: 60–76.

Habermas, J. (1973) *Legitimation Crisis*. Berlin: Surhkamp Verlag.

Hacker, S.J. and P. Pierson (2002) 'Business Power and Social Policy: Employers and the Formation of the American Welfare State', *Politics & Society* 30 (2): 277– 325.

Haldane, A. (2009) 'Small lessons from a big crisis: Remarks at the Federal Reserve Bank of Chicago 45th Annual Conference', Reforming Financial Regulation, 8 May 2009.

Haldane, A. (2010) 'The Contribution of the Financial Sector Miracle or Mirage?' Speech by Andrew Haldane, Executive Director, Financial Stability, of the Bank of England, at the Future of Finance conference, London, 14 July 2010.

Haldane, A. (2012) 'On being the right size', Speech by Andrew G. Haldane, Executive Director, Financial Stability, Bank of England, at the Institute of Economic Affairs' 22 Annual Series, The 2012 Beesley Lectures, at the Institute of Directors, London, 25 October 2012.

Haldane, A. (2013) 'Have we solved "too big to fail?"', CEPR Policy Portal, http://voxeu.org/article/have-we-solved-too-big-fail

Haldane, A. et al. (2016) 'QE: the story so far', Bank of England Working Paper 624.

Halvorsen, S. (2012) 'Beyond the Network? Occupy London and the Global Movement', *Social Movement Studies* 11(3): 427–33.

Hardie, I. and S. Maxfield (2013) 'Market-Based Banking as the Worst of All Worlds: illustrations from the United States and United Kingdom', in Iain Hardie and David Howarth, eds, *Market-Based Banking and the International Financial Crisis*. Oxford University Press, pp. 56–78.

Hardie, I. et al. (2013) 'Banks and the False Dichotomy in the Comparative Political Economy of Finance', *World Politics* 65(4): 691–728.

Harris, J. and P. Bromiley (2007) 'Incentives to Cheat: The Influence of Executive Compensation and Firm Performance on Financial Misrepresentation', *Organization Science* 18(3): 350–67.

Harvey, D. (2005) *A Brief History of Neoliberalism*. Oxford.

Hau, H., et al. (2013) 'Bank Ratings: What Determines Their Quality?' *Economic Policy* 28(74) (April): 289–333.

Hay, C. (2002) *Political Analysis: A Critical Introduction*. Basingstoke: Palgrave.

Hay, C. (2011) 'Pathology Without Crisis? The Strange Demise of the Anglo-Liberal Growth Model', *Government and Opposition* 46(1): 1–31.

Hay, C. (2013) *The Failure of Anglo-Liberal Capitalism*. London: Palgrave Macmillan.

Hayek, F. (1976) *The Road to Serfdom*. London: Routledge.

HC Note (2013) The Independent Commission on Banking: The Vickers Report, Review of Recommendations, House of Commons Library.

Henning, P. J. (2014) 'US finds fresh use for seldom-used statute in subprime cases', *NY Times DealBook*, 11 August 2014.

Hermalin, B. E. (2001) 'Economics and Corporate Culture'. In: C. Cooper, S. Cartwright, and P. C. Early, eds, *The International Handbook of Organization Culture and Climate*. Chichester: John Wiley and Sons, Ltd.

Hillman, A. and G. Keim (2001) 'Shareholder value, stakeholder management, and social issues: what's the bottom line?' *Strategic Management Journal* 22(2): 125–39.

HM Treasury (2007) 'HM Treasury Annual Report and Accounts 2006–07', London.

HM Treasury (2010) 'Department for Business Innovation and Skills, Financing a Private Sector Recovery', July 2010, London.

HM Treasury (2011) 'Bank Executive Remuneration Disclosure: consultation on draft regulations', December 2011, London.

HM Treasury (2012a) 'Review of Treasury response to crisis', July 2012, London.

HM Treasury (2012b) 'Sanctions for the directors of failed banks', July 2012, London.

HM Treasury (2013a) 'Government response to the Parliamentary Commission on Banking Standards', July 2013, London.

HM Treasury (2013b) 'Financial Services Bill, Government Amendments: Groups Restructuring Powers ('Electrification')', Briefing for Peers, October 2013, London.

HM Treasury (2015) 'Senior Managers and Certification Regime: extension to all FSMA authorised persons', October 2015, London.

HM Treasury (2016) 'Chancellor Letter to Treasury Committee', 15 February 2016.

HMT (2011) 'Financial Regulation: a preliminary consideration of the Government's proposals', Seventh Report of Session 2010–11, Treasury Committee.

HMT & BIS (2013) 'Banking reform: a new structure for stability and growth', February 2013, London.

HMT & BIS (2013) The Government's response to the Parliamentary Commission on Banking Standards.

Hoenig, T. (2012) 'Financial Stability Through Properly Aligned Incentives', Thomas M. Hoenig, Director, Federal Deposit Insurance Corporation, Delivered to the Exchequer Club, Washington, DC 19 September 2012.

Holloway, J. (2010) *Crack Capitalism*. Pluto Press.

Hope, D. and D. Soskice (2016) 'Growth models, varieties of capitalism and macroeconomics', *Politics and Society* 44(2): 209–26.

House of Commons (2009) HC Debate. 9 December 2009, http://www.publications.parliament.uk/pa/cm200910/cmhansrd/cm091209/debtext/91209-0007.htm

House of Commons (2010a) Budget 2010, HC61, June 2010, https://www.gov.uk/government/uploads/system/uploads/attachment_data/file/248096/0061.pdf

House of Commons (2010b) Debate, 12 July 2010, http://www.publications.parliament.uk/pa/cm201011/cmhansrd/cm100712/debtext/100712-0003.htm

House of Commons (2015) 'Taxation of banking', Briefing Paper 05251, 4 September 2015.

House of Commons (2017) 'Financial services: contribution to the UK economy', House of Commons Briefing Paper, 31 March 2017.

Houston, J. and C. James (1995) 'CEO compensation and bank risk: is compensation in banking structured to promote risk-taking?' *Journal of Monetary Economics* 36: 405–31.

HSBC (2006–17) Annual Reports, 2006–17.

HSBC (2006–17) Proxy Statements, 2006–17.

Huffington Post (2010) 'White House Taps Warren to Set Up Consumer Financial Protection Bureau', 15 September 2010.

Huffington Post (2011) 'Banks Extract Fees on Unemployment Benefits', 1 November 2011.

Huffington Post (2015) 'Osborne's Present to Senior Bankers', 24 December 2015.

Hycner, R. (1985) 'Some guidelines for the phenomenological analysis of interview data', *Human Studies* 8(3): 279–303.

IEA (2017) 'The Case Against "Rebalancing the Economy"', Institute of Economic Affairs, 14 November 2017.

Institute for Fiscal Studies (IFS) (2007) 'Government and the Financial Sector: Green Budget 2009'. London: Institute for Fiscal Studies.

IFS (2017) 'What's been happening to corporation tax?', Institute for Fiscal Studies, 10 May 2017.

IFS (2018) *Problem Debt and Low-income Households. Institute for Fiscal Studies Report*. London: IFS.

IIA (2013) 'The three lines of defense in effective risk management and control', January 2013, Institute of Internal Auditors.

Illinois Attorney General (2016) 'Attorney General Madigan Settlement Over Mortgage-Backed Securities Recovers Funds for State's Pension Systems', 11 February 2016.

IMF (2008) 'Global Financial Stability Review', October 2008, Washington DC.

IMF (2010) 'A Fair and Substantial Contribution by the Financial Sector', Final Report for the G20, June 2010, Washington DC.

IMF (2014) 'Fiscal Policy and Income Inequality', IMF Policy Paper, 23 January 2014.

IMF (2015) 'United States: financial sector assessment program', IMF Country Report No. 15/170, July 2015.

IMF (2016) 'Monetary Policy and the rise of nonbank finance', chapter 3 of the IMF Global Financial Stability Report 2016.

IMF (2018) 'Can Accommodative Monetary Policies Help Explain the Productivity Slowdown?' Remarks by Maurice Obstfeld, IMF Economic Counsellor and Director of Research, Joint BIS-IMF-OECD Conference on Weak Productivity: The Role of Financial Factors and Policies, co-sponsored by the Global Forum on Productivity, 10 January 2018.

Ingham, G. (1984) *Capitalism Divided? The City and Industry in British Social Development*. London: Macmillan.
International Compliance Association (2017) ICA website, available at https://www.int-comp.org/ (last accessed 15 March 2019).
Interview 20150618 Interview with Senior Official, 18 June 2015, London.
Interview 20160601 Interview with Senior Official, 1 June 2016, London.
Interview (2016) Interview with Senior Official, 19 April 2016, New York.
Interview 20150625 (2015) Interview with John Vickers, 25 June 2015, All Souls College Oxford.
Interview 20150703 (all interviewees will remain anonymous for legal reasons).
Interview 20160415 (all interviewees will remain anonymous for legal reasons).
Interview 20160416 (all interviewees will remain anonymous for legal reasons).
Interview 20160418 (all interviewees will remain anonymous for legal reasons).
Interview 20160421 (all interviewees will remain anonymous for legal reasons).
Interview 20161018 (all interviewees will remain anonymous for legal reasons).
Interview 20161101 (all interviewees will remain anonymous for legal reasons).
Interview 20161107 (all interviewees will remain anonymous for legal reasons).
Interview 20161109 (all interviewees will remain anonymous for legal reasons).
Interview 20161114 (all interviewees will remain anonymous for legal reasons).
Interview 20161121 (all interviewees will remain anonymous for legal reasons).
Interview 20161123 (all interviewees will remain anonymous for legal reasons).
Interview 20161128 (all interviewees will remain anonymous for legal reasons).
Interview 20161130 (all interviewees will remain anonymous for legal reasons).
Interview 20161216 (all interviewees will remain anonymous for legal reasons).
Interview 20170130 (all interviewees will remain anonymous for legal reasons).
Interview 20170213 (all interviewees will remain anonymous for legal reasons).
Interview 20170215 (all interviewees will remain anonymous for legal reasons).
Interview 20170313 (all interviewees will remain anonymous for legal reasons).
Interview 20170411 (all interviewees will remain anonymous for legal reasons).
Interview 20170504 (all interviewees will remain anonymous for legal reasons).
Interview 20170511 (all interviewees will remain anonymous for legal reasons).
Interview 20170627 (all interviewees will remain anonymous for legal reasons).
Interview 20170629 (all interviewees will remain anonymous for legal reasons).
Interview 20170718 (all interviewees will remain anonymous for legal reasons).
Ipsos MORI (2009) 'New study reveals banking crisis has reduced trust in all businesses', IBE and Centrica study, 8 December 2009.
Ipsos MORI (2012) 'Banking Standards: written evidence from Ipsos MORI to UK Parliament', http://www.publications.parliament.uk/pa/jt201314/jtselect/jtpcbs/27/27iv93.htm
Ipsos MORI (2015) 'Veracity Index: Politicians are still less trusted than estate agents, journalists, and bankers', 22 January 2016.
IRS (2013) 'Deduction for Indemnification of Liability', Office of Chief Counsel Internal Revenue Service Memorandum, 7 December 2013.
Jaffer, K. et al. (2014a) 'Why trustworthiness is important'. In: *Capital Failure: Rebuilding Trust in Financial Services*, by Nicholas Morris and David Vines, Oxford: Oxford University Press.
Jaffer, K. et al. (2014b) 'Changing Bank Income Structure: Evidence from Large UK Banks?' *Asian Journal of Finance and Accounting* 6(2).

Jensen, M., and K. J. Murphy (1990) 'Performance Pay and Top Management Incentives', *Journal of Political Economy* 98, 225–64.

Jessop, B. (1993) 'Towards a Schumpeterian Workfare State? Preliminary remarks on post-Fordist political economy', *Studies in Political Economy* 40(1): 7–39.

Jimenez, G. et al. (2014) 'Hazardous Times for Monetary Policy: What Do Twenty-Three Million Bank Loans Say About the Effects of Monetary Policy on Credit Risk-Taking?' *Econometrica* 82(2): 463–505.

Jordà, O., M Schularick, and A. Taylor (2015) 'Betting the house', *Journal of International Economics* 96: S2–S18.

JPMorgan (2006–17) Annual Reports, 2006–17.

JPMorgan (2006–17) Proxy Statements, 2006–17.

Kahneman, D. and A. Tversky (1974) 'Judgment under Uncertainty: Heuristics and Biases', *Science* 185(4157): 1124–31.

Kaplan, S. and J. Rauh (2010) 'Wall Street and Main Street: What Contributes to the Rise in the Highest Incomes?' *Review of Financial Studies* 23 (3): 1004–50.

Karpoff, J. M. (2012) 'Does Reputation work to Discipline Corporate Misconduct?'. In: *The Oxford Handbook of Corporate Reputation*. Oxford: Oxford University Press.

Karpoff, J. M. et al. (2013) Jonathan M. Karpoff, D. Allison Koester, Scott Lee, and Gerald S. Martin, 'Database Challenges in Financial Misconduct Research'. Georgetown McDonough School of Business Research Paper.

Kaufman, G. and L. Mote (1994) 'Is banking a declining industry? A historical perspective', *Economic Perspectives* 18(3): 2–21.

Kay, J. (2009) *Narrow Banking: the Reform of Banking Regulation*. London: Centre for the Study of Financial Innovation.

Kay, John (2012) 'The function of the financial services sector', https://britac.ac.uk/sites/default/files/BAR20-07-Kay.pdf

Kay, J. (2016) *Other Peoples' Money: Masters of the Universe or Servants of the People?* London: Profile Books.

Kenworthy, L. and L. A. Owens (2011) 'How Do Economic Recessions Influence Public Opinion?' In: *The Great Recession*, edited by David Grusky, Bruce Western, and Christopher Wimer. New York: Russell Sage Foundation.

Kindleberger, C. (1967) *Europe's Postwar Growth: the Role of Labor Supply*. Harvard University Press.

Kotz, D. (2008) 'Financialization and Neoliberalism.' Mimeo available at: http://people.umass.edu/dmkotz/KotzPapers.html (appeared in Relations of Global Power: Neoliberal Order and Disorder), ed. G. Teeple and S. McBride. Toronto: University of Toronto Press 2010.

KPMG (2016) 'The Three Lines of Defense: making the transition to a mature risk management model', KPMG.

Kreps, D. M. (1990) 'Corporate Culture and Economic Theory'. In: J. E. Alt and K. A. Shepsle, eds, *Perspectives on Positive Political Economy*. Cambridge: Cambridge University Press.

Kriesi, H. (2012) 'The Populist Challenge', *West European Politics* 37(2): 361–78.

Krippner, G. (2005) 'The financialisation of the American economy', *Socio-Economic Review* 3: 173–208.

Krippner, G. (2011) *Capitalizing on Crisis: The Political Origins of the Rise of Finance*. Cambridge, MA: Harvard University Press.

Kroeber, A. L., and C. Kluckhohn (1952) *Culture: A Critical Review of Concepts and Definitions*. Cambridge, MA: Peabody Museum of American Archaeology.

Kroszner, R. and P. Strahan (1999) 'What Drives Deregulation? Economics and Politics of the Relaxation of Bank Branching Restrictions', *The Quarterly Journal of Economics* 114(4): 1437–67.

Krugman, P. (1994) *The Age of Diminished Expectations: US Economic Policy in the 1990s.* MIT Press.

Kurucz, E. et al. (2008) 'The Business Case for Corporate Social Responsibility' In: *The Oxford Handbook of Corporate Social Responsibility*, by Andrew Crane et al. eds, Oxford University Press.

Labaton Sucharow (2015) *The Street, The Bull, and the Crisis: a Survey of the US and UK Financial Services Industry.* The University of Notre Dame and Labaton Sucharow LLP.

Lagarde, C. (2014) 'Economic Inclusion and Financial Integrity: an Address to the Conference on Inclusive Capitalism', Speech by Christine Lagarde, Managing Director, International Monetary Fund, 27 May 2014.

Langley, Paul (2006) 'Securitising Suburbia: The Transformation of Anglo-American Mortgage Finance', *Competition and Change* 10(3): 283–99.

Langley, P. (2010) *The Everyday Life of Global Finance.* Oxford University Press.

Lapavitsas, C. (2013) 'The financialisation of capitalism: profiting without producing', *City* 17(6) 792–805.

Lapavitsas, C. and I. Levina (2010) 'Financial Profit: profit from production and profit upon alienation', Discussion Papers 24, Research on Money and Finance.

Lasn, K. (2011) 'The origins of Occupy Wall Street explained', Salon, 4 October 2011.

Latham and Watkins (2010) 'A Tale of Two Clawbacks: The Compensation Consequences of Misstated Financials', Client Alert, Number 1070, 10 August 2010.

Lawsky, B. M. (2015) 'Superintendent Lawsky's remarks, entitled "Financial Federalism: The Catalytic Role of State Regulators in a Post-Financial Crisis World"', 25 February 2015, http://www.dfs.ny.gov/about/speeches/sp150225.htm

Levin, I. (2014) 'Remuneration in Banking: Two Lessons from History and Current Policy', Political Economy Research Institute, UMASS Working Paper No. 359.

Levine, Matt (2016) 'Compliance Therapy and Software Rules', https://www.bloomberg.com/view/articles/2016-05-31/compliance-therapy-and-software-rules

Levine, Matt (2017) 'Dog leasing and bank fines', https://www.bloomberg.com/view/articles/2017-03-02/dog-leasing-and-bank-fines

Lexology (2011) 'New York Department of Financial Services to have authority beyond legacy regulators; new legal risks emerge for insurers', http://www.lexology.com/library/detail.aspx?g=7608586b-5a7e-4ddc-ac30-b013c7234b44

Lindh, S. and S. Schich (2012) 'Implicit Guarantees for Bank Debt: Where Do We Stand?' *OECD Journal of Financial Market Trends* 1 (June): 45–63.

Lindley, J. and S. McIntosh (2014) 'Finance Sector Wage Growth and the role of Human Capital', Sheffield Economic Research Paper Series No. 2014002, https://www.sheffield.ac.uk/polopoly_fs/1.342913!/file/serps_2014002.pdf

Lipset, S. and W. Schneider (1983) *The Confidence Gap: Business, Labor, and Government in the Public Mind.* Johns Hopkins University Press.

Lloyds (2006–17) Annual Reports, 2006–17.

Lloyds (2006–17) Proxy Statements, 2006–17.

Lo, A. (2016) 'The Gordon Gekko Effect: the role of culture in the financial services industry', New York Federal Reserve Economic Policy Review, August 2016.

Lombardi, M. et al. (2017) 'The real effects of household debt in the short and long run', BIS Working Papers, no. 607, January.

Longstreth, F. (1979) 'Chapter 5: The City, Industry and the State', in Colin Crouch, *State and Economy in Contemporary Capitalism*. London: Croom Helm, pp. 157–90.

Lord Griffiths (2017) 'Restoring Trust in the Banking System', Lord Griffiths of Fforestfach, International Advisor, Goldman Sachs Mais Lecture at Cass Business School. 24 May 2017.

Luyendijk, J. (2015) *Swimming with Sharks: My Journey into the World of the Bankers*. London: Guardian Faber Publishing.

Macartney, H. (2009) 'Disagreeing to Agree: Financial Crisis Management within the "Logic of No Alternative"', *Political Quarterly* 29(2): 111–20.

Macartney, H. (2010) *Variegated Neoliberalism: Convergent Divergence in EU Varieties of Capitalism*. London: Routledge/RIPE Studies in Global Political Economy.

Macartney, H. (2011) 'Crisis for the State or Crisis of the State?', *The Political Quarterly* 82(2): 193–203.

Macartney, H. (2014) 'From Merlin to Oz: the strange case of failed SME lending targets in the UK', *Review of International Political Economy* 21(4): 820–46.

Macartney, H. (2016) 'Too Big To Separate? EU ring-fencing and the defence of Too Big To Fail banks', co-authored with Iain Hardie, *West European Politics*.

Macartney, H. and P. Calcagno (2019) 'All Bark and no Bite: the Political Economy of Bank Fines in Anglo-America', *Review of International Political Economy* (forthcoming).

Maddaloni, A. and J-L. Peydro (2011) 'Bank Risk-Taking, Securitization, Supervision, and Low Interest Rates: Evidence from the Euro-Area and the US Lending Standards', *Review of Financial Studies* 24(6): 2121–65.

Magdoff, H. and P. Sweezy (1983) 'Production and Finance', *Monthly Review* 35(1): 1–11.

Madigan, L. (2016) 'Attorney General Madigan Settlement Over Mortgage-Backed Securities Recovers Funds for State's Pension Systems', 11 February 2016, Illinois Attorney General.

Mankiw, N. G. and M. P. Taylor (2008) *Economics*, 2nd revised edn, Cengage.

Martens, P. and R. Martens (2015) 'Brooksley Born: still telling the uncomfortable truth about Wall Street', *Wall Street on Parade*, 7 May 2015.

Marx, K. (1990[1867]) *Capital: A Critique of Political Economy (Volume 1)*. London: Penguin.

Maxfield, S. et al. (2017) 'An empirical investigation of the financialization convergence hypothesis', *Review of International Political Economy* 24(6): 1004–29.

Mayer, T. (1975) 'Should large banks be allowed to fail?', *Journal of Financial and Quantitative Analysis* 10(4): 603–10.

McGuire J., A. Sundgren, and T. Schneeweis (1988) 'Corporate social responsibility and firm financial performance', *Academy of Management Journal* 31: 85.

McKinsey (2016) *A Best Practice Model for Bank Compliance, January 2016*. McKinsey & Company.

McKinsey (2017) *The Productivity Puzzle: a Closer Look at the United States*. March. McKinsey Global Institute: Discussion Paper.

Mehran, H. and J. Tracy (2016) 'Enhancing Financial Stability in the Financial Services Industry: The Contribution of Deferred Cash Compensation', *Federal Reserve Bank of New York Economic Policy Review* 22(1).

Merton, R. C. (1977) 'An analytic derivation of the cost of deposit insurance and loan guarantees', *Journal of Banking and Finance* 1: 3–11.

Middlemas, K. (1979) *Politics in Industrial Society*. Deutsch.

Milgram, S. (1963) 'Behavioral Study of Obedience', *The Journal of Abnormal and Social Psychology* 67(4) (October): 371–8.

Miller, G. P. (2015) 'Compliance: past, present, and future', *University of Toledo Law Review* 48: 437–52.

Miller, G. P. (2017) *The Law of Governance, Risk Management, and Compliance.* New York: Wolters Kluwer.
Mirrlees, J. et al. (2010) 'The Mirrlees Review: Conclusions and Recommendations for Reform', *Fiscal Studies* 32(3): 331–59.
Mitchell, R. K. et al. (1997) 'Toward a theory of stakeholder identification and salience: defining the principle of who and what really counts', *Academy of Management Review* 22(4): 853–86.
Moeller, S. B. et al. (2003) 'Do shareholders of acquiring firms gain from acquisitions?' NBER Working Paper No. 9523.
Mondaq (2013) 'United States: FIRREA: The DOJ's Expansive (And Expensive) Tool Of Choice', 9 October 2013.
Montgomerie, J. (2009) 'The Pursuit of (Past) Happiness? Middle-class Indebtedness and American Financialisation', *New Political Economy* 14(1): 1–24.
Moosa, I. (2016) 'The hubris of excessive remuneration in the financial sector: the case for regulation', *Journal of Banking Regulation* 18(4): 287–301.
Moran, M. (1991) *The Politics of the Financial Services Revolution.* Palgrave.
Moran, M. (2009) *Business, Politics, and Society: an Anglo-American Comparison.* Oxford University Press.
Morgan, D. and K. Stiroh (2005) 'Too big to fail after all these years', Federal Reserve Bank of New York Staff Report No. 220.
Morgan, G. (2012) 'Supporting the City: economic patriotism in financial markets', *Journal of European Public Policy* 19(3): 373–87.
Morgan Stanley (2006–17) Annual Reports, 2006–17.
Morgan Stanley (2006–17) Proxy Statements, 2006–17.
Moschella, M. and El Tsingou (2013) 'Regulating finance after the crisis: Unveiling the different dynamics of the regulatory process', *Regulation and Governance* 7(4): 407–16.
Mounck, Y. (2014) 'Pitchfork Politics: the populist threat to liberal democracy', *Foreign Affairs* 93(5): 27–36.
Mudde, C. and C. Kaltwasser (2017) *Populism: a Very Short Introduction.* Oxford: University Press.
Mueller-Armack, A. (1947) [1989] 'The meaning of the social market economy', in A. Peacock and H. Willgerodt, eds, *Germany's Social Market Economy: Origins and Evolution*. Basingstoke: Palgrave.
Müller-Armack, A. (1978) 'The Social Market Economy as an Economic and Social Order', *Review of Social Economy* 36(3): 325–31.
Müller-Armack, A. (1979) 'Thirty Years of Social Market Economy', in J. Thesing, ed., *Economy and Development.* Mainz: Hase und Köhler, pp. 146–60.
Mynsky, H. (1977) 'The Financial Instability Hypothesis: An Interpretation of Keynes and an Alternative to "Standard" Theory', *Challenge* 20(1): 20–7.
NCUA (2016) Incentive-based Compensation Arrangements, https://www.ncua.gov/About/Documents/Agenda%20Items/AG20160421Item2b.pdf
New America Foundation (2015) 'America's Debt Problem: How Private Debt is Holding Back Growth and Hurting the Middle Class', December 2015, http://privatedebtproject.org/cmsb/uploads/america-s-debt-problem-final-website-version.pdf
New York DFS (2015) Department of Financial Services, 'NYDFS Announces Barclays to pay $2.4bn, terminate employees for conspiring to manipulate spot FX trading market', http://www.dfs.ny.gov/about/press/pr1505201.htm
New York Fed (2014a) 'Workshop on Reforming Culture and Behaviour in the Financial Services Industry', 28 October 2014, https://www.newyorkfed.org/medialibrary/media/newsevents/events/banking/2014/Summary-Culture-Workshop.pdf

New York Fed (2014b) 'Reforming Culture and Behavior in the Financial Services Industry', 20 October 2014, List of Attendees, https://www.newyorkfed.org/medialibrary/media/newsevents/events/banking/2014/Participant-List-Culture-Workshop.pdf

New York Fed (2015a) 'Reforming Culture and Behavior in the Financial Services Industry: Workshop on Progress and Challenges', 5 November 2015, List of Attendees, https://www.newyorkfed.org/medialibrary/media/newsevents/events/banking/2015/Participants-in-Attendance

New York Fed (2015b) 'Reforming Culture and Behavior in the Financial Services Industry: Workshop on Progress and Challenges', Workshop Summary, https://www.newyorkfed.org/medialibrary/media/newsevents/events/banking/2015/culture_workshop_summary_2015.pdf

New York Fed (2018) 'Household Debt and Credit Report', Federal Reserve Bank of New York, Center for Microeconomic Data, https://www.newyorkfed.org/microeconomics/hhdc.html

New York Post (2015) 'Banks eye less aggressive superintendent to lead DFS', 22 November 2015.

New Yorker (2013) 'The Justice Department's "War" on Wall Street: still no criminal charges', 8 August 2013.

NMSS (2018) Joint State-Federal National Mortgage Servicing Settlements website, http://www.nationalmortgagesettlement.com/about

NPR (2011) 'New Consumer Protection Agency Faces Opposition', National Public Radio, 21 July 2011, http://www.npr.org/2011/07/21/138550502/new-consumer-protection-agency-faces-opposition

NY Assembly (2011) Public Integrity Reform Act of 2011, New York State Assembly.

NY Post (2015) 'US slaps Germany's Commerzbank with $1.45B money-laundering fine', 12 March 2015.

NY Times (2000) 'The Dot-Com Bubble Bursts', 24 December 2000.

NY Times (2001) 'S.E.C. Opens Investigation into Enron', 1 November 2001.

NY Times (2008) 'On Wall Street, bonuses, not profits, were real', 17 December 2008.

NY Times (2009a) 'Obama plans major shifts in spending', 26 February 2009.

NY Times (2009b) 'Bankers reaped lavish bonuses during bailouts', 30 July 2009.

NY Times (2010a) 'Short List Emerges for Consumer *Guardian*', 16 July 2010.

NY times (2010b) 'Batting Cleanup at Bank of America', 11 December 2010.

NY Times (2011) http://www.nytimes.com/2011/02/02/nyregion/02budget.html?_r=0

NY Times (2012a) 'Standard Chartered Signs Pact with New York Regulator', 21 September 2012.

NY Times (2012b) 'Expanding Reach; Cuomo Creates Second Cop on Financial Beat', 29 January 2012.

NY Times (2012c) 'Holder Defends Efforts to Fight Financial Fraud', 23 September 2012.

NY Times (2012d) 'Richard Cordray named consumer chief in recess appointment', 4 January 2012.

NY Times (2012e) 'Jamie Dimon shows some love for Volcker rule', 21 May 2012.

NY Times (2013) 'British Commission Calls for New Laws to Prosecute Bankers for Fraud', 18 June 2013.

NY Times (2016a) 'Goldman Sachs to pay up to $5billion to settle claims in faulty mortgages deal', 14 January 2016.

NY Times (2016b) 'In Settlement's Fine Print, Goldman May Save $1 Billion', 11 April 2016.

NY Times (2017) 'Household debt makes a comeback in the US', 17 May 2017.

NYC Mayor's Office (2018) 'NYC Opportunity 2018: Poverty Report', Mayor's Office for Economic Opportunity: the City of New York.

O'Connor, J. (1973) *The Fiscal Crisis of the State*. London: Transaction Publishers.

O'Hara, M. and W. Shaw (1990) 'Deposit insurance and wealth effects: the value of being "too big to fail"', *Journal of Finance* 45(5): 1587–600.

Obama, Barack (2010) 'Wall Street Reform: The Dodd–Frank Act', https://obamawhitehouse.archives.gov/economy/middle-class/dodd-frank-wall-street-reform (last accessed 15 March 2019).

Obama, Barack (2011) State of the Union address, https://www.whitehouse.gov/the-press-office/2011/01/25/remarks-president-state-union-address

Obama, Barack (2012) State of the Union address, https://www.whitehouse.gov/the-press-office/2012/01/24/remarks-president-state-union-address

OBR (2017) 'Forecast Evaluation Report', October 2017, http://obr.uk/docs/dlm_uploads/FER-October-2017-speaking-notes.pdf

OCC (2016) 'Survey of Credit Underwriting Practices', Office of the Comptroller of the Currency, Washington DC.

OECD (2011) 'G20 High Level Principles on Financial Consumer Protection', http://www.oecd.org/daf/fin/financial-markets/48892010.pdf

OECD (2015a) 'In it together…why less inequality benefits all', https://www.oecd.org/unitedkingdom/OECD2015-In-It-Together-Highlights-UnitedKingdom.pdf

OECD (2015b) 'Income inequality data update and policies impacting income distribution', http://www.oecd.org/unitedkingdom/OECD-Income-Inequality-UK.pdf

Offe, C. (1974) 'Structural problems of the capitalist state: class rule and the political system: On the selectiveness of political institutions', *German Political Studies*, 1: 31–54.

OIG (2014) 'The Board Should Enhance its Supervisory Processes as a Result of Lessons Learned From the Federal Reserve's Supervision of JPMorgan Chase & Company's Chief Investment Office', Office of Inspector General, https://oig.federalreserve.gov/reports/board-supervisory-processes-jpmorgan-chase-oct2014.pdf

ONS (2015) *Average weekly earnings: Bonus payments in Great Britain, 2014–15*, Office of National Statistics: London.

ONS (2018) 'Unemployment rate: Labour market statistics time series dataset', https://www.ons.gov.uk/employmentandlabourmarket/peoplenotinwork/unemployment/timeseries/mgsx/lms

Osborne, George (2010) Speech by the Chancellor of the Exchequer at the Lord Mayor's dinner for bankers and merchants of the City of London, Mansion House.

Osborne, G. (2012) Statement by the Chancellor, 2 July 2012, https://www.gov.uk/government/speeches/statement-by-the-chancellor-of-the-exchequer-rt-hon-george-osborne-mp-on-libor

Osborne, G. (2013) Budget Speech 2013, available at: https://www.gov.uk/government/speeches/budget-2013-chancellors-statement

Osborne, G. (2014) Budget Speech 2014, https://www.gov.uk/government/speeches/chancellor-george-osbornes-budget-2014-speech

Osborne, G. (2015) Budget Speech 2015, https://www.gov.uk/government/speeches/chancellor-george-osbornes-budget-2015-speech

Owens, L. A. (2012) 'The Polls—Trends: Confidence in Banks, Financial Institutions, and Wall Street 1971–2011', *Public Opinion Quarterly* 76(1): 142–62.

Palley, T. (2008) 'Financialization: what it is and why it matters', IMK Working Paper, No. 04/2008, Institut für Makroökonomie und Konjunkturforschung (IMK), Hans-Böckler-Stiftung, Düsseldorf, http://nbn-resolving.de/urn:nbn:de:101:1-20080818136

Pava M. and J. Krausz (1996) 'The association between corporate social responsibility and financial performance: the paradox of social cost', *Journal of Business Ethics* 15: 321–57.

PBS (2015) 'How $80 Billion in Corporate Fines Can Become $48 Billion in Tax Breaks', 4 December 2015.

PCBS (2012) 'Parliamentary Commission on Banking Standards', first Report, http://www.publications.parliament.uk/pa/jt201213/jtselect/jtpcbs/98/98.pdf

PCBS (2013a) 'Banking reform: towards the right structure', second report, http://www.publications.parliament.uk/pa/jt201213/jtselect/jtpcbs/126/126.pdf

PCBS (2013b) 'Changing Banking for Good', Parliamentary Commission on Banking Standards, HL Paper 27-I HC 175-I.

PERC (2015) 'Financial Melancholia: Mental Health and Indebtedness', Political Economy Research Centre, London, http://www.perc.org.uk/project_posts/financial-melancholia-mental-health-and-indebtedness/

PERC (2016) 'Financial Melancholia: Mental Health and Indebtedness', Report by Political Economy Research Centre, July 2015.

Persaud, A. D. (2015) *Reinventing Financial Regulation: A Blueprint for Overcoming Systemic Risks*. Apress.

Pew (2016) 'Consumers Need Protection From Excessive Overdraft Costs: An evidence-based case for regulation to limit the number and amount of fees', Pew Charitable Trusts, http://www.pewtrusts.org/en/research-and-analysis/issue-briefs/2016/12/consumers-need-protection-from-excessive-overdraft-costs

Philippon, T. (2008) 'The Evolution of the US Financial Industry from 1860 to 2007: Theory and Evidence', http://pages.stern.nyu.edu/~tphilipp/papers/finsize_old.pdf

Philippon, T. and A. Reshef (2012) 'Wages and Human Capital in the US Financial Industry: 1909–2006', *Quarterly Journal of Economics*.127(4):.1551–609.

Piketty, T. and E. Saez (2003) 'Income Inequality in the United States, 1913–1998', *Quarterly Journal of Economics* 118(1): 1–41.

Pollin, R. (1996) 'Borrowing more but investing less: economic stagnation and the rise of corporate takeovers in the US', MS, Dept. of Economics, University of California-Riverside.

Postone, M. (2016) 'An interview with Moishe Postone: That Capital has limits does not mean that it will collapse', *Crisis and Critique Magazine*.

PRA (2015) 'Supervisory Statement SS28/15: strengthening individual accountability in banking', July 2015, Prudential Regulatory Authority, London.

Project Merlin (2011) 'Project Merlin: banks' statement', 9 February 2011, http://webarchive.nationalarchives.gov.uk/20130129110402/http://www.hm-treasury.gov.uk/d/bank_agreement_090211.pdf

Promontory (2016) Promontory Financial Group website, available at http://www.promontory.com/default.aspx

PWC (2009) 'Bringing back best practices in risk management: banks' three lines of defense', PWC, https://www.strategyand.pwc.com/media/file/Bringing-back-best-practices-banks-three-lines-of-defense.pdf

PWC (2017) 'Bank regulatory compliance services', PWC, https://www.pwc.com/us/en/financial-services/regulatory-services/bank-regulatory-compliance.html

Quinn, R. E. (1988) *Beyond Rational Management: Mastering the Paradoxes and Competing Demands of High Performance*. San Francisco: Jossey-Bass, Inc.

Quinn, R. E. and K. Cameron (1983) 'Organizational Life Cycles and Shifting Criteria for Effectiveness', *Management Science* 29(1) (January): 33–51.

Radice, Hugo (2011) 'Cutting government deficits: Economic science or class war?' *Capital and Class* 35(1): 125–37.

Rajan, R. G. (2005) 'Has Financial Development Made the World Riskier?', Technical report, National Bureau of Economic Research, 2005.
Rakoff, Judge J. (2014) 'The Financial Crisis: Why have no high-level executives been prosecutes', NY Review of Books.
Rakoff, Judge J. (2015) 'Justice Deferred is Justice Denied', The New York Review of Books, 19 February, http://www.nybooks.com/articles/2015/02/19/justice-deferred-justice-denied/
Reinhart, C. and K. Rogoff (2008) 'Is the 2007 US subprime financial crisis so different? An international historical comparison', *American Economic Review* 98(2): 339–44.
Resnick, P. et al. (2006) 'The value of reputation on eBay: A controlled experiment', *Experimental Economics* 9(2): 79–101.
Resolution Foundation (2014) 'To avoid squeezed households struggling, we must beware of premature interest rate rises', Resolution Foundation, 6 August 2014.
Resolution Foundation (2018) 'An unhealthy interest? Debt distress and the consequences of raising rates', Resolution Foundation, 12 February 2018.
Reuters (2008) 'US fines Nigeria's United Bank for Africa $15 mln', 28 April 2008.
Reuters (2010) 'Banker bonuses, salaries surge: survey', 12 February 2010.
Reuters (2012) 'U.S. tests rare legal path in financial crisis cases', 12 April 2012.
Reuters (2015a) 'Traders questioned as NY probe of automated FX heats up', 5 October 2015.
Reuters (2015b) 'Britain scraps "guilty until proven innocent" rule for bankers', 15 October 2015.
Reuters (2016) 'Bank culture just one side of a strategic trilemma', 7 January 2016.
Reuters (2017) 'Americans' debt level notches a new record high', 15 August 2017.
Rodrik, D. (1995) 'Political economy of trade policy', in G. Grossman and K. Rogoff, eds, *Handbook of International Economics*. Elsevier, pp. 1457–94.
Röpke, W. (1957) *Welfare, Freedom and Inflation*. London: Pall Mall Press.
Röpke, W. (1998) *A Human Economy*, 3rd edn, Wilmington: ISI Books.
Röpke, W. (2017) *The Moral Foundations of Civil Society*. London: Routledge.
Ross, S., R.Westerfield, and J. Jaffe (1996) *Corporate Finance*, 4th edn, Homewood, IL: Irwin.
Royal Bank of Scotland (2006–17) Annual Reports, 2006–17.
Royal Bank of Scotland (2006–17) Proxy Statements, 2006–17.
Rüstow, A. (1932/1963) 'Die StaatspolitischenVorraussetzngen des wirtschaftspolitischen Liberalismus', in A. Rüstow, ed., *Rede und Antwort*. Ludwigsburg: Hoch.
Rüstow, A. (1942) 'General Social Laws of the Economic Disintegration and Possibilities of Reconstruction', Afterword to W. Röpke, in *International Economic Disintegration*. London: W. Hodge.
Ryner, M. (2010) 'An Obituary for the Third Way: The Financial Crisis and Social Democracy in Europe', *The Political Quarterly* 81(4): 554–63.
Samuelson, P. (1992) 'My Life Philosophy: Policy Credos and Working Ways', in Michael Szenberg, ed., *Eminent Economists: Their Life Philosophies*. New York: Cambridge UP, pp. 236–47.
S&P (2016) 'S&P Global Market Intelligence', cited in https://www.wsj.com/articles/bank-overdraft-fee-revenue-bounces-back-1489656603
Salz Review (2013) 'Salz Review: an independent review of Barclays' business practices', http://www.euromoney.com/downloads/2013/Barclays-Salz-review.pdf.
Salz Review (2013) 'Salz Review: An independent review of Barclays' business practices'. London: Barclays.
Schein, E. H. (2004) *Organizational Culture and Leadership*. San Francisco: Jossey-Bass.

Schnittker, C. (2016) 'Falling off a cliff: what happened to UK corporate debt? A transatlantic comparison', Bank Underground, 22 January 2016, Bank of England blog, London.

Schularick, M. and A. Taylor (2009) 'Credit Booms Gone Bust: Monetary Policy, Leverage Cycles and Financial Crises, 1870–2008', CEPR Discussion Paper No. 7570.

Scully, R. E. (2011) 'Executive Compensation, the Business Judgment Rule, and the Dodd–Frank Act: Back to the Future for Private Litigation?' SEC The Federal Lawyer, https://www.sec.gov/comments/df-title-ix/executive-compensation/executivecompensation-58.pdf

SEC (2001) 'Cautionary advice regarding the use of "proforma" financial information in earnings releases', United States Securities and Exchange Commission Release Nos. 33-8039, 34-45124, FR-59, 4 December 2001.

SEC (2010) 'Corporate Governance Issues, Including Executive Compensation Disclosure and Related SRO Rules', United States Securities and Exchange Commission, https://www.sec.gov/spotlight/dodd-frank/corporategovernance.shtml

SEC (2011) 'The Role of Compliance and Ethics in Risk Management', speech by Carlo V. di Florio, Director, Office of Compliance Inspections and Examinations, NSCP Meeting 17 October 2011. https://www.sec.gov/news/speech/2011/spch101711cvd.htm

SEC (2012) 'SEC Charges J.P. Morgan and Credit Suisse with Misleading Investors in RMBS Offerings', 16 November 2012, https://www.sec.gov/news/press-release/2012-2012-233htm

SEC (2016a) 'Agencies Invite Comment on Proposed Rule to Prohibit Incentive-Based Pay that Encourages Inappropriate Risk-Taking in Financial Institutions', Joint Release by FDIC, FHFA, Federal Reserve, NCUA, OCC, and SEC, 16 May 2016, https://www.sec.gov/news/pressrelease/2016-89.html

SEC (2016b) 'Incentive-based compensation arrangements', Notice of Proposed Rulemaking and Request for Comment, Joint Proposed Rule by the OCC, Federal Reserve, FDIC, FHFA, NCUA, and SEC, https://www.sec.gov/rules/proposed/2016/34-77776.pdf

Shambaugh, J. et al. (2017) 'Thirteen Facts about Wage Growth', Economic Facts September 2017, The Hamilton Project, https://www.brookings.edu/wp-content/uploads/2017/09/thp_20170926_thirteen_facts_wage_growth.pdf

Shapiro, D. (1984) 'Should a guilty plea have preclusive effect?' *Iowa Law Review* (70): 27–8.

Shields, S. (2012) *The International Political Economy of Transition: Transnational Social Forces and Eastern Central Europe's Transformation*. London: Routledge.

Shields, S. (2014) *The International Political Economy of Transition*. Routledge.

Siegert, C. and M. Willison (2015) 'Estimating the extent of the "too big to fail" problem: a review of existing approaches', Bank of England, Financial Stability Paper No. 32, http://www.bankofengland.co.uk/financialstability/Documents/fpc/fspapers/fs_paper32.pdf

Smith, A. (1976[1776]) *The Wealth of Nations*. Oxford: Oxford University Press.

Smith, R., C. Staikouras, and G. Wood (2003) 'Non-interest income and total income stability', Working Paper No. 198, Bank of England.

Smithers, A. and S. Wright (2000) *Valuing Wall Street: Protecting Wealth in Turbulent Markets*. New York: McGraw Hill.

Sprague, S. (2017) 'Below Trend: The U.S. Productivity Slowdown since the Great Recession', Bureau of Labor Statistics, US Department of Labor, Washington, DC.

Squam Lake Group (2013) 'Aligning incentives at systemically important financial institutions: a proposal by the Squam Lake Group', *Journal of Applied Corporate Finance* 25(4): 37–40.

Stanley, L. (2014) '"We're Reaping What We Sowed"': Everyday Crisis Narratives and Acquiescence to the Age of Austerity', *New Political Economy* 19(6): 895–917.

St Louis Fed (2011) 'Economic Snapshot: Prepaid Market is Small But Growing Rapidly', second quarter 2011, Federal Reserve Bank of St Louis, https://www.stlouisfed.org/publications/inside-the-vault/fall-2011/prepaid-market-is-small-but-growing-rapidly

St Louis Fed (2018) 'Household Debt Service Payments as a Percent of Disposable Personal Income', Federal Reserve Bank of St Louis, https://fred.stlouisfed.org/series/TDSP

Stern, G. H. and R. J. Feldman (2004) *Too Big To Fail: the Hazards of Bank Bailouts*. Washington: Brooking Institute Press.

Stern, R. L. and M. Schifrin, (1987) 'Crime wave', Forbes, June 29.

Stigler, G. (1969) 'Does economics have a useful past?', *History of Political Economy* 1(2): 217–30.

Stiglitz, J. (2015) 'Inequality and economic growth', Political Quarterly 86(S1): 134–55.

Stiglitz, J. (2016) 'Inequality and Economic Growth', *Political Quarterly* 86(S1): 134–55.

Stiroh, K. J. (2004) 'Diversification in Banking: Is Noninterest Income the Answer?,' *Journal of Money, Credit and Banking* 36(5): 853–82, October, Blackwell Publishing.

Stiroh, K. J. and A. Rumble (2006) 'The dark side of diversification: The case of US financial holding companies', *Journal of Banking and Finance* 30: 2131–61.

Stockhammer, E. (2004) 'Financialisation and the slowdown of accumulation', *Cambridge Journal of Economics* 28(5): 719–41.

Stockhammer, E. (2005) 'Shareholder value orientation and the investment-profit puzzle', *Journal of Post Keynesian Economics* 28(2): 193–215.

Strange, S. (1998) *Casino Capitalism*. Manchester: Manchester University Press.

Streeck, W. (2014) *Buying Time: the Delayed Crisis of Democratic Capitalism*. London: Verso.

Sweezy, P. (1994) 'The Triumph of Financial Capital', *Monthly Review*, June 1994.

Tax Journal (2012) 'Sector focus: the UK banking sector', 9 November 2012.

ten Have, S., et al. (2003) *Key Management Models: The Management Tools and Practices that Will Improve Your Business*. London: FT Prentice-Hall.

Tenreyro, S. (2018) 'The fall in productivity growth: causes and implications', speech by Silvana Tenreyro, given at Peston Lecture Theatre, Queen Mary University of London, 15 January 2018.

Thain, Colin (1984) 'The Treasury and Britain's Decline', *Political Studies* 32(4): 581–95.

Thakor, Anjan (2016) 'Corporate Culture in Banking', Economic Policy Review, August 2016, New York Federal Reserve.

Thanassoulis, John (2011) 'The Case for Intervening in Bankers' Pay', University of Oxford Department of Economics Discussion Paper Series No. 532.

The *Guardian* (2008a) 'Voters blame bankers: and everyone else', 21 October 2008.

The *Guardian* (2008b) 'Alliance & Leicester fined £7m for PPI sales', 7 October 2008.

The *Guardian* (2008c) 'Wall Street banks in $70bn staff payout', 17 October 2008.

The *Guardian* (2009) 'The case for a windfall tax on bank bonuses is unanswerable', 7 December 2009.

The *Guardian* (2010a) 'New poll reveals depth of outrage at bankers' bonuses', 21 February 2010.

The *Guardian* (2010b) 'JP Morgan fined £33m by Financial Services Authority', 3 June 2010.

The *Guardian* (2011) 'Vince Cable: I sympathise with Occupy London protesters', 13 November 2011.

The *Guardian* (2012) 'US regulators have Britain's "wild west" bank culture in their sights', 7 August 2012.

The *Guardian* (2013a) 'Ex-compliance officer: "I had to tell the trader what to do—I had two minutes"' 28 January 2013.

The *Guardian* (2013b) 'The biggest problem in banking is measuring performance', 25 September 2013.
The *Guardian* (2013c) 'Equity sales director: "Something happens to your brain after a big bonus"', 8 May 2013.
The *Guardian* (2013d) 'Bankers face jail term for "reckless misconduct"', 1 October 2013.
The *Guardian* (2013e) 'Literacy and numeracy: which country tops the league?' 8 October 2013.
The *Guardian* (2013f) 'RBS fined £390m / $612m for rigging LIBOR interest rate: as it happened', 6 February 2013.
The *Guardian* (2013g) 'Finance industry wages rise faster than any other sector', 26 February 2013.
The *Guardian* (2014) 'Barclays condemned over £2.4bn bonuses', 11 February 2014.
The *Guardian* (2015a) 'Is the government still behind the banking ringfence?' 20 July 2015.
The *Guardian* (2015b) 'UK banks receive first report cards from Banking Standards Board', 29 December 2015.
The *Guardian* (2015c) 'FCA's £819m in fines revenue gives Osborne room to fund worthy causes', 5 July 2015.
The *Guardian* (2015d) 'OECD: large banking sectors widen inequality and slow growth', 18 June.
The *Guardian* (2015e) 'FCA's £819m in fines revenue gives Osborne room to fund worthy causes', 5 July 2015.
The *Guardian* (2016a) 'World's 20 biggest banks rack up £252bn "conduct costs" in five years', 18 July 2016.
The *Guardian* (2016b) 'Debt-fuelled growth could trigger financial crash, governments told', 26 June 2016.
The *Guardian* (2016c) 'Wells Fargo executives forfeit millions and CEO to forgo salary amid inquiry', 28 September 2016.
The *Guardian* (2017a) 'Britain's growing debt problem demands a fresh set of eyes', 24 September 2017.
The *Guardian* (2017b) 'Bill sets out plan to tackle "extortionate" UK overdraft fees', 23 April 2017.
The *Guardian* (2017c) 'John McDonnell warns over "alarming increase" in UK household debt', 27 December 2017.
The *Guardian* (2018a) 'Complaints about high-cost credit climb to record level', 29 May 2018.
The *Guardian* (2018b) 'Doorstep lending crackdown to save vulnerable from debt', 27 May 2018.
The *Independent* (2009) 'Backlash over bankers' bonuses', 8 February 2009.
The *Independent* (2011) 'St Paul's protest is not the Big Society', 8 November 2011.
The *Independent* (2015) 'Levels of UK household debt at record high, says think tank', 4 June 2015.
The *Independent* (2017) 'UK wage growth lags inflation as savers feel pinch of post-Brexit pound sterling slump', 18 October 2017.
The Nation (2017) 'Special Investigation: How America's Biggest Bank Paid Its Fine for the 2008 Mortgage Crisis—With Phony Mortgages', The Nation, 5 October 2017.
The New Yorker (2015) 'The Push Against Performance Reviews', 24 July 2015.
The *Telegraph* (2008) 'Barclays' shareholders angry at generous terms of £7bn Middle Eastern fund raising', 31 October 2008.

The *Telegraph* (2009a) 'Vince Cable, Shadow Business Secretary, cited in "Banks 'Hoarding Credit' as Lending Falls a Record £8.4bn"', 2 September.

The *Telegraph* (2009b) 'Bailing out Britain's banks: RBS, Barclays, Lloyds, HSBC react', 19 January 2009.

The *Telegraph* (2009c) 'Barclays chief executive John Varley says sorry for banks crisis', 9 February 2009.

The *Telegraph* (2009d) 'Bonus culture to blame for banking crisis, say MPs', 15 May 2009.

The *Telegraph* (2010) 'Coalition Government could "water down" City pay code', 22 December 2010.

The *Telegraph* (2011) 'Is Cameron able to rescue the Big Society?', 7 February 2011.

The *Telegraph* (2012) 'Simplify bank regulation, Haldane says', 31 August 2012.

The *Telegraph* (2015) 'The "age of irresponsibility is over" says Bank of England head as he promises crackdown on rogue traders', 10 June 2015.

The *Telegraph* (2016) 'Mark Carney warns Britain is suffering first lost decade since 1860 as people across Europe lose trust in globalization', 5 December 2016.

The *Telegraph* (2017a) 'Bank of England warns more defences may be needed against consumer credit', 24 July 2017.

The *Telegraph* (2017b) 'Atlantic divide as European bank bonuses lose pace with US rivals', 1 July 2017.

The *Telegraph* (2017c) 'Unwinding QE could trigger financial crisis, warns JP Morgan', 4 October 2017.

The Times (2009) 'I'm doing "God's work": Meet Mr Goldman Sachs', 8 November 2009.

ThinkProgress (2011) 'Former JPMorgan Banker: Exploiting Consumers is "The Purpose of the Banking Organization"', available at https://thinkprogress.org/former-jpmorgan-banker-exploiting-consumers-is-the-purpose-of-the-banking-organization-7e06447d9cf5/ (last accessed 18 March 2019).

ThisIsMoney (2018) 'Ditch big banks to boost your rate: Savers can raise returns by up to £145 a year on each £10,000 by switching', 27 November 2018.

Thomas, C.W. (2002) 'The Rise and Fall of Enron', Journal of Accountancy, 1 April 2002.

Time Magazine (2011) Time Poll, 9 October 2011, http://swampland.time.com/full-results-of-oct-9-10-2011-time-poll/

Tobin, J. (1984) 'On the Efficiency of the Financial System', *Lloyd's Bank Review* 153 (1984): 14–15.

Tower Hamlets (2018) 'Healthy Life Expectancy in Tower Hamlets: Annual Public Health Report of the Director of Public Health', available at: https://www.towerhamlets.gov.uk/Documents/Public-Health/Tower_Hamlets_Public_Health_Report_2018.pdf (last accessed18 March 2019).

Treasury Committee (2016a) 'Tax deductibility of fines imposed by regulators on banks', Treasury Committee Letter to Chancellor, 5 February 2016.

Treasury Committee (2016b) 'Tax deductibility of fines imposed by regulators on banks', Treasury Committee Letter to Chancellor, 6 April 2016.

TSC (2008a) Uncorrected transcript of oral evidence: Rt. Hon. Alistair Darling, MP, Mervyn King, and Lord Turner of Ecchinswell, 3 November 2008, http://www.publications.parliament.uk/pa/cm200708/cmselect/cmtreasy/uc1167-i/uc116702.htm

TSC (2008b) 'Uncorrected Evidence', Bradford and Bingley, 18 November 2008.

TSC (2009a) 'Banking Crisis: regulation and supervision: responses from the Government and Financial Services Authority to the Committee's Fourteenth Report of 2008–09', Treasury Select Committee, http://www.publications.parliament.uk/pa/cm200910/cmselect/cmtreasy/47/47.pdf

TSC (2009b) 'Too important to fail: too important to ignore', Ninth Report 2009–10, http://www.publications.parliament.uk/pa/cm200910/cmselect/cmtreasy/261/261i.pdf

TSC (2009c) 'Pre-budget report 2009', Treasury Select Committee, http://www.publications.parliament.uk/pa/cm200910/cmselect/cmtreasy/180/9121602.htm

TSC (2009d) 'Banking Crisis: reforming corporate governance and pay in the City', Ninth Report of Session 2008–9, http://www.publications.parliament.uk/pa/cm200809/cmselect/cmtreasy/519/519.pdf

TSC (2010a) Royal Bank of Scotland, Northern Rock, Lloyds Banking Group, http://www.publications.parliament.uk/pa/cm200910/cmselect/cmtreasy/259/10011202.htm

TSC (2010b) June 2010 Budget, http://www.publications.parliament.uk/pa/cm201011/cmselect/cmtreasy/350/35007.htm#note135

TSC (2012) 'Fixing LIBOR: some preliminary findings', http://www.publications.parliament.uk/pa/cm201213/cmselect/cmtreasy/481/481.pdf

Tung, F. (2011) 'Pay for Banker Performance: structuring executive compensation for risk regulation', *Northwestern University Law Review* 105(3): 1206–51.

Turner Review (2009) 'The Turner Review: a regulatory response to the global banking crisis', March 2009, http://www.fsa.gov.uk/pubs/other/turner_review.pdf

UK Parliament (2017) 'Household debt: statistics and impact on economy', House of Commons Briefing Paper No. 7584, 10 May 2018.

Uppal, R. K. (2011) 'Fee-based activities in Indian banks', *International Journal of Research in IT & Management* 1(1).

US Census (2017) 'Income and Poverty in the United States: 2017, current population reports', https://www.census.gov/content/dam/Census/library/publications/2018/demo/p60-263.pdf

US Congress (2015) Truth in Settlements Act of 2015, https://www.congress.gov/bill/114th-congress/senate-bill/1109

US Department of Justice (2009) 'Credit Suisse Agrees to Forfeit $536 Million in Connection with Violations of the International Emergency Economic Powers Act and New York State Law', Justice News, Department of Justice, https://www.justice.gov/opa/pr/credit-suisse-agrees-forfeit-536-million-connection-violations-international-emergency

US Department of Justice (2014) 'Bank of America to Pay $16.65 Billion in Historic Justice Department Settlement for Financial Fraud Leading up to and During the Financial Crisis', Justice News, Department of Justice, http://www.justice.gov/opa/pr/bank-america-pay-1665-billion-historic-justice-department-settlement-financial-fraud-leading

US Department of the Treasury (2015) 'TARP's Bank Programs: a success story', 10 July 2014, https://www.treasury.gov/connect/blog/Pages/TARP-Bank-Programs-A-Success-Story.aspx

US Senate (2013) 'JPMorgan Chase Whale Trades: A Case History of Derivatives Risks and Abuses', US Senate Committee on Homeland Security and Governmental Affairs, Permanent Subcommittee on Investigations, 15 March 2013.

USDC (2015) 'Criminal charges against Anthony Allen, Paul Thompson, Tetsuya Motomura, Anthony Conti', 16 October 2014, United States District Court, Southern District of New York, https://www.justice.gov/sites/default/files/criminal-fraud/legacy/2015/05/22/10-25-14anthony-allen-indicted.pdf

USPIRG (2015a) 'Settling for a lack of accountability? Which Federal Agencies Allow Companies to Write Off Out-of-Court Settlements as Tax Deductions, and Which Are Transparent about It', US Public Interest Group: Washington, http://www.uspirgedfund.org/sites/pirg/files/reports/USPIRG_SettlementsReport.pdf

USPIRG (2015b) *Big Banks, Big Overdraft Fees: The CFPB Defends Consumers Against Harmful and Deceptive Fees*. US Public Interest Group: Washington, https://uspirg.org/reports/usp/big-banks-big-overdraft-fees

USPIRG (2016) *Big Banks: Big Overdraft Fees: US Public Interest Research Group Report*. Washington: USPIRG.

Van den Steen, Eric J. (2010) 'On the origin of shared beliefs (and corporate culture)', *RAND Journal of Economics* 41 (4): 617–48.

Van der Pijl, K. (1998) *Transnational Classes and International Relations*. London: Routledge.

Verburg, R. (2000) 'Adam Smith's growing concern on the issue of distributive justice', *European Journal of the History of Economic Thought* 7(1): 23–44.

Volcker, Paul (2005) Foreword. In: G. Stern and R. Feldman, *Too Big To Fail: the Hazards of Bank Bailouts*. Washington, DC: Brookings Institute Press, pp. vii–x.

Waddock S., and S. Graves (1997) 'The corporate social performance-financial performance link', *Strategic Management Journal* 18(4): 303–19.

Walker, D. (2014) 'Trust and trustworthiness in banks and bankers', speech by Sir David Walker, Barclays Chairman at the Federal Reserve Bank of New York workshop on reforming culture and behaviours in the financial services industry, 20 October 2014.

Walker Review (2009) 'A review of corporate governance in UK banks and other financial industry entities: final recommendations', 26 November 2009, http://webarchive.nationalarchives.gov.uk/+/http:/www.hm-treasury.gov.uk/d/walker_review_261109.pdf

Wall, L. D. (1993) 'Too Big To Fail after FDICIA', *Federal Reserve Bank of Atlanta Economic Review* 78: 1–14.

Watson, M. (2006) 'Civilizing market standards and the moral self', in B. Bowden and L. Seabrooke, eds, *Global Standards of Market Civilization*. Routledge, pp. 45–59.

Warren, E (2018) *This Fight is our Fight: the Battle to Save Working People*. Harper Collins.

Washington Post (2005) 'Timeline of Enron's Collapse', 2 November 2005.

Washington Post (2011a) 'Senate blocks Richard Cordray confirmation to head consumer watchdog agency', 8 December 2011.

Washington Post (2011b) 'Bank of America to add $5 monthly debit card fee as era of low-cost banking ebbs', 29 September 2011.

Washington Post (2013) 'Senate confirms Cordray to head Consumer watchdog', 16 July 2013.

Washington Post (2014a) 'A watchdog grows up: The inside story of the Consumer Financial Protection Bureau', 11 January 2014.

Washington Post (2014b) 'Watch the US transition from a manufacturing economy to a service economy', 3 September 2014.

Weigand, R. (2013) 'The Recovery of US Commercial Banking: An Analysis of Revenues, Profits, Dividends, Capital and Value Creation', *Banks and Bank Systems* 8 (3): 76–88.

Weigand, R. (2015) 'A tale of two banking systems: the performance of the US and European banks in the 21st-century', *Investment Management and Financial Innovations* 12:1.

Wells Fargo (2013) Annual report.

Wells Fargo (2006–17) Annual Reports, 2006–17.

Wells Fargo (2006–17) Proxy Statements, 2006–17.

White House (2011) 'President Obama Nominates Richard Cordray to Lead Consumer Financial Protection Bureau', 18 July 2011, The White House.

White House (2012) 'Consumer Financial Protection Bureau 101: Why We Need a Consumer Watchdog', 4 January 2012, The White House.

Widmaier, W. W. (2004) 'The social construction of the "impossible trinity": The intersubjective bases of monetary cooperation', *International Studies Quarterly* 48(2): 433–53.

Williamson, S. D. (2017) 'Quantitative Easing: How Well Does This Tool Work?' Federal Reserve Bank of St Louis, Regional Economist Q3 2017.
Woll, C. (2014) *The Power of Inaction: Bank Bailouts in Comparison.* Ithaca: Cornell University Press.
Wood, D. and R. Jones (1995) 'Stakeholder mismatching: a theoretical problem in empirical research on corporate social performance', *International Journal of Organizational Analysis* 3(3): 229–67.
Wren-Lewis, S. (2015) 'The Macroeconomic Record of the Coalition Government', *National Institute Economic Review* 231(1): R5–R16.
WSJ (2002) 'Systemic Failure by SEC is Seen in Enron Debacle', 7 October 2002.
WSJ (2008a) 'Bankers cast doubt on key rate amid crisis', 16 April 2008.
WSJ (2008b) 'Study casts doubt on key rate', 29 May 2008.
WSJ (2010) 'Fight Over Consumer Agency Looms as Overhaul is Signed', 22 July 2010.
WSJ (2011) 'Cuomo Takes Office, Calls New York State's Reputation a "National Joke",' 2 January 2011.
WSJ (2012) 'Nearly 150 Protesters Arrested on Occupy Wall Street Anniversary', 17 September 2012.
WSJ (2014a) 'Bank of America to Pay $17 Billion in Justice Department Settlement', 20 August 2014.
WSJ (2014b) 'Goldman Sachs Set to Shun U.K. Banking Standards Review Council', 19 October 2014.
WSJ (2015a) 'As Regulators Focus on Culture, Wall Street Struggles to Define It', 1 February 2015.
WSJ (2015b) 'S&P Near $1.37 Billion Settlement of Crisis-Era Suits', 28 January 2015.
WSJ (2015c) 'N.Y. State Suspends Promontory From Some Consulting Work', 3 August 2015.
WSJ (2015d) 'Regulators Intensify Scrutiny of Bank Boards', 30 March 2015.
WSJ (2015e) 'Where did the money go? Total bank fines infographic', http://graphics.wsj.com/bank-fines-where-did-the-money-go/#thirdPage
(*WSJ* (2016a) 'Look Who's Getting That Bank Settlement Cash', 28 August 2016.
WSJ (2016b) 'Big Banks Paid $110 Billion in Mortgage-Related Fines. Where Did the Money Go?' 9 March 2016.
WSJ (2016c) 'Nuns With Guns: The Strange Day-to-Day Struggles Between Bankers and Regulators', 30 May 2016.
WSJ (2016d) 'Digging into the biggest U.S. bank fines: Where did the money go?' Infographic, http://graphics.wsj.com/bank-fines-where-did-the-money-go/#firstPage
WSJ (2017a) 'Bank Overdraft: Fee Revenue Bounces Back', 16 March 2017.
YouGov (2016) 'One in three middle-class Brits would struggle to pay a £500 bill', YouGov poll, 8 June 2016.
Young, B. (2017) 'Is Germany's and Europe's Crisis Politics Ordoliberal and/or Neoliberal?', in T. Biebricher and F. Vogelman, eds, *The Birth of Austerity: German Ordoliberalism and Contemporary Neoliberalism.* New York: Rowman and Littlefield, pp. 221–38.
Zysman, J. (1983) *Governments, Markets, and Growth: Financial Systems and the Politics of Industrial Change.* Ithaca: Cornell University Press.

Index

Note: Figures and Tables are indicated by an italic '*f*' and '*t*', respectively, following the page number.